Revise

Read through your rough draft five times with *only one thing in mind each time*. Do not recopy the draft unless it becomes impossible to read.

Revise for Ideas:

- For depth and honesty
- To clarify
- To make sure the thesis still fits the paper
- To cut irrelevant sections

Revise for Details:

- Add details for support
- Sharpen details for vividness, concreteness
- Cut details that don't fit the main idea

Revise for Order:

- Each paragraph should be about one idea
- Paragraphs should divide logically
- Add transition words to move from point to point

Revise for Word Use:

- Conciseness
- Vivid verbs
- Metaphors
- Precise word use
- Variety in vocabulary

Revise for Spelling, Punctuation, Sentence Structure:

- Search for errors you made in previous papers
- Circle all words, punctuation, or sentences you're not 100 percent sure of and look them up in a dictionary or Chapter 16

Refer to Chapters 7, 8, and 16.

Warning: Writing Is Not This Orderly. The Sentence General has determined that the writing process is sloppy. A write-by-number approach may be dangerous to your best writing. You are normal if you do not follow this process exactly. The process may more accurately be described by the diagram below.

Correction Symbols Your Professor May Write on Your Papers

AB—Abbreviations, See **page 453**.

Agree or Ag—Agreement. Nouns, verbs, or pronouns don't match each other. See **pages 447–448**.

Awk—Awkward. Something is clumsy, and your professor doesn't have a category for it.

C—Comma error. See **pages 430–436**.

Cap—Capitalization. See **pages 441–443**.

Format—See **page 453**.

G—Good work here.

Irr. Verb—Irregular verb form. See **pages 449–451**.

MM—(1) Mixed metaphor. See Chapter 8.

   OR (2) Misplaced modifier. See **pages 446–447**.

Org—Organization. Two points mixed together or one point split apart. See Chapter 5.

¶—Paragraph needed. See Chapter 4.

?—Confusing section. Look for missing words awkward sentences, illogical idea, or misused words.

Red—Redundant. Needs cutting. See Chapter 8.

R.O. or C.S.—Run-on or comma-spliced sentence. Needs a period or semicolon. See **pages 444–446**.

Ref—Reference. Usually unclear pronoun reference. See **page 448**.

SF—Sentence fragment. See **pages 443–444**.

SS—Sentence structure. May be awkward or nonparallel construction. See Chapter 8.

Tense—Verb tenses don't match. See **page 447**.

Thesis—Thesis needed or unclear. See Chapter 5.

Trans—Transition needs improvement. See Chapter 4.

Vague—Need clarification or more detail. See Chapter 2.

Wordy—Be more concise. See Chapter 8.

WW or Usage—Wrong word used. See Dictionary of Usage, **pages 454–459**.

OTHERS:

IDEAS AND DETAILS

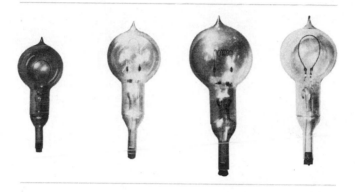

"Tell as much of the truth
as one can bear, and
then a little more."
—James Baldwin

IDEAS AND DETAILS

A GUIDE TO COLLEGE WRITING

FIFTH EDITION

M. GARRETT BAUMAN

Monroe Community College

THOMSON

HEINLE

Australia • Canada • Mexico • Singapore • Spain • United Kingdom • United States

THOMSON ™
HEINLE

Ideas and Details: A Guide to College Writing / Fifth Edition
M. Garrett Bauman

Publisher: Michael Rosenberg
Acquisitions Editor: Dickson Musslewhite
Development Editor: Laurie Runion
Editorial Assistant: Stephen Marsi
Production Editor: Diana Baczynskyj
Director of Marketing: Lisa Kimball

Senior Manufacturing Manager: Marcia Locke
Compositor: Argosy
Project Management: Argosy
Photo Manager: Sheri Blaney
Cover Designer: Dick Hannus
Printer: Webcom Limited

Cover Images: © Corbis

Printed in Canada.
1 2 3 4 5 6 7 8 9 10   06 05 04 03

For more information contact Heinle, 25 Thomson Place, Boston, Massachusetts 02210 USA, or you can visit our Internet site at
http://www.heinle.com

For permission to use material from this text or product contact us:

Tel   1-800-730-2214
Fax   1-800-730-2215
Web   www.thomsonrights.com

ISBN 0-8384-0768-4

Library of Congress Cataloging-in-Publication Data
Bauman, M. Garrett.
  Ideas and details : a guide to college writing / M. Garrett Bauman.—5th ed.
      p. cm.
Includes bibliographical references and index.
  ISBN 0-8384-0768-4
  1. English language—Rhetoric. 2. Report writing.
I. Title.
  PE1408.B4617 2003
  808'.042—dc21
                                    2003005018

For Carol
Who lives as I would write

And for Alan Barker Shaw
That most generous of colleagues and teachers

PREFACE

The single most common cause of writer's block and of poor writing is trying to manipulate words when the writer has nothing much to say. The goal of this book, therefore, is to help writers activate their brains to stir up more and better ideas and details. Its thesis is simple and straightforward: Good writing combines fresh ideas energized by vivid details. Within this principle, seemingly endless variation occurs, whether you are supporting a thesis about why smallpox vaccines are dangerous or describing the way a puddle ripples in the breeze. Chapters 1, 2, 3, and major portions of most chapters, are devoted to providing thinking options for writers.

In emphasizing the process of writing, this book takes a no-frills approach to theory; it reduces terminology and the number of steps so students are not intimidated and can see the essentials. Offering options instead of prescriptions empowers writers to try different techniques and liberates teachers. My style is personal to let students know there is always a voice behind writing.

Chapters 4 and 5 discuss options for paragraphing and organization. Chapter 6 discusses options for introductions, drafting, and overcoming writer's blocks. Chapters 7 and 8 deal with revision, including advice for peer review and conferences. Chapters 9–14 cover the most widely taught types of essays, and Chapter 15 offers additional student essays demonstrating these forms. Chapter 16 is a brief handbook that focuses on the essential rules and is based on the premise that less is learnable; more is ignorable.

Ideas and Details focuses on student writing, including 35 complete student essays and dozens of short samples. Each chapter also contains practice writing assignments that require immediate application of the ideas. These five- to ten-minute exercises encourage students to write, so the professor can spend less time going over the text and more time applying the concepts in hands-on participation. These and the end-of-chapter suggestions often form sequences that lead to essays.

Here's what's new to the fifth edition of *Ideas and Details*:

- New student writings on the following topics: stereotypes about modern witches, Quakers and feminism, ghetto language, nude modeling for art classes, a letter asking a boss for a promotion, a night in the life of a bartender, dealing with a father's stroke, a dramatic evangelical church service, weird dental patients, a letter from a pregnant woman to her lover, personal ads, how to slaughter a chicken, and a gay pickup story. They should provide lively reading and class discussions.

- Most chapters now evaluate a sample student essay for how well it hits or misses the chapter's principles. These evaluations are based on the chapter's peer review checklist. A second sample essay allows students to practice for peer review workshops, using my comments on the first essay as a model.

- All 112 brain teasers in *Ideas and Details* are now labeled with an icon for easier location.

- More than 100 new practice, writing, and discussion questions offer more applications for students and more options for professors.

- Chapter 14, on research papers, has been thoroughly updated for the latest documentation formats. New, reliable Web sites (with URL addresses) for college research have been added. Professor Christopher Otero-Piersante, who coauthors this chapter with me, takes students through the research process with a sample topic—modeling topic selection and narrowing, using brain teasers, researching gold mines and dead ends, note taking, as well as writing trial theses and outlines. Professor Otero-Piersante, who began teaching writing with an early edition of *Ideas and Details,* is as committed as I have always been to keeping the book compact, honest, fun to use and accessible to students. That focus has not changed.

- *InfoTrac*® College Edition access: Each student now receives four months of access to *InfoTrac*® College Edition with a new copy of *Ideas and Details. InfoTrac*® College Edition is a college-level database of nearly 13 million sources from leading periodicals in many fields. Unlike the Internet, *InfoTrac*® College Edition's sources are more reliable; there are no advertisements; bibliography information is clearly labeled for documenting research papers; it is updated daily; sources do not vanish; and it is indexed specifically for college research. *InfoTrac*® College Edition effectively expands *Ideas and Details* without additional size or cost, allowing the professor to decide what supplementary use, if any, to make of it. A professor can create common reading assignments from anything available on the database or use specific reading suggestions listed throughout *Ideas and Details.* There are sample professional informative, descriptive, narrative, persuasive, and literary essays with discussion/writing suggestions for how to use the readings to develop topics, to analyze rhetorical principles, to creatively "co-author" with the published writers, and to evaluate the model essays using the criteria developed in the chapter. Most chapters also direct students to *InfoTrac*® College Edition sources that provide more information on topics covered in *Ideas and Details,* so they can read Russell Baker on punctuation, Donald Murray on revision, or a half-dozen authors' ideas for brain teasers.

- In the new Chapter 17, there are guidelines for using *InfoTrac*® College Edition as well as two additional applications. Students can learn to write resumes, poetry, letters of complaint, proposals, and many other forms of writing I cannot cover in this text by accessing articles listed from writers' trade journals such as *The Writer* or *Business Communicator.* There are also additional research and writing projects that can be done on *InfoTrac*® College Edition—knowing there is enough information there for a freshman or sophomore paper. In summary, *InfoTrac*® College Edition access is a window from *Ideas and Details* into a much wider world. As in previous editions, I have tried to provide guidance and opportunity, but left the creative applications to the professors and students who use the book.

ACKNOWLEDGMENTS

I have been blessed by wonderful colleagues, editors, students, and friends during the writing of this book. I would first like to thank the Monroe Community College Foundation for supporting the early booklet version, and I want to especially thank James Davis and Judith Hall for their administrative support and editorial suggestions. Cheryl Desmond and Suzanne O'Brien deserve special thanks for meticulous manuscript preparation beyond the call of duty.

My colleagues Lee Adnepos, Nancy Bailey, Elizabeth Behr, Gail Bouk, Patrick Callan, Stasia Callan, Carol Cloos, Donna Cox, Alan Glossner, William Goglia, Judy Hall, Erika Hartmann Hayes, Robert Herzog, Tony Leuzzi, Thom Metzger, Martin Napersteck, Christopher Otero-Piersante, Elaine S. Rich, Mark Spall, Ann Tippett, Holly Wheeler, and Carolyn Wendell provided detailed critiques and feedback. To my students and other professors' students who sent me letters responding to the book, I am deeply grateful. A special thanks goes to Holly Wheeler's students, who have sent me dozens of sincere and valuable reviews. I want this book to be for students, and they help me see through their eyes. My wife, Carol, has been of invaluable help in reading and researching and especially in telling me how a student would feel about the issues.

In transforming *Ideas and Details* through five editions, I thank Dickson Musslewhite, Stephen Marsi, Michael Rosenberg, Lisa Kimball, and Diana Baczynskyj for their encouragement, wise and experienced suggestions, and clarity of intent. I am especially indebted in this edition to developmental editor Laurie Runion, who—while moving cross-country with a van full of cats and remodeling an old house—never missed a beat. Her insights, guidance, and ability to adapt to changing situations have been invaluable.

I am deeply indebted as well to my colleagues at other colleges who honestly and meticulously reviewed the book and made it better, sometimes by demolishing walls, sometimes by realigning bricks. I thank them all.

Anjili Babbar, *University of Rochester*

Betty Bamburg, *University of Southern California*

Paula Bennett, *Seattle Central Community College*

Therese Brychta, *Truckee Meadows Community College*

Lucy Coombs, *Central Maine Technical College*

Christopher Gould, *University of North Carolina*

Jeanne Grinnan, *SUNY Brockport*

Paula Guetschow, *University of Alaska*

Zita Ingham, *Arkansas State University*

Pat Kile, *Richard Bland College of the College of William and Mary*

Lynn McDonie, *Antelope Valley Community College*

Janice McKay, *SUNY Brockport*

Tim McLaughlin, *Bunker Hill Community College*

Carolyn Mee, *Beaver College*

Michael Miller, *Longview Community College*

Amy J. Pawl, *Washington University*

Roxanna Pisiak, *SUNY Morrisville*

Paula Ross, *Gadsen Community College*

Susan A. Schiller, *Central Michigan University*

Mary Sottman, *South Puget Sound Community College*

Ellen Tiedrich, *Gloucester County College*

Arthur Versluis, *Michigan State University*

Troy T. Wolff, *Shoreline Community College*

Jeb Wyman, *Seattle Central Community College*

—**M. Garrett Bauman**

CONTENTS

Chapter 5 Order from Chaos: Thesis and Outline   91

Chapter 6 The Draft: That Frenzy Near Madness   109

Chapter 7 Revising Drafts: Writing Is Revising   125

Chapter 8 Writing with Style   143

Chapter 13 The Literary Essay and Review   271

Chapter 14 Research: Written with Christopher Otero-Piersante   301

Chapter 16 Handbook of English   **427**

CHAPTER 1

The Honest Writer

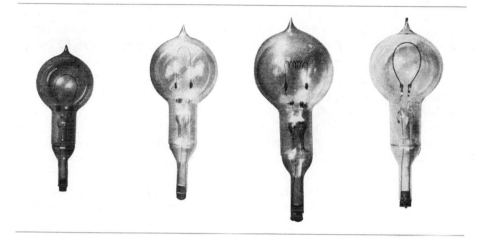

From the cowardice that dares not face new truths,
From the laziness that is content with half truths,
From the arrogance that thinks it knows all truth,
Good Lord, deliver me.

—KENYAN PRAYER

Everything that can be invented has been invented.
—CHARLES DUELL, COMMISSIONER OF U.S. PATENTS, 1899

Many students enroll for college writing courses with apprehension. Writing is hard work—and there's lots of it in such a course. You probably will have to expose your feelings. And some students say English teachers want to change their style—but isn't style something that's personal?

Let's look at these three issues a little closer. First, **writing *is* hard work,** even for professional writers. All writers have crumpled papers or made trips to the refrigerator when the words refused to cooperate. Sometimes, I seem to change ten words for every five I write. But writing can be made easier by practicing and by learning shortcuts that this book and your professor will suggest. Compare learning to write to learning to play tennis or the guitar or learning to drive a car. How graceful were you the first time you tried these activities? And when you moved up to the next level of difficulty, didn't it seem almost as hard as starting over? Writing is at least this complicated; there are 750,000 words in the English language—750,000 choices. Your professor hopes to make you practice as hard and often as *both* of you can stand it. For research shows that the best predictor of success in college is effort. Not IQ, not the college you attend, not your SAT scores, age, sex, or race. Take comfort in that. *You* control your own effort.

Second, what about the papers in which you might have to **expose your feelings or ideas** that may sound strange to others? If you can open up, you'll learn one great truth about writing: *Telling the truth as you really see it is the only way a writer ever says something worth reading.* Alice Walker, the author of *The Color Purple,* writes openly about being blind in one eye and about growing up in a poor family. She says she was so embarrassed about her "crooked eye" that for six years she did not raise her head, for fear people might notice the "blob" on it. In life these things are embarrassing, but in writing, they make us feel and understand. A reader *wants* a writer to give of himself or herself—to know the writer's truth. As readers we respect such truth and the person who dares to tell it.

Almost all mediocre writers share two qualities—they're vague and they're half-hearted. This is not intentional, of course. Perhaps they want to be safe. Perhaps they fear making mistakes or saying something unacceptable and so choose a vague, comfortable half-truth. A writer should be sensitive to readers' reactions; however, the writer's first job is to create stimulating ideas for the reader to consider. You cannot do that timidly. Besides, your professor will be grading you on how forcefully your opinions are presented and supported—not on your opinions themselves. Your teacher wants the real you to emerge, and if you want to write moving, interesting papers, the kind you enjoy reading, trust your professor and classmates with your story. Zora Neale Hurston's mother, a poor black woman of the last century, told all her children, "Jump at the sun." Zora, who later became a great writer, commented, "We might not land on the sun, but at least we would get off the ground." Use this course to jump at the sun.

Third, will your professor try to **change your style?** Let's hope so! You had a writing style when you were 14. Would you like that same style to represent you on professional reports, letters, and college papers? Your style has changed as you've matured, for change accompanies all growth. Your professor will encourage further change and maturity by asking you to experiment with a variety of styles and techniques so you can find your best. She also wants you to be able to adapt to the many writing tasks life will throw at you after college.

Your professor wants you to become the writer *you* want to be. And like all intellectual activity, writing should make a person feel more alive, growing. Consider that the great novelist Marcel Proust was still revising his work on his deathbed, hopeful, alive for the perfect word that would, as he said, "move the world." Near the end he revised a death scene because, now that he was in the same predicament, he saw more honestly how the character felt. Doing so helped him to continue to grow until his last hour.

Perhaps a writer ought to be an optimist, hoping that in the next words, the next sentence, the next idea, something will make a difference to a reader. If you don't stretch yourself to say something beyond what you already know, the writing will be flat. College should be a great stretching experience, whether you are 18 or 68. You really don't know how far you can stretch. Perhaps there is a novel or speech in your future; perhaps a letter to the newspaper that will change someone's life; perhaps a report that will get you promoted; or a letter that will calm a family feud. One thing is sure: Safe, predictable ideas won't change either you or your readers.

Trying different styles also prepares you to write for different audiences. Your tone must differ when writing to an angry customer, to an admissions officer you don't know, or to your favorite cousin. When you choose simpler words to speak to a child, use technical terms to discuss a research project with a professor, or eliminate slang when speaking to your grandparents, you are adapting style to your audience. Which is the real you? *All* of them. In being sensitive to your audience, you stretch yourself into a person encompassing many different people.

As with learning any complicated skill, writing can paralyze you at first. I can't do all this at once, you think. You're right. That's why when people learn something new they sometimes seem to get worse for a while. Often this is only an illusion. You may simply be setting higher goals for yourself that you must work up to. If you hit the target every try, it's too close. Some assignments and techniques in this book may seem artificial at first, but with practice they will become part of your unconscious process. If I write for a while without giving an example—as I have been—a little twitch reminds me. At other times a subconscious detector tells me I'm stamping out the same bland verbs over and over. But every writer has to struggle *consciously* to learn these things before they become automatic. This book will focus on the essential concepts you need.

■ **PRACTICE 1-1:** On the first page of your notebook, complete this sentence: "One hard aspect about writing that I want to work on this semester is . . ."

■ **PRACTICE 1-2:** On the first page of your notebook, complete this sentence: "One topic I'd like to dare to write about is . . . ."

A PROFESSIONAL ATTITUDE

The writing you do in this course should be considered professional writing. It is real writing for a real purpose, not practice exercises. I say this because nothing you learn in college will be as important to your professional success as the ability to write well, no matter what career you choose. You may be able to land a first job after college without strong writing ability, but promotions and recognition will get harder at each level. Engineers, businesspeople, nurses, counselors, technicians, and teachers write far more than you might think—and always there is more writing as careers advance. The computer age has made writing more important than ever. Fax, e-mail, and the Internet are replacing the telephone and the personal visit.

Let me use as an example a friend of mine who is not a college graduate. Rick is a carpenter—a physical labor job, right? That was true as long as Rick worked for a boss. But he wanted to be independent, keep more of the profits, and do more creative carpentry. So he established a small, three-person building company—and found himself writing more and more and hammering less and less. He writes letters to inspectors *explaining* variations in housing codes; he writes *persuasive* complaint letters to customers and suppliers when he feels cheated; he writes accurate and vivid *descriptions* of additions or remodelings so customers can visualize them; he's become sensitive to audience, tone, and word choice, knowing they sell his houses as much as his reputation for craftsmanship. He's come to realize his business success has a lot to do with his success as a writer.

From a career standpoint, you owe it to yourself to learn to write effectively for these reasons:

- A boss may avoid asking you to do work that would otherwise enhance your career if you cannot write well. Although no one may ever say so, poor writing embarrasses both the writer and the company.

- Writing well makes you self-reliant; you don't have to depend on a secretary to fix your work. You can control your own destiny.

- A boss or client feels rapport when reading clear, organized writing, but alienated when reading stuffy, disorganized, or vague reports and letters.

- Good writers create new ideas; think of the benefits this brings a career. In Chapters 2 and 3, you will learn to write on almost any topic thrown at you in college or at a job.

Almost any business or professional person today will put writing ability high on the list of what is desired in an employee. Many rank it above even courses in your career field.

Never underestimate the usefulness of good writing. I usually ask my students to do some real professional writing tasks for real audiences, and some have met with the kind of success that makes them realize the power the written word gives them. Mike, who was recently promoted to manage a computer chip lab, wrote a paper for class that became a safety brochure for his company. Rob was upset at the city law forbidding people to keep cars without license plates in their driveways. He'd gotten a ticket. For a class paper, he wrote a proposal to have the law changed so people who couldn't afford big garages could keep a rust-bucket car for the winter and a cleaner car for the summer without paying for two license plates and two insurance policies. The city council agreed and changed the law. Darlene, a single parent returning to college, had a male boss who made sexist remarks and discriminated against her in assigning tasks. She wrote a tactful letter of complaint to him (it's easy to blast someone and get fired). Her letter was so well explained and supported that the man not only treated her better, but admitted it opened his eyes to the way other working women were mistreated. These are examples of professional writing in its broadest sense.

Of course, your college writing must show professional polish. This means not just the kind of grammar and spelling you'd want on your résumé, but also a professional attitude toward ideas, details, and honesty. Professionals revise (literally, re-see). Your professor may challenge you to look again at words, ideas, and details in an effort to help you think more professionally. This is natural; expect it.

Some college writing assignments in courses across the curriculum may seem boring or irrelevant to you. A paper on "Plato's Concept of Justice" in a philosophy course or "Prison Conditions in the Nineteenth Century" in Criminology may not excite you. But a person with a professional outlook will be able to get into almost any topic assigned. If you believe the world is interesting, you will find interesting things to think and say. If you expect boredom, you will probably find it. Although I cannot promise this will always be true, most topics are made exciting by the concentration and curiosity the writer brings to them. A professional thinker takes this approach.

Why does college require so much writing? Because you learn more about a subject by writing about it. Studies have consistently shown that you will retain three to five times as much knowledge by writing about a topic than by simply reading or hearing about it. You make ideas part of you by actively describing them in your own words. If you really want to learn the material in your psychology or biology course, don't just highlight the book. Write out a few paragraphs after finishing your reading.

■ **PRACTICE 1-3:** Think of a financial or job situation in your life now in which a strong letter might solve a problem or do you some good. Who would you write to and why?

THE STRUGGLE AGAINST SILENCE

Personal reasons to write well are as important as professional reasons. You can write to touch someone you care about. You can write to discover who you are and what you believe. You can write to preserve important moments in your life. Writing for yourself also means you are taking control of events, making your life more your own. As Mexican writer Carlos Fuentes once said, "Writing is a struggle against silence." The writer does not just accept life, but works to understand and respond to it.

Chances are, in trying to stretch you, your professor will require both professional and personal writing. But most college writing will require a deeper honesty than you may have been asked for to this point. Not that people try to be dishonest. What I mean is that **in college it may not be enough to just write what you** *already know or already feel* **about something; instead you must** *discover more* **about your subjects.** It is dishonest to think that what you already know and believe about a subject is the entire truth. Sometimes you will discover new ideas through research, but many times they can come through looking closer at your own experiences and feelings—probing deeper into what you may have accepted too easily in the past.

I recall an older student who was in a wheelchair. Tom had been shot three times in the lower spine, shattering two vertebrae and leaving him unable to walk. This happened in 1973 during the Vietnam War. Tom had spent many years in veterans' hospitals. He decided to attend college, even though he had been a high school dropout. He sat in the front corner of the classroom—isolated—wearing purple and silver mirror sunglasses that hid his eyes. The few things he said were sarcastic snaps, and the other students shrank away from him. He was in the class but not part of it. His papers were poor in grammar, but even worse to me, they were bland. "Nothing ever happened to me in my whole life but one thing," he said after I returned a D-minus paper to him. "I don't care about this stuff."

"So write about that one thing that did happen to you," I said.

"No way!" Tom said. "I don't want to. If I do, a lot will come out I don't want out again. It's no good. You don't know what I might do if I get upset." During the semester Tom had trouble with the police regularly. Once he showed me a bruised knee he said the police had given him during a brawl when he refused to leave a buddy's room in the spinal ward of the hospital.

"You're kind of proud of that, aren't you?" I asked.

He admitted he was. "I guess I like fighting cops."

"Do you know why?" I asked.

It was then that Tom reached up and slid off his mirror sunglasses, slowly, reluctantly. I suppose he wanted to see me better, but I saw his eyes for the first time. They were old, exhausted eyes. "Yeah," he answered, "I know why."

After this, Tom slowly began exploring his inner landscape—his own heart. It is the most wonderful and terrifying subject any of us have. Tom wrote several papers that erupted, that gripped his readers. He read one to the class, and people sat near him to be in his workshop group so they could find out more. **His writing made him real to them,** and they wanted to know what he'd been through. They didn't pity him; they simply hungered for his experience, because real writing makes a reader live more, too. He explored the day he was wounded, what Vietnam meant to him, the father who deserted him, his own son he hadn't seen since becoming disabled, a girl he loved. He made us laugh when he described how scared walking people are of those in wheelchairs, how when he noticed the look of fear on them he'd pretend he was going to run them over. Tom's life poured out on paper, and the class read it and cared. Tom taught them they could write for real, and some people who had previously hidden behind safe topics took a chance, too.

Tom turned his pain into power and freed himself. He'd feared going over these events because they hurt, but he learned that holding them inside hurt him again and again, while they lost their terror and control over him as he shaped them into words. Tom still had a long way to go at semester's end, but he told me, "At least my mind's started walking again."

Tom's is an exceptional story of self-discovery, but most writing teachers can tell stories about how writing has freed writers from self-imposed handicaps.

■ **PRACTICE 1-4:** In half a page, tell about a time when your own habits, fear, or laziness held back your growth as a person. Remember Tom.

WHAT DO YOU KNOW?

Let me reinforce this point another way. In college most of your papers will be essays. The word *essay* comes from the French *essai,* which means *to try* or *to attempt.* Michel de Montaigne, a French writer who in the sixteenth century invented the term to describe what he wrote, saw the essay as a trial of an idea, an attempt to express something as clearly and honestly as possible. He was reacting to the fake, predictable, and overly idealistic writing of his peers. For de Montaigne writing was liberation—a way of freeing himself from what he was supposed to think. Not only society, but our own habits, fears, and laziness prevent us from seeing and thinking freshly and honestly. For instance, when we become accustomed to seeing work as duty and drudgery, we may block out the pleasures work gives us. We may forget that we work because we love someone or that work makes us stronger, more capable people and makes us proud. Can you think of two other benefits from work besides money?

When de Montaigne tried an idea, he wasn't satisfied until he turned it upside down, cross-examined it mercilessly, wrung every last possible drop of truth from it, and exposed every possible half-truth or lie hidden in it. He even cast a medallion that he wore on a cord around his neck. It read *"Que sais-je?"* or "What do I know?" This curious phrase changes meaning as you emphasize "I," "what," and "know." See if you can discover those different meanings.

De Montaigne's unrelenting honesty comforts me. He makes me believe humans can find truth, can write it, and perhaps can even live by it. Use this book and your writing course to free yourself of old ways and dead notions and to find ones you can live by today.

Here are some examples of things we think we know but don't question carefully. Let's start with a cold scientific fact: Water boils at 212 degrees Fahrenheit. It's one of those things you memorize in elementary school. But water does not boil at 212 degrees on a mountaintop or below sea level. Nor if it's salt water or carries dissolved minerals. Nor in a vacuum. The truth is more complicated than the simple fact I'd like to believe. Besides, how do *I* know it's 212 degrees? I've never tested it.

Next, consider this story. In 1969, I watched live television pictures of the first man stepping on the moon. I saw Neil Armstrong's boots kick up gray lunar dust as he planted a flag there. I went outside and stared at the pale moon and wondered if I'd ever walk there. The next day I went to my summer job at the warehouse and asked people what they thought about the moon landing.

They laughed. "You really believe a man's on the moon?" one guy said. "It's all made up in Hollywood."

"Sure," another said. "You go to college to believe *that*?" I sputtered and argued feebly for a few minutes, then gave up. Did I *know* men were on the moon? No. And I didn't know enough to prove it to these people, most of whom had not graduated from high school. In fact, how did I know it wasn't a Hollywood trick? I do *believe* men landed there in 1969, but back then I was basically taking the government's and the media's word for it.

My point is simply that a lot of what we think of as factual truth is based on blind trust of authority and our own prejudices and preconceptions without firsthand observation, hard logic, or research. We hear and we believe. One last example: Most people assume that people who become rich from humble beginnings must be smart and honor-grade students. But Tom Stanley, who studied thousands of self-made millionaires, discovered that millionaires are only slightly above average in both intelligence and grades.

■ **PRACTICE 1-5:** What are two ideas or facts you accept only because you have been told to believe them? Try for one from your personal life (something family or friends have told you) and one from social, historical, or scientific areas. Raise questions about them.

Let me end this chapter with a few ideas that are, I hope, as honest and direct as I can be about writing. First, in your personal and professional life there will be times when you will be asked to use language to comfort sleeping minds—to reassure and soothe your listeners with predictable statements. This is civilized dishonesty. We all do this. But it is not the best that is in us. Use this course to strive for a deeper honesty, one that does more than avoid the obvious lie—one that tries to touch the heart of a topic. In the long run, these will be the only things you write that will matter to you or anyone else. **The enemy in college (and life) is not other people or our duties, but our own passivity.** To listen without speaking, to follow the feet ahead of us instead of peeking behind the blackberry bushes—that is our enemy. Each half-truth we accept or repeat without really putting it on trial shrinks our intellect. Intensity expands our intellect—and our well-being. Psychologists such as M. Scott Peck say that the intense, sometimes painful pursuit of truth leads to happiness and mental health, while unhappiness and mental illness are more likely to come to those who passively accept things as they *seem* to be.

Second, **talent in writing is overrated.** Ninety-nine percent of all writing tasks do not require natural genius, just a reasonable intelligence and a willingness to work. You *can* do that. *Will* you? Annie Dillard, a Pulitzer Prize winner, goes so far as to say, "There is no such thing as talent. . . . We all start out dull and weary and uninspired. . . . Genius is the product of education." She says people want to believe in genius because they can blame their genes instead of working to improve themselves. So don't begin with excuses. Your professor will not ask you to write Pulitzer Prize–winning books. But if you work hard, you will write better than you think you can. Teaching yourself to write or speak well or to do any task well is often teaching yourself to find what is interesting in the job at hand. **The effort to revise also separates good writers from the pack.** The funny thing is, anybody can revise a paper one grade better with an hour's work. Few do. And revision separates the really honest writer—the one who will put his first thoughts on trial—from the writer who chooses a lesser honesty.

Third, **write for a real purpose to a real audience.** When your writing course allows, write your papers about topics that matter to you and imagine sending them to a particular person. Write your paper on alcoholism to your friend's alcoholic father; write your paper on energy taxes to your senator or to the owner of a local trucking company or even to the pollution-sensitive owl in your backyard; write your paper on prenatal care to your sister and her new husband. If you cannot think of an audience, imagine that listening carefully as you write is someone who is not judging you but rather who needs help visualizing your ideas, asks questions, wants to learn something from your paper.

Most students want simple formulas for writing. I'd like to give them to you, but they don't exist. Good writing balances rules and creative freedom. This book will strive for clear guidelines, but remember that rules often rule out great possibilities.

InfoTrac® College Edition: Readings on Honesty and Creativity

Throughout *Ideas and Details,* I will suggest that you read some published writings that offer new perspectives on topics discussed in the book. You can find them in *InfoTrac®* College Edition, an electronic database of more than 12 million articles. Four months of access to this database comes with this book. Some of these articles will reinforce *Ideas and Details;* others will challenge my ideas. That's good for your learning and for honesty.

See page 464 for tips on how to use your *InfoTrac®* College Edition access.

Honesty

Stephen L. Carter, "The Insufficiency of Honesty." *Public Management.* Oct. 1996.

The differences between honesty and integrity.

Antonella Surbone, "Truth Telling to the Patient." *Journal of the American Medical Association.* 7 Oct. 1992.

In Italy patients are not told they have terminal illness. Should they be told?

Vincent Bozzi, "Good-looking Lies." *Psychology Today.* Jan.1986.

Clues that give liars away.

C. O. Mathews, "The Honor System." *The Journal of Higher Education.* Sept. 1999.

Research into academic honesty.

Genius, Talent, and Creativity

Kim Kiser, "Lessons from Leonardo." *Training.* June 1999.

Seven ways to develop the genius inside you.

Mihaly Csikszentmihalyi, "The Creative Personality." *Psychology Today.* July–August 1996.

Ten contradictory traits of creative people.

Michael Michalko, "A Theory About Genius." *The World and I.* July 1998.

Thinking strategies that geniuses use.

Highlights of Chapter 1

- Writing courses create three major apprehensions: that it will be hard work; that you may have to expose your feelings; and that your style may change.

- All of these can be positive if you see them properly. Learning a difficult skill makes you a valuable person; exposing feelings may give you more control over the events of your life and may touch other people; and being open to new styles helps your writing mature and reach new audiences.

- This course is an introduction to a professional attitude toward writing that will advance your career for years to come.

- The personal writing you do will stretch you and give you the intellectual independence de Montaigne advocated.

- Both types of writing require de Montaigne's energetic engagement in the trial of an idea. What do you know?

Writing Suggestions and Class Discussions

1. In your opinion, what makes a piece of writing outstanding? List four or five qualities and star the most important. Bring in a short, published example to read to the class, noting specific sections you believe are particularly good.

2. *Try,* in de Montaigne's sense of the word, any current issue (the Mideast, using cell phones in cars, or genetic engineering, for examples). Suspend judgment and biases. Instead, focus on honest questions and ask, "What do I know?" whenever you write something you've heard others say. Play around, and take all sides.

3. Write several paragraphs describing your relationship with a past teacher of writing. Which guidelines for writing do you remember best? What did you like or not like about that teacher's approach to writing?

4. Honesty Assignment: Briefly describe an embarrassing moment and one thing it taught you that you may not have realized at the time. (One of mine was during my first lecture to a large college class. I leaned forward on the lectern—to show how relaxed I was—and the entire table and lectern collapsed with a crash, my notes floating down amid the class's roaring. It knocked some of the stuffiness out of me and made me realize how tentative my position as professor was.)

5. Honesty Assignment: Think about one weird idea you have—something not socially acceptable today, something even your friends would think strange. Explain it in one paragraph.

6. Write a "personals" ad for yourself—but be 100 percent honest about who you are and whom you seek.

7. Honest writing often balances two realities—our inner, private one and an outer, public one. Write a paragraph or two about an intensely important moment of your life as honestly as you can. Then write, again as honestly as you can, how someone else might have seen your experience differently.

8. How will you use writing in your future? List all the kinds of professional writing you may face in your career. Be specific about whom you will be writing to and why.

9. Make a list of ten things you really care about, that are important in your life. They may be people, ideas, beliefs, objects, goals, or whatever else matters. Write one or two sentences about each. Your teacher may ask you to share these with the class or a small group and help you develop them into topics for future papers.

10. Label each of your topics from #9 as descriptive, narrative, informative, or persuasive. If one could fit two categories, mark it that way.

11. Think about a person who died or passed permanently out of your life. In freewriting style, not worrying about grammar or sentence structure, record what you remember of that person. Don't stop until you have several insights that you didn't know before you started. Stretch your knowledge and feelings.

12. How will you use writing in college? List five writing tasks you will have to do in your major field and in other courses while in college.

13. Read pages 350–356 on the journal and write a journal entry.

14. Read pages 392–393 on the professional letter and write a brief professional letter to a business, government, or college official.

15. In peer groups, take one of the following clichés and test it for honesty. First, decide what the quotation means by paraphrasing it in your own words. Next, give an example of how it might be true. Then explain why it might be an incomplete truth. Remember, your job is to discover how much truth is in the saying, not to simply label it true or false.

    "What goes around, comes around."

    "Every cloud has a silver lining."

    "You can't teach an old dog new tricks."

    "You can't tell a book by its cover."

16. Read the following essay on pages 13–15 that was written by a student in response to Writing Suggestion 3.

17. Read the following student responses to Writing Suggestion 6 on page 16, thinking about the signals being sent:

Student Essay

Chicken at Wegman's

Jennifer M. Horton

She always arrived after the bell rang. Of course we chattered and shuffled our papers and sat on our desks, but when she appeared in the doorway we all settled.

"Oh, you are so good to me," she would purr in her Lithuanian accent, for she knew she was the only teacher to whom we granted such respect.

To look at her, one might expect to see her buying grapes or yellow daffodils at a fruit stand. She was a big woman with a round, wise face. Her almond-shaped eyes were sharp, icy blue. They were eyes that had seen much of life—her family had escaped the Soviet Union during World War II, but her father and brother had been killed along with millions of other refugees. She had high cheekbones and straight, short gray hair. When she spoke, her consonants were sharp but not harsh. They gently clicked and ticked across her teeth. Her vowels were slow and smooth, and she rolled her "r's" when she got excited. She had no use for an extravagant wardrobe. Simple skirts and sweaters suited her best, but they were always warm pinks, bright blues, or mustard yellows.

Mrs. Lilvinas was our Advanced Placement English teacher during our senior year of high school. Most of us had come to the course on recommendation from previous teachers. Most of us had understood the intricate books we had read. Most of us could write a well-developed essay explaining the political symbolism of Madame DeFarge's crocheting. We joined the A.P. elite, but few of us expected what was to come.

continues

We learned to be alert in her class, never knowing what morsels we might find in her lectures. She challenged us every day to work harder, learn more, and be better than we had been the day before. "Today you will write for me," she would say as she passed out the assignments. "You will tell me how Faulkner uses time as a structuring device in the first half of his book." Some of us cringed silently; others moaned audibly. "Thank you, Mrs. Litvinas," she prompted us. "Thank you for helping me to become a better person."

"Thank you, Mrs. Litvinas," we all mumbled in singsong, then laughed at ourselves.

I can still hear her. Each day she passed out an in-class writing assignment, she would plod up and down the aisles, saying, "If you have not read, you will write on your paper, 'My character needs improvement.' When you finish that, you may sit quietly and contemplate your immortal soul. Do not philosophize! I do not care to read your little philosophies. I want to know if you have read the book. You must read the books in order to pass my class. If you do not read, you will never survive me. I will break you!" Her voice still rings in my mind.

Sometimes she'd mock our papers by reading in a nasal tone, "And so therefore I believe that I think that in conclusion . . ." and pound her fist on the podium. "No! Don't insult me with that garbage. We both know you can do better. All of you."

When our papers were returned, more often than not they were covered with red markings: a "NO!" beside one passage, a triumphant "YES!" beside another, or perhaps an "I know where you stopped reading."

In class she would say, "Be glad there is still room for improvement. Life would be so dull if you were already perfect." When we discussed the "lock theory" in *Darkness at Noon* or Faulkner's southern code of honor or Ionesco's social criticism, she would slice the air and say things like this: "Nothing is a throw-away. Only a small writer would put that sentence there for no reason. You must drink every word in. You must read it over and over until it becomes part of you." And so we drank and drank until we overflowed with Shakespeare and Conrad and Chekhov and Forster. We became, as Mrs. Litvinas would say, "masters of the craft."

Strangers might think Mrs. Litvinas mean, maybe crazy, but those of us who knew her loved her. We waited for her philosophical wanderings. "You must be with people who make you more," she insisted with a broad sweep of arm. "None of this drinking beer at parties. Get a bottle of wine and take your mother on a picnic. You have got to realize, ladies and gentlemen, that there is more to life than chicken at Wegman's" [a local supermarket].

This was her favorite line and we all knew what she meant about what was important in life. Those of us whom she touched with her strength, knowledge, wisdom, and love went out into the world perhaps a little better prepared to face the challenges that life offers.

Discussion/Writing

1. What makes this essay honest and not fake praise of a teacher?
2. How do you react to Mrs. Litvinas's teaching methods? Honestly look for both good and bad aspects.
3. Describe a teacher you had whose strong personality left you with mixed feelings. Balance your honest gut feelings with an honest, objective evaluation.

Student Sample

Personal Ads

Submitted Anonymously

1. Single black male, age 23, looking for a woman who is independent and likes to watch sports. Must be good looking, like Halle Berry or Toni Braxton and must be around the age of 25–29. If you are this person, call 1-800-TOO-CUTE!

2. Single female—athletically bodacious, confident, self-secure and outgoing—looking for large, healthy, fit man who enjoys clean fun, romance, the great outdoors and a cold beer.

3. I am a single, white female who is loving, caring and honest. I'm looking for a younger guy who will like me for who I am and not try to change me. I enjoy hiking and skiing and it would be nice if this person would too. I also enjoy spending time at home with my family.

4. Exploring South American jungles! Climbing the Alps! Swimming the crystal blue waters of Hawaii. All this is within your grasp and whatever else! Imagination is the key to open my heart.

5. Boring and stupid young male looking for a boring and stupid young female. Call me for a boring and stupid time.

6. Single white male, age 18, wants a sweetheart. I enjoy sports but will spend lots of time cuddling with my special girl. I hope she'll be caring and maybe a little lonely when I'm not around.

7. Smart, funny, sometimes sassy Queen looking for a strong King to rule in my castle. Wannabes need not apply.

Discussion/Writing

1. Closely analyze two of these personal ads for the signals they send to their audience. Pay special attention to the values behind the words, how the style (vocabulary and tone) reveals the writer, what is left out, and perhaps what might appeal to readers and turn them off. How honest do they seem?

2. Here is a sample analysis of the first ad as a model: His **style** is specific and factual with a little corny humor in the phone number. The use of the word "must" twice suggests a rigid outlook and maybe more. If I were his **audience**—a gorgeous, independent, older woman—I'd probably think this guy wants a fantasy, not a real person. What's **not said?** He talks a lot about what he wants, but says almost nothing about what he offers the woman. His **values** emphasize physical appearance and self-centeredness, and I suspect most women will be **turned off** by his desire for a Hollywood face. **Honesty?** Does a Toni Braxton look-alike read the personals? I'm a little suspicious of "independent," too—does he want money or self-reliance?

CHAPTER 2

The Two-Part Secret of Good Writing

Ideas and Details

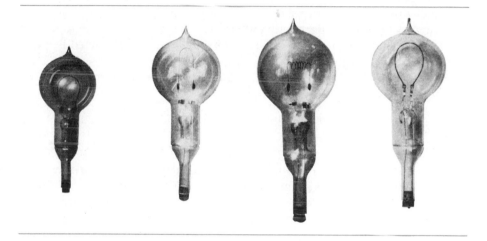

Eternity is in love with the productions of time.

—WILLIAM BLAKE

You probably didn't expect the best kept secret of writing to be given away so soon, but here it is. All successful writers—whether businesspeople or professionals—have this ability, and many writers who have serious flaws in other aspects of their writing can get by with just this one skill: **the ability to combine ideas and details.** Another way of saying this is that the successful writer must continually move between the general and the specific.

Ideas and details are the heart of your writing. They alone cause readers to say, "This is great!" or "Let's take this to the board of directors." No one I know ever received an award, a job offer, a kiss, or a promotion for perfect spelling or punctuation. Readers of magazine essays, love letters, and business reports care about interesting ideas brought to life with vivid details, and that is what your reader will pay attention to unless distracted by poor spelling and organization.

Let's look at what *ideas* and *details* mean, why they're both necessary, and how you can work with them comfortably.

IDEAS

An idea summarizes; it concludes, highlights, or generalizes. It's usually abstract. Here's an example to study. Thomas Paine, who wrote many books and pamphlets in support of democracy at the time of the American Revolution, once said:

> Where there is bread, there is one's fatherland.

If your first reaction to this sentence was like mine, you found it vague or confusing. Most ideas take time to unravel. I would loosely interpret Paine's sentence to mean that people's patriotism and loyalty are given to those who satisfy their material needs. Let me share some other thoughts that occurred to me while thinking about this. If a government stops supplying our needs, do we become less loyal? Is our love of country really disguised self-interest? I wonder if the loudest patriots are the wealthiest? Would Americans trade their precious freedoms and Bill of Rights for bread if times were tougher? Is company loyalty no more than fear of losing a paycheck? I don't *think* I'd care less for my own family and friends if they didn't do things for me, but would I? Are people that self-centered?

I'm not sure if I agree with Paine's idea, but notice what's happening. *My comments are already moving away from the general to the specific.* Paine's idea stands above specifics. It can apply to many possible situations and leaves room for readers to supply their own examples. But because it is not specific, its meaning is vague. In the original essay this quotation was tied to specific details: Paine used it to summarize some of his reasons why a people should have the right to revolt against a king and be free—when the king did not feed, clothe, educate, or protect them—as happened in 1776. As with any good idea, the details gave it vitality.

■ **PRACTICE 2-1:** Below are four more idea sentences. Any could be the seed from which an entire essay grows. Examine them carefully to see what *expectations* a reader would have after reading them. What kind of details does the writer need to explain them?

- Robin Williams may be the funniest person alive.
- Technology today is humanity's greatest hope and greatest threat.
- Growing up on a farm prepared me for life.
- The Internet is not just a communication tool; it has changed our families and our values.

DETAILS

Let's look at *details:*

> A young man strolls a sandy beach at dawn, picking his way along the line of discarded shells, seaweed, and crab legs brought by high tide. He picks up several souvenirs. He plans to display them on his bookshelf when he returns from vacation. A fisherman casts in the surf a few yards off, and nearby is a pool of water left by the retreating tide. The young man notices a fish in the tidal pool.
>
> "It's a bottlenose skate," the fisherman says. "A lot of them get trapped by the tide."
>
> The fish is flat like a flounder, white on the bottom, brown on top with a long, whiplike tail. It thrashes the water.
>
> "Skates are garbage fish," the fisherman says. "They compete with the game fish." The young man looks closer.
>
> The pool is sinking into the sand and the skate gasps. It thrashes, searching for deeper water, then settles into a three-inch deep puddle. "A half-dozen get stranded every day," the fisherman says. "People don't eat them. Look—" he gestures down the beach where gulls are pecking at another skate, which is still alive.
>
> The young man bends, touches the skate. It's slimy. He tries to grasp it, but his hand slips off.
>
> "All right," the fisherman says, setting his pole in its holder. "Get the other side." Between them, the men drag the skate down to the surf. The skate jerks free as it hits water. It surges, tail splashing. The young man's souvenirs jangle into the frothy water and are lost.
>
> The skate disappears.

This little story is a collection of sights, sounds, and touches. It is easier to visualize the first time through than Thomas Paine's sentence because it is concrete and specific. We're not talking about dozens of possibilities here, but of one day at one beach with one fish. **Details can be facts, descriptions, stories, examples.** They give us life close up, one piece at a time. Ideas give us life from the mountain top, in grand scale. Details make a reader visualize, so what you write seems present and real. **An idea does something else for a reader—it gives a sense of purpose and more**

significance to the details than first meets the eye. You might consider details and ideas to be sight and insight—the physical presence and the mental meaning. Readers need both to feel satisfied with a piece of writing.

The story about the skate might end as it is, leaving the reader to figure out what insight is behind these details. Fiction usually does not tell, while narrative essays often make the meaning clearer by climaxing the story with a generalization. Let me suggest some. One thing seems clear—the young man understands better the life that inhabits his souvenirs. In a sense both men have been fishing. Has the older man been resensitized to the lives he takes for sport, or is he just being polite? The loss of the shells in the frothy sea and the fact that gulls eat many skates each day suggest it is futile to save one life. Is it?

Notice that we had to move to details with Thomas Paine's idea to clarify and develop it. The story about the skate was a collection of details; to clarify and develop it, we must move toward ideas that give meaning and purpose to the details. Alone, neither is enough.

Read the following, and try to figure out what each paragraph needs to satisfy a reader:

1. Is it fair for a woman who gets raped and pregnant to have to deliver her rapist's baby? Then there's the possibility she may be in danger of dying herself. But there are lots of women who use abortion like birth control and don't give a damn that a little life is involved. And I personally know of at least one anti-abortion protester who had an abortion herself! On the other hand, if we say a woman has total rights over her own body, doesn't that also give her the right to use drugs, be a prostitute, or commit suicide?

2. Education today needs to be more personal. Too much that goes on in schools is theoretical and professional; students and teachers both forget they're dealing with people because they focus too much on the job.

The overall effect of **1** is confusing; it has interesting examples, but it's difficult to figure out what the writer's main point is. The writer needs to help pull details together with *a unifying idea*. Example **2** is just the opposite. It has a clear, forceful idea, but hasn't come to life with details to illustrate what it means. See if you can complete paragraph **2** with vivid details from your experience and provide an idea that would tie **1** together. As you write, don't hesitate to *add details or change the idea a bit*. That is how writing gets better!

Aside from the specific facts and skills college teaches, it also aims to move you smoothly into a professional mode of thinking. The amateur thinker thinks only when inspired—which makes that person unreliable. Wouldn't you be shocked if a doctor, teacher, or accountant said, "Sorry, I'm uninspired today. Try me tomorrow." We expect professionals to be able to think as part of their jobs.

This is especially true of writing tasks. You may not be able to write a poetic masterpiece every day, but you should be able to put together a clear, interesting piece of writing almost any day you're asked. We'll be discussing other techniques for doing this throughout the book, but the first and most important is learning to **think in both general ideas and specific details in each writing task.** Ideas and details enhance each other, build each other up. They create inspirations.

The professional thinker (and you should see yourself this way) tests ideas against details and draws ideas from details. If your employer asks, "Do you think we ought to start a day-care center for company employees?" you've been given an idea to work with. Your first step is to test it against some details—how many employees would bring their children to the center, how much will it cost, is there room, and a dozen other specific questions. This should help develop the original idea.

If your boss says, "We get 40 percent more damaged merchandise returned from our shipments of widgets to New England than anywhere else in the country," you've been given a fact (a detail) in search of an idea to explain it. Could it be transport (bad New England roads); personnel (a truck driver on that route who throws boxes); manufacturing (widget psychopaths on the assembly line); or something else?

■ **PRACTICE 2-2:** For each of the following concrete details, create an idea that draws a conclusion or generalizes:

- In 1971, 62 percent of new college freshmen said they thought an important part of college was to "develop a philosophy of life." In 2002, 29 percent agreed.
- There are many more cells in each human body than there are known stars in the universe.
- Only accidents kill more college students than suicides.
- 2 + 2 = 4 (Hint: The most obvious details may lead to the most profound conclusions.)

WHAT MAKES A GOOD IDEA

What makes a good idea? The best ideas are original, but since true originality is rare, your teachers will probably be happy if you present an **unusual or fresh idea** and avoid clichés and commonplace ideas. Fine, but how do you get unusual ideas? It's easy to grab the first idea that comes to mind. The problem is, those ideas come to everybody else's mind first, too. Chances are, if you take the first idea off the top of your head, you'll be saying something trite and dull. Look at your facts or story more closely—what truth might be lurking there that isn't obvious? Here's an example. When asked to tell a story about themselves, many students write about being in car crashes. Ninety percent of the time the professor can predict the theme or idea—bad news for a writer. After the wounded are put in the ambulance and the tow truck hauls the once-sparkling car to the dump, the writer will say that he or she has learned how serious driving is and will drive more carefully in the future.

That may be true, but the essays you remember say things like this: "Being in an accident made me realize how close I am to death *all* the time and not really aware of it. A loose bolt, a piece of glass, a flying rock, one drink too many, and I'm gone forever." If the writer then goes on to speculate how people block this out of their minds and still drive, the writer is brewing a good idea.

■ **PRACTICE 2-3:** Think of an additional, less obvious meaning to be drawn from car accidents.

Being **brutally honest** leads you toward good ideas. Social pressure to say the acceptable thing and fear of embarrassment or of being different hold back fresh ideas more than a lack of brain power. No one deliberately tries to come up with boring ideas, but too often we censor ourselves. There will be more on this in the next chapter, which is devoted to getting ideas. But for now ask if your idea has an unusual twist or slant to it. If not, dig deeper.

A second aspect to a good idea is **complexity,** because the truth is usually complicated. One way to make your ideas deeper is to **develop several competing ideas.** Your writing will seem shallow if you imply there's only one way of seeing the topic. If you believe in simple explanations, I'd like to discuss selling my old car to you. To develop the habit of deeper honesty, force yourself to look for ideas that compete with your first ones. Put them on trial. This means you must dig up ideas that potentially contradict your first idea or offer alternatives to it. For example, if I believe young teenagers try drugs because of peer pressure, I should look for competing explanations before I plunge into a blind defense of that idea. Less parental supervision, films emphasizing risk taking and pleasure seeking, and despair about getting a job in an era of business downsizing are ideas that compete with peer pressure to draw teens to drug use. Can you think of one more competing explanation for why teens use drugs?

Why should you challenge your own idea? First, you will impress *author credibility* your reader with your openness and insight. Second, you will write a more honest paper. Third, you will anticipate objections your reader may consider and you can answer them. You can write, perhaps, that peer pressure is involved in other causes of teen drug use. For example, peers fill the void left by missing parents and by employers who'd rather fire than hire people.

There will also be more on this in the next chapter, but let me take some time here on competing ideas because it's so important. Students frequently tell me they've been working hard on their next paper, pull out a sheaf of scribbled notes, and then say they're frustrated because since they've been thinking so honestly, they can no longer figure out which side to take in an argument. They say they've become confused and can't recognize the truth now that they're searching for it.

One student had decided to write about television advertising. "Everybody hates TV ads," Carrie told me. "They try to get you to buy things you don't need or even things harmful to you. They lie and deceive. But everybody knows that." Carrie looked frustrated. "I can't write a paper telling people what they already know."

"So what do you think ought to be done about commercials?" I asked.

"Well, first I thought we could just not allow them anymore. But who'd pay for the shows on TV? Maybe we could charge people to watch, like with cable TV. Then I thought, well, what about poor people? And legally, don't the advertisers have a right to say what they want?" She sighed. "But what about *my* right not to hear the same dumb ads over and over? I'm so sick of dogs selling beer! Well, then I thought, why not just turn off the TV set? Maybe enough people not watching would make them create better commercials. Suppose a lot of us wrote letters. . . ."

"How about that?" I said.

"Oh, no! People are too lazy. I don't know if *I'd* even bother. The other night I caught myself laughing at a new ad. And I hum the jingles sometimes. I don't know what to write. It's just a mess. I need another topic."

"What? And waste all this good thinking?" I told Carrie to be glad, not upset. Her conflicting emotions and ideas had made her better informed, even though the only research she'd done—the most important kind—was in her internal library.

The temptation for a writer in Carrie's position is to glance at her watch and say, "I've got to get this paper done by Friday. I'm just going to pick a side, call it 'Just Say No to Commercials,' and state that the answer to bad advertising is to twist that little dial to the off position." Then the real idea she's come so close to shrivels and dies. But don't kid yourself. A FAKE paper will still be hard to write because it's tough work to tell only half the truth.

The honest response to confusion is to accept it. Don't worry. Most people are confused when they think. All research into creativity and idea-getting shows that you must tolerate chaos for a time until the confusion rearranges itself into a good idea. You have time to sort out the contradictions later in the last three stages of writing: organizing (Chapters 4 and 5), drafting (Chapter 6), and revising (Chapters 7, 8, and 16). In the thinking stage of writing, don't pick *one* side but gladly choose two or three sides before deciding what the truth is. If one fixed idea comes to you at the start of your paper and never changes, red lights and buzzers should rattle your head to warn you that you're not really thinking.

Work patiently through competing ideas, testing each with details to see if it is supportable. If one answer doesn't emerge during the thinking or outlining stage, perhaps it will in drafting or revision. If *the* answer doesn't come by then, the worst you have is a paper that says, "There's no simple answer to television advertising—the sellers, the station owners, and even the viewers are all to blame. No one solution can satisfy the rights of everyone involved." This is essentially what Carrie wrote. **Sometimes, the contradiction is the answer.**

Despite what I've just said, here's a warning: Deliberately trying to be complex *just to be complex* usually leads to confusing writing. Complexity should be the *result* of honestly exploring an idea—of opening yourself to see as many possibilities in it as you can. It's not something you add to a paper like a pinch of salt.

■ **PRACTICE 2-4:** Which of the following ideas promise the most originality? Which could you expand into an essay? Do any go too far?

- Suicide *is* a reasonable response to misery.
- It's tough to be a teenage parent.
- Racial discrimination continues to make this society unfair.
- Discrimination hurts the haters as much as those who are hated.
- We love innocence in others, but not in ourselves.

WHAT MAKES A GOOD DETAIL

What makes a good detail? **Vividness! Details must be specific, dramatic if possible, and direct, not secondhand.** Suppose you wanted details to bring the following idea to life: "College athletics do more harm to the student than the supposed benefits of character building we hear about so often." Which of the following gives the most vivid details to support the idea?

> **A.** College athletes spend so much time practicing they have very little time left for studies and they're too tired to do a good job anyway. What does playing basketball, tennis, or football teach them about their field of study? Yes, they're taught competition, winning at any cost, but will

that get them a good job when they graduate? Most athletes take easy courses and do poor work. They miss the real meaning of college. A lot of them never even graduate, and when the coaches get four years' effort out of them, they couldn't care less what happens to them.

B. Bill Peterson has just limped back to his dorm from football practice, where he has spent two hours slamming his body into a metal sled. The coach has yelled at him, "Hit harder, Peterson! Drive into his guts!" He's limping because the all-star fullback stepped on his ankle. "Pull those legs in when you go down, Peterson," the coach said. "You could trip the runner."

Peterson is a starter this year but has no hope whatsoever of playing pro ball or of making the big money. At the dorm, he picks up his history notebook and heads for his night class—scheduled around football practice. He sighs. The professor has been talking about Thomas Jefferson and the American Constitution as the first institutionalized statement on the dignity and nobility of man. "What a crock!" Peterson says. "Maybe I'll sit in the back and catch a few 'Z's."

Is there any doubt that **B** involves readers more, makes us think more? **A** is general and **B** is specific. **A** relies on abstract terms like "the real meaning of college"; **B** makes those ideas concrete by talking about Jefferson's concept of "the dignity and nobility of man." **A** is bland (athletes are "too tired" or "have very little time"); **B** is vivid, *showing* us how tired Bill is, not just *telling* us.

Finding the powerful detail can be just as creative as developing an interesting idea. Our eye, as well as our intellect, must be trained to see better. One of my students who wrote of hugging an old woman said, "Her chest was as hard and flat as a weatherbeaten plank." The story of years of living was in that comparison. Another student, writing about working in a nursing home, gave intimate, honest details: "I have put diapers on a 100-year-old woman, helped quiet an old man after a bad dream when he called on his long dead wife, and put countless people on bedpans only to have them miss and urinate on me instead."

Good detail may look a bit different in informative writing, but it follows the same principles. If I announced that you will probably earn more money after finishing your associate or bachelor's degree, you might not even bother to yawn. But if I gave you the details, told you that college graduates' starting salaries for 2002 average $31,000 per year to high school graduates' $16,000, I've given you something specific to visualize (you can visualize $15,000, can't you?).

The chapters on descriptive, narrative, informative, and persuasive writing will suggest specific ways of creating vivid details for specific writing assignments. But for now, remember that details plant the reader's feet on the ground. Support each of your ideas with at least a couple of examples, descriptions, or facts. Only then will the reader be able to see your idea clearly.

■ **PRACTICE 2-5:** Rate the vividness and specificity of each of the following details. Then rewrite two of the weaker ones for more specificity:

- Nurse O'Hare is a real witch.
- Many homeless people are mentally disturbed.
- Wedge shoes make women resemble flamingos trying to walk during an earthquake.
- In the last decade more women and minorities than ever before attended college.
- Today 27 percent of men and 24 percent of women have college degrees. Twenty-six percent of whites, 14 percent of blacks, and 12 percent of Hispanics have college degrees.
- The price of computers has dropped a lot in the past five years.

THE DIFFERENCE BETWEEN A TOPIC AND AN IDEA

Students often ask, "What's the difference between a topic and an idea?" and "How can I tell if my details are detailed enough?" Good questions. Let me respond through an example.

Suppose you decide to write a paper for your English class on growing old. Perhaps you've been noticing your grandmother slowing down and remember bicycling and swimming with her. Your topic is "growing old." But it's not an idea yet. **An idea must make a point about the topic.** An idea generalizes or summarizes. And there are hundreds of possible points one *could* make about growing old:

- Growing old stinks.
- Growing old is the high point of life.
- Growing old teaches us about the youth we rushed through.
- Society treats growing old as if it were a disease.
- Growing old comes as a surprise to most people.

These are all complete ideas—they generalize and require supporting details. The first two—first off the top of my head—are superficial. They show a simplistic lack of depth because I haven't subjected them to competing ideas. But all have moved beyond the vague topic stage.

If I decide to write on "Growing old comes as a surprise to most people," I might start by scratching down some supporting details:

"Suddenly, you can't do what you always did, and other people just assume they ought to help you."

Is this detailed enough? No! It's **fuzzy detail.** It does support my main idea and it sets up the transition to real details, but it's just not vivid. **You will know you're specific enough when your details do some or all of the following:**

- You name names.
- You refer to a *single* instance, not a group.
- You use exact statistics or numbers.
- You quote people directly.

For example, sharper details for my growing-old idea would be: "At 72, Evita Perez's knee began swelling up after grocery shopping, and her daughter began raking leaves and cleaning out gutters when she visited. Evita laughs about shrinking two inches so that she can no longer reach the top shelf in the kitchen. 'I woke up one day, and the floor had dropped!'"

■ **PRACTICE 2-6:** Write down a *topic* (like "growing old" or "terrorism") that you care about. Then list three preliminary *ideas* you have about the topic. Now pick one and write three hard details to support it. Bonus: Honestly question your idea by stating a competing idea and a detail that supports the competing idea.

SHOULD YOU START WITH IDEAS OR DETAILS?

Should you start with an abstract idea and then add details to liven it up? Or should you start thinking about papers with details and develop the overall idea from them? Both sides have their advocates and **either method will work as long as you move back and forth between ideas and details.** Remember: The thinking process is not neat; neatness is for the final draft. But let's consider the pros and cons of each method as a starting point.

In life outside school we usually learn things by starting with details and drawing conclusions. As children, we first touch hot stoves or we slobber out half words, and later theories about heat and language emerge. The idea of death was not real to me until, at age 13, I saw my Uncle Samuel looking like wax in a casket. Divorce was an empty abstraction until I lived through one.

As we experience things one by one, our brains develop ideas to explain our experiences. Most of our self-learned ideas grow this way over years.

On the other hand, most teaching starts with ideas and asks you to apply them to specifics. Moral guidance from religion or family begins with abstract ideas like "Thou shalt not kill," rather than letting you kill to see how it feels and discover what punishment follows. Biology professors give you the abstract plan behind a frog's internal muscle and digestive systems and then ask you to dissect a specimen, rather than handing you a frog and scalpel to let you figure out the principles by trial and error.

For a writer, sometimes details offer the best place to start—when you're doing personal writing, for instance, where recalling specific places, people, and incidents will lead you to ideas. William Faulkner was fond of saying that he started his great novel *The Sound and the Fury* because he had a picture in his mind of a little girl with dirty underwear. She had climbed a tree to peer into the second-story window of a house. Faulkner claims he wrote the book to figure out how and why that little girl came to be there.

Your professional writing tasks may more often start with an idea given to you. Your employer may ask you to come up with a plan to reduce employee absenteeism or to persuade a client to stay with your firm. Your job is to supply details. This might also be true with informative essays or reports in which the topic is assigned to you.

Details are easier to get than ideas. They tend to come to us whole. Ideas, however, rarely, if ever, emerge complete—like a light bulb flashing on. We need to play around with an idea, rub it up against details before we can say clearly what it is.

Think about how you might create ideas and details when you consider topics for papers. Examine the following as potential essay topics. What will be hard or easy in each?

- Democracy
- Your favorite vacation spot
- Airport terminals
- Artificial intelligence

Democracy is the most abstract and general topic. Therefore, an idea will be easy to get and details harder because the topic does not help you visualize it. But much has been said about democracy, so even though *an* idea will be easy to get, saying something fresh will be harder. However, that means competing ideas will be readily available. Your favorite vacation spot and airport terminals are both visual, so you'll have an easy time with details, but a harder time creating an abstraction about them. The vacation is one of the most common topics ever assigned, so a fresh idea will be even harder. Beware the topic that looks familiar or easy at first glance! The airport topic is more unusual, so as long as you stay away from the obvious approaches (hijacking problems and delays), almost anything you say will be fresh. Artificial intelligence (or computer intelligence) is less abstract than democracy but not nearly as specific as the other two. Visualizing will be a problem. Since it's a technical topic, details will be hard to get unless you're well read on computers or do some research.

■ **PRACTICE 2-7:** Evaluate the following topics as I've done with the previous four for ideas and details. Which would be the best topic for you? How could you tweak one to work better for you?

- Earrings
- Pet food commercials
- What conservatives stand for
- One of your family legends

THE THREE-TO-ONE RATIO

One last point: There's a classic formula for details and ideas. It says **about 75 percent of your writing should be details, 25 percent ideas.** There's nothing sacred about this formula, but it's a handy guideline. Many college students think abstractions sound more intellectual, more important than homely details. Your professor is likely to tell you, however, that most papers suffer from too few details rather than from too few abstractions. Almost every professor wants more and livelier detail.

In this way writing is like life itself. We need principles or ideas to guide us, but we spend most of our time dealing with little details of eating, working, and loving. We could ponder the meaning of love forever, but eating M&Ms and holding hands in a park gives substance to our abstract idea of love. Likewise, we don't continually ponder the direction of our career but do concrete tasks in front of us: answer the phone, plan the next meeting, and collect our paycheck. Once in a while, we need to step back, to see if the details of our job or love life match our ideas, make one life. It's the same with writing.

Highlights of Chapter 2

- Good writing combines ideas and details, and the writer who hopes to be in touch with a reader must continually move back and forth from abstract ideas to concrete details.
- Ideas give meaning and purpose to writing. They tie things together. Details help readers visualize ideas. They are memorable and touchable.
- Honest ideas should be both fresh and complex. Strive to develop competing ideas in the thinking stage of writing.
- Good details should be specific and vivid. The more nitty-gritty they are, the better.
- You can start with either details or ideas in developing topics to write about, but both are necessary and usually writers have several supporting details for each idea they present.

Writing Suggestions and Class Discussions

1. "If this were my last day alive, I would . . ." Make a list of ten specific things you might do. Then pick two or three and list specific details about them in note form. Be vivid, concrete, and honest. Don't write to impress people.

   Now, create a single unifying idea that best summarizes the philosophy of your last day. Write a short paper based on these notes.

2. What follows are some famous generalizations—ideas that need details. Pick one and use it for your core idea. Illustrate the idea with three or four concrete details and build it into a coherent paragraph. To sharpen your honesty skills, try to find an exception to the idea and work that in too.

   "Heaven is under our feet as well as over our heads."
   —Henry David Thoreau

   "Imitation is suicide."—Ralph Waldo Emerson

   "Fear not that your life shall end, but rather fear that it shall never begin."—Cardinal Henry Newman

   "Most folks are about as happy as they make up their minds to be."
   —Abraham Lincoln

   "Failure is impossible."—Susan B. Anthony

   "We see things not as they are; we see them as we are."—Anaïs Nin

   "The man who sees the world at 50 the same as he did at 20 has wasted 30 years."—Muhammad Ali

3. The following generalizations are all about love. Pick two to work into a coherent paragraph. You'll need to supply details—examples, facts, stories, or descriptions—to make them more concrete. Some of the quotes go together easily, but you may find it more interesting to put contradictory quotations together. You may agree or disagree with the statements.

   "Love is perhaps the only glimpse we are permitted of eternity."
   —Helen Hayes

   "Love is the delusion that one woman differs from another."
   —H. L. Mencken

   "It is impossible to repent of love. The sin of love does not exist."
   —Muriel Spark

   "A broken heart is wonderful five years later, when you see the guy in an elevator and he is fat and smoking a cigar."—Phyllis Battelli

   "Love is an act of endless forgiveness."—Peter Ustinov

   "Love is what you go through with somebody."—James Thurber

   "The face of a lover is unknown—because it is invested with so much of oneself."—James Baldwin

4. Quote a favorite line of yours from a song, then explain what it means to you, giving specific details.

5. What follows are collections of details about AIDS in search of an idea. Create two ideas that the details suggest.

   ■ AIDS may be transmitted from mother to fetus.

   ■ AIDS may lie dormant in a person for as long as ten years, while the person infects other people.

   ■ Three quarters of North Americans say they run "no risk" of getting AIDS.

   ■ AIDS is now the leading cause of death for women aged 25–39 and children aged 1–4 in New York City.

   ■ Most Americans say they have "little or no sympathy" for those who get AIDS from homosexual activity. Twenty-five percent of these say God is punishing them through AIDS.

   ■ In 2002, 3 million children worldwide had HIV/AIDS.

   ■ People between the ages of 13 and 24 accounted for 15 percent of all HIV cases and 4 percent of AIDS cases in 1998.

   ■ Twenty-four percent of all people with AIDS in 1999 were intra-venous drug users.

   ■ Sixty percent of AIDS cases are caused by heterosexual intercourse.

   ■ Many people in developing countries resist using condoms.

   ■ In 2001, 5 million people were newly infected with HIV worldwide.

6. For one of these topics, generate a list of details that can be used in a paper: quotes, stories, facts, descriptions. But also list ideas as they occur to you. Try for three ideas and nine or ten details on the topic you choose. Mark each item on your list as an "I" or a "D."

   ■ Teaching morals to today's children

   ■ Physical education classes

   ■ Cell phones

   ■ War movies

   ■ Abuse of the elderly

   ■ Choose a topic yourself

7. Follow the instructions for 5. This time consciously start with ideas first, freely moving to details.

   ■ An ethnic group to which you do *not* belong

   ■ Relations between western and Islamic nations

   ■ Personality of the last person you dated

   ■ Dentists

   ■ Thick pan pizza

   ■ Choose a topic yourself

8. Write down three *competing* ideas to explain one of the following:

    ■ Why men under 25 cause far more automobile accidents than women under 25

    ■ Why bad things happen to good people

    ■ If teenagers today know more about sex than other generations ever did, why there are more teenage pregnancies than ever before

    ■ Why peace seems impossible between Palestinians and Jews

9. Idea to details writing. Express in one sentence one of your guidelines for living: how to be happy, what is important in life, what is right, what is real, how individuals relate to society, family, nature, or God. Now illustrate your sentence with three specific examples. To be more fully honest, also consider a competing idea or objection someone might have to your philosophy.

10. Details to idea writing. Describe a powerful dream you've had. Start with vivid details: who's in the dream, where it occurs, objects, events, how you feel, odd or unrealistic aspects. Then interpret the dream— look for symbols, how the dream relates to your awake life. Suggest *several* possible ideas before concluding.

11. Write a list of ideas and details for a personal topic that interests you. Label each item as an "I" or "D."

12. Write a list of ideas and details for a professional writing task you might have someday. Imagine, for instance, that you have been asked to deliver a speech to your local business group or library or church group, or to write a press release or a memo on hiring procedures.

13. Write a list of ideas and details for a college paper due in another course. Label each item as an "I" or "D."

14. What is one idea you have mixed feelings about and would like to explore more deeply? Explain why you have mixed feelings and give a few details. (One of mine is how much freedom a teacher ought to allow students in writing assignments. One side of me says students should develop their own topics completely from scratch. It's democratic. The other side of me says students need to be shown they *can* write on anything and that in their careers they will most often be assigned topics. It's less democratic, but more practical.)

15. Write a two- or three-page essay based on any one of the previous writing suggestions. Aim for a fresh idea with some complexity and plenty of vivid details.

16. Evaluate the following list as potential paper topics. How hard would it be to come up with a fresh, complex idea and vivid, specific details for each? Also consider how these topics match your experiences, knowledge, and biases: What are your *personal* strengths and weaknesses in each?
    - The national budget
    - Concepts of beauty and ugliness
    - Stereotypes of grandparents
    - Exotic pets like pythons and ferrets
    - Lesbian parents
    - Your first encounter with violence

17. Write a letter to your boss asking for a promotion or raise. Present several reasons (ideas) why you deserve this reward and support each idea with specific details. For a sample student letter, see page 401.

18. Write a brief summary of a key concept you're learning about in another course. Write out the main idea so it's accurate and clear, then illustrate the idea with several examples. Imagine your audience is a student in the class who doesn't understand the concept.

19. Write a brief criticism of an afternoon talk show. Make an overall point about what you don't like, then support it with at least three specific examples.

20. Read the following student essay. As you read, pay attention to how it moves between general ideas and specific details.

Student Essay

Nosy People

Melissa Waheibi

Most people are nosy. We enjoy peeking over the neighbor's fence. We want to know what's cooking in the kitchen. We want to know what's on television tonight. We ask for a mirror while getting our hair cut, just to see how it's coming along. While having dinner at our favorite restaurant, we want to know where that amazing aroma is coming from, and why our dinner doesn't smell like that. We watch the news to see if the latest war has ended yet, how our stocks are doing, and to check out tomorrow's weather. This basic nosiness is fine. It doesn't interfere with anyone and keeps us informed.

continues

Then there is unhealthy nosiness. Do we really have to know why Larry got fired? Do we really have to know where the big boss went on his vacation? Do we really have to search through the closets to find Santa's bag of goodies? And do we really have to know who hosted that huge party everyone attended but us?

Some nosiness gets us in trouble. Let me confess. I was baby-sitting at a neighbor's house, and after I put the kids to bed, I sat next to the wooden crate that held their photo albums. I peeked. At the bottom of the crate, I noticed a fat manila envelope. As I opened it, my uneasy stomach told me I shouldn't be touching it. Inside, I found about 30 letters the father had sent the mother while they were at college. Of course I shouldn't have read them. But I did. And I found out that . . . (you would be disappointed if I didn't tell, right?) . . . they got engaged because she was pregnant! I shouldn't know that! That's personal stuff! I think they even suspect I looked because I haven't been asked back. My stupid, nosy nature got me in trouble, and I'm out 20 bucks a week.

Some people say they're not nosy, just concerned. Like when we pace the halls of a hospital, constantly wondering what is going on in the nearby operating room. But is it out of deep concern that we slow our car to gaze at a nasty accident? Is it out of deep concern that we make our friend promise to come out of the dressing room in her new corduroys? I'm sure some good Samaritans pull over to assist at accidents. And I'm sure some true friends really are concerned that those corduroys don't make her look fat. But mostly, that's not why we look.

I was watching Ricki Lake one night, and I was horrified—not at what I saw—but at myself. I found myself screaming at the screen, "You're so stupid! Why did you sleep with him? You knew he was married!" One third of television shows between 9 A.M. and 6 P.M. on the big networks are talk shows. We have Sally Jesse, Regis and Kelly, Maury Povich, Vicki Lawrence, Jenny Jones, The View, Leeza, Oprah, Rosie, Montel, and Ricki Lake. Why do we care what other people are doing with their lives? How did that become our business? Is it because we're concerned, or does watching them make us feel good because our lives aren't as screwed up as theirs are?

Nosiness is a human trait. It may grow from concern for others, but often causes problems and shows us in an unfavorable light. Society would run a lot smoother if we learned to mind our own business.

Commentary

Ideas: This is a wonderful topic for originality and there's an intimate honesty about it that appeals to me. Her "confessions" open us up to recognize ourselves. She also has several competing ideas to explain types of nosiness. But I feel let down at the end; I really want a strong main idea to tie it together. She is excellent at showing people *are* nosy, but the paper needs to go deeper into *why*. Why is being nosy "unhealthy"? Why do we look at horrible things and pry into secrets even when we know it's wrong?

Think of how *you* might answer these questions.

Details: Melissa does a fine job here. There are plenty of details for each idea. Many are vivid and honest. She uses hypothetical situations, actual examples and facts for nice variety. Can you add two or three new details to hers?

Structure: This essay is organized as a classification essay. Each new paragraph focuses on a different type of nosiness.

Style: I'm not sure about using the "we" and "us" approach. I like the way it includes the reader with the writer as co-spies, but many examples might not apply to some readers. But there's probably enough so we find ourselves saying, "Uh-oh, she caught me!"

For other sample student writing to study for ideas and details, see "Being Ghetto," page 89, "Letter to Senator Perry," page 396, or "Quakers: America's First Feminists," page 341.

InfoTrac® College Edition: Readings that Combine Ideas and Details

See page 464 for tips on how to use your *InfoTrac*® College Edition access.

> Aline Alexander Newman, "Animals at Play: Dogs Leap for Frisbees and Cats Chase Their Tails. But Pets Aren't the Only Animals That Just Want to Have Fun." *National Geographic World.* July–August 2002.
>
> *How animals play and what it means.*

> "When Anaesthesia Fails to Anaesthetize." *Discover.* August 1986.
>
> *What if you were awake during an operation?*

> Marion Davis, "Millions of Children Witness, Experience Domestic Violence."*Knight-Ridder Tribune News Service.* Nov. 1999.
>
> *Facts, quotes, stories, and examples to make you feel their pain.*

> James Kitfield. "Devastation in a Truck." *National Journal.* 1998.
>
> *Dealing with truck bomb attacks.*

> Mark Krupnick, "The Art of the Obituary." *The American Scholar.* Autumn 2002.
>
> *A dying author explains how to write obituaries. A long reading.*

InfoTrac® College Edition Discussion/Writing

1. List the main ideas in one of the essays, then state what the overall idea (the thesis) is. How fresh or unusual is it? How does the author achieve (or fail to achieve) greater honesty than average?

2. Now look at the details. First, reskim the essay to get a sense of how many examples, quotes, facts, descriptions, stories, and other hard, specific detail there is. What's the rough percentage of space devoted to ideas compared to details? How many are new to you? Which are the most interesting?

3. What details or ideas could you add to this topic? Write a short paragraph in which you raise a new issue or comment on what is presented (an idea); then list some examples, quotes, stories, or other details you or someone you know witnessed that might bear on the topic. Be creative—stretch the concept of the original essay!

CHAPTER 3

Getting Ideas

Brain Teasers to Help You Write on
Almost Anything

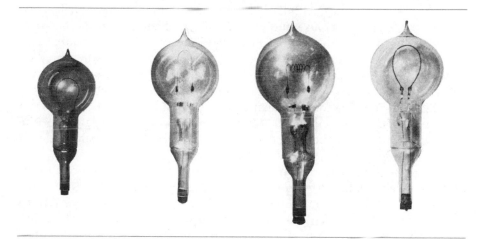

Writing is thinking.

—ANNE MORROW LINDBERGH

There are no limits set to thought.

—EDITH HAMILTON

Not all those who wander are lost.

—J. R. R. TOLKIEN

A former editor-in-chief of *Ladies' Home Journal* once said that she learned to be an idea person when she first started working as a young assistant editor. Each Monday, she and every other staff member had to bring to a meeting a list of 25 great ideas for articles. This gave her boss hundreds of ideas from which to choose for the dozen or so needed each month. It also gave the young assistant editor a headache. For the first few weeks she felt as though each idea was an elephant being born.

Then the ideas began to come easier. Some weeks she began having 30 or 40 ideas—better ones her boss could use. The important trick she learned was to let her subconscious mind work on the problem all during the week and not sit down at 3 o'clock on Friday afternoon to create 25 ideas. All week long she'd jot an idea or two down as it came to her—stimulated by all sorts of things—a taxi ride, a meal in a Hungarian restaurant, an unusual garden she saw, a newspaper article. Soon she realized that almost anything could become an idea for a magazine article. "Just knowing I had such an assignment made me remember things I'd otherwise have forgotten," she said. One of the side benefits of becoming an idea-creating person was that she lived more intensely, appreciated life more.

This is *incubation*. You plant a seed of an idea, and your subconscious brain—which has far more brain power than your conscious brain—will work on the problem. The solution that suddenly comes to you does nothing of the sort. It has been planted in the subconscious, which thinks about it while you go about your normal life, unaware of its activity except in flashes here and there. When the idea has ripened, it rises to the conscious level. My point is this: You don't have to wait helplessly for a magic moment to strike in order to write. You can arrange your own inspiration. In fact, it might be most accurate to say that working with ideas creates inspirations. Inspiration comes to those who sniff around a lot for hidden bones. It isn't luck when they dig up a great idea.

There are two things to remember about using your subconscious brain power. The first is that better ideas come if you **make a conscious assignment to your subconscious.** If you ignore the task, your subconscious will work instead on your bowling form or try to recall the telephone number of that great-looking person you met last week. The subconscious likes to be tickled once or twice a day with reminders if it's to keep going.

The second thing to remember about incubation is that **ideas often don't come out fully formed** like a newborn baby. They usually emerge in misshapen bits and pieces—the arm or leg of an idea. I'm using this grotesque image to describe ideas because most people don't want to accept such fragments as the offspring of their minds. Have faith. Be prepared to write down the idea fragments as they're delivered. You don't need 3 × 5 cards or a computer—although they work for some people. I'm a bit sloppy myself. I use any handy paper, and as I sit to write my first draft, it looks as though I've spread out the trash in front of me. The novelist H. G. Wells had an unusual system to keep new ideas organized as they emerged in bits and pieces. He kept a dozen big barrels around his home, one for each book he planned to write. When fragments of an idea or details came to him, he'd jot them on a slip of paper that he tossed into the appropriate barrel. When a barrel filled, Wells knew he had enough material to write a book.

There's no need to buy barrels. Two pages of notes are plenty to create a two- or three-page paper for a college course.

"Two pages of notes?" I imagine some students protesting. "Why not just write the essay? I thought you were going to save us work in this book?"

This whole chapter will address this question, but a few comments are in order now. First, I want to help you do a *good* job, an honest, deep piece of writing. Writing a draft without notes is easy if you want to do poor work, but it's the most agonizing way I know to create a good final essay because the revisions go on forever, trying to make up for the thinking that should have been done first. **A little sweat in the notes saves bleeding in the revision.** Notes nail down details, connect ideas, and help us concentrate. Researchers into creativity in many fields have shown that this is how the best idea people operate. They've proved it's dependable, saves time, produces more interesting ideas, and helps blocked writers get going again. Why shouldn't it help you? And remember this—all these notes are *easy writing* because you pay no attention to spelling, word choice, or complete sentences.

So when your boss or professor assigns a writing task, start *that day.* Suppose your anthropology professor tells you to write on "Cultural Differences Within the United States." In your next class, listen to the roll call. Do Mozzamil and Mustapha want to be called "Mo" and "Steve"? Does a woman with the French name "Lemieux" pronounce it "Leemo" instead of "Laymeoo"? Does the woman of Indian background touch other women while talking? Perhaps that afternoon you go to the dentist and get a shot of Novocaine. As the needle punctures your gum and the pain shoots through your cheek, you recall that the Chinese use acupuncture, which is painless. Perhaps you run into a woman in a bicultural marriage. Ask her a few questions. Talk to the Japanese fellow on your volleyball team. Eat at a Thai or Mexican restaurant. Read the "World News" in the city paper. AND WRITE DOWN ANYTHING RELEVANT. These activities will be fuel for your subconscious, and when you write your paper, deeper, more original ideas are more likely to arise as well. Inspiration results from many good ideas banging into each other.

Now, let me tell you how I got the ideas for the previous paragraph, because I wasn't doing it for a college paper. I knew I needed an example to illustrate my idea on incubation so you could visualize it, so I went to a sheet I keep marked "Examples." I made this up when I began the book. It's about 40 to 50 items long most of the time, and I add and subtract from it continually. I picked "Cultural Differences" more or less at random after considering "Grandmothers" (too easy and sentimental) and "Lasers" (too narrow). Nothing much came immediately. The next day when I took attendance in my class, I noticed the names from so many cultures. Later that afternoon I saw my wife talking with an Indian woman in the parking lot—

she touched my wife's arm and hair as they spoke, a cultural difference with westerners. That night our daughter Amy brought a friend to dinner, an exchange student from South Africa named Despo. We had a heated discussion about apartheid with Despo, who offered some unusual comments about American racism. That never appeared in my paragraph, for I couldn't see how to make such an encounter seem like an average occurrence in most people's lives. As I wrote these details into the paragraph, they brought to mind an American woman married to an Arab man and the incident of the Novocaine. (I didn't really go to the dentist, but recalled a lecture I'd heard a year earlier in which the speaker talked about why Americans never invented painless anesthesia while the Chinese never invented chloroform.) From this messy, haphazard material, the paragraph emerged. I rewrote it as a student might see the assignment, but the incubation process was exactly the same for me—and cost me little brain-squeezing pain.

■ **PRACTICE 3-1:** Take five minutes maximum to recall some specific cultural differences you've noticed where you live. Write in list form and do not worry about spelling or sentence structure. Tomorrow, add new things that occur to you from school, your job, travel, or television. Add to the list throughout the day until class time.

IMPROVING YOUR IDEAS

It's easy to come up with dull ideas—they're the first ones off the top of our heads. The tops of our heads are notoriously dull—clichés, television jingles, routine responses, and pass-the-salt ideas live there. The Greek writer Euripides once said, "Among mortals, second thoughts are best." Believe him! Second, third, and fourth thoughts create the unusual angles and viewpoints that make ideas creative. Put ideas on trial, as de Montaigne said; call them into question, as Edith Hamilton said. This is what the successful people who compete against you are doing.

So *how* do you go deeper, draw out your more original ideas? You can order yourself to be profound. Richard Wilbur tells the story of a poet who dove under water and held his breath until he thought up a line of poetry and sputtered verse as he gasped to the surface. It kept him in great shape, but really didn't lead to great poetry. Or, like most professional writers, you can *make a habit of creativity* through regular note-taking and incubation; you can get yourself into the groove of having ideas just as ballplayers groove a batting swing. Columnist Ellen Goodman says she goes "through life like a vacuum cleaner, inhaling the interesting tidbits in my path, everything I observe or read." Other long-term ways of being and staying creative are keeping a journal and reading stimulating books. They will reward you in many ways and lead to many inspirations in the long run. But these methods won't help you get next Friday's paper done.

For an immediate improvement in your ideas, use **brain teasers—systematic ways of stimulating and exploring regions of your mind to find out what ideas lurk there subconsciously.** These are the ways people think. (Brain teasers will be indicated throughout the book by the icon you see here in the margin.) At first, these brain teasers may seem artificial and awkward to use, but when you practice with them for a semester or two, they will become a part of the way you think, will help you create ideas quicker and with less agony. They will make it possible for you to think or write on almost anything. Brain teasers also help you to be more honest, for they draw out complex, conflicting ideas you may be holding back.

Brain teasers go beyond what you tried in the last chapter. There you *randomly* bounced between ideas and details—a kind of free brainstorming. It's a great technique to get started and may be enough to bring some papers to the Order and Draft stages. But there will be times when simple brainstorming doesn't evoke fresh enough ideas, times when you want more focus. Brain teasers will get you going again, and some even organize papers. If you feel blocked or empty, try one or two brain teasers to reenergize yourself. You can use several to get started on any topic.

All the brain teasers follow the same process. First, **make long lists.** Since your brain contains thousands of ideas, you must never settle for the first few that appear. Write down the obvious stuff, but keep going, for the longer the list you create, the more you'll have to choose among and the more likely that better ideas and details will turn up. Sure, you'll throw away some of these lists, but we're only talking about a rough list anyway. I recommend a half-page minimum for a brain teaser list. One page is better. It takes time to wake our deepest brain. Why a list and not freewriting? Items on a list are easier to organize than a paragraph. Also, freewriting tends to focus you on one idea; a list leads you to many alternatives. If you really like to freewrite, first do a short brain teaser list, then freewrite on the best idea your list generated.

Part of the problem any writer has is translating a nonverbal concept into words. How many times have you thought, "I know what I want to say, but I can't put it into words." Second, then, to eliminate this problem, **make a list of ideas in rough form—not worrying about wording or grammar.** Turning the ideas into words becomes a separate step. A little sloppiness is good compost: Don't rewrite brain teasers for neatness. If you use a computer for brain teasers, be sure to turn off the spell checker and grammar checker, which will distract you. In the early stages of writing, concentrate on *what* you want to say (the ideas and details), not on the structure (which comes next), the words (which come during the draft and revision), or the mechanics (which come last). Brain teasers are *not* word association but a list of ideas. One-word items are too vague to help a lot. Phrases of three-to-ten words or occasional sentences will tweak your brain more.

Third, **you must not prejudge ideas or details as you compose an idea list.** Write everything down, no matter how dumb some items sound. Judge later when you choose which ones will appear in the paper. If you judge at the list-making stage, you may shut off the flow of ideas. Good ideas have a way of hiding underneath weaker ideas. Research into the creativity of scientists, businesspeople, artists, writers, and many others proves that self-criticism kills creativity if done too early—save criticism until later. To summarize:

- Make a long list (half to one page).
- Concentrate on ideas/details, not words.
- Move quickly, and do not prejudge items.

TEN BRAIN TEASERS

 ## 1. Use Your Senses

List sense details about your topic—smell, taste, touch, and sound, as well as sight. This will help you get into the topic and supply you with vivid details for the draft. Our senses connect our mind to the world around us, so by recalling sense impressions you recreate the subject for yourself, engaging brain and feelings, stirring subconscious memories. Drenching yourself in sense impressions is enjoyable once you catch on—one of the secret pleasures of most professional writers. Sure, you look like you're lolling in a chair doing nothing, but you're really stretching your arms on a sugar sand beach as the waves hiss over your toes.

Let's try an example. List all the sense details you can about your mother (or another relative). Imagine your mother. Start visually—picture her face, the way she walks, favorite gestures, the way she looks when angry, sad, or laughing. Then become more specific—try her teeth, hair style and color, her favorite clothes. Bring up other things.

Now move to touch sensations—the way she felt your forehead for a fever, a time she struck you in anger, the temperature and texture of her skin, what it feels like to kiss her cheek.

Now sounds—the tone of her voice, the noise of her steps, peculiar expressions she uses when she speaks, unusual sighs or other noises like snores, wheezes, or gurgles. (Yes, mothers do these things. Be honest.)

Now smells—smell her perfume or kitchen or work odors, the unique odor of her room.

You can't just read my words to understand; try it with a pen or keyboard now. Write down as much as you can about your mother, letting your mind go. Probe deeply for the forgotten or unusual detail. Think sensuously. Recall key scenes. For me, my earliest memory is of my mother pushing my baby brother in a carriage across a busy street, me wondering where my father was; another key scene was the first time she learned to drive a car with a stick shift and made the car jerk up and down the street like a bucking bronco; a third was the night in a darkened hallway when she leaned against me and told me my father was dying of cancer.

Not only does a sense brain teaser prepare details and get you into a topic, but it also leads inevitably to ideas. Write any *ideas* that occur to you as well as details. For example, I noticed in my three key incidents that my mother always comes to my mind with my father, and it makes me recall that he so dominated her life that she really had little life of her own at times. This is an abstract idea, not a sense detail, and could become the main idea of an essay. This is exactly how brain teasers move writers from notes to a paper idea.

Using senses doesn't just apply to personal topics like mothers. Suppose you're writing about public smoking laws. Use your senses to visualize scenes of smoke-filled cafeterias or restaurants. If you're a nonsmoker, get down all the smell and breathing sensations you've experienced in a smoke-filled room—your burning eyes, your raw throat, the film on the windows, the stale odor of your sweater afterward. If you *are* a smoker, use your senses to describe the personal agony you suffer wanting a light—your dry throat, your nervous hands, your eyes involuntarily glancing at the door. The sense brain teaser is an excellent way to start almost any topic. It draws you into your topic and provides sharp details. It will not help you organize papers.

■ **PRACTICE 3-2:** Make a half-page list of sense details about bus or airplane travel. Move quickly; pay no attention to spelling or writing complete sentences. Be as specific as possible. In class your teacher may ask you to read your list and discuss how to develop it into a paper.

■ **PRACTICE 3-3:** Write a half-page list of sense details about a topic of your choice. Other brain teasers in this chapter will develop the same topic in different ways, so pick a topic you care about.

 ## 2. See the Topic from Alternative Viewpoints

This brain teaser gives you *perspective* by making you see the topic from outside your own narrow viewpoint. This is another secret of honest writing. When using alternative viewpoints, you must try to see the topic as someone else would, to inhabit another's mind and eyes for a little while and not impose your views on others. It helps open our own eyes.

For example, if you want to write on a personal relationship that has soured, first list all the people whose viewpoint might be different from yours:

- Igor (your ex-boyfriend)
- Igor's mother
- Igor's friends
- Your parents
- Your friends
- Igor's new girlfriend, Bertha
- Your new companion, Lars
- Your children (if any)

Now spend time with each viewpoint, trying to see the breakup as each of them would; what would they think in their secret hearts about it; how would they explain its causes or place blame? Remember that each of them will have a different focus. Lars may care less about the past than the future; friends may think Igor was tied down to you; your mother might take your side, but underneath her sympathy perhaps she hopes the experience teaches you a lesson about jumping too quickly into relationships. Ask yourself as you proceed how much truth is in these ideas.

If you still don't feel as though you have enough ideas, you can create a list of *character types* who always have viewpoints on any topic. This is a kind of cross section of human opinions. How would the following view your topic:

- An accountant
- A socialist
- A lawyer
- Your religious leader
- Your favorite singer
- Someone in the year 2050
- An ecologist
- A psychologist
- A child
- A politician

You are doing a little bit of stereotyping here, but just imagine what a lawyer might say about the breakup. He or she would consider it a legal/contract problem. What new facets would that bring up? Your religious leader might relate the breakup to your moral and spiritual beliefs. Obviously some of these character types may not be very helpful on this topic: the ecologist and socialist perhaps. The person from the future may simply say, "It won't matter by then," and suggest not worrying about it. Give each one a few minutes. If nothing comes, move to another. We all have little bits of all these perspectives inside us. To cultivate your deep, honest ideas, give each perspective a chance to speak. See who speaks loudest and clearest to you and listen for new ideas. Alternative viewpoints help free you from your usual self so you can probe your deeper, more unusual self.

Here are three examples of people thinking from alternate viewpoints. Loren Eiseley, the great nature scholar, said, "In the world of the spider, I do not exist." The aging actress Shelley Winters once said, "I think onstage nudity is disgusting, shameful, and damaging to all things American. But if I were 22 with a great body, it would be artistic, tasteful, and patriotic." Last, there's a story anthropologist Bronislaw Malinowski tells. While working with cannibals, he informed an old chief that the millions of dead in European wars were not eaten by the victors, but buried. The old cannibal shook his head. "How barbaric!" he said. All three make us think by shifting our perspective.

The competition among the different viewpoints will lead to more honest and sophisticated ideas. Good ideas toughen up under pressure from other ideas; poor ones crumble. Alternative viewpoints also help you relate better to your audience because you will think of things your reader may want discussed. As the English novelist W. Somerset Maugham once said, "The measure of a writer is the number of selves he encompasses." Can you, for instance, visualize the world your parents saw when they were your age? How did they feel then about music, war, computers, jobs, and college? What hopes and fears filled their thoughts?

Suppose you're writing on a less personal topic for a communication course, such as how television affects our view of marriage. You can start by listing some alternative viewpoints:

- Young children
- Advertisers
- Teenage couples
- Program writers
- Actors/actresses
- Lesbians and gay men
- Marriage counselors
- Religious leaders
- Senior citizens
- People in troubled marriages
- People in wonderful marriages

Go over each one, writing down the viewpoint of each and giving a specific detail. For example, senior citizens might complain that older married couples are often portrayed as grouchy and unloving. Remember, no matter how you feel about this conflict, each person or group will feel it is doing what's right and will justify these feelings. When you finish, you can begin sorting through the viewpoints to decide which to use. If you decide on your message before honestly exploring all sides, you'll be a little bit like the Queen in *Alice in Wonderland* who wants to have the punishment first and then the trial.

Examining alternative viewpoints is best for honesty, for widening your perspectives, and for audience awareness. It may help you organize but may tend to pull a draft in different directions.

■ **PRACTICE 3-4:** Your college is suffering budget problems and is considering reducing costs by eliminating the required writing course. List five people or groups who would have different perspectives on this plan. Explain each of their viewpoints in a half-page list.

■ **PRACTICE 3-5:** Imagine the perspectives four or five different people might have on the topic you chose in Practice 3-3. Fill a half-page with their viewpoints.

3. Attack Stereotypes, Unquestioned Ideas, and Slogans

Stereotypes, unquestioned ideas, and slogans are enemies of creativity—blocks that prevent honest, imaginative thinking. All three encourage us to think in accepted, common patterns—which as you know is not really thinking.

Stereotypes place people or ideas in closed-minded categories:

> "Poor people don't want to work."
>
> "A woman can't build a house."
>
> "They're white; they're probably racists."
>
> "Fat people are so jolly."

Sentences like these portray a writer who does *not* look carefully at life, a writer who sees groups and generalities, not individuals. Stereotypes are comfortable lies that make the world seem more simple and predictable than it really is. They're hard to break because they make thinking easy. But when you break them, your writing leaps to life. Do poor people really not want to work? The fact is that 40 percent of poor people do work, 45 percent are children, and 12 percent are disabled.

Leo Buscaglia, the famous "love doctor" psychologist, said he liked to touch students so they knew he was real—a human and not a faceless professor. He told students when they came to his office, "I'm gonna hug you!" and it terrified some, he said, because it broke the safe stereotype.

A creative thinker must peek behind **unquestioned ideas** once in a while to keep from being closed-minded. Doing this has led to some of humankind's most creative concepts. The Declaration of Independence challenged the divine right of kings—the unquestioned belief that a king received his right to rule from God. Thomas Jefferson questioned this by stating that "all men are created equal" and that a king should rule, not by God's authority, but by "the consent of the governed." What changes so few words have made in the world!

For centuries the dissection of the human body was forbidden. Until this unquestioned idea was challenged and the body dissected, people believed our emotions came from our hearts (not our minds) and even thought a man's erection came from air in his lungs!

Unquestioned ideas are invisible to us because almost everyone takes them for granted, like eyesight or the ability to walk. When I mentioned Thomas Jefferson's famous phrases, did you go one step further and ask if "all men are created equal" and "consent of the governed" have also become unquestioned *today*? If challenging these ideas is upsetting, it's because our belief in them is deeply ingrained.

Slogans are stereotyped use of words. If you find yourself concluding, "Man does not live by bread alone," or "Just say no," watch out! You're not thinking; you're repeating something off the top of your head. While stereotypes are comfortable and unquestioned ideas are invisible, slogans come to us with a sense of discovery: "Ah, I've got it!" But it usually means just as we had the chance to move into new territory, we found our way back to the worn, common road of thought. Students sometimes protest, "But this slogan is true! I've seen it!" Perhaps. But if it's true, put it into your own words at least to make it your truth.

I've lumped stereotypes, unquestioned ideas, and slogans together because the same brain teaser applies to each. To get fresher, more honest ideas, imagine yourself as a puncturer of balloons. **Become a cynic who suspects all commonly held ideas and sayings to have little lies in them that need exposing.** Think like the philosopher Nietzsche, who said, "Joyous distrust is a sign of health."

To attack these three idea killers, first list all the stereotypes, unquestioned ideas, and slogans you can about your topic, all the "common" truths. These are the things you'd write in your paper if you wanted to create a below-average paper. Next, find *exceptions* to items in this list. Think of people, cases, incidents that may contradict the common belief. Write as long a list as you can. After you've attacked the stereotypes, unquestioned ideas, and slogans, you can honestly decide what you really think and will have plenty of material for an outline/draft.

For example, let's assume your sociology professor assigns a paper on "Women in the Workplace." Here are some stereotypes, unquestioned ideas, and slogans I've heard about this topic:

- Women can't do the heavy work a man can. (stereotype)
- A woman's place is in the home. (slogan)
- Working mothers hurt kids by not being home. (unquestioned idea)
- Men will not go to a woman doctor. (unquestioned idea)
- Keep women barefoot and pregnant. (slogan)
- Equal pay for equal work. (slogan)
- Would you want women shot if they were allowed in combat? (unquestioned idea)
- Women are too emotional to be president. (stereotype)
- All male bosses are chauvinists. (stereotype)
- Women bosses aren't feminine. (stereotype)

Notice that these stereotypes, unquestioned ideas, and slogans come from *both* sides of this controversial topic. Now, the creative task is to puncture these balloons.

Some, like "a woman's place is in the home," are easy to attack. Suppose Queen Elizabeth I, Venus Williams, Catherine the Great, Marie Curie, Jane Goodall, and Oprah Winfrey had stayed home? My list could go on for pages. What a drab world we'd have without these perspectives and personalities. See if you can poke other holes in this slogan. Notice that the "pop" is more powerful if you use specific examples.

Other statements are harder to attack. I do think it's awful to shoot women in battle. I've been brought up to believe women should be treated with a gentler touch than men. Maybe, however, I need to get behind the "manners" I've been taught. Are those manners sexist? Maybe the real issue is that it's awful to shoot men in battle, too.

I found "equal pay for equal work" to be the hardest slogan to criticize. I agree with this slogan. But my job in this brain teaser is to question what I believe on the surface. So here's how I might puncture that slogan: How do we ever know work done is equal? Doctors may earn as much in two hours as a truck driver does in a week. People with seniority often earn far more for doing the same job as newer employees. What about quality of work? Many mediocre workers get the same pay as outstanding workers.

My conclusion: Equal pay for equal work sounds good in theory, but I discovered that variables not related to the worker's gender make such an idea hard to define, to put into effect, or to enforce. I'm not happy with this conclusion because I want to believe in the possibility of gender fairness, but until I think some more about it, I'll be forced to qualify that generalization. Can you find some exceptions to *my* conclusion?

You can research facts to attack stereotypes, unquestioned ideas, or slogans, too. It is commonly thought, for instance, that American workers are overpaid, underworked, and inefficient compared to workers in Japan and Germany. But in a few minutes I dug these facts from a brochure of the U.S. Bureau of Labor Statistics: German workers were paid an average of $22 per hour, U.S. workers an average of $15, and Japanese workers an average of $13. American workers labor 100 fewer hours per year than the Japanese, but 400 more than the Germans. And American worker productivity is 22 percent higher than the Germans and 24 percent higher than the Japanese. These put a few dents in the stereotypes at least.

This brain teaser shows us some of the walls we or our upbringing have built around our inner world. Tearing down these walls, or at least peeking around them, is one way people think. Loren Eiseley, the great nature and science writer, once warned any thinking person "not to love anything *official* too fondly . . . otherwise one is easily destroyed." Attacking stereotypes is good for creativity and challenging established ideas and a great approach to most college papers. It may irritate traditional audiences.

■ **PRACTICE 3-6:**

- List five stereotypes about men and **attack** two of them with examples, facts, or logic.

- Treat "all men are created equal" as an unquestioned idea and poke two holes in it with specific cases in which this is not or should not be so.

- List five common slogans used to debate public policy (for example, "Guns don't kill people; people kill people") and pop holes in two of them.

■ **PRACTICE 3-7:** List three stereotypes, unquestioned ideas, or slogans about the topic you chose in Practice 3-3. **Then attack them.**

4. Classify Your Topic

To classify is another way to think. Classifying breaks a subject into categories and places individuals in each category. For example, biology divides all living creatures into two main classifications: plants and animals. It further classifies types of animals according to whether they are mammals, fish, or insects. The thinking you do here is to figure out sensible, inventive categories that show underlying qualities among members of the same group that may not be obvious at first glance. People classified whales as fish, for instance, until realizing that some not-so-obvious qualities, such as lungs and feeding offspring with milk, made whales closer to land-inhabiting mammals than to fish.

In a classification brain teaser, break your subject down into categories several times until you come up with a creative pattern. For example, suppose your topic is "Dreams." You could break dreams down into daydreams and night dreams. Too general and obvious? Yes. Suppose I classify night dreams as follows:

- Dreams in which you're chased
- Sexual dreams
- Falling dreams
- Replay-of-the-day dreams
- Dreams in which you can't run or speak

To finish this brain teaser, I'd list examples and descriptions of each. Suppose your topic is "Education." Off the top of my head:

- Elementary school
- High school
- College

I hope this classification bores you. It bores me. But it is a starting point. So I try working just on high school. How about:

- Good high schools
- Bad high schools
- Average high schools

Nope. Still flat. The categories are too vague. How about this:

- Preppie high school
- Learn-nothing high school
- Vo-tech high school
- Parochial high school

This is getting better. I can think of people and facts to put under each. I might get even more specific by classifying types of parochial schools.

Let's go back to our main topic, "Education." I could have taken a different route. Instead of schools, I could have classified students, courses, or teachers. Take a minute or two to imagine several classifications for each.

The more specific your subject, the more you can do with it. This seems like a contradiction, since you might think the broader the topic, the easier it is to think up things to write. Not true. It's easier to think up common thoughts on big topics, but harder to say something fresh. Suppose you start with "Technology" as a topic. The possibilities are too overwhelming. Narrow it to medical technology and you can classify it more vividly. Narrow medical technology further to "Types of Gynecologists" or "Types of Sports Doctors," for instance, and the paper almost begs to be written.

You might have one objection to classifying—it seems to create stereotypes! It puts individuals in categories. Isn't that what we were fighting in the last brain teaser? Yes, it was. However, our main objective in this chapter is increasing the ways we have of thinking. Attacking classifications that have become stereotypes is one way people think; creating classifications is another. Classification need not be stereotyping—if you keep in mind and remind your reader that individuals do not all fit their categories perfectly. Classification helps us see patterns; it is only dishonest if it's applied too strictly. Classifying works well for scientific and technical writing and many college assignments. It is a strong organizer.

■ **PRACTICE 3-8:** Classify types of television comedies, love songs, art works, or country music. Have at least five categories. Now pick one of these types and classify it into at least three subcategories. Give a specific example of each.

■ **PRACTICE 3-9:** Classify the topic you chose for Practice 3-3. Break it into at least three categories and list examples for each category.

5. Compare and Contrast Your Topic

You can get more ideas by comparing your topic with something else. This is another basic way people think. We contrast socialism with capitalism, murder with manslaughter, retailing with wholesaling, the Yankees with the Mets. To understand our world, we stretch one thing to meet another, creating meaning. If you must write a paper on John Steinbeck's novel *The Grapes of Wrath*, you might discover ideas by comparing it to another novel. Steinbeck's novel is about poor people struggling to survive tough economic times, so it might compare well with Alice Walker's *The Color Purple*. Start listing differences:

Steinbeck	Walker
People are Okies, white Midwesterners	People are black Southerners
The antagonist is the capitalist system (banks, sheriffs, the rich)	The antagonist is the heroine's chauvinist husband
Characters travel across country	Character makes an inner journey
Pessimistic ending	Heroine succeeds in the end

This list should continue for half a page. What do I do next with this list? Well, I might create my main essay idea by combining a number of these contrasts, or I might go into one difference in depth: say, to figure out why Steinbeck's characters fail and why Walker's heroine succeeds.

Sometimes comparison or contrast is implied in the question given to you—"Contrast the Democratic and Totalitarian View of the Press," or "What Similar Techniques Do the French Painters Monet and Renoir Use?" Other times you may be given a topic and can discover a useful comparison to bring it to life. If you must write a paper on "Modern Nursing Ethics," think of several possible comparisons:

- Two nurses whose ethics are different
- Two situations that require different ethics
- Nursing ethics of a hundred years ago compared with today's ethics
- The contrast in ethics between doctors and nurses
- Similarities between nursing ethics and those of another profession

You would then explore *one* of these in depth, listing as many comparisons and contrasts as possible.

A list of similarities and differences takes the pressure off; you can say, "I'm only listing things." But when done, you'll have some ideas and details and the basis for organizing your paper as well. Comparison or contrast can open up almost any topic in any situation. Its drawback may be that you must work hard to get beyond superficial comparisons.

■ **PRACTICE 3-10:** Think of three possible comparison and contrast approaches to *one* of these topics: men's clothes, e-mail, or Christmas shopping. Pick your best and create a half-page list of specific points to support your idea.

■ **PRACTICE 3-11:** Think of a comparison or contrast approach to your topic from Practice 3-3, and list a half-page of specific details to support it.

6. Create Metaphors

A metaphor is a special comparison, not between things in the same category (two novels, for example), but between things in different categories (for example, a novel and a beverage):

- "Reading her book is like drinking a cool, clear glass of water."
- "Her party was like an insane asylum."
- "Rap music is a sermon delivered with hammer blows."
- "Love must be made fresh every day—like bread."
- "Old-age homes are like warehouses."
- "The city is wearing a veil of fog this morning."

Why make such comparisons? Because it's fun, and it stirs a reader's imagination and visualization. The metaphor brain teaser helps you because it suggests many ideas.

Let's return to the topic of "Education" again to show how you could use a metaphor brain teaser to come up with new topics that did not appear in the classification brain teaser. Start by listing all the comparisons you can think of, not worrying if some sound silly.

Let's try narrowing our topic to "College" and see what bubbles up:

College is like: a factory

the army

a farm or garden

a beehive or ant nest

the ocean

a circus

a meal

a tree

No apologies—this is my rough list. Now I glance over the list, adding a few details to each item to see which ones have the most potential. In trying to compare college to a factory, I think of college courses in which the same work is done in mass-production lecture halls, or how class recess resembles a shift change. The *idea* behind this metaphor suggests that college is routine, uncreative, time serving. Someone who felt this way may have the concept for a paper here.

I liked the circus metaphor, especially thinking about the last week of classes when everyone's a bit wild—people dress outrageously and "clowns" try out their routines in class. As an instructor, I feel like a ringmaster trying to keep the show going. Some students give beautiful performances, while that tiger in the front row snarls over his last paper. To explore this concept further, I'd want to make a list of all the circus things I can think of and try to find equivalents in college life. See if you can add to the following list and if you can find college equivalents for these items:

- Three rings
- Buying a ticket
- High-wire act
- The elephants bellowing
- The sideshow
- Monkeys
- Peanuts, popcorn, and cotton candy
- The bleachers
- The cages
- The freak show
- Cleaning up the elephants' mess
- The whip and chair

The overall mood a piece like this would create is light, a kind of gentle, sarcastic humor that doesn't take college too seriously, but as an entertaining game—much different from the grim metaphor of a factory.

Recently I asked a composition class to help a student with her paper on teenage suicide by suggesting metaphors. Let me recreate the discussion to show you how ideas emerged.

Me: What can you compare suicide to?

Student A: An ending.

Me: Okay, what kinds of endings are there? Let's think of endings, and then see if we can come back to suicide.

Student B: A rear end.

Student C: A cliff edge.

Student D: A book ending.

Student A: Yeah, like a book with the last pages ripped out—that's suicide.

Student B: How about a dead-end road?

Student A: Or a road that leads nowhere.

Student E: Suicide's more an escape.

Me: From what? Metaphors ought to be visual.

Student F: An escape from prison. Life's like a jail to some people. They want to be free.

Student E: Suicides like to control what happens to them. They feel like victims until they plan to kill themselves. Then they're in charge.

Me: So what's *that* like?

Student G: Like—writing a play. They make everything happen as they want—for once.

A metaphor brain teaser can lead to a main idea and be the backbone of your essay, but it can also be used simply to create a few sparkling details. It's good for creativity, visual detail, and humor. In college and business writing, you may want to keep metaphors on a short leash.

■ **PRACTICE 3-12:** Pick one of the metaphors for college (or invent one of your own) and make a half-page list of specific equivalents.

■ **PRACTICE 3-13:** Create one or more metaphors for your topic from Practice 3-3 and give a half-page of details.

 ## 7. List Examples

This brain teaser provides you with *details*. Simply list all the specific examples about the topic you can think of. If you're writing about abortion, list all the cases you've ever known: ones from the news, people you know, stories mentioned by friends or teachers. **An example must be a single concrete instance, never a generality.** This brain teaser tells you quickly which topics you don't know enough about before it's too late. If it's an assigned topic, it'll tell you what research you need to do.

If I were going to write a paper on alcoholism, for instance, these examples occur to me:

- Matt—A gentle young man who was attending AA during a course he took from me. Several times his writing and class comments were incoherent. He was quiet and lonely.
- Rico—An older man who declared he was a recovering alcoholic. He told me about the hell of shakes and fits he used to go through and how desperate he was to make up for the time he was "dead" for his four children.
- Jeanette—The mother of a teenage alcoholic. Her son had ruined her family, bringing her almost to divorce. She threw him out of the house.
- Ed—A 50-year-old man who stole money from his daughter for booze.

Once I started this list, I realized I knew far more alcohol-related stories than I thought—another ten or so besides these. Catching one example often hooks more. To develop this list into a paper, I might narrow it to teenage alcoholism or the effect of alcohol on families.

Examples are essential to support or visualize most writing. This brain teaser is a good one to use early in writing a paper, but will not help you organize.

■ **PRACTICE 3-14:** List a half-page of your own examples for a paper on alcoholism or drug abuse. Fill out some of the examples with details. To move you toward an idea, state a *point* the examples seem to suggest.

■ **PRACTICE 3-15:** List a half-page of examples for the topic you chose for Practice 3-3.

8. Make a Bug List

One way to approach any topic is to criticize or complain about it. You begin this brain teaser by saying, "What really bugs me about _____ is _____. Then you list all the complaints you can think of. A bug list helps you formulate a problem, and solving a problem is a great topic for many college papers. One tested method to impress your boss is to solve a chronic work problem. In both cases, you start with a bug list and move to solutions.

In preparing to write this book, I made a bug list about texts. Some are too filled with terminology, some too complicated, some too theoretical, and some too impersonal. The bug list told me what I wanted to avoid.

One of my recent students worked at a nursing home, and I suggested for one paper that she use a bug list to decide what she could write on. Christine listed dozens of complaints: about the elderly residents themselves, about the way the home was managed, about the families of the residents, and, most creatively, about her own flaws as an employee. She decided there was no easy way to make the home more humane and caring. She wasn't aware of this until she went through an exhaustive list of complaints. Old Mr. Fitzwater was just a miserable grouch, whose bad humor couldn't be blamed on family or staff. And there was that gloppy un-food served each day—she'd spit it out, too, if someone tried to feed it to her. And while she understood why an orderly might feel irritated by continual messes, she didn't like employees handling the old people as if they were machines to be oiled. She even found complaints about the building's design that encouraged isolation; it was more tomb than home. Now Christine could not cure all these ills in her paper, but by listing the problems, she saw how some things could be fixed, and she even brought them to her supervisor. And she found a new bug: He was afraid to do anything about her bugs.

Dissatisfaction has solved many problems, so put yourself in a sharp, critical mood for this brain teaser. Mention little things as well as large, abstract things so you have both details and ideas. Be honest. In reviewing your brain teaser list later, you may decide to tackle a lot, as Christine did, or you may focus on just one interesting or creative criticism and seek a solution for it. Bug lists are excellent for career problem solving and argumentative papers. If not used with other brain teasers, however, they can lead to excessively negative writing.

■ **PRACTICE 3-16:** Make a half-page bug list about public transportation, the World Wide Web, or a fast-food restaurant.

■ **PRACTICE 3-17:** Write a half-page bug list about the topic you chose for Practice 3-3.

9. Use Humor and Fantasy

Go wacky and wild. Think of all kinds of fantasy situations about your topic or the humorous side to it. This form of thinking is often downgraded because it sounds unintellectual or silly, but fantasy and humor have solved many personal and world problems. The German poet Goethe once said, "The intelligent man finds almost everything ridiculous." Dorothy Parker, the great humorist, said, "Wit has truth in it." And psychotherapist Sheldon Kopp said, "Laughter is the sound of freedom." Think how a grin or joke can often end arguments. Think of all the comic movies, plays, and books that have changed people's ways of thinking. One of the greatest antiwar plays ever written was *Lysistrata*, a story about the women of two warring armies who go on a sex strike until their husbands agree to stop fighting. No sex for any man, the women on both sides vow. It's a hilarious fantasy that makes a serious point about the stupidity of war—that killing and love-making don't go together—and Aristophanes wrote it 2,400 years ago.

Some people will find this brain teaser hard. But anyone can develop this part of his or her thinking repertoire. Being able to let go, without prejudging dumb ideas, is the key. Included in this book—in Chapter 14—is an essay by a student on "Pigs as Pets" that grew from such a fantasy. It's funny, but it also makes serious points about the human attitude toward animals.

Here are a few ways to help loosen your imagination:

1. **Reverse expectations of the normal rules of reality.** Gary Larson, who created "The Far Side" cartoon, does this with deer who hunt people, salmon who wear tourist caps and ride a boat upstream to the spawning grounds, and ants in lab coats trying to figure out how to get rid of their pests—humans.

2. **Break a social, scientific, or mathematical law** related to your topic and imagine the results. Do you hate the federal 65/55 MPH speed limits? Imagine the results of having no speed limit. Do you hate high taxes? Imagine a world without them, or a world of 100 percent taxation, or a world without money.

3. **Create a new rule or law and imagine its effects.** Suppose libraries could be recorded on microchips that could be implanted in each human brain at the age of 10. What would happen? If you're interested in world harmony, you might imagine a world government or the outlawing of foreign travel.

Humor or fantasy can spark personal writing, fiction, and satire, and occasional flashes enliven professional writing. It's creative, but risky. Know your audience first.

■ **PRACTICE 3-18:** Think of a fantastic or humorous way of stopping terrorism, preventing divorce, or reducing traffic deaths. Fill out your idea with a half-page list of details.

■ **PRACTICE 3-19:** Think of a fantasy or humorous approach to your topic from Practice 3-3. Fill a half-page with details.

10. Anticipate Your Audience

This brain teaser makes you think about how your reader may react to your topic. Answering these questions suggests strategy as well as new ideas and details:

- Who is my audience? Describe its concerns or features.
- What does my audience already know about the topic?
- What does my audience already believe about the topic?
- How might my audience respond to my opinion? Be specific, especially about objections they'd have.
- What does my audience want (need) to learn?
- What might my audience resist hearing? How can I overcome this bias?

For example, suppose I'm thinking about writing about garbage. Perhaps I spent a summer working at a landfill, took a course in the environment, and think it's an unusual topic. Here's how I might anticipate my audience.

My audience is my English professor and a peer group in class. I'd bet they don't *know* much about garbage. Most people leave full bags at roadside each week without worrying where the garbage goes. But one woman in class made a few comments about nuclear waste. My professor's hard to read; she said she enjoys nature but hasn't said anything specific about pollution. I'll assume she's more interested in good writing than in my environmental views. Probably most people in class *believe* we have too much garbage, but they don't know the details. I'd guess most would like to stop unnecessary garbage but won't put much time into it. About half would resist my pet idea of having lots more mandatory recycling, especially the Republican guy in the front who speaks out against government rules. Maybe I could say something about how rules are necessary until people get more responsible. To convince them, I'll have to motivate them. Plain numbers—tons of aluminum thrown away—won't grab them. They may be more impressed by the loss of trees and ugly strip-mining pits. They'll be most influenced by threats to their health by incinerators burning garbage and poisons leaking into our drinking water or even the rising cost of garbage collection. I'd like to get them to change their personal buying habits, but I'll have to do it in a way that doesn't sound as if I'm accusing them.

Doing this audience analysis clarified my topic, created some ideas, and uncovered objections I must answer in the paper. Because it stresses strategy, it's effective with argumentative writing. The downside: This brain teaser may draw you away from your beliefs and into saying what you think your audience wants to hear.

■ **PRACTICE 3-20:** Suppose you're writing a letter to your classmates about changing a government policy. After stating your point, describe your audience's beliefs, knowledge, and possible reactions to your idea. You may also ask a peer group to give a "live" reaction.

■ **PRACTICE 3-21:** Describe a potential audience's reaction to your topic from Practice 3-3.

If you can only remember one thing from this chapter, remember this: The more brain teasers you devote to a topic, the wiser you'll be writing the paper. Your idea will be tougher, more resistant to attack if you scrutinize it from many perspectives. Another way of saying this is that you have to kiss a lot of frogs before you find your prince or princess idea. People's typical response to a problem like writing a paper is to get *rid* of it; brain teasers help you learn to embrace a problem and make something positive out of it.

Brain teasers should be fun—you are playing the mind's video game, punching all the buttons and switching electricity through the cobwebs of the skull. Enjoy the show. There is no perfection, no rule for neatness or order.

Brain teasers give you control over your thinking. You can passively accept whatever ideas come to you, not knowing if they're the best or most honest you have, or you can reject intellectual helplessness. Active use of your brain's capabilities leads to self-reliance and confidence. **You edge a few inches closer to mental freedom when you can challenge an idea you find appealing.**

Writing is about interesting ideas brought to life with vivid details. All the structure, word manipulation, and grammar in the world won't breathe life into an idea-dead paper. Spend time creating lots of ideas, because good ideas make structure, word choice, and grammar easier.

OTHER BRAIN TEASERS IN THIS BOOK

Bouncing between ideas and details (page 20) Good for all types of writing. Helps focus and support writing.

Freewriting (page 96) Good for getting the flow started, working toward a focus. For people who don't like lists. Hard to revise.

Looping (page 96) Good for shaping freewriting toward a draft. Lacks overview of the whole paper.

Clustering (page 102) Good for visually oriented people; shows relationships among items so outlining is easier.

Thesis development (page 92) Good especially for research, college papers, and persuasion. Focuses your purpose before drafting. Weak for narrative and descriptive papers.

Overcome writing blocks (page 116) Good to help overcome fears and poor writing environments.

Six brain teasers for introductions (page 110) Good for focusing your idea as well as getting started.

Workshop with others (page 131) Great for new perspectives when you get stale reading your own work.

Iceberging and other eye-training brain teasers (page 169) Good for creating sharp detail and symbolism.

People-describing brain teaser (page 192) Good for narratives, but also for career writing when analysis of people is required.

Informative brain teasers (page 217) Process, cause, effect, and essentials. Good to organize and focus college and business writing.

Persuasive brain teasers (page 245) Facts, values, logic, Maslow's hierarchy, and refutation. Good for arguments.

Literary essay brain teasers (page 274) Gut reactions, critical perspectives, and explication. Good for any topic analyzing a text.

Using sources, asking questions, and commenting on texts (page 303) Good to fill in missing material and to surprise readers with facts. Can control the paper or downgrade your own ideas if overused.

Use Peer Review Checklists (in most chapters) These jog your mind to look at things you may overlook.

Journals (page 350) Good for personal writing, but can develop professional or college writing if focused. Uses incubation to stir the brain. Weak for tightly directed assignments.

Read student essays (page 349) Be inspired by your peers' writing.

Read professional writings (page 392) Be inspired by sources you can access on *InfoTrac*® College Edition.

Two Sample Brain Teasers

BUG LIST—GROCERY STORES

—Long express lines/people with 20 items

People with checks, coupons, food stamps, and unscannable items in express lanes

– Trashy newspapers:

"Aliens in Congress!"

"Lawyer Eats Baby!"

continues

"Liz's Face Falls Off"

—Too much plastic packaging

—Plastic bags—tear, dump groceries in car

—After your hands are full, the cashier tries to hand you the little receipt slip

—Carts in the parking lot. Wind blows them. Scratch cars

—People, especially kids with colds, grab bulk cookies with their bare hands

—Big Ruth!

—Not enough cashiers

—Carts with stuck wheels

Humor—Funerals

—"Doesn't he look good!" He's dead!

—Telling strangers how sorry you are

—Praising the dead one, even when he was a rat and everyone in his family is glad he's dead

—Soft pillows for the dead

—Old men carrying the coffin

—Justin saw a casket dropped and the corpse rolled into the church aisle. Half the crowd screamed. The rest laughed

Commentary

Format: Both brain teasers are good starts. They're in list form so the ideas can be extracted. Both are specific without being wordy. The length of each item is good, although "Big Ruth" and "Old men carrying the coffin" are too vague to mean much to me. The funeral list is too short. There's just not enough there yet.

How the authors might focus their brain teasers for a paper: The funeral notes emphasize ironies—contrasts between appearances and reality. This would make a good theme. But it needs more details. The author might try attacking Unquestioned Ideas and Slogans ("he's gone to a better world" or "her suffering's over"), Examples, Alternate Viewpoints, and Anticipating Your Audience to get more ideas. The bug list on grocery stores is an easier topic and may be too broad, but it has some sparkling details to work with. To be a successful paper, it will have to be narrowed down. Two focuses I see in it deal with customer behavior and improving the environment of the store. She has avoided the obvious path of attacking the checkout people. If the author wants more to think about, she could try Using Senses, Breaking Unquestioned Ideas, and Contrast (between two stores). What else would you suggest?

■ **PRACTICE 3-22:** Which brain teasers would you recommend to someone thinking about writing on the following topics? Why? What kind of paper focus do you envision?

- Trailer parks
- Gangsta rap
- The drug ecstasy

ROADBLOCKS TO GOOD IDEAS AND DETAILS

Despite all these brain teasers, there will be times you will find yourself staring at a blank piece of paper at 2 A.M. or at a few sentences that are so bland and empty you can't build a thing on them. All writers have these awful moments, so nothing is wrong with you as a writer if you have blue dry spells.

Fear of Risk

Despite the desire to do well, many people are just afraid to put anything on paper that is daring or a bit odd. They're afraid of being judged as weird or of revealing something secret about themselves. When they sit down to write, the flow of ideas is blocked by this internal censor. Sometimes the mind will let safe ideas through and you can manage to write something. Other times, the hold-back message shuts down the flow of all ideas. You want to write, but nothing comes.

Solutions: Tell yourself **to write down the most outrageous things about your topic**—the wildest, grossest, most absurd things. You reduce the fear of risk by telling yourself this is a throwaway list that no one else will see.

If I'm writing about pollution control, for instance, and I'm blocked, I can let loose the little demon in me to say irresponsible, risky things:

- Let's pollute faster so we kill off humanity—the world may be better off without us.

- There ought to be pollution hit squads. Instead of taking polluters to court, these action groups could break polluters' windows or dump garbage, oil-killed animals, or chemical wastes on the lawns of the company's president. We could picket their houses, churches, and clubs.

- To cut down on garbage, we could forbid all wrappers on things that don't need to be sanitary, such as clothes.

- Use big machines to crush garbage into blocks and build houses with them.

Next, I evaluate my absurd, secret list. Bullet 1 is just nastiness talking; 2 is illegal and mean, but modified a bit, it might be usable. Perhaps we could pass laws to hold individual employees responsible for company pollution and prosecute, fine, and jail them as individuals. Bullet 3 may also have merit if I tame it down a bit; 4 sounds like a technological problem (to make odor-free garbage houses), but turning junk into treasure is a concept I might be able to use with other items—such as automobile tires or bottles.

Insecurity About Your Ability to Think

People with this block are amazed that anything at all appears on paper. When *any* idea appears, they are so thrilled they don't dare put it aside or try for another option. They feel compelled to accept any idea as a gift of the gods. *These writers do not see writing as a skill to be learned because they think of it as a one-time miracle.*

Solutions: Writing is a learnable skill to be relied on, and a wealth of ideas exists in everyone's brain. In his book about human intelligence, *The Dragons of Eden*, Carl Sagan calculated that the human eye can absorb 5,000 bits of information per second and that all this data is stored in the brain, which recombines each bit many times with others, forming ideas and adding to them second by second. The average human brain contains an unimaginably large number of pieces of information and ideas—2×10^{13}—which is *far* greater than the total number of all electrons, protons, and neutrons in the universe! Be impressed with your own brain power. Rely on it.

If you're a thank-God-I-have-an-idea person, you're too humble. Use brain teasers regularly for several months until you build up your confidence that you do have many ideas to choose from. You must demystify creating ideas. Having ideas is human nature; it comes with our genetic code.

InfoTrac® College Edition: Readings on Brain Teasing

See page 464 for tips on how to use your *InfoTrac®* College Edition access.

Donald M. Murray. "Write What You Don't Know." *The Writer.* May 1998.

How to "harvest ignorance" and make the familiar feel new.

Linda Conway Correll. "Using a Shoe to Stretch Your Mind." *College Teaching.* Summer 1997.

"Creative aerobics" to generate ideas.

James M. Higgins. "Storyboard Your Way to Success." *Training and Development.* June 1995.

A corporate technique for group creativity and problem solving.

Robyn D. Clarke. "For a Better Way to Brainstorm." *Black Enterprise.* Jan. 2000.

Using drawing to think visually.

John Travolta. "From an Actor's Notebook." *Rolling Stone.* 18 July 1985.

The actor's story of the inspiration and incubation of a writing project.

"Managing, American Indian-Style." *Fortune.* 14 Oct. 1996.

Using a tribal brain teaser to solve problems.

"'The Wreck': Meeting the Needs of the Audience." *Business Communication Quarterly.* Sept. 2000.

A classroom game in which you must explain your car wreck to various audiences. A business perspective.

Highlights of Chapter 3

- Brain teasers are ways people think. They are learnable and can be used to teach yourself to think more clearly, more creatively, more quickly.
- Use your subconscious brain for incubation unless you enjoy frustrating yourself. Think early and often and take notes painlessly. Remember: Ideas create inspirations, not the other way around.
- Continue with a particular brain teaser until you hit a dead end or until you catch fire. When you catch fire, follow the ideas and details until the heat dies down.

- Trust yourself—you *do* have ideas.
- Coming up with ideas regularly is a part of most jobs for college gradu-ates. You won't even be asked to write a report for the boss until you come up with good ideas first.
- Use these brain teasers *any* time you get stuck for ideas or details. They can help you choose a topic, develop a topic, or jump-start a stalled draft.
- Brain teasers improve honesty. They are not formulas because each per-son uses them differently. They help you probe deeper into your unique experiences and views. Risk letting your mind free.

Writing Suggestions and Class Discussions

1. Incubation Exercise: Your teacher will assign a paper. At each class meeting bring in a half-page list of new ideas and details for that paper.

(Note for numbers 2–11: All brain teasers should be in list form and *note* form, not in paragraph style.)

2. Sense Brain Teaser:
   a. Fill one page listing sense details about your first home. Try for all five senses, being as specific as possible. Allow these details to bounce into ideas, but keep returning to the senses.
   b. Same as a, except list sense details about the first time you ever saw death. Recall hidden details.
   c. Same as b on any topic of your choice.

3. Alternative Viewpoint Brain Teaser:
   a. In a sentence or two describe one failure you have had. Then list your feelings about its significance, causes, and effects. Now write out how two other people close to you saw your failure differently. Try to think as they would. Now make a fourth and fifth list choosing two of the types of people on page 46 for your alternative viewpoints.
   b. Take any controversial issue today and write half-page lists for the viewpoints of each of the parties involved. Concentrate on honestly seeing the issue as they do.
   c. Do an alternative viewpoint list for any topic you choose.

4. Attack Stereotypes, Unquestioned Ideas, and Slogans Brain Teaser:
   a. Take some unquestioned idea (playing the national anthem at sporting events, for instance)—and see if you can expose some un-reasonableness about it.
   b. In a paragraph describe a situation in which someone stereotyped you because of your age, sex, race, physical appearance, or other reason. Then list all the exceptions to this stereotype that you can think of—in yourself or others.
   c. Pick a popular slogan that bothers you and list five to six objections to it.

5. Classification Brain Teaser:

   a. Classify a type of film into subclassifications. For example, classify three types of action films or four types of "chick flicks." List several examples for each type.

   b. Classify reasons why people succeed in their careers; what different qualities does success require? Give details for each.

   c. Classify any topic of your choice. Give details for each category.

6. Comparison/Contrast Brain Teaser:

   a. In your Popular Culture class, you are assigned to write on clothes styles of today versus five years ago. Fill a page with points of comparison, being sure not just to compare details, but also how the clothes' styles reflect changes in attitude or values.

   b. Compare or contrast two consumer products of the same type (two models of car or two microwaves, for instance).

   c. Write a comparison or contrast brain teaser for any topic of your choice.

7. Metaphor Brain Teaser:

   a. Life is like _____. List ten possible metaphors to finish the sentence. Then pick one and fill the rest of the page with details that could develop it. No clichés.

   b. A teen's first sexual encounter is like _____. List ten possible metaphors. Then pick one and fill the rest of the page with details that could develop it.

   c. Create a metaphor list on any topic of your choice.

8. List Examples Brain Teaser:

   a. You are assigned the topic "Computers and Children" in your introduction to computers course. List at least ten specific, concrete examples you could use in this paper. Allow your mind to produce ideas as the examples come. Circle any ideas that seem to tie the examples together.

   b. List ten examples of teenage crime. As you review your list, add explanations for its causes or ideas on how to stop it.

   c. List ten examples on any topic that interests you.

9. Bug List Brain Teaser:

   a. Make a 15-item bug list on one of the following topics:
      - Recreational motor homes
      - Evangelists
      - Television advertisements
      - Your job
      - One flaw in your personality

Now circle the two or three items that have the most potential for a paper and try to probe deeper into them by providing details and more explanation.

    b. Write a bug list on a topic of your choice.

10. Humor/Fantasy Brain Teaser:

    a. List all the humorous things you can about one of these topics:

- Blind dates
- Family holidays
- Funerals
- School cafeterias

    b. List a page of humorous or fantasy ideas about any topic of your choice.

11. Anticipate Your Audience Brain Teaser:

    a. In one sentence summarize a paper assignment you've been given for a college course. Then list the qualities you believe the professor expects in an "A," a "C," and an "F" paper.

    b. List a page of audience analysis about any topic of your choice.

12. Peer Review: Bring to class a brain teaser you're thinking about expanding into a paper. Read it to your group, explaining as you go. Write down the group's suggestions and circle important items. Finally, write one sentence that explains your paper's tentative main idea. Share it with the group.

13. Which two brain teasers do you think would dig up the strongest ideas or details for the following topics? Without actually doing the brain teasers, describe what each will provide for your paper:

- A report to your boss about which software program the company should purchase
- A letter to a girlfriend/boyfriend breaking off the relationship
- A research paper for sociology class on the minimum wage
- A cover letter for a job application
- Your own home page to put on the Internet

14. Using any *three* brain teasers, develop two pages of ideas/details on one of these topics:

- MTV
- Pornography
- City life
- A book you read recently
- People and their pets
- A first job

15. Using any *three* brain teasers, develop two pages of ideas/details on any topic of your choice. This can be a personal, college, or career topic. Try to choose something you care about or must write anyway.

16. Develop a rough outline from one of the brain teasers in 2–11 and write the rough draft of a two- or three-page paper from it.

17. You wake up one morning and discover one of three changes in your life:

    - You have aged 25 years. If you're over 50, you lose 25 years!
    - Your sex has changed.
    - Your species has changed.

    Thinking from alternative viewpoints, describe the next 20 minutes of your life accurately. These may be read aloud to peer groups and debated.

18. Your peer group's job is to write a bug list of what's wrong with high school, then solve two or three of the problems.

19. Your peer group's job is to break television stereotypes of cowboys, businesspeople, one ethnic minority, teenagers, or police officers. Choose one, state the stereotype, then break it.

20. This is your fantasy: You are director of community relations for a successful corporation. The company wants to donate $1 million to your community for goodwill. You are to advise them how best to donate the money. List various possibilities, then give reasons for your choices. A peer group may debate these lists.

Student Essay

The following essay began from a sense brain teaser list. Read the essay and then the notes and comments.

Spring Break: Mazatlán, Mexico

Tinamarie Ciccarone

Waiting for the train, I felt like a young child going to the circus. This was my first vacation alone—destination: Mazatlán, Mexico. Like the other hundreds of students, my mind filled with visions: the sun setting into the ocean, the serene beach at night. I was going to have the best time of my life. The Mexican train was scheduled to arrive at 3 o'clock, but that hour

---

continues

came and went. The train station was falling apart: chipped paint, holes in the wall, and the unspeakable rest room. Hyper students and baggage crammed the lobby.

As the hours crept by, I encouraged myself by flipping through the brochures of our hotel. The Riviera was the best beachfront in Mazatlán. I dreamed of crystal water and hours of undisturbed tanning on white sand. My excitement rebubbled, and when the train finally arrived in the darkness like a wobbly earthworm, our eyes widened and faces glowed. We chose seats in the dark and fumbled baggage into the racks above. My aching backside was thankful for a padded seat and we slept.

I opened my eyes at 7 A.M. and scanned the car for the first time in the light. The vinyl orange seats were layered with grime, and my white sweatshirt had become gray overnight. Some seats were loose and shook their occupants. The floor—the original color of which could not be determined—was black, sticky, and wet from spilled beer. Food wrappers, empty beer bottles, and cigarette butts collected under the seats. Someone three seats down dropped a powdered sugar doughnut. An army of ants seized it.

Pretty soon a guy with a bunch of keys hanging from his belt came through, yelling, "Cerveza! Cerveza!"

I limped stiffly down the aisle. The bathroom knob resisted turning, and the door hesitated before giving in to my push. A wretched smell rushed my unprepared nostrils, and I gagged. I took a deep breath and entered. What else could I do?

The bathroom walls were gray with dirt and slime, the floor wet with either vomit or urine or a putrid combination. The tiny window was closed, trapping the deadly smell. The toilet was black and unusable. The sink was filled with solid human waste. Before I could add to the vile mess on the floor, I jumped out and slammed the door behind me. I stumbled to the booth connecting the cars and sucked in breath after breath of fresh air. Unbelievable! I could not use the bathroom, wash my hands, or change my clothes for another twenty hours.

As I gazed at the countryside, I saw the Mexican people for the first time. We were snaking through a small village. Dozens of identical-looking children, barely clothed, sat in front of houses no bigger than my father's utility shed. Holes in the brick walls served for windows and door. Clothes-lines draped across the front yards. The passing train excited them. They shouted, waved, and ran alongside. I waved back and they shrieked joy-fully, like puppies behind a fence at my attention. As they vanished in the distance, I walked back to my seat, angry, disgusted, and confused about how I felt. A tear collected—for who?

By the time we arrived, I knew a little bit what life was like for unwealthy, ordinary Mexicans. I had not used a bathroom for 27 unbearable hours. I ate and drank tiny portions, making sure not to run out of food. My body, like everyone else's, smelled like a gym locker. My hair was ragged and tangled and my clothes were now brown. I never thought I'd reach Mazatlán, but of course we did.

Being young, somehow I managed to do some of the wild, fun things I'd planned. I spent hours on the sandy beach, the sun's warmth pene-trating and soothing me. The sparkling ocean was filled with sailboats, water skiers, and swimmers. Fancy, modern hotels and sophisticated nightclubs strung along the beach let us in.

continues

But I could see now what else infested Mazatlán. Locals scavenged like rats. Children begged money or food. Sometimes they trailed behind an old, hunched woman, but mostly they hunted alone. By the end of the week I no longer could see the beach's beauty. The hotels were no longer brilliant towers. The ocean lost its gleam, and the sun became plain hot. The happy, carefree college students seemed like mere shadows. What I saw were human beings who did not live like human beings, did not look like human beings. Finally all I could see were the children. Like stray cats, they sniffed through every garbage can in the back alleys, hoping for something, anything. None of them had return tickets in their purses.

Discussion

This is a vivid, honest essay with strong details. Tinamarie used the Sense Brain Teaser to help prepare herself to write the previous paper. This is how her notes looked. I've omitted the scratchouts and fixed the spelling to make it readable, but it was a healthy jumble in the original.

Brain Teaser for Spring Break 2003

SIGHTS—Train—shabby, dirty, old, worn down, broken windows, opaque with grime and dirt.

Original color gone; the floor was sticky, black, wet in spots.

Food wrappers and garbage under seats.

Spiders, bugs crawled on windows and floor.

The bathroom!!! Filthy, stinky, no toilet seat.

Toilet was black not gray or brown—Black—The sink was gray with a large hunk of human waste.

Flies gathered for a hearty meal.

Mazatlán—the beautiful ocean and beach.

Nice restaurants and nightclubs on one side vs. the poor, hungry, dirty

people begging for food and money.

Their broken-down buildings, streets, and sidewalks.

SOUNDS—the train was obnoxious, frightening like it was forcing its mo-

tion, like it was going to fall apart.

Constant banging from the connecting doors between cars.

Loud, rock-n-roll.

Rowdy laughter, drunken shouts on the train.

The guy who walked up and down the aisles selling beer had a bunch

of keys hanging down. You could hear those keys jangle from the other

end of the car. He yelled out "Cerveza!" in a scratchy, harsh voice over

and over.

SMELLS—the BATHROOM was unbearable! stench of human waste.

Air stale and uncirculating.

B.O., spilled beer, rotten food.

Commentary

Notice that Tinamarie did not use all her brain teaser sense details—some good ones like the flies in the bathroom and the noise of her peers never made the essay. She might have forgotten them or she might simply have found her theme didn't need them. Don't worry about using everything on your brain teaser lists. Notice that other things she barely mentions in her list become much more important in the finished essay—especially the children. A brain-teasing list is valuable not only for what you write down, but for how it helps incubate new ideas when you begin the draft or outline.

Finally, she mixes sentences, phrases, and sometimes single words, allowing ideas to flow as they want. Using the five senses as headings kept her on track when one sense ran dry.

Student Essay

Myths About Wicca

Bianca Guevara

Most religions suffer public misconceptions, but few religions today are as misunderstood as Wicca. Wicca believes in peace, balance, and nature, not worship of evil spirits or the devil. Most people who practice Wicca do consider themselves to be witches, but not the kind of stereotyped witches who fly on brooms. Wiccans do perform magic (or "magik" as they spell it), but not the kind that turns people into monkeys.

One of the biggest misconceptions is that Wiccans worship Satan. There is no such thing as Satan in Wicca. Satan belongs to the Christian faith. No one is really sure exactly how that myth got started. Some think it was the medieval Christian church's way to deter people from practicing Pagan religions. Other people believe that the church may have used a Pagan god (who happens to be a male with horns) as their symbol of Satan. In truth, the Wicca religion has nothing to do with evil. It is a peace loving religion, where everything and everyone is equal to each other.

A second myth is that Wicca is a purely Goddess religion. This isn't true either. In Wicca, there are two deities: the god and the goddess. Both of the deities play an important role in the religion. The fact that there are two deities represents the balance between man and woman in the universe. Wiccans believe that everything (trees, animals, ocean, wind, etc.) has a spiritual connection to the god and goddess. All things and creatures must be respected, loved, and cared for.

Another common misconception about Wicca is the use of the word "witch." It's true that Wicca followers consider themselves "good witches."

But they don't practice black magic—that belongs to Satanism cults. Why, then, do they consider themselves to be witches? Because the word Wicca came from the Anglo-Saxon word for witch ("wicce"). And witchcraft means the Old Religion. There are male followers of Wicca, too. It is said that a man in England, during the 1950's, revised the art of Wicca. Although there is no real proof where Wicca came from, most people consider it a neo-Pagan religion, or the feminist religion movement based on a variety of ancient pagan religions throughout Europe.

What about the art of Witchcraft and voodoo "Magik"? Well in Wicca they do practice magic, cast spells and perform rituals. However, this kind of magic is not as extravagant as some people think. Wiccans do not believe they can change the universe with their own hands. Their magic is more like prayer, as in Christianity or Judaism. When they ask a high priestess or priest to perform a spell, it's equivalent to asking your priest to say a prayer for you. The difference is that a magic spell is more immediate and more obvious than a prayer. When Wiccans perform magic, they are asking the God and Goddess for help, as some people would ask the Christian God's help. But they believe that the spirit of the God and Goddess is within them, which makes the magic being performed more significant. Special tools such as crystals, candles, or certain stones may be used when performing this magic; this is because everything has an energy and spirit. You can use elements of the earth—but never animals—to create the kind of energy you want. For example, if Wiccans want to protect a loved one while in the hospital, they would perform a magical spell for protection. They might lay a stone that represents protection in the sick person's room or light a candle of a certain color. Wiccans do not

continues

perform magic that would bring harm to anyone or thing, nor do they use magic to intervene in someone else's actions no matter how harmful those actions may be. They strongly believe in free will. As their old saying goes: "An it harm none, do what ye will." There is also the threefold law, which means that anything you do comes back to you three times. This is like the Buddhist principle of Karma.

This is just the very basic idea on Wicca. There are many different interpretations of the religion by the people who practice it. Like Christianity, Wicca has its own sects (covens). People of all races and classes practice Wicca. It doesn't discriminate against the CEO of a huge company or the clerk at a natural food shop. Since Wicca is recognized as a religion by the government, its high priestesses can perform legal marriage ceremonies. Every day Wicca is growing, with followers from all creeds, races and religions, despite the myths that surround this peaceful religion.

Discussion/Writing

1. List the main stereotypes the author breaks. What other stereotypes about Wicca might she have considered?
2. Find a part of her essay that needs more detail to convince you. Explain why.
3. What are three or four myths about your religion (or, if you don't profess religious belief, myths about agnostics or atheists)? Show why they're faulty.
4. What other brain teasers might be good to approach a topic like Wicca? Explain why.
5. These student essays illustrate the other brain teasers:

    Alternate Viewpoints: "Bastard," (page 138)

    Classification: "Nosy People," (page 35)

    Comparison/Contrast: "Food for Thought," (page 372)

Create Metaphors: "Pa's Secret," (page 356)

Using Examples: "Being Ghetto," (page 89)

Bug List: "Letter to Brad A. Walker," (page 394)

Using Humor: "Pigs as Pets," (page 336)

Anticipate Your Audience: "Dear Greg," (page 403)

InfoTrac® College Edition: Readings that Demonstrate Brain Teasers

In reading any of the essays that follow, pay attention to the way the author is thinking—look for the brain teaser below the surface that shapes and controls the finished writing. Is it possible to see two or three brain teasers in one work? Sure. "Would You Trust Your Boyfriend to Take Birth Control?" uses alternative viewpoints, examples, and contrast, for example. My own essay, "Moonwalking," uses metaphor almost as much as sense detail. See page 464 for tips on how to use InfoTrac® College Edition access.

Using Senses

Hamish Guthrie. "Resurrections." *Queen's Quarterly.* Summer 2002.

This poem evokes the feel of the sea and the past.

M. Garrett Bauman. "Moonwalking." *Sierra.* Jan.–Feb. 1994.

Your senses intensify when you walk in the woods at night.

Alternative Viewpoints

Steve Johnson. "Air Cadet's Dreams Shot Down by Harassment Allegation." *Knight-Ridder/Tribune News Service.* 27 May 1998.

Several perspectives on a sexual harassment incident.

"Would You Trust Your Boyfriend to Take Birth Control?" *Cosmopolitan.* Jan. 2000.

There are more ways to respond to this question than you might think.

Attacking Stereotypes, Unquestioned Ideas, and Slogans

Grace Marmor Spruch. "The Legend of Christopher Columbus." *The American Scholar.* Autumn 2002.

People knew the earth was round long before 1492. Here's why we assumed that they didn't know.

continues

Classifying

Karen Parr. "If the Scent Fits . . . Seeking Your Signature Fragrance?" *In Style*. 1 Nov. 2002.

Five types of women and the perfumes an expert says best suit them.

Comparing/Contrasting

Emma Dawson. "Forget Frilly Fashions: Today's Youngsters Go for Sophisticated Styles." *Knight-Ridder/Tribune News Service*. 13 Nov. 2002.

The author contrasts girls' dress styles today with the last generation's.

Thinking in Metaphors

"An Image to Relish." *Science News*. 31 Aug. 2002.

Why is a dying star like a hamburger?

Examples

Matt Weiser. "The Hidden Life of Your Television." *Sierra*. July–Aug. 2002.

Televisions are more dangerous than you think.

A Bug List

C.M. Smith. "Aimee Mann's Cliché Death List." *Guitar Player*. Oct. 1993.

Corny song lyrics that deserve the death penalty.

Humor/Fantasy

Karen Dave. "The Dog's Visit." *Chicago Review*. Summer 2002.

What is going on in this woman's love life?

InfoTrac® College Edition Discussion/Writing

1. Create a list of ten paper topics you could write that are take-offs from these readings. For instance, Johnson's article on a sex-harassment accusation might inspire you to write about an incident you witnessed. Dave's fantasy story about dogs might lead you to think of how your cat (or goldfish) could symbolize you. Make a half-page list of ideas and details for the topic you like best.

2. Choose one of the essays and quote several examples of how it uses a brain teaser technique in the finished writing. Point out the metaphors or name the categories in the classification essay.

3. Think up additional brain teaser material you could add to one of the essays. Write a half-page list. For instance, if you chose Guthrie's poem about the sea, list more sense details about the ocean; if you choose Smith's essay on song clichés, list more clichés from today's songs that bug you and say what's stupid about them.

✓ **PEER REVIEW CHECKLIST FOR BRAIN TEASERS**

Author:_____

Reviewer:_____

1. Is the brain teaser long enough (at least one-half to a page long)?

2. Are most items phrases (not simple words and not paragraphs)?

3. Are most items detailed enough? Circle those that need more specifics.

4. Add two or three new ideas or details of your own to the list.

5. What focus or main idea might tie most of this list together?

6. Suggest another brain teaser that might open the topic further.

CHAPTER 4
Paragraphs

Ideas and Details in Miniature

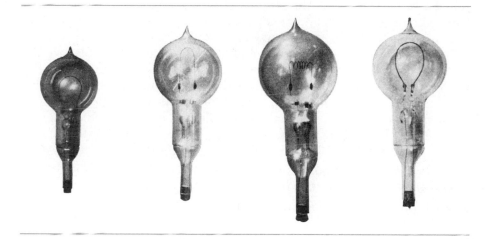

. . . If design govern in a thing so small.

—ROBERT FROST

So far this book has tried to open up your thinking process to create more and better ideas and details through the controlled chaos of brain teasers. In Chapters 4 and 5 we will begin shaping these creative lists into more finished writing. Paragraphs are good places to begin thinking about order, for like essays, paragraphs combine ideas and details. In an essay the key idea is traditionally called a "thesis"; in a paragraph, the key idea is traditionally called a "topic sentence." The rest of an essay or paragraph consists of details that enliven or support the key idea. In theory, everything in an essay or paragraph must *relate* to the key idea.

In actual writing, of course, paragraphing isn't so neat. What fits together and what doesn't involves interpretation, and it may be tough to realize you are repeating yourself. It's also true that many paragraphs by reputable authors lack topic sentences, contain two ideas, or use repetition for effect. It's simply the nature of writing to break rules. *As long as your reader can follow you,* you'll get away with breaking rules. But it's also fair to say that most good writers *do* follow two guidelines most of the time:

- **Each paragraph should combine one idea with as much vivid detail as you can pack into it.**
- **Each paragraph should stick to one key idea.**

THREE WAYS TO BUILD PARAGRAPHS

Here's an example from a student's essay on being a waitress:

> When you wait on tables, remember that people are unpredictable. With this in mind you won't get flustered, annoyed, or irritable when customers ask for margarine instead of butter, whole wheat instead of white, cottage cheese instead of coleslaw, and French fries instead of salad with their linguini alfredo. Nor will you think anything of it when a person orders pumpkin pie topped with chocolate ice cream or scrambled egg beaters (cholesterol-free powdered eggs) with greasy home fries and bacon.
>
> —Lisa M. Agban

This paragraph states its **key idea in the first sentence** and then enlivens it with six compact examples of diners' unpredictability. This common paragraph pattern can be visualized like this:

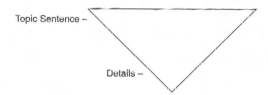

Topic Sentence –

Details –

The "broadest" part of this paragraph, its topic sentence, comes first, at the heavy end of the inverted triangle. The "smaller" or narrower details represent the narrow end of the triangle. But a sentence about how waitressing hurts your feet or about salary would simply not fit in this paragraph. A sentence about the unpredictability of customer tips *would* fit. The topic sentence-to-details paragraph is common because it makes sense; it's clear from the beginning where you're going, to both you and the reader. Here's another example of the same pattern from an essay about the destruction of rain forests:

> Rain forests contain nearly half of all the plants and animals in the world—] Topic Sentence
>
> many of which have unique medical properties that humans must save from
>
> extinction. Some rain forest plants are used to treat Hodgkin's disease, mul- – Details
>
> tiple sclerosis, and Parkinson's disease. A delicate, tiny blue periwinkle – Detail
>
> flower found only in Madagascar, for example, is the key element in a drug
>
> used to treat leukemia. Ecologist Norman Myers estimates there are five – Detail
>
> million rain forest species found nowhere else in the world, and many are
>
> becoming extinct before we ever discover what wonder drugs they contain.
>
> —Sally Lujetic

While topic sentence-to-details paragraphs are most common, good writers occasionally **start with details and build to their key idea,** as in this student essay about working in an insurance agency:

> The face of the clock, reflecting the cool, gray wall, reads 8:55. Outside
>
> the office, a face presses against the glass door—its nostrils flared, accus-
>
> ing like some grimacing, tribal mask. Do I look intimidating sitting amid

continues

disordered files, vagrant pens, computers, and fax machines, and muttering words like "subrogation" or "earned premium"? Inside the bright but still inaccessible office, I almost feel guilt for allowing this person to stand outside while I sit inside. Like a near-realized sneeze, the feeling passes, and I pretend nobody's waiting to get in. When the indifferent clock reads 5:05, similar masks reappear at the door, along with pummeling fists. Sorry! The office is closed. "C-l-o-s-e-d," I mouth to the irate face outside. The clock's indifference has completely become mine.

—*Irene Kuzel*

This intimate, honest paragraph gains power from the delayed message; the sharp details of the author's thoughts and description of the customer, office, and clock make us *want* a conclusion in the last sentence. If we were to visualize this paragraph, it would look like this:

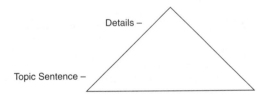

This paragraph shape works well to build up suspense in narrative paragraphs. Here's another example of the same pattern:

My first day of school, I wore a frilly pink dress with lacy crinoline puckering out around my bottom. The night before, Mom had to hide it so I wouldn't wear it to bed. I felt so pretty that day, as if I could stand on tippy toes forever like a ballerina. Mom held my hand, smiling. When the school bell rang, I thought everything was going to be okay, but Mom fainted with one of "her things." I tried to catch her, but she slipped through my small, helpless hands to the pavement. A trickle of blood ran down her sleepy face. Epilepsy, we'd been told. I knew she didn't <u>want</u> these things, but why did she have to have one _now_? A girl with pretty, carrot-colored hair stared with sympathetic, mocking eyes and asked, "Is that _your_ mommy?" So badly did I want to be accepted by the other children, I lied as I walked away. "Oh, no," I said, "That's not _my_ mommy," words that haunted me for years afterward.

—_Christine Bailey_

This paragraph starts simply, complicating and expanding to larger issues. As an introductory paragraph to an essay, it tempts us to read on for more detail.

Informative or persuasive paragraphs can also use the details-to-topic sentence format, as in this one on the issue of gun control:

Carol Kolen, a Chicago psychologist, was attacked several years ago at the University of Illinois Medical Center by two men, one carrying a gun. She fought off the rape but was severely beaten. Then one Saturday morning last year, she was attacked outside a neighborhood church. She bought a gun, and practices regularly at indoor shooting ranges. [_Narrative detail_] Many people install costly security systems in their homes, double-check their locks, won't walk to the store after dark, and panic if they lose sight of their child in a [_FACT details_] mall. But does it make a difference if your assailant aims a gun into your back, swings a steel bat at your head, or pokes a knife in your chest? No. [_Descriptive detail_] The threat lies in the assailant—not the weapon. [_Topic sentence_] In a society as violent as ours, the law should not take away our right to protect ourselves from criminals. Recent bills like the Metzenbaum/Stark bill before the Congress jeopardize our safety, security, and freedom as citizens. [_More specific restatement of topic sentence_]

—_Barbara Collins_

This paragraph plants the reader visually with a specific incident, then gives four other examples before widening to the key idea—that a gun control bill before Congress was unsound. The details-first paragraph makes sense because readers are more easily interested by stories and examples than by abstractions.

Later in the same essay Barbara relies on a third type of paragraph construction—one in which **the topic sentence is surrounded by details:**

Defenders of gun control say there are too many killings not to outlaw guns. But many killers today are on drugs. According to my sociology professor, 75 percent of all murders last year were committed by people under the influence of drugs. The person high on cocaine or in need of a fix won't stop to wonder if his victim will fight back or is armed. His lowered inhibitions make for haste—and you can't scare him away with threats or a stick. You have to shoot because when a drug addict needs drugs, that is the only thing that matters. When I worked at a drug rehabilitation center in Scotia, NY one summer, a polite, sensitive 16-year-old boy sobbed to me his story of cocaine addiction. One day his friends bought from a local Brooklyn dealer and after discovering the cocaine was actually cleansing detergent, they hunted the dealer down in a park where they beat and kicked him. Then one of the boy's friends handed the boy a gun and said to shoot the dealer. In his rage and frustration, he did.

This paragraph begins with a statistic and hypothetical examples, makes its main point in the middle, and then concludes with a specific example. It could be diagrammed like this:

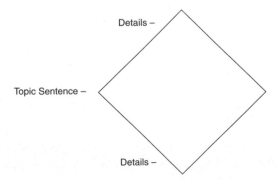

Some paragraphs may not need a definite topic sentence, and **the three patterns only suggest options for arranging details and an idea.** Most writers do not say to themselves, "Aha, now I'm going to write a details-to-topic sentence paragraph." But writers *do* sense the placement of details and idea. **You must always move your reader between the general and the specific.** You want to avoid paragraphs that simply state and restate the main idea and never reach specific details.

Start a new paragraph when you change the subject, change the speaker, change the place, or change the time.

TRANSITIONS

Most sentences and paragraphs naturally flow smoothly. But if you find the jump between two sentences or paragraphs difficult or awkward, try using transitions to connect them.

Repeat key words. Pick up a key word from the previous sentence. Such a word (in this sentence, it is "word") helps writers sew sentences together.

A common way of doing this without being wordy is to use pronouns that recall the previous sentence:

"*This* is why we must . . ."

"Because of *this* man . . ."

"*It* is a problem . . ."

Or use specific transition words:

Time Transitions: now, then, meanwhile, before this happened, afterward

Space Transitions: on the other side of the room, farther down the trail, nearby

Contrast Transitions (to highlight opposition): however, despite this, although the police say, on the other hand

Example Transitions (when giving evidence): for example, in fact, for instance, one case involves

Addition Transitions (amplifying a point): in addition to, besides, on top of this, also

Concluding Transitions (to end a section or essay): thus, therefore, finally

Place Marker Transitions (to move the reader from point to point): second, next, lastly

These are key trail markers for readers. By numbering your points clearly, you prevent readers from thinking you only have one mixed-up argument; transitions help readers see how things fit with each other. Transitions are invisible—like punctuation. Don't fear boring a reader with them. Many times you will use transitions naturally. However, if people seem confused about how your paragraphs or sentences connect, consciously include more transitional expressions. As an example, read the last three sentences of this paragraph without my two transitions, "however" and "as an example."

InfoTrac® College Edition: Reading on Paragraphing and Topic Sentences

For tips on using *InfoTrac®* College Edition, see page 464.

David A. Fryxell, "Many Happy Returns." *Writer's Digest.* August 1995.

This professional writer challenges traditional ideas.

Highlights of Chapter 4

- Each paragraph should combine one idea with vivid details.
- If your paragraphs are skimpy—one or two sentences long—consider adding more detail.
- If your paragraphs sprawl over a page or two, see if you have mixed two or more ideas into one paragraph.
- In revision, add transitions to show how the parts of paragraphs are related.
- Vary your paragraph patterns by occasionally starting with details and building to the key idea.

Writing Suggestions and Class Discussions

1. Write a topic sentence-to-details paragraph on one of these topics. Do a half-page brain teaser first and include at least four details in the paragraph. Be creative with the topics:

   - Oil
   - Your favorite television program
   - Zoos
   - Presidential politics
   - High school dances/balls

2. Write a details-to-topic sentence paragraph on one of these topics. Do a half-page brain teaser first and include at least four details in the paragraph. Be interesting:
   - Bridges
   - Math teachers
   - A scar or flaw in your body
   - One bigot you've met
   - Thanksgiving rituals

3. Write a topic sentence-surrounded-by-details paragraph on one of these. Do a half-page brain teaser first and include at least four details in the paragraph. Be creative:
   - Halloween
   - Litter
   - Laundromats
   - Something in school that's hard to learn
   - The human hand

4. Bring your best paragraph to class for a peer review, revise it, and turn in a finished copy.

5. Write a "paragraph anthology" of three paragraphs on unrelated topics. Give each a title. Each paragraph should be about half a page in length. Underline your key idea.

Student Paragraph

Being Ghetto

Shawn'ta Brown

Being ghetto is a funny, creative state of mind, and its language changes like the weather. You don't say "nice," but "fly," "fresh," "butta," or "hott." A loser was first a "nobody," then a "derelict," and now is a "scrub." A girl who sleeps around went from being a "harlot" to being a "ho," "a chicken head," and now a "pigeon." Clothes are "gear." A car is a "whip." When you're rocking in fresh gear, there's nothing better than a hott whip and a girl that loukdld so fly. But being ghetto is hard on English grammar, which is why it doesn't sound butta to management. "Gimme

continues

dat thang ova dere" won't get you a job. If the boss asks, "How are you doing today?" don't be creative and say, "Holla at me, baby girl. Ya boy could neva be betta!"

Discussion/Writing

1. Describe the "shape" of this paragraph by locating its idea sentences and detail sentences. What is its plan?
2. Write a paragraph of your own, making a point about another style of language (computer jargon, professor-speak, or your Italian grandmother's style, for example).

✓ **PARAGRAPH PEER REVIEW CHECKLIST**

1. Underline what you believe to be the topic sentence. If the rest of the paragraph does not stick to it, suggest changes.

2. What is the most interesting part of the paragraph?

3. How well supported is the topic sentence? Suggest one more detail the author could include.

4. How could one of the details be made more vivid?

5. What is the "shape" of the paragraph?

6. Mark all transitions used. Where might others be used?

CHAPTER 5

Order from Chaos

Thesis and Outline

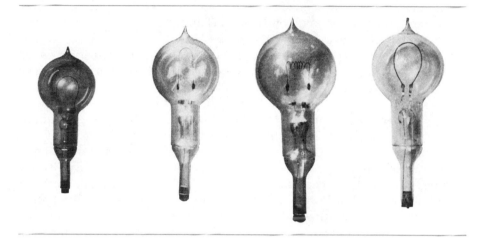

A place for everything, everything in its place.

—BEN FRANKLIN

A system-grinder hates the truth.

—RALPH WALDO EMERSON

In the quotes on page 91, Franklin and Emerson summarize the debate about organizing. On one hand, writing needs order. Ideas presented randomly as they flow from brains—or brain teaser lists—are often chaotic. On the other hand, excessive organization can kill the very truth writers hope to convey, for truth has a nasty habit of resisting preplanned schemes. This chapter seeks a reasonable middle ground between these extremes: the minimum organization needed to focus your topic. Why "minimum"? Because except in rare cases, no one ever exclaims, "Your organization really grabbed me." Fresh ideas and vivid detail do that.

That's why brain teasers are crucial. Nothing makes organizing a paper easier than creative, vivid brain teasers; nothing makes organization harder than a vague, skimpy list of preliminary ideas.

Let's start with an attitude. Organization must come from you. Don't cram your ideas into somebody else's box. Nor can you ignore organization, for it rarely occurs magically without conscious effort. The writer who plans how the essay will be structured and who studies a draft's structure will discover the holes in ideas ("I never did say *why* Matt Damon was so powerful as an actor"), unbalanced emphasis ("Oh, no! I spent four paragraphs on one movie and only one paragraph on the other") and redundancy ("I'm saying the same thing about Angelina Jolie in the second and fifth paragraphs—I ought to combine them"). The writer who plans will discover these things—before the reader does! In other words, developing a thesis and outlining not only should refine existing ideas, but also should create new ideas and details: *Structure is a brain teaser, too.*

A WORKING THESIS

A thesis is the key point your essay makes—the assertion, message, core idea, or purpose the rest of the essay illustrates or proves. This is where conscious organizing usually begins because a thesis creates the relationship between a paper's parts. Here are sample thesis sentences:

- Fathers and mothers who try to fulfill their lost chances through their children often crush the children's personalities.
- The 2000 presidential election proved just how political the U.S. Supreme Court has always been.
- The abstract painting exhibit on campus is awful.
- Bill Clinton was a better president and worse man than most leaders.
- My roommate models her life on a TV soap opera.

Some of these are personal, some informative, some argumentative, but as theses, they share two qualities. First, they give the essay a flag to rally around. They lead a reader and writer to anticipate and visualize the essay to come. Second, they are assertions—complete statements.

■ **PRACTICE 5-1:** What do the five theses promise a reader?

■ **PRACTICE 5-2:** Make up two trial thesis sentences on any topic you choose, then say what each promises your reader.

Statements such as "My essay is about welfare" or "Welfare is an important topic of concern today" fail as theses. What *about* it? There's no flag. Is the writer really going to tell us welfare is important? That's obvious. The real message hasn't emerged yet. A thesis asserts a viewpoint: "Two solutions look more promising than others to solve our welfare mess: Workfare and Entrepreneurism."

Not all essays need a working thesis. Narratives usually *imply* their messages, and simple reports don't need formal theses. In "How to Repair Your Bike" or "A Summary of the Minutes of the Student Senate Meeting," the MAIN POINT is obvious. However, almost all analytical, persuasive, and informative writing does require a thesis.

Try to develop a working thesis sentence during or after your brain teasers, but before beginning your first draft. You will probably modify it several times during the writing. This is a good sign that your thinking is not too rigid; until final revisions, you should still be learning about the ideas.

A thesis develops in two stages:

1. **Narrow the original topic** until it is vivid and small enough to handle in your allotted space.

2. **Make an assertion or express a viewpoint** about this narrowed topic.

Sample: A Working Thesis

Suppose the professor for your psychology course assigns a paper on love. The topic makes you—and me—panic. Thousands of books, poems, and articles have been written on the subject. How can you say anything significant in four or five pages? Well, you can, and here's how.

First, *narrow* the topic before doing brain teasers. Love? What kind? Sexual? Brotherly? Love of country? Can you list three other kinds? Your brain teaser will be hopelessly vague unless you're more specific than "love." To narrow, think a bit about the *circumstances* of the paper:

■ For whom am I writing? (audience)

■ Why am I writing this? (purpose)

■ What obvious topics should I avoid? (freshness)

These three questions apply to most writing tasks and will save you wasted work on doomed topics. In this case, your psychology professor is the audience. You may grab an uninformed audience with a general topic, but not her. Your purpose is to show you've learned something; you can't

just throw back her lectures. To be fresh, avoid topics and approaches common to other students. With this in mind, I hear this message: Avoid the
topic of sexual love. Many psychology classes dwell on it, and I'd guess most
students will choose it or parent–child love. I would pick the less traveled
topic. "Love of Country" cries out. Honestly, I'm skeptical that I can write
something decent about this, but let's try.

To narrow it more for vividness, I do some brainteasing—*asking questions:*

Is love of C. different in socialist countries than in democracies?

How is L. of C. different in monarchies?

In Hitler's Germany?

Should I deal with how governments encourage patriotic love?

Should I deal with the people's *need* to love?

Should I contrast L. of C. in different countries?

Should I deal with L. of C. in different races or cultures?

Would people today really say "I regret I have but one life to give for my
country" like Nathan Hale?

This brain teaser helps me understand what's involved in this topic; I'm
learning more. At this point I'm going to try an example brain teaser on Love
of Country:

U.S. purple mountains/fruited plains—L. of C. based on beauty.

What do the Soviet, French, or Nazi Germany patriotic anthems say?
Research?

The frenzy of Hitler's speeches—the spell and regimentation. The goose
step parades, the *sieg heil* salutes. What was behind that frenzy?

The shame of Germany after WWI—a broken country.

The Soviet May Day parades with missiles, tanks, and blocks of soldiers.
The gray mass of people—somber—dull.

U.S. parades on Memorial Day—dancing, fun, music, entertainment. A
sprinkling of soldiers. More loose and individualistic.

The tomb of the unknown soldier—all countries.

The editorial in my local paper critical of the U.S. on July 4th.

State-controlled press for Nazis and Chinese.

Japan: highest L. of C. was *Kamikaze* pilots.

U.S.: draft resisters during the Vietnam War said that they loved the U.S.

I learned or reminded myself of much while doing this and think I'll narrow my topic further to "a comparison of the psychology of love of country
in Nazi Germany to America today." My brain teasers kept returning to this,

and I'm reasonably sure no one else in class will have such a topic. If I'm not sure the professor will accept it, I'll ask her for approval.

Now I'm ready for the second step in creating a thesis: *to make an assertion*. Since I've decided to write a contrast paper, I should do a contrast brain teaser for more detail. Here's a start on it:

Nazi Germany	*U.S. Today*
Poverty-stricken	Prosperous
Ambition to be on top	Already on top
Chaos, emotional insecurity	Orderly society, more secure
Resents outside intrusion	U.S. intrudes in other lands
Fervent, frenzied L. of C.	Cool, cynical L. of C.
L. of C. meant obedience	L. of C. means . . . who knows?

In psychology class perhaps you've studied Abraham Maslow's hierarchy of needs,[1] and you recognize that some of these contrasts fit his categories. The Germans may have been patriotic because they were broken by World War I and poor; they had strong safety and esteem needs that Hitler appealed to by promising prosperity and a powerful empire. The United States already has considerable material and national security, so its love of country can afford more open-minded cynicism. So here's my **trial working thesis:** "Nazi German and modern American love of country differ because the needs of the citizens differ."

This section you've just read is pretty much as it came from my head so I could demonstrate how the process works. It *is* sloppy, and I had no idea what thesis was coming. If I'd taken different paths (for instance, developing the contrast in Soviet and U.S. parades that I found tempting), the thesis might be radically different. I've tried to reveal the connections between topic choice, brain teasers, and thesis formulations, but I know at each stage there are unseen jumps of thought. You must make these on your own; they are what make ideas truly your own. To develop a good idea, you must play back and forth between thesis and brain teasing.

Here are **alternative ways to narrow a topic** and conjure up the thesis lurking in your early thoughts. Write the following sentences, and finish the incomplete idea.

"What I really want to say is . . ."

"Reader, what I really want to tell you is . . ."

"What interests me most about my topic is . . ."

---

[1] Maslow believed there is a hierarchy of human needs: moving from the basic biological needs (hunger, thirst, and safety) to the more complex psychological needs (self-fulfillment, appreciation of art).

If you're still stuck, back up. **Make a short list of key words** from your brain-teaser lists and formulate a thesis sentence from them. Or first create a trial title for your paper—a phrase of three or four words—and build a thesis sentence from it. Imagine you have 15 seconds to convey your main idea. If you use a computer to create a thesis sentence, I recommend not trying to edit your first attempts. Just hit return and start over. After you write four or five versions, edit the best one.

■ **PRACTICE 5-3:** Choose a topic for your next paper and suggest three ways of narrowing it. Then write a possible thesis sentence.

LOOPING

Some students skip a working thesis, saying, "I'll just write a draft and fix it later." A few people can do this—but if you question them closely, virtually all of them really have done brain teasing and thesis work in their heads beforehand. Most writers who skip thesis preparation start confidently for a sentence or two. Then the next paragraphs fumble into new ideas or repetition. Somewhere halfway through the paper, the writer realizes what the thesis might be, and the paper smooths out a bit near the end. Revision of this tangled stuff is torture; the ideas smear together and the details are skimpy. It's almost a sure route to a poor grade. In effect, the writer is using the draft to generate ideas, organize them, and find the right words to express them. It's too much to ask of one sitting.

You *can* freewrite to generate ideas and structure, however, by **looping.** To loop, write freely for ten minutes, without censoring ideas, much as you do during a brain teaser, except that instead of listing, write full sentences, letting one flow to the next. Then *extract* the key sentence or concept from this freewriting and copy it on another sheet of paper. Write for another ten minutes using the extracted sentence as a guide, then extract the best key sentence from *that* freewriting until you formulate a thesis. Looping works well for people who like writing connected sentences rather than the helter-skelter of brain teasers.

Rethink your thesis at all stages of writing a paper. A perfectly formulated thesis that never changes during draft and revision is a red flag. You may be grinding down the truth for the sake of the system. Slop around in the topic before settling on a working thesis. Find out what's there, pile up some building blocks, and—with a *working* thesis—have a rough plan before constructing the essay. As Shakespeare's King Lear said, "Nothing will come of nothing." All this work on theses has *not* led to just one sentence! It spades up new ideas and makes the glue that will hold everything together.

■ **PRACTICE 5-4:** Create a working thesis sentence for one of these topics. First list three to five potential narrow topics within the general one, and choose the one you think will be the freshest. Then do a half-page brain teaser. Finally, write a working thesis. Show your work on paper.

Or, try looping; write three free-form paragraphs, extracting a key sentence from the first to start the second, and from the second to start the third. Your thesis must still be narrow and stated as an assertion.

- Freedom of the press
- Tourism
- Underwear ads in newspapers and magazines
- Single fathers or single mothers
- Choose your own topic

OUTLINES

Like theses, outlines create a Ben Franklin–Ralph Emerson debate. I've heard students say of former high school teachers, "My God! She said we had to have fifty 3 × 5 index cards and a two-page outline. The outline had to have five divisions and each division had to have at least two subheads and *they* had to have two subheads and they. . . ." However, I've heard other voices: "My teacher said not to worry about an outline: Just write what we feel and it'll be true. Just be loose. Well I'm real loose—I'm totally disorganized. I need help." I advocate a middle ground. Here's why.

The detailed outline on multiple levels looks like this in the abstract:

```
   I.
  II.
      A.
         1.
         2.
      B.
         1.
            a.
            b.
         2.
 III.
      A.
      B.
         1.
            a.
            b.
            c.
         2.
```

Its relentless order seems as inevitable as fate. It gives a writer who molds ideas and details to it a false sense of security—**just because you are organized doesn't mean you've said anything worthwhile.** It may also paralyze many writers who assume their ideas are bad because they don't easily adapt to the outline.

Third, it may kill spontaneity in the draft. Advocates of this system *want* to eliminate the dangers of spontaneity—disorganization, uncertainty about what to say in the next sentence, redundancy. But they kill spontaneity's virtues, too—coherence of mood, surprise, discovery. Overoutlining often creates dead, lifeless drafts. The writer simply colors inside lines already drawn.

Finally, ruthlessly detailed outlines create unnecessary labor because they're seldom used in practice. As philosopher Søren Kierkegaard once commented, "Most systematizers are like a man who builds an enormous castle but lives in a shack nearby." Most advocates of intricate outlines don't use them themselves. They usually write from humbler shack outlines. We get hung up on detailed outlines because humans like abstract order and want to believe that creativity can be planned perfectly. It can't. Actual writing based on a minutely detailed outline usually is dull. Most good writing by scientists, businesspeople, and essayists fails to meet the standards of a multidivision outline.

The other extreme, starting without any outline, may work for some people, but it, too, is flawed. Without any plan, you *are* going to stumble, wander around, repeat yourself. If you want to do a good job, you will do heavy rewriting to separate the brilliant tidbits from the garbage and simply to see what you've said. This path, of course, is the one writers must take when composing at the last minute. This approach gives the writer the illusion that a draft is being produced because pages fill up.

THE SCRATCH OUTLINE

The scratch outline is a single-level outline that only shows main headings (only the "I," "II," and "III" in the example). For a two- or three-page paper, three or four headings will do. For a four- or five-page paper, five headings will do. An essay entitled "The Dangers of Seatbelts" might be outlined this way:

- Introduction
- Pregnant women
- Fire during an accident
- Drowning during an accident
- Back problems

The writer then assigns details from brain-teaser lists to the appropriate heading and starts drafting. The scratch outline *does* offer direction but *does not* stifle creativity. Within each section, *details are fluid* so you have some spontaneous creation and still know where you're going next. A scratch outline can be seen as a whole; headings can be easily added or rearranged. Most professional writers use this kind of bare-bones outline.

To turn your brain teasers or other notes into a scratch outline, I'm going to suggest three options professional writers use. Let's assume that my topic is "death" and that I've already narrowed it down to deathbed moments.

Use Brain Teasers with Built-in Outlines

Classification, Comparison or Contrast, and Alternate Viewpoints create structure by their nature. You may have to consolidate or rearrange a bit, but they point you toward a narrow thesis and an outline. For example, if you do a classification brain teaser on "Death," you may **classify different ways people behave while dying:**

- Calm—death is natural, a part of life
- Begging forgiveness—to make up for wrongs
- Humor—playing a joke
- Philosophical—the "deep thoughts" death
- Religious—death leads to afterlife

This is already an outline. You only need to make a thesis assertion and find examples to illustrate each heading, and you're ready to write. As examples, you might use stories from deaths you've witnessed or from famous people. For humor, I recall that the comedian W. C. Fields—a life-long atheist—was found on his deathbed reading a Bible. "What are you doing?" a friend asked Fields. "Looking for loopholes," Fields answered.

Distribute your examples to the headings. If you have headings with no examples, you drop them. If you have interesting examples with no heading, try to invent a new one. For instance, I just recalled that Revolutionary War hero Ethan Allen was lying on his deathbed when someone whispered to him, "Sir, the angels are waiting for you."

General Allen snarled, "Goddammit, let them wait!" I might add a new category called "Defiance."

Your thesis might assert which approach to death makes the most sense and defend it. ("Of all the ways people die, going with a joke makes the most sense.") Or it might explain the motivation behind each type of death. ("The way you die tells the world how you lived.")

One danger of using brain teasers with built-in outlines is falling into a cookie-cutter approach: stamping out outlines without thinking of your message first. *Never let a pattern interfere with what you think is true.*

■ **PRACTICE 5-5:** Make a scratch outline on "Interracial Dating" or "Athletes as Role Models," using any of the organizing brain teasers.

■ **PRACTICE 5-6:** Make a scratch outline for your topic in Practice 5-3, based on one of the organizing brain teasers. Note: You may have to rewrite your thesis to fit the brain-teaser format.

Use Bullets to Outline Your Brain Teasers or Freewriting

A "bullet" is a little dash, star, or box like the ones that mark lists in this book. Read through your brain teasers or freewriting, and on a separate sheet of paper, write the highlights in list form, starting each one with a bullet. Imagine that your notes are a lecture from which you're trying to pick out the key points for a test. These should be ideas, not details—for they are your potential outline headings and should summarize other items. If you end up with more than four or five headings for a short paper, try combining some. Fewer than three headings means you may need another idea or two. For the topic of deathbed behavior, I might end up with something like this:

- Defiance
- Humor
- Religious
- Philosophical

To get my bullet outline ready for a draft, I have two options. First, I can use my four headings as labels and **label each item on my original brain teaser list.** I circle labels so they stand out on a messy brain teaser. On a computer, insert the heading in bold before each item. An examples brain teaser listing famous deaths might be labeled like this:

(DEFIANCE)
Beethoven shaking his fist at the sky a moment before death.

(RELIGION)
John Donne lying in his coffin to have his picture painted.

(HUMOR)
Dylan Thomas's last words: "I've just drunk 18 straight whiskies—that's a new record."

(PHILOSOPHICAL)
Gertrude Stein's last words: "What's the Question?"

(PHILOSOPHICAL)
Thoreau—when somebody asked if he'd made his peace with God, he answered, "I wasn't aware we'd quarreled."

(HUMOR)

W. C. Fields, looking for loopholes.

(DEFIANCE)

Ethan Allen telling the angels to wait.

(??)

Houdini (escape artist) saying, "I think this thing's got me."

(HUMOR - RELIGION)

Ramon Narvez (espionage agent) was told by his priest to forgive his enemies. "I have no enemies, Father," he said. "I have shot them all."

When you sit down to write your draft, compose a sentence or two that describes what you want to say about the defiant death, for example, and then scan your notes for each defiance label and add them as details.

A second option to finish a bullet summary outline is to **rewrite the brain teaser details under the headings.** Read through your brain teasers and rewrite each item under one heading. This is easy on a word processor. Just cut and paste the brain-teaser material under the headings. If you're hand writing, leave enough room between headings, or give each heading a separate sheet of paper. Here's how this method would look:

Defiance

Beethoven

Ethan Allen

Humor

Dylan Thomas

W. C. Fields

Religion

John Donne

Narvez(??)

Philosophical

Gertrude Stein

Thoreau

When you compose your draft, everything is in place, but you have to do more rewriting of notes beforehand. With both options, if you find details that don't fit the headings, you must cut them or create a new heading. You can also begin to scratch out the dumb stuff you encouraged during the brain teaser.

Use Clustering, a Visual Diagram

Write your general topic in the center of a clean page and then draw lines out, like radiating spokes from a wheel hub, to related ideas. It stimulates ideas (as a brain teaser does), yet keeps the key topic at the center of focus. Each item must connect to another by a line—either to the central topic or to any radiating headings. Go through your brain-teaser lists and assign each item a place on the cluster sheet. Try connecting each item to headings first. If it doesn't belong, connect it with a line to the main topic. When done, you'll have a visual representation of your ideas—where you have the most ideas, what fits with what.

An outline for this topic developed from **clustering** would look like this:

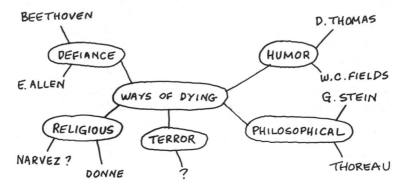

Your last step is to decide what order the outline headings should follow. Don't worry about the order of details. Rearrange the headings a few times to see how they'll flow when you write the draft. Most writers save their most creative idea for last.

■ **PRACTICE 5-7:** Suppose your research for the classification of deaths topic uncovered these examples:

- John Greenleaf Whittier's last breath: "My love to the world."

- Mark Twain's last written note: "Death, the only immortal who treats us all alike, whose pity, peace and refuge are for all—the soiled, the pure, the rich and the poor, the loved and the unloved."

- Emily Dickinson's last words were disputed: either she said "Oh, is *that* all?" or "I must go in; the fog is rising."

- Theodore Dreiser prepared these last words, but did not say them: "Shakespeare, here I come!"

- O. Henry's last words: "Turn up the lights. I don't want to go home in the dark."

- Thomas Jefferson died on July 4, 1826. His last words: "Is it the fourth?"

- Wilson Mizener to a priest: "Why should I talk to you? I've just been talking to your boss."

- I. J. Rodale, organic health food advocate, uttered these words on a national TV interview just before he dropped dead: "I'm so healthy that I expect to live on and on."
- James Thurber's last words: "God bless . . . God damn!"

Incorporate these examples into a scratch outline. You may use some categories developed in the chapter, but create at least two new ones.

■ **PRACTICE 5-8:** Do a page of brain teasers for your topic from Practice 5-3 and distribute the material to your scratch outline from Practice 5-6.

Sample Draft from Outline

The Fine Art of Dying

How will we spend our last breath when facing the brink of eternity? As the soul shakes free, will we defy death? Or reach into philosophical depths for the meaning of life? Will we pass silently away? Or congratulate death with a sporting handshake and a joke? Or will we go with faith in a new life?

I suspect the few people who think about dying imagine approaching the grave with dignity, summoning up spirited words or actions that will reveal their true hearts. The notorious atheist W. C. Fields was found reading the Bible on his deathbed by a friend who had come to pay his last respects. The religious friend smugly asked what Fields was doing with the Holy Book. "Looking for loopholes," the comedian replied. Death himself must have grinned at such pluck and integrity.

Perhaps the simplest dignified response to death has been defiance. On the brink of reckoning, people dare the cosmos to take them. Beethoven sat bolt upright when he spotted a flash of lightning. Long cursed with deafness by the Powers-that-Be, he shook his fist at the heavens, sank back, and expired. There was music in this gesture, one last

continues

measure beating valiantly against the silent tomb. Told to confess his sins, 15th-century Italian painter Perugino refused because he didn't believe in an afterlife. Were demons gleefully stoking a fiery pit for the unrepentant? Good! He would find out, he vowed.

For those of a philosophical mind, Gertrude Stein's death. . . .

Commentary

Because you went through the notes and predraft writing with me, you can see them behind this draft. Notice how the introductory paragraph sets up the classifications to come. Instead of simply saying, "I will discuss five types of deaths in this essay: defiant, philosophical, silent, humorous, and religious," the writer poses questions to get readers to think about which option they would choose. These questions set up the categories. W. C. Fields is used to visualize a specific example early but also to create the thesis, that our death shows how much integrity we have had in the way we have lived. This point needs to be made in each of the categories. Notice that each of the next paragraphs focuses on one of the outline headings, and examples illustrate each.

Concluding Comments: Outlines are like bones. Nobody sees them, but a person would sag into a baggy lump without them. You need some skeleton to help your essay stand up. Your thesis is also almost invisible—like a brain—but it makes your essay walk straight instead of reeling and wobbling. How do you know if you're organizing too much or too little? If you feel lost during drafts, try more organization. If you feel bored and confined, try more brain teasers and maybe looser organization. The one thing you cannot do is simply write the way you always have if it's not working. The writer who really wants to improve can do so at *every* stage of writing: thinking up fresher ideas and details, making theses and outlines, writing the draft, and revising.

InfoTrac® College Edition: Reading on Outlines

For tips on using *InfoTrac*® College Edition, see page 464.

Patricia A. Delwiche, "Passing Notes in Class." *College Teaching.* Summer 1998.

A group technique for classes to create outlines for college papers.

Highlights of Chapter 5

- Organization balances spontaneity and control. You can kill thinking with a stranglehold outline and you can become hopelessly lost without some plan.

- Writing brain teasers with plenty of ideas and details will do more to solve your organizational problems than any organizing formula I can offer.

- Developing a thesis is the first step to organizing many papers. This sentence states your paper's key idea. Consider your audience, your paper's purpose, and freshness when you shape this sentence.

- After you have a trial thesis, read over your brain-teaser notes to make sure it fits what you have. This sentence may be the most revised sentence in your paper.

- I advocate a scratch outline, but try a variety of methods during this course. You may have been using the wrong method for yourself.

- Persuasion and research require more outlining than narration and description. Try looping, clustering, labeling, and drawing lines if you never have before. Give yourself a lot of options.

Writing Suggestions and Class Discussions

1. Narrow three of these topics into ones you can handle in two or three pages. Concentrate on freshness—anticipate the obvious things others might say. Some topics may seem "boring"; you must *make* them interesting. Prepare brain teasers for each as you work along. *Or* try looping to narrow two of these topics.

    - Road construction
    - Disaster films
    - Courage that's overlooked
    - A book you've read
    - Prejudice you've suffered
    - High school versus college
    - Open topic

2. Now, write a working thesis for each of your narrowed topics. Be sure it's a complete sentence and makes an assertion the rest of the essay can relate to. If you "looped" in 1, you're done!

3. For your best thesis sentence in 2, write a scratch outline. Aim for three or four main headings and assign your best brain-teaser material to them. Use any outlining method discussed, but tell which kind. Bring all work to class.

4. Write a draft for the outline.

5. Evaluate the following as potential theses. What strengths and weaknesses do each have? Imagine what you'd have to do as a writer to fulfill reader expectations for each.

   - Pets bring out the worst in their owners.

   - Japanese products have been extremely successful in the United States.

   - Noise pollution is bad.

   - Statistics on teenage pregnancy don't tell how it hurts one young woman at a time.

   - Chevrolets are better than Fords.

   - I'm going to write about my first love and my latest love.

   - The New York Yankees and the Boston Red Sox are rivals.

   - San Francisco is the Paris of the United States.

   - We ought to extend mandatory recycling to tires.

6. Write a brief, *tactful* letter of complaint to a company or organization that has mistreated you. Make a half-page list of ideas and details, formulate a thesis that specifies what you want from the organization, then outline your letter. Consider your reader's viewpoint.

7. Write a three-year review of your life. Your object is to *evaluate* your last three years, not simply to tell what happened. Although the topic is already narrowed, you need to create a thesis and an outline with details for each heading.

✓ **PEER REVIEW CHECKLIST FOR THESIS/OUTLINES**

Author: _____

Reviewer: _____

Paraphrase the author's thesis in your own words to give him or her a new option.

1. Is the thesis as narrow and clear as the samples in this chapter? If not, suggest other angles.

2. Does the thesis have spark? Freshness? Suggest how to improve it.

3. What promises does the thesis make for the coming essay?

4. Does the outline make sense? Try rearranging the main headings. Try adding or combining headings. Even if it looks perfect, suggest one change the author can chew on.

5. Are there enough details for a vivid essay? Add some and sharpen some by asking the author to explain orally what will be said about a heading or two.

CHAPTER 6

The Draft

That Frenzy Near Madness

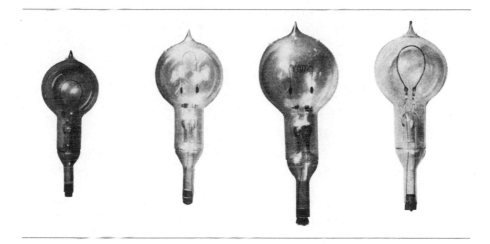

There was a world in my eye.

—ALICE WALKER

Planning to write is not writing. . . . Writing is writing.

E. L. DOCTOROW

"Why is it that I can never get a paper going! I thought I was into the topic—I did some brain teasers and made an outline. Yet my pen just wants to doodle when I sit down to write the draft. Everything I start to write looks awful—if anything comes at all." I've heard this many times over the years, and I've often felt exactly the same way myself. Most writers sometimes experience choking uncertainty when starting a draft. It may be fear of commitment to one idea or switching from the note-taking method of thinking to thinking in sentences. Whatever the reasons, here are a few ideas to make the draft go easier.

THE CONCRETE INTRODUCTION

Warm-ups Are for Leftovers

The introduction can be particularly hard because most people don't put much prewriting thought into it. A typical outline just says "intro." Yet we instinctively know that our introduction will set the tone for the whole paper, will grab or sedate a reader, and will either point us in the right direction or bog us down in swampy confusion. So, as our first task in the draft, we must write a key paragraph without the prewriting help the rest of the paper has. No wonder writers hesitate at that first sentence. I do. I've already thrown out two introductions to this chapter.

Many introductions are "warm-ups" as the writer gropes for the right tone, the properly phrased thesis, and an interesting lead-in. When I tell students their introductions are too long or vague and that they should get to the point quicker, they sometimes respond that the reader has to get used to them. But what's really happening is that the *writer* is getting used to the topic. Nothing gets a reader used to you faster than a sharp opening; nothing makes a reader feel uneasy sooner than an introduction that mushes around a topic. How does this one make you feel?

> Homelessness is a very important topic today. The future of our society depends on solving this problem. So many people are suffering, and homelessness is different than it was ten years ago. It's time we did something to cure this blot on society.

This introduction evaporates if you try to squeeze a specific idea out of it.

To avoid introduction paralysis, start your paper not by warming up but by being already hot. Warming up is for leftovers; an introduction should set a fresh appetizer before your reader.

One strategy is simply **don't write the introduction first.** Start by drafting the first main heading in your scratch outline, and write the introduction after the rest of the draft is done. As your draft evolves, the introduction you do write later will fit the paper better. The weakness of this approach is that you may miss the self-guidance the introduction provides.

You can compromise by starting the paper with this simple working sentence: "The purpose of this paper is . . ." Obviously, you'll have to improve this bland opening during revision.

Many professional writers try another method for the first paragraph. Their first few sentences attract and stimulate the reader's *interest*. Once interested, a reader is ready for your thesis, so **a good introduction frequently starts with several concrete, perhaps puzzling details, then presents the paper's main idea in the last sentence of the opening paragraph.** All six of the introduction types below share this principle.

One specific technique is to start with an **anecdote**—a short story related to your main idea. It can be a personal, researched, or fictional story. Here's an example that could substitute for the vague introduction on homelessness.

> Hattie McBride's dress was torn and dirty. She pushed her shopping cart into an alleyway, pulled out the folded cardboard from the lower rack and spread it under a fire escape. She rummaged among the wadded clothes and utensils on top until she pulled out a bottle of cheap wine. After settling down on the cardboard, she sighed. She was a grandmother and once owned her own home. Now, like thousands of other street people, she's become a social problem. Let's look at one solution for people like Hattie.

These details should make a reader hungry for the idea that would explain them—the thesis sentence, which comes next.

Another opening starts by asking **a good question.** That's the trick—a *good* question. Obvious questions or those needing only "yes" or "no" responses don't arouse our interest. Examples of bad questions: "Would you like to be a street person?" or "Are most homeless people happy?" There's mild interest in these, but they don't push the reader toward a theme, just a yes or no response. A better question is one with open-ended answers, such as this:

> Every time I walk downtown and see men, women, and children shuffling around in rags and scavenging like stray dogs, I wonder why. Why would a person *choose* to grub in garbage dumpsters, sleep in abandoned cars, and huddle around wine bottles? What can be done to help reclaim these people into society? After talking to some of these people and reading about the topic, I think there are three main reasons why people end up on the street, and that there *is* hope for some of them.

These questions are specific and involve readers by *asking them to account for a situation, not simply respond true or false*. Whether readers do think of an explanation or are simply puzzled, your audience will be primed to listen to what you have to offer, and that's the introduction's job. Notice also how concrete details attract our eye as these questions develop.

A third technique is to start with a **striking fact or facts:**

> Nearly two-thirds of all homeless people once held responsible jobs and 25 percent are employed; one-tenth hold college degrees; over half have families, most of whom know about their present condition. Homeless people should bother us not because they've degraded themselves, but because they point out how industry, education, and family have failed.

The same pattern holds here: vivid details followed by the author's thesis. A striking fact must be something unexpected. The following doesn't qualify: "Many automobiles produced in our high-tech society continue to be unsafe." But this does: "Twenty percent of the cars we drive today have life-threatening flaws in their construction." Always remember the power of the specific.

A fourth technique is to start with **a quotation** that leads to your thesis:

> "For God's sake, get them off the beach!" said one of the contest organizers. "Get the security people—now!" It seems during a publicity session at the 1989 Miss America Contest in Atlantic City that several homeless men crawled out from under a lifeboat the gorgeous women were using as a photo prop. The men had slept all night under the boat. Police officers escorted them off so the photos of sea, casinos, and American beauties could continue to maintain the image of America the beautiful, home of the brave and free. Cruel as the organizer's words sound, they may reflect a typical American attitude toward the homeless: We don't want to think about you.

Strong quotations dramatize an idea—interest readers by creating conflict or mystery. You read on to find out why the person said it or what the author of the paper will say about the quotation. That leads to your thesis.

Fifth, **open with a problem or dilemma**—viewpoints that contradict each other. Present several sides of a controversial situation before working toward your solution in the thesis:

> Being homeless means being powerless. No money, no stake in your society, no knowledge of how to escape. Most citizens are ashamed of homelessness, especially of homeless children. Yet without an address you can't vote, receive welfare, and, often, attend school—things that give you power. However, there is good reason to require addresses. Society must protect itself from being cheated by fake voters, welfare frauds, and parents sneaking children into better schools outside their towns. In a conference in Washington, D.C., advocates of the homeless think they have found a way around the address dilemma: Social Security numbers assigned on birth certificates.

Problem/dilemma introductions clarify issues and entice your audience.

Sixth, ask yourself, "What will people first think about this topic?" and **speak directly to the reader's concerns.** This is how I began this chapter, imagining negative thoughts some students have starting a draft. First, vividly identify with your readers' viewpoint, then lead them toward considering a new idea. Addressing the reader as "you" may help:

Perhaps you've seen the wino curl on the grate by the post office, the plastic sheet "tents" spread over bushes outside an office building at night for homeless people, the man who emerges from a doorway to ask for a dollar you're too afraid not to give him. Perhaps in disgust you want to shout at them, "You shouldn't live this way! No human being has to accept this!" I felt this way, too, until I met Robert Cole, the philosopher of the homeless.

Three final points. **One,** avoid the dictionary definition introduction: "*Webster's Dictionary* defines homelessness as 'the state or condition of being without a domicile; indigent.'" This does not move the paper anywhere; it's superficial and corny. The two cases for which it might work would be if you were really going to pick apart the definition in your paper (Is it really a condition or is it an attitude? What is a domicile?) or if the definition had things in it most people wouldn't know. This means you really must create your own definition that offers some ideas that are different from what a reader expects. Writers who start with predictable dictionary definitions usually ignore them and move on. So will the reader.

Two, your introduction hooks the reader, but it also *promises* the reader what will come. As in the striking fact example, you may even list the main points to be covered. But be careful not to promise what you can't deliver—the essay will be like a flashy car that gets repossessed during a big date.

Three, be brief. A play reviewer once estimated he spent a year and a half of his life waiting for curtains to rise. Don't do that to a reader.

WHAT TO FOCUS ON WHILE WRITING THE DRAFT

Once you get past the introduction, you may be fortunate enough to experience that frenzy near madness—a compelling rush of energy and insightful concentration that carries writers along. You may need only to refer briefly to your notes to start another cascade of sentences. If this happens and the draft still sparkles in the cold light of the next morning, consider yourself lucky.

But the frenzy of inspiration has a finicky way of not showing up or of teasing a writer with a two- or three-sentence burst and then vanishing. The writer who depends on inspiration will have some lucky effortless compositions but much more despair and frustration. The fact is that most writing— just like most living—is done at an ordinary pitch of mental excitement and must be done in a professional manner. Fine frenzies are memorable and cherished because they are not everyday happenings. All writers must learn to write without them. Ironically, it's when I'm plugging away at an ordinary pitch of concentration that inspiration sneaks into my fingers and brain. While I cannot promise that this fickle muse will carry you off, you can improve the odds of an inspiration through concentrated prewriting and focus during the writing of your draft. Here are four suggestions:

1. **Most importantly, concentrate on the logical, smooth flow of ideas and details.** Think visually as you bounce between ideas and details. As you clarify a generalization, supply details to visualize it. As you give examples, think of the conclusion you can draw to round out the paragraph.

2. **Use your outline intelligently.** Your scratch outline headings should become topic sentences for paragraphs most of the time, and the listed details will fill out your paragraphs. But don't think of this as a coloring book in which you're simply filling in spaces. You should think up new examples and recast ideas as you write. Don't let an outline chain you. But also don't run off in totally new directions for long sections without referring back to the outline—you could end up confused or with what should be two papers. If you really see a whole new direction for the paper as you draft, take a few minutes to throw together another scratch outline, scrap the old draft, and chase after your new thoughts.

3. **Move fairly quickly as you write the draft.** It helps things stick together. If your mood changes between writing parts of the draft, the tone may change. Ideas that you mean to bring up later (but that aren't written down) tend to be forgotten during interruptions. Ernest Hemingway believed that the best time to interrupt the draft for the day was at a spot where he knew exactly what the next sentence would say. That way, the following day, it would be easy to recapture the feel of his work and start up. Other writers tend to stop at a tough spot, hoping incubation will solve the problem for them overnight.

   There are some writers who work slowly. The French writer Gustave Flaubert was known for drafting only one paragraph per day during the composition of *Madame Bovary*. But for almost all writers I'd recommend a fast pace—a two- to three-page paper should be drafted in one sitting if you've done good prewriting work, and a four- to six-page paper should be no more than a two-sitting effort. It takes a certain sustained effort to engage your mind in the topic. The speed record may be held by Isaac Asimov, who claimed he could draft a nonfiction book in 70 hours. That's hot!

4. **To ease the flow of words, imagine speaking your draft to someone** as you compose. If it's a personal essay, imagine the person to be a friend. If it's an argumentative or informative essay, imagine speaking to your intended audience. If you don't remind yourself this way that you're writing for people, you may treat writing as a mechanical process, and the sparkle of a human voice will evaporate from the draft. Visualizing your audience helps you fill in gaps, keep a consistent tone, and suggest new ideas as you compose. Some writers say their sentences aloud and then type them. Others compose aloud from the outline into a tape recorder and then transcribe to paper, just to get this effect of audience. As I "talk" to my reader, I imagine her saying things like "What's that word mean?"... "Get to your point!"... "How does all this relate to me?" ... "Keep my interest—give me a story."... "Where did you get that fact?"

What Not to Focus on in the Draft

- Do not think about mechanics, spelling, or sentence structure.
- Do not work hard at word choices and style.

Why not? Because secondary matters bog down a writer during the draft and interrupt the smooth flow of ideas and details. If a great metaphor or vivid verb comes to you, fine. Take it. But don't spend five minutes during the draft searching for one. Save this effort for revision.

Drafting on a Computer

To keep you focused, I recommend turning off beeping spell checkers. They're just interruptions now. Likewise, don't dawdle over font sizes or title page graphics. You really haven't started writing until you write words. Right now it's ideas and details that count. If you want to start with a **proper format,** set your margins at 1¼ inches, lines at double space, font at something plain in size 12. Left-justify and use black ink.

Do save your work on a disk! And double-check that it's saved before you exit. Computers now eat the papers that dogs used to eat in the days of typewriters, but most teachers are as hard-hearted as ever about deadlines. If your computer has an automatic save feature, activate it. One summer a three-second power outage from a lightning storm caused eight pages of hot new work to vanish before my eyes. I'd like to spare you that. If a paper seems to have been eaten, it might only be hiding under other windows. Reduce whatever is on your screen to see what's behind it or check your file menu.

When You Get Stuck

Notice, it's not "if" you get stuck. All writers spin their wheels in the mud of a draft occasionally. You can continue to gun the engine and splatter goo, hoping you will wiggle loose, or you can try alternative strategies to get you to the dry land of the next sentence. **Here are some specific tips I use when I get stuck.**

1. *Use brain teasers* discussed in Chapters 2 and 3.
   - Move from ideas to details or from details to ideas.
   - Think with your senses to visualize the topic.
   - Imagine an alternative viewpoint to your last sentence.
   - Classify or compare the last point you made.
   - Think of a metaphor for your last or next point.
   - Attack stereotypes about issues you've just raised.
   - Try a humorous or fantastical touch.
   - Give an example.
   - Think about what bugs you about what you're saying.

2. *Study your scratch outline* and think up a transition phrase to move you to the next point:

   - "On the other hand . . ."
   - "The next reason to support this proposal is . . ."
   - "Secondly . . ."
   - "However . . ."
   - "Despite this fact . . ."
   - "The next morning . . ."
   - "When I saw Bill again . . ."

3. *Reread the last page you wrote.* When you reach the blank space, you may build up enough momentum to leap across it.
4. *Reread your thesis* and ask how the next point should relate back to it.
5. *Ask what your reader would want to know at this point.* Would she have a question to ask? Would he be confused or want to protest? Use the responses as a cue.
6. *Skip the tough section and move to the next.* Fill it in later. You may discover that it's illogical or doesn't belong in the paper.
7. *Write several alternative sentences* to see which sounds best.

BLOCKS DURING DRAFTING

As I mentioned in Chapter 3, fear of risk and insecurity about your ability to think can disable a writer. These can also occur during the draft. You suddenly fear you're going to say something really dumb or embarrassing, and your pen hesitates. You think, what will my professor think if I say I've used cocaine? Or that my uncle abused his children? Is my idea juvenile? Maybe I should be safer, hide more. Maybe I should just scrap it all and start over.

These are common fears. You must risk sounding silly to get anything drafted. The fact is, no first draft sounds polished. And dealing with embarrassing facts forces you to be more honest about the topic. In any case, there's time to reconsider these things in revision. At the draft stage, trust yourself and keep moving.

Some delay is good for incubation, but inability to start can be a lack of commitment. If you sigh a lot and say to yourself, "I just don't want to do this," remember the story of Cortez. In the year 1519, the Spanish explorer landed his soldiers in Mexico, then burned all the ships. He told his men there was no alternative to fighting for their goals, no escape. They fought hard! You, too, must burn your ships to be really committed to college. You *are* going to graduate. Not writing this paper is *not* an option. Behind you lies only empty water. Ahead, on the other side of this paper, lies your fortune. Write!

Unfortunately, additional blocks may emerge during drafts.

Fear of Messiness

We've heard it so often: "Neatness counts." And neatness does count in writing, but *only in the final draft.* Many people want to write drafts logically, grammatically, progressing word by word to a perfect conclusion. They're doomed. Within a few sentences they see the imperfections, the ideas that contradict each other, the detail that doesn't fit exactly, the awkward sentence. "All right," they say to themselves, "I'll write slower, more carefully." Before long they're up to their hips in quicksand and the writing stops. Why? Because they're asking too much of themselves. Even an average genius cannot think, organize, draft sentences, and consider words and grammar at the same time. Shakespeare and Mozart *may* have churned out masterpieces with little revision, but the history of literature by writers as great as James Baldwin, E. B. White, and Mark Twain is a history of messy cross-outs, redrafts, thrown-away pieces, and ink spots. Bob Dylan said, "Chaos is a friend of mine," and Thomas Wolfe claimed he cut 100,000 words from one novel (that's about 150 papers of the length you might write in this course). If ideas, details, honesty, organization, brilliant word choices, and grammar could come at once, we'd all be bestselling authors.

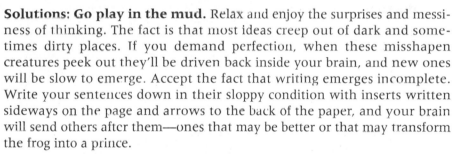

Solutions: Go play in the mud. Relax and enjoy the surprises and messiness of thinking. The fact is that most ideas creep out of dark and sometimes dirty places. If you demand perfection, when these misshapen creatures peek out they'll be driven back inside your brain, and new ones will be slow to emerge. Accept the fact that writing emerges incomplete. Write your sentences down in their sloppy condition with inserts written sideways on the page and arrows to the back of the paper, and your brain will send others after them—ones that may be better or that may transform the frog into a prince.

Poor Work Environment

Your sister plays loud head-banger music. Your desk is too low and makes your back ache. The room is stifling hot. You just ate and feel sleepy. Your paper's going nowhere. Anything relating to your physical environment can affect your ability to write. Some people like to be comfortable and cozy. That makes me fall asleep; I like a hard chair in a cool room. Some people must turn on music or the television. Others can't concentrate through such distractions. Some people require absolute silence and privacy. Others like to sense people moving around them because utter silence is intimidating. Some people are morning people, some evening people. And so on.

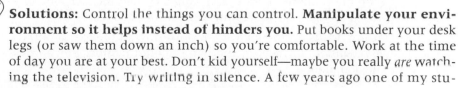

Solutions: Control the things you can control. **Manipulate your environment so it helps instead of hinders you.** Put books under your desk legs (or saw them down an inch) so you're comfortable. Work at the time of day you are at your best. Don't kid yourself—maybe you really *are* watching the television. Try writing in silence. A few years ago one of my students had a mother who interrupted him just as he sat down to write. She'd want to talk or make him do chores or complain about some aspect of his behavior. Mike began to suspect she saved these things until he opened his books. I suggested Mike finish his work at school. He did, and his writing improved one grade almost immediately.

People serious about thinking and writing give their minds the best environment they can, instead of letting a poor environment control them. If you really want to write, you will get it done. When your little brother dumps cola on your keyboard, remember Cesare Cantio—who wrote a novel in prison using a toothpick for a pen and candle smoke for ink.

NAIL YOUR CONCLUSION

Don't dawdle. A murky, wordy ending obscures your message. You want a sharp, crystal sentence or two that highlights your key idea. I'll give you specific suggestions for conclusions to narrative, persuasive, and research papers in later chapters, but one all-purpose conclusion simply **returns to a concrete example, fact, anecdote, question, or dilemma from your introduction.** An essay on the homeless might conclude this way:

> Hattie McBride died of malnutrition on her cardboard mat under the fire escape. If the work-for-shelter program and tenement rehabilitation plan I proposed were enacted, we might not find more Hatties dead in alleys.

InfoTrac® College Edition: Reading on Writing A First Draft

For tips on using *InfoTrac*® College Edition, see page 464.

Donald M. Murray, "The Craft of Telling." *The Writer.* June 1994.

How to start and keep going on a draft—advice from a Pulitzer Prize winner.

Highlights of Chapter 6

- Introductions should interest a reader with details, then present the thesis that leads a reader to the main body. You can do this by telling a story, asking a good question, presenting a striking fact, quoting someone else, opening with a problem, or addressing your reader's concerns.

- While drafting, focus on the logical, smooth flow of ideas and details. Move quickly without being bogged down in minor matters, and address your intended audience.

- While drafting, do *not* focus on style, words, mechanics, or spelling.
- When you're stuck, use the brain teasers from Chapter 3, refer to your outline and thesis, reread the last page you wrote, ask what your reader would want to know next, or search for a transition word to the next point.
- Two common drafting blocks are fear of messiness and poor work environment. Tell yourself not to be afraid of a little dirt; and change your work environment if it hurts your work.

Student Essay Introduction

Tougher Punishment for Sex Offenders

Pamela Fleming

Silver, a 30-year-old executive, was raped and beaten in her home by an ex-boyfriend and another friend. During the assault she sustained a black eye, busted lip, and bruises to her arms and thighs. She was choked, leaving welts around her neck. Caramel, a student, was raped by an acquaintance in the front seat of her car after he asked for a ride. During the attack, she sustained bruises on her left breast, along with aches all over her body. Both women were subjected to this ordeal at the hands of men they had once trusted.

Since sex offenders disregard the physical and psychological pain they inflict, here is a way of dealing with them. I propose that sex offenders be punished to fit the crimes they commit. A convicted first offender might be sentenced to ten years in prison without chance of parole and should receive a penile electric shock once daily during that time. Repeat offenders should be incarcerated for twenty years and given two shocks daily.

Commentary

The opening two examples vividly *grab our attention,* and the proposal is equally vivid. It's (pardon the pun) shocking and should be controversial reading. It uses the classic introductory *pattern of details moving to thesis.* But it's spread over two paragraphs. In a short paper (two to three pages), I'd like the introduction in one paragraph. It promises to convince us to agree with her punishment scheme—a tough sell, perhaps. *Issues she might cover* are the 8th Amendment to the U.S. Constitution, which prohibits "cruel and inhumane punishment." Another is the possibility that a rapist would be more likely to kill a woman rather than risk her testifying against him under Fleming's plan. She addressed these in her paper. The *length* could be reduced by cutting the last sentence of the first paragraph. It's not really part of her point. Suggestions for *wording:* "Sustained" is used twice and is vague. The beginning of the second paragraph could be cut to start "Here is how I propose dealing with rapists." The first part of that sentence argues the point before saying what it is. Overall this is a powerful introduction that will require strong support to sustain it.

Writing Suggestions and Class Discussions

1. Evaluate the following introductions. The Peer Review Checklist on page 122 will help guide you.

As Sir Walter Raleigh stepped up to the executioner's block, he ran his finger along the ax blade. "This is sharp medicine," he said, "But a sound cure for all diseases." Raleigh, most historians now agree, was innocent of treason, but capital punishment prevented him from being discovered innocent. I think we ought to have capital punishment today, but I think there ought to be a two-year delay to allow other evidence to turn up.

—*Gabriel Derida*

Imagine the police pounding on your door one fall day. You answer and your stomach knots. A red-haired officer softly tells you your daughter who had been running in the park has been raped and beaten with jagged rocks and a pipe by a pack of school-age boys. This nightmare became

---

reality to the parents of a 28-year-old jogger in New York City last year. What runs shivers down my spine is that one of the kids involved said, "It was fun." Our efforts to rehabilitate teens like this have been futile. We need to take a new approach to teen crimes of violence.

—*Lisa Neal (student essay)*

The program *20/20* showed a four-year-old boy who'd been abused by his mother's boyfriend. Beatings with a heavy object caused permanent brain damage. His back had inch-and-a-half deep whip marks from a leather belt. And the abuser carved his initials into the boy's backside. This boy will never ride a bike, walk, or even talk. He is fed intravenously and must urinate through a tube in his penis. He received a lifetime of retardation and pain. Yet the abuser received 15 to 20 years in prison, and the mother who let this happen received five years. Another baby burned to death after kerosene had been poured over him. The only two adults in the house were never even put on trial. Beyond how they could do this and what we can do to help, the question we must ask is: What is wrong with our judicial system?

—*Tara Geska (student essay)*

This is addressed to heterosexuals. Twenty years after lesbians and gay men threw coins, bottles, and parking meters at the cops who attempted to arrest them for being queer, many of you still see no reason to fight for our rights. Most of you are not by our side. Yet homophobia hurts you almost as much as it hurts us.

—*Allan Richards (student essay)*

2. Bring to class two magazine articles that strike you as having strong introductions and explain why they work well.

3. List three environmental conditions that encourage *your* thinking/writing. List two things that hinder your thinking/writing. Discuss how to change the poor conditions and create or maintain the good ones.

4. For your next paper, bring to class two alternative opening paragraphs, using two of the six methods suggested. Both introductions should be on the same topic but use different approaches.

5. Suppose you had to write a paper on family stress for a sociology class. Write three trial introductions, using a different technique in each. For the last sentence of the paragraph, invent a thesis or main idea that leads from the details to the paper.

6. Write introductions for two of these topics. Try to hook the reader's interest, then lead toward a thesis the paper will develop:

   - Men's or women's hairstyles
   - 2 A.M.
   - Animal experimentation
   - Dates who drink
   - Birthdays
   - Survivor shows on television

✓   **PEER REVIEW CHECKLIST FOR INTRODUCTIONS**

Author of Introduction:_____

List three possible titles for your paper:

_____

_____

_____

Reviewer:_____

1. Which title do you find most intriguing and why?

   _____

   _____

2. Does the introduction grab your attention and set up the paper? Why or why not?

   _____

   _____

3. What promises or expectations does this introduction give a reader for the essay? Suggest issues or questions the author should cover.

_____   _____

_____

4. Make a suggestion to improve the wording of the introduction. Mark your suggestions on the draft itself.

_____

_____

5. What is the sharpest detail that draws your eye into the introduction? If you think the introduction needs better detail, suggest what might be done.

_____

_____

6. Is it too long or too short? If so, suggest how the author might revise

_____   _____

_____   _____

CHAPTER 7

Revising Drafts

Writing Is Revising

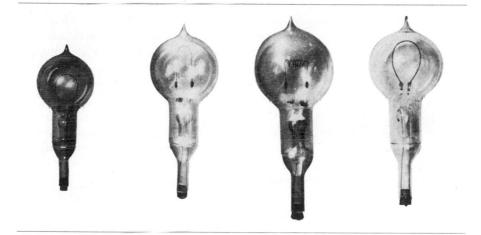

The manuscript revealed the usual signs of struggle—bloodstains, teethmarks, gashes, and burns.

—ANNIE DILLARD

My pencils outlast their erasers.

—VLADIMIR NABOKOV

Many people assume a writer's job is 95 percent done when the first draft is complete. Now, they think, we'll correct spelling and typos, read it over to see how it flows, and then crank out a clean copy.

I wish writers could operate that way. But experienced writers—whether they publish essays, write business reports, or compose senior theses—know that "revision" means "re-seeing." A writer is simply not doing the job if re-seeing is limited to fussing over spelling and a few surface blemishes. That's amateurish. You must re-see and re-feel the entire paper, back down to its roots. Ralph Ellison revised *Invisible Man* for ten years, and Boris Pasternak said of his first draft of *Doctor Zhivago,* "Everything is corroded. . . . It is disgusting." The person who writes a company's annual report or the committee that writes your college catalogue may revise for months. The inspired genius who whisks out immortal masterpieces on the first draft is 99.99 percent myth.

For virtually all writers, including Nobel Prize winners like Pasternak, revision means a total, word-by-word re-seeing of the draft. Revision means rewriting good parts as well as bad. Only during revision does most writing move from poor to acceptable or from acceptable to good or outstanding. Your professor does not expect from you the fanatical dedication of published writers such as Ernest Hemingway, who revised the last paragraph of his great World War I novel, *A Farewell to Arms,* 39 times. But your professor *does* want you to revise more than just the surface, to take the manuscript through at least one complete revision. Your writing *will improve* through honest, close revision, and only then will you know how good you are as a writer.

REVISION MYTHS AND REALITIES

Revision draws from a different part of your brain than brain teasing or drafting. Creating is self-centered, accepting, and sloppy; revising is reader centered, judgmental, and orderly. Although most people find one easier, we're all capable of both.

The lonely writer tapping away in solitary confinement is largely myth. Most writers in professional situations depend on advice and criticism from others during the revision process. They give us perspective on what we are too close to notice; they remind us what we forget to mention or point out what might confuse a reader. Even Shakespeare had help. His acting company commonly deleted scenes and suggested changes during rehearsal for such classics as *Hamlet* and *Romeo and Juliet.* Most bosses ask to see drafts of proposals, reports, or significant letters their employees write—and will suggest changes. Or they may ask *you* for suggestions on *their* drafts. Grant writers, legislators, and scholars all ask peers for criticism before the public sees the written document. The word "criticize" in this sense does not mean to rip the writing apart but to highlight weaknesses *and* strengths and to make *positive* suggestions.

Let me illustrate how a writer combines personal revision and outside criticism by using this book as an example. In 16 years of college teaching, I'd written hundreds of assignments, course outlines, and instructions.

Some bombed! In one research assignment, my directions for using the microfilm machine were vague enough that one student ended up shooting a reel of film from the viewer like a spider gone berserk. Each semester I revised flaws and pursued new ideas, finally expanding these into a short "Guide to Writing" used only at my college. Teachers and students told me what worked and what didn't. One class sent me 24 letters! More revision.

When I mailed sample chapters for an expanded book to publishers, my future publisher sent these to teachers at other colleges for their reactions and criticism. The reviews broadened my limited viewpoint. More revision. New chapters had to be written; others combined, relocated, or eliminated. One chapter expanded from 10 to 40 pages and helped me discover exactly what process of writing I believed worked best. More reviews (nearly 50 pages in all) and more new voices in my ear helped me. For this fifth edition, more new voices and ideas helped me revise. More than 40 professors and editors and hundreds of students have their fingerprints on this book, and they have helped me write better than I can alone.

I was happy to have new things to think about, because with each draft of a piece of writing, I exhausted myself. Do you know this feeling? After working for hours on a draft, do you feel wrung out, as though you have said everything you possibly can about the topic? Well, peer criticism jump-starts a writer's dead battery if it's the right mix of honest encouragement, suggestion, and flaw finding.

An important part of your college education is to learn how to handle both kinds of revision—revision on your own and revision with the help of others. Let me suggest some things to look for and a process to follow when revising first drafts.

REVISING ON YOUR OWN

I recommend a five-step revision process, but keep in mind this is an *ideal process that rarely if ever can be followed exactly.* Like thinking, revising is a sloppy process. That said, you'll find a revision checklist on the inside front cover of the book. Consider this another brain teaser to remind you to think in all the ways you should during revision.

Start by revising major things first—the ideas and details—and then work on secondary items such as organization and word use. Correct punctuation and spelling last. Why? So you don't waste time correcting spelling if you later decide you need a better word or waste time thinking up a great adjective if the entire sentence gets thrown out. Imagine a draft essay as a building to be rehabilitated. There's no point painting until the room walls are patched, and that shouldn't begin until the supporting girders are square and plumb. Occasionally, changing a word or phrase can clarify your main ideas, and if it seems important, go ahead. But don't spend your early revision time tinkering.

You may want to read your draft over for general flow, but if you **read through for one focused thing at a time,** you'll do more real thinking and less falling in love with what's already there. Writers often get "sick" of drafts because they're following the draft, instead of demanding specific things of it. If you keep rereading and waiting for a "bump" to jolt you, you will fall asleep. I recommend reading through and revising the draft once for each of the following aspects.

- Ideas
- Details
- Order
- Words
- Mechanics

A two- to three-page paper can be revised for all of these in an hour, and careful revision is almost sure to raise your grade one level.

■ **PRACTICE 7-1:** Try the five-step process that follows in class or at home with the draft of a paper. Stop and do each step separately before reading on.

1. REVISE IDEAS

Honesty, Freshness, Coherence

Clarify the *main* idea. First, read through your draft quickly. Now, without referring back to the essay, try to state your main point or purpose. Write it out in one sentence. You may be surprised that you'll be able to say it more sharply after reading the paper. Compare it to the existing thesis sentence and substitute the new one if it's better or revise the old, if necessary. If you had trouble writing a statement of purpose, your paper may ooze in several directions.

If your paper lacks sharp focus, try this technique: Read through the paper again, copying down sentences that seem to state purpose. Try to combine these sentences into one statement. If this works, great. Replace the existing wobbly thesis. If you can't combine the purpose sentences, you'll have to accept the fact that you mixed two or three paper ideas together. You must then divide the essay into parts, some of which will become your paper and the rest of which will leave the house in a brown bag.

Second, when revising for ideas, **test your main idea for *honesty* and *freshness.*** I read through once ruthlessly to see if I've slipped into superficial thinking or oversimplification. Qualify or moderate extreme sentences. Be particularly alert for contradictions or potential rebuttals to your arguments. Don't ignore them. Your paper will be stronger and more honest if you confront and respond to them (see "refutation" in Chapter 12). For example, as I reread this section, I worry that I'm simplifying revision by making it seem too mechanical, too much like a write-by-number activity. No techniques substitute for your intense concentration or involvement in your ideas. A checklist is only a reminder of things to look for.

Third, **read through the draft as your reader will.** If you have a particular reader in mind, *be* that person. What will confuse him? What points
will she deny or contradict? What have you left out that will be important
to her? This is a wonderful brain teaser for revision.

■ **PRACTICE 7-2**: Reread your last paper and (1) underline key sentences
that reveal purpose; (2) combine these into a one-sentence statement of
purpose; (3) find two places in which you could have raised an objection or
modified an idea for more honesty or freshness. Make the revision.

2. REVISE DETAILS

Visualize and Support

Read the draft again, just for details. Are they vivid and convincing? **Support each major generalization by adding examples, sense details,
descriptions, and facts.** Suppose you had written the following in a draft
of a paper on Tennessee Williams's play, *The Glass Menagerie:*

> Laura lives in a fantasy world in this play. For instance, there's her glass
> menagerie, the old phonograph records she plays, and her visits to the green-
> house. She can't even attend business college.

The right information is here, but it's not vivid enough to make us see
Laura's fantasy world. Let's expand just *one* of the details:

> Laura lives in a fantasy world. The greenhouse she visits is full of exotic
> flowers—tropical plants that can't exist in the cold world of St. Louis where she
> lives. Their fantasy world is protected from reality by artificial heat and fragile
> glass, just as Laura can go on living only because her mother and brother protect
> her from the cold reality of the Depression.

In revising for detail, remind yourself that a reader is hungry for facts,
quotes, pictures, and examples. Feed him details.

■ **PRACTICE 7-3:** Find three places in your last paper that could use more
details. Pause a moment to visualize completely, then add them.

3. REVISE ORGANIZATION

Make It Easy on the Reader

Check the essay's *overall organization.* While doing this it's better not to
read in the normal sense—just skim the main sentences. If it's more than three
pages, I usually take notes on a separate page by jotting down a heading for
each paragraph or section. This helps me see more clearly what my main

points are, if I'm repeating myself, or if I should combine two sections. Now's the time to cut redundant paragraphs or draw arrows to move things around.

Next, **check that each *paragraph* sticks to one idea.** Are the *transitions* smooth between them? (If not smooth, add key markers like "On the other hand," "Another reason to support this proposal is . . ." or "Once outside, Fergusen saw . . ."). If you see a lot of skimpy one- and two-sentence paragraphs or one paragraph runs over a page, a red signal light should buzz. You may be able to join the bitty paragraphs or insert paragraph breaks into the elephant-sized ones, but it may be a sign that as you motored through the first draft, your thinking became scattered. **Make sure every sentence points at the same target.**

Finally, flip directly from your introduction to your conclusion. Is your main point consistent? If not, scream, and then revise.

■ **PRACTICE 7-4:** Revise your last paper just for organization. Outline the paper, check paragraph unity, and add transitions where needed.

4. REVISE WORD USE

Waxed Words Sparkle

At this point you should know which sentences and paragraphs will be in the final paper. Now focus on polishing words. Look small. Tinker. Wax and polish. Do you repeat the same words, or challenge the reader with a few exotic *palabras?* Be ruthless to clichés—they are corpses in your living essay. Did you define key terms? Be more concise. Punch up bland verbs. Substitute slashing, red-eyed adjectives for dull ones. Create a metaphor to make a boring paragraph crack with lightning. Consider sentence variety. Unlike the previous sentence, which was a short, imperative sentence, this complex one delays the main subject and verb with an introductory phrase. Both kinds snap the reader to attention. Chapter 8 is devoted to word polishing.

■ **PRACTICE 7-5:** Pick any paragraph from a previous paper and improve three word choices and perk up a vague or dull spot with a metaphor.

5. REVISE MECHANICS

My grandmother told me always to wear clean underwear. She wanted to be sure that if I was hit by a car and taken to the hospital they'd know I was from a decent family. I think of my grandmother when I revise for mechanics. I do it for decency's sake.

Reading through the paper lightly for mechanics will only catch the errors you *don't* normally make. That's fine, but the deadly errors are the ones you make regularly and don't see. Go through the paper once searching just for the errors teachers repeatedly mark on your papers. This must be a conscious effort, or you won't improve. If your vices are sentence fragments and apostrophes, go through the draft once, searching only for the little vermin. Work with the handbook in Chapter 16; don't guess. If you're a weak speller, check any word you wouldn't risk in a $1,000 bet. After two or three papers, they won't be *your* errors.

■ **PRACTICE 7-6:** List your three most common grammar, punctuation, or other small errors. If you don't *know* what they are, examine your last few papers. Use this as your own individual checklist. Write it in your notebook.

REVISING WITH OTHERS: PEER EDITING AND TEACHER CONFERENCES

By this time, you should have exhausted your own resources. Your draft should be scratched up with improvements. Now your professor may mark your paper, ask you to give it to other students to read (peer editing), or talk it over with you (conferencing). These can be your most valuable opportunities to really learn to write. Peer editing and conferencing do more than help with one paper. They teach skills that will serve you a lifetime: Giving and receiving positive criticism leads to renewed enthusiasm and ideas in marriage, career, sports, and friendship as well as writing. You'll write for a real reader, not a cardboard one; you'll see how others write; and you'll learn from them.

How to Give Peer Criticism

When called on to critique another student's paper, **your goal should be to help the writer create better ideas, sharper details, smoother organization, and more vivid word choices.** You may also repair punctuation and spelling.

The reviewer/editor must be honest. The person who writes on your paper, "I love it!" or "I wouldn't change a thing!" may flatter you momentarily, but doesn't help you one bit. You may be shy or feel unqualified to criticize, but making an honest effort to help someone else improve a paper will teach you to revise better yourself. You'll learn to see some of the hidden possibilities behind existing words, to see your own drafts more objectively. Teachers who encourage peer editing expect *both* parties to learn.

You must be tactful, of course. The person who scrawls changes all over the paper and says, in effect, "revise everything" is just as dishonest as the person who wants to award the Nobel Prize. Help the writer to his or her destination.

Because most writers need help recognizing what they have written and help understanding how a live audience reacts, **it's probably best to start your comments simply by mirroring back to the writer the message or feeling the essay gave you.**

You can do this with a line like this: "What I remember best about your essay is . . ." or "The main point I get from this is . . ." or "The most visual part of your essay is . . . ."

Or you might make a bullet summary of the main point as you read. After the author lets you know you're aboard the same spaceship, you can move to suggestions for ideas, details, organization, and wording. Work together. If you were confused at a certain point, for instance, brainstorm with the author for several possible clarifications. Whatever you react to strongly in any way should be discussed with the writer. Try to *enjoy* peer editing; allow yourself the pleasure of inhabiting someone else's mind for a while.

How to Receive Peer Criticism

Remember, your peer editors try to be honest. If they feel confused, you may point out things that you think clarify the point, but you can't tell them they're not confused. What peer editors tell you is something you can never see for yourself: how another person receives your communication. You can never be your own reader.

Strike a balance between total acceptance and total rejection. If you're too pliable, you may accept changes you shouldn't. It's *your* paper; don't let a strong peer dominate your idea. On the other hand, some closed-minded writers seem to say, "It's written this way because that's the way I wanted it. It's my paper, isn't it?" This person supposes the paper came out exactly as intended. I'm skeptical because it's never happened to me or any other writers I know. More importantly, papers *shouldn't* come out exactly as intended; to me that's a sign that I haven't *learned* as I moved through the stages of writing. **Your paper is not a monument to what you thought at one moment, but an attempt to communicate an idea as freshly and vividly as possible to someone else.** Listen to what your readers say. Before rejecting changes, first ask the reviewer, "Why do you say that?" You don't have to follow each suggestion slavishly, but do welcome new possibilities as potential friends.

Bring questions to a peer editing session. Ask about things you've wrestled with or wondered about. For example, "Is this a corny sentence?" or "It seems too long. What should I cut?" or "I'm worried I sound too harsh. What do you think?" Only by showing yourself eager to find weak spots will reviewers really open up to you. It's fairly easy to stifle criticism in workshops—just get defensive. But then you won't get any help either.

A SAMPLE REVISION

Here is the opening paragraph from a letter written as a class paper by Tina C. Maenza. First is the rough draft as brought to a peer review session:

Dean H. Freericks
Assistant Vice President for Facilities Management
John Beane Center
SUNY AB
Buffalo, NY 14261
Dear Mr. Fredericks,

    As you probably are already aware of there is a major problem with student parking at our school. At the end of every class one can be sure to find a line of students in their cars waiting for people to leave so they can park. Not only is this an inconvenience, but it causes arguments among students racing for empty spots, and it makes us late for class. You should consider building parking garages or consider some other possible solutions to this problem.

The reviewer thought the thesis was clear, but suggested that the author "put in a story, more details" to catch the reader's eye. She also pointed out a few flaws in the letter format, the choppiness of the first sentence, and exaggeration in line 2 ("every" and "be sure"). Here is the same text with the author's revisions penned in:

>   *de*   *July 14, 2003*
> Dean H. Freéricks
>
> Assistant Vice President for Facilities Management
>
> John Beane Center *Looking at their watches every 30 sec.,*
>   *they wonder just how late they will be to*
> SUNY (AB)   *class today. Teachers are not sympathetic*
>   *+ some threaten to penalize tardy students*
> Buffalo, NY 14261 *by reducing their grades.*
>
> ← Dear Mr. Fredericks,   *What can we students do?*
>   *exists*
> ← As you probably are already aware of, there ~~is~~ a major problem with
>   *almost*   *almost*
> student parking at our school. At the end of every class one can be sure to
> find a line of students in their cars waiting for people to leave so they can
> park. Not only is this an inconvenience, but it causes arguments
>   *making*
> among students racing for empty spots and ~~it makes~~ us late for class.
> You should consider building parking garages or consider some other
> possible solutions to this problem.

Notice that the author revised additional items beyond the ones suggested. Next is the final draft with more improvements. The new visual details certainly help, as do the ironed-out sentences and "little" corrections, including the reader's name!

July 14, 2003

Dean H. Fredericks

Assistant Vice President for Facilities Management

John Beane Center

SUNY at Buffalo

Buffalo, New York 14261

Dear Mr. Fredericks:

As you probably already are aware, a major problem exists with student parking at our school. Following most classes, one can almost be sure to find a line of students in cars waiting for people to leave so they can park. Looking at their watches every thirty seconds, they wonder just how late they will be today. Most teachers are not sympathetic, and some threaten to penalize tardy students with reduced grades. What can students do to make class on time when we drive? Besides being an inconvenience and making us late, it causes arguments among students racing for an empty spot. Please consider building parking garages to solve this problem.

Teacher Comments

Your teacher will probably be the most attentive reader you will ever have. If you write a boring or confusing letter to customers or supervisors, they will stop paying attention. Your professor will persevere and mark the rough, confusing, or vague spots. *Improvement* is the point of this effort. Therefore, **the most important marks on your papers are not the grades but the comments.** Each one is a guide for future papers. Study each comment on returned papers carefully. If you don't see where you went wrong or how you could improve a section marked "awkward" or "vague" or why a teacher wrote "good" somewhere, find out. Ask. Be hungry for feedback; that's how you move forward. If you think of comments as simple test scoring, you've thrown away a road map. If you don't understand, look the problem up in this text, talk to your professor, or go to your college's writing center. Take the time to figure out the symbols and abbreviations your teacher uses. Some common ones are listed in a table opposite the title page.

If your teacher has conferences about rough drafts, think of them as opportunities. Come with prepared questions. "Why does my opening sound flat?" or "Did I overdo the facts on the dangers of nuclear waste?" *Take notes* and mark sections your teacher discusses so you remember. As with peer editors, be open to suggestions and try to re-see your work objectively through your professor's eyes. However, if the professor seems to have the wrong idea about where you want to go with the essay, make clear what you really want to accomplish and ask for suggestions on how to get there.

THE FINAL DRAFT

1. **Title** the paper and make the title work for you. The best titles convey information and also a concrete image to hold the eye. Which of the following titles promise boredom and which promise an experience?

   - English Paper #2
   - Air Pollution
   - Whose Poison Gas Is It
   - Death Stalks Your Home

   Good titles often come from phrases near the end of your paper, from metaphors you use, or dialogue you quote. Why waste time thinking up a bunch of titles? Well, Margaret Mitchell's first titles for *Gone with the Wind* were duds: *Ba! Ba! Black Sheep* and *Tote the Weary Load*. The title symbolizes the whole work. Each semester, students ask, "Does my paper have to have a title?" The answer is "Yes—just as you have to have a name, so you can be picked out in a crowd." So make the title memorable!

2. **Format.**
   - Use black ink.
   - Write your name and class in a corner.
   - Center the title one-quarter of the way down the page.
   - The title should be capitalized but not underlined or in quotation marks.
   - Number the pages.
   - Double-space and use only one side of the page.

- Leave one-inch margins.
- Staple or paper-clip your essay.

3. **Proofread** after typing or printing and make corrections—that's what professionals do. If you have more than a few mistakes, print a corrected copy. Here are some basic proofreader's correction marks:

⁋	New paragraph
No ⁋	No paragraph
⎿⏋	Reverse order of items enclosed
∧	Insert mark (write new items above line)
ℐ	Delete mark
≡	Capitalize letter
lc	Lowercase letter
#	Space needed
Stet	Ignore the changes

Revising on a Word Processor

Word processors are wonderful, but there are some drawbacks. First, because small changes are easy, you'll be tempted to focus on small items. You may be deceived by a neat surface appearance into not really studying the logic and sentences. You've got to dig up a draft, no matter how polished the work *appears*. Second, word processors with spell-checkers may give you the illusion that your spelling is fixed. However, if you type "affect" where "effect" belongs or "kiss" instead of "kill," the machine recognizes a legitimate word and won't alert you to your error. Grammar-check programs can help fix some errors, but they are wrong about half the time. Use them, but also learn to rely on your own knowledge—and on dictionaries.

Since you can do so much revision with a computer with such little pain, you should experiment: Combine paragraphs, separate them, move them around, add details, rephrase. You can ask most computers to count the number of times you used "I" or "was" if you're afraid of monotony. You can usually reformat with different fonts—but please!—only one font per paper, and avoid the script fonts that are hard to read. This is one place I advise you to be bland. **Choose Courier or Times New Roman font.** To keep this rich activity safe, print a copy of each draft. **And save it to both disk and hard drive.**

InfoTrac® College Edition:
Reading on How a Professional Writer Revises

For tips on using _InfoTrac®_ College Edition, see page 464.

Donald M. Murray, "The Maker's Eye." _The Writer._ Oct. 1998.

Seven things to think about when you revise—from a Pulitzer Prize winner.

Highlights of Chapter 7

- Welcome revision. Your essay will survive being picked apart and glued back together. That is how ideas are made better and how professional writers operate—whether they write memos or publish books.

- Peer criticism requires both honesty and tact. Use the specific suggestions in this chapter to get started.

- Revise with specific things in mind, not just for general flow. Revise your papers one time each for ideas, details, order, words, and mechanics. Use the specifics in this chapter as a checklist. But remember: No checklist or process for revision can substitute for your intense concentration and involvement in your subject.

Writing Suggestions and Class Discussions

1. Make up three questions about the draft of an essay you're working on. Leave room for responses and attach them to your rough draft for your peer editor or professor. Try for a mix of broad questions on thesis or organization and specific questions about particular words or sentences.

2. To have a sample to practice revision, write a half-page paragraph on one of these topics:

   - Adult toys
   - Children and toys
   - Wise elders
   - What I don't like about my present job
   - "_____" is a great song because . . . .
   - Open topic

3. Revise the paragraph from 2 on your own:
    ▪ Rewrite the main idea/topic sentence without looking at the original and compare it to the original. Use the clearest one or make changes.
    ▪ Sharpen the details—make at least two points more specific.
    ▪ Circle all transitions and improve if necessary.
    ▪ Improve three word choices and rewrite any clichés. Then find two or three needless words and cut them.
    ▪ Check all spelling and grammar.
4. Bring your revised, retyped paragraph to class for a peer editing session. Attach two questions about the paragraph for the reviewers. Using peer suggestions, revise and submit a finished paragraph.
5. Write a draft of a home page for yourself for the World Wide Web and collaborate in revising it.
6. Your peer group will write an ad for a commercial product. Your client wants one picture and about 100 words to appear in the Sunday newspaper. Your group will submit a draft to the client (played by your professor), and then revise.
7. Read the following student essay. How would you advise the writer to revise it?

Student Essay and Analysis

Bastard

Miguel Martinez

I have always been awed by the strange bonds fathers are supposed to have with their sons. Literature, television, and film have shown these relationships to be complex and intense. Even my friends in school would relate stories of massive power struggles. The part about love they left out but I knew it was there.

I grew up believing my father to be dead. At least that's what my mother told me when I asked her. I know the only reason I did ask was I had just entered kindergarden and my classmates were always talking about this strange being, a sort of god, they called Daddy. Contrary to popular belief, those of us having only one parent do not feel that anything is missing. At least I didn't until I found out I was an oddity. There is no biological instinct inside us saying that there should be someone else. There was just me and my mother. Period.

Off I went through school. My mother was involved with other men, and we lived with two of them. They were never 'Dad,' just 'Uncle.' These relationships didn't work out, and when I was six, my mother gave up on men entirely. We moved to the east side of the city, and she started working. For the next ten years, my mother and I didn't see much of each other. She was a waitress, keeping odd hours, and I was in school or playing. She did make a big point of eating together, even if it was in the greasy spoons she worked in.

When she was able to spend more time with me, I was sixteen, and pretty set in my ways. I suppose I should have let her have her way, but the arrogance of youth took hold again. I left. I didn't have anywhere to go, I just wanted to travel. I spent the next 8 months traveling the country. I did return eventually, only to find my mother filled with a sense of failure. It hurt knowing I had caused someone such hard feelings. She begged me to enter the Navy, and while I wasn't a big fan of the military, I went. The night before I was to leave for boot camp, my mother sat me down and asked if I ever wondered who my father was. I told her, quite honestly, that I didn't, that she had said he was dead. Well, she gave me his name and told me he was living in South Carolina. She told me he didn't care about me, as he had always known who I was, but never made any attempt to contact me.

continues

The news didn't faze me. Friends will ask if I have any urge to find him. I get satisfaction from their expressions when I tell them I have his address and phone number. But just as they can't understand my apathy toward him, I can't understand their reliance on fathers.

Here are comments on the draft by the writer, peer editors, and professor:

The Writer's Concerns About This Draft

1. I didn't explore the aspect I wanted to—it seemed too general and jumpy in what I was trying to get at.
2. One sentence that drove me crazy was 'Off I went through school' (third paragraph). It just didn't flow.

Peer Editor Comments Made by Students Reading the Draft

1. The only 'jumpy' part was the fourth paragraph. Time seemed too compressed. You were six and then entered the Navy.
2. You need more detail on growing up without a father. The most vivid detail was your not asking about your father. The least was why your mother wanted you to join the navy. I'd like to see more about why you didn't miss or need a father.
3. Paragraph 3—for <u>ten years</u> you didn't see much of your mom???
4. First paragraph needs more detail.

Teacher's Comments

1. It's strong in honesty. Daring. Potentially a powerful paper.

2. But it doesn't follow its nose to the end of the idea. Your purpose is unclear, as you suspect. Are you dealing with (1) the mother-son relationship; (2) the life of a single mother; (3) the social problems of bastards; (4) your lack of need for a father, or . . .? All these are here, but you need to decide what main point the others will support. Conclusion is inconclusive.

3. Paragraphs 1 and 2 are good—a snappy start.

4. #4 needs more detail—it's abrupt, seems to start a new idea.

5. #4 Last sentence is awkward.

You will find a revised, final draft of this essay on page 360 in Chapter 15. Although the student followed some reader suggestions, notice how he found new areas to explore simply as a result of talking about the essay and hearing what other people saw there.

A draft and revised informative essay can be found on page 372.

✓ **PEER REVIEW CHECKLIST FOR REVISION**

Author of Paper: _____

Reviewer: _____

Instructions:

1. Read the paper slowly and carefully.
2. Mark parts that were confusing or problems with a "?".
3. Mark strong sections with a "G" or "*".
4. Check the appropriate boxes and write out comments.
5. Return this sheet to the author and discuss your reaction.
6. Do not mark small things like spelling yet.
7. This sheet should be attached to the final draft.

	Strong	Average	Weak
Ideas: Originality/Freshness			
Depth/Complexity			
Audience: Well Targeted			

continues

	Strong	Average	Weak
Details: Number of Details			
Vividness			
Organization: Main Point Is Clear			
Smooth Flow Between Ideas			
Word Use: Concise and Vivid			
Mechanics			

The strongest part of this paper to me is:

I'd like to know more about:

Here are two additional suggestions I have:
1.
2.

✓   **PEER REVIEW CHECKLIST QUESTIONS FOR REVISION**

Author: _____

One question or problem the author wants the reviewer to help with:

One sentence the author is not satisfied with (mark it and explain why it bothers you):

Reviewer: _____

My response to the author's first concern is . . . (discuss and brainstorm with author):

Here's a possible rewriting of the weak sentence:

I feel the purpose (thesis) of your essay is:

One area that could use more detail or support is:

What idea could be added or cut to enhance the paper's purpose?

Find a paragraph needing smoother transition and suggest it. (No, it's not perfect!)

Suggest at least three word or sentence structure changes.

CHAPTER 8

Writing with Style

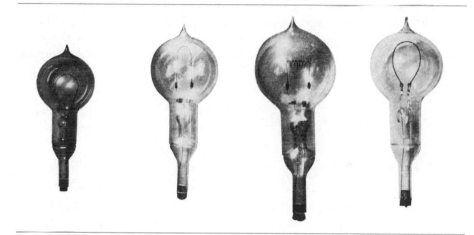

To improve one's style means to improve one's thoughts.

—FRIEDRICH NIETZSCHE

The language must be careful and appear effortless. It must
not sweat.

—TONI MORRISON

She would write 8–10 words, then draw her gun and shoot them
all down.

—E. B. WHITE ON KATHARINE WHITE'S WRITING

After revising your draft for ideas, details, and organization, comb through your words. Words help ideas croak or sing, convey an authoritative or awkward tone, and arouse or sedate readers. A smooth, clean style proves a writer sweats the words. It isn't luck. It isn't a genetic gift.

The quotation from Nietzsche heading this chapter reminds us, however, that glittering words cannot somehow brush fancy makeup over a bad idea or no idea. Revising words means revising ideas, for words and ideas are inseparable and together create style. Katharine White reminds us that we must struggle to find the right word. And Morrison reminds us we must sweep away the signs of our struggle.

HONESTY

Vocabulary

Some writers think big words sound more sophisticated or intellectual. They click the thesaurus icon on their computer for fancy synonyms. With happy enthusiasm, they might revise my previous sentence this way: "They inaugurate a scrutinization of a thesaurus in diligent quest for ostentatious synonyms." I hear readers snoozing. An expanded vocabulary does create options, but the big-word approach usually doesn't work. First, if the writer doesn't *really* know her words, they tend to be used off-center: sometimes confusing a reader or showing the writer's *un*sophistication. Second, big words rarely impress good readers, who want a smooth journey, not a sojourn over gargantuan, albeit splendiferous, boulders. Usually the simplest, most direct word possible is best. The fancy word draws attention to itself—and away from your ideas and details. Use the occasional fancy word or technical term when you need to; don't sprinkle them like salt over the entire paper. Write within yourself.

This does not mean you can get away with dull or monotonous words. Your vocabulary should be colorful and vivid, but that rarely requires big words.

■ **PRACTICE 8-1:** Revise the following for clear vocabulary:

- The industrial unit will downsize operations to maximize return on investment.
- My antagonist inaugurated a campaign to terminate my presidency of the Ostentatious Vocabulary Association.

Accuracy

Honest writing demands accuracy, and this means **revising the sloppy word choices** we *all* make in rapid draft composition. If you don't find three or four inaccurate word choices in each paragraph of a draft, you're either a genius who will soon be famous and rich as if by magic, or you're not searching hard. Ask if each word presents exactly the tone or picture you want. It's obviously wrong to misstate a fact or statistic, but **it's also dishonest to exaggerate or use absolutes:**

- Al *always* arrives late.
- Marcie's *never* had a sick day in her life.
- You'll *love* the new Ford carburetors.
- Drug dealers are murderers, *pure and simple.*

Absolutes are words like "always," "never," "all," "every," or "none." Leaving no room for exceptions, they sound dramatic and make writers feel forceful, but they are often dishonest. Notice, I did not say "always dishonest." Some absolutes are true: *All* humans die. Ask yourself in revision if an "often" or "usually" might better describe Al's lateness or if a "hardly ever" or "as long as I've known her" might more accurately describe Marcie's health.

To say someone will "love" a carburetor will probably be an exaggeration for all but the most fanatical car owner. It might be more accurate to simply describe its outstanding features. Why is it exaggeration to say drug dealing is murder, pure and simple? Because it's neither pure nor simple but requires distinctions—drug dealing differs from, say, strangling someone, or from selling automobiles that may also end up killing the user—and you must show *how*.

Being tough with words will make your ideas tougher too. Question key words ruthlessly. **Hunt for "weasels":** words that seem to say something but weasel out of it. (For example, "Computers *may* help you write one to two grades better." Bananas *may* help you write two grades better, too.) Inaccurate language makes you appear an unreliable and sloppy thinker.

■ **PRACTICE 8-2:** Revise these sentences for accuracy:

- The antiabortionists never consider the lives of pregnant teenagers.
- The United States has been completely humiliated by a bunch of rag-tag terrorists.

Euphemisms and Crude Language

Euphemisms are expressions that make things sound nicer or grander than they are. When a used car is called "pre-owned" or "pre-enjoyed," a trucker a "commodity relocation engineer," or a garbage collector a "sanitary engineer," the writer is prettying up the truth. During the Vietnam War, American generals denied they invaded Cambodia, a neutral country; they announced they had "launched a protective reaction strike," suggesting self-defense.

Notice that many euphemisms hide behind crooked use of big words. In a famous letter leaked to the press during the Vietnam War, orders were given to assassinate a secret agent, but the words "assassinate" and "kill" never appeared. The agent was to be "terminated with extreme prejudice."

Euphemisms have their place in conversation. If your friend Bob is fired, you may choose to say he "lost" his job, "was laid off," or "was furloughed" to spare his feelings. But unless you need to spare your *audience's* feelings, writing demands a stricter standard of honesty. If Bob was fired, say he was fired. Consider whether it's more accurate to describe an agent as "shot," "murdered," "assassinated," "blown away," "offed," or "eliminated." How do these each have different implications? At a funeral, the dead person may be euphemistically referred to as "the dearly departed" or "the late Bertha Smith," certainly not as "the stiff" or "the corpse." The dead are "conveyed to their final resting places," not "hauled to the worm farm."

Notice that some alternatives to the euphemisms here are unnecessarily brutal. **Crude expressions,** like euphemisms, give you power or distance over unpleasant facts; euphemisms deny them; crude words exaggerate them so they can be laughed at. **In revising for honest words, ask if your choices are** *appropriate to the subject*—not sickeningly sweet, not unnecessarily crude. The honest writer can't be so polite the message is wimpy or so impolite the message is forgotten. Obscenities, therefore, should only be used if necessary to duplicate the way a person speaks; the drama they create is usually dishonest—a cheap way to shock the reader. They are inappropriate in professional communication.

■ **PRACTICE 8-3:** Revise these sentences for euphemisms or crude language:

- When buying a reconditioned car, delve into the mechanical functioning as well as the amenities or you may own a less than wonderful vehicle.

- The judge thinks a surrogate mother is just a uterus with legs. (Taken from an actual television news broadcast.)

Clichés

Clichés are dead places in your essay. Like all inaccurate word choices, they come more easily than the perfect word and often creep into rough drafts. Revision must root them out and plant live words in the empty holes. Some writers may defend clichés by saying, "Everyone knows what a cliché means." I disagree. For example, is the expression "toe the line" or "tow the line?" Visualize it and you'll see different images for each spelling. A student who described a nasty woman as "an old batilacks" had no idea the original expression referred to a weapon, a "battle axe." Nor do readers pay close attention to clichés. They know there's no new idea, no new, interesting word use that requires attention. Do you really want your readers to drift away? Complete these images:

Hungry as a _____

Gentle as a _____

Quiet as a _____

Eats like a _____

Busy as a _____

Slippery as _____

Most people will complete these images with the same one or two words; the expressions are that predictable. Clichés slide easily in *and out* of readers' minds. If you want to show how slippery a political issue is, for instance, don't compare it to a "greased pig" or an "eel." Compare it to a wet gangplank, a slimy creek bed, an icy wheelchair ramp, or a salesman asked for a refund. As Hollywood producer Sam Goldwyn used to say, "We have to get some fresh platitudes." Start by picturing what you're describing. Feel, see, hear, taste, or smell it as a *thing*, not as a word.

New clichés are born each year, sounding exciting and creative. Lately you may hear someone say, "Give him props. His music's butters. It's mad phat. And that girl's a dime." Translation: "Give him credit. His music's great. It's very cool. And the girl's outstanding (a ten)." I like "butters" and "mad phat." For today, it's creative. But if these expressions last they'll sound as stale and corny as "souped-up car," "pinko," "sexpot," "mod," and "D.A." do today. (Ask your professor what these expressions meant—he or she may have been around then!)

■ **PRACTICE 8-4:** Invent two creative alternatives for each of the clichéd expressions listed above. Be visual and fresh.

■ **PRACTICE 8-5:** Revise these clichés to be more fresh and visual:
- Don't put all your eggs in one basket.
- Curiosity killed the cat.
- Fight fire with fire.
- The economy is going down the tubes.
- It's never too late to learn.

Sexist Language

Aside from the ethical argument that sexist language is wrong and that by using it you personally contribute to bias against women, sexist language can alienate readers (both male and female) who find it offensive. You may also create a picture of yourself as a sloppy thinker who stereotypes and generalizes without much thought. If you always refer to lawyers or scientists as "he," for instance, you should know that nearly 50 percent of all current law students and 40 percent of all advanced degree science students are women. Here are three options for dealing with the "she-he" problem:

- When the sex of an example is irrelevant, use "he or she" or a pronoun without sex reference. "A student should prepare his schedule . . ." could be "Students should prepare their schedules . . ." or "A student should prepare his or her schedule . . ."

- You may sometimes use "he" and sometimes "she," as this book does. Just remember, some nurses are male, some mechanics are women.

- Use a gender-neutral term instead. "Salesman" can be "salesperson;" "postman" can be "postal worker" or "mail carrier."

Do these little variations matter? Some people might claim that everybody knows "mankind" includes both males and females, as do jobs that end in "man." But even though we "know" it, hearing "man" used thousands of times in our lives to describe the species, respected positions, and important activities probably has hammered values into all of us. Many researchers believe these small messages affect our self-image, confidence, and the dreams and goals we set for ourselves. Whether you agree with this or not, it's undeniable that most educated people, most businesses, and most public institutions are sensitive to sexist language. The penalties far outweigh the rewards for using such language today.

■ **PRACTICE 8-6:** Revise these sentences to make them less sexist.

- An athlete must accept his responsibility to be a role model.
- The chairman must control his audience.

VIVIDNESS

Someone might ask, "If I weed out big words, extreme words, clichés, and sexist and crude language, won't my style be dull?" No. You're cleaning away the debris to make room for real style. Honesty and vividness come from concreteness and from improving key words—especially verbs, modifiers, and metaphors.

Concreteness

During revision, replace general or vague words with concrete words that are specific or appeal to the reader's senses. This is the difference between pretend meaning and real meaning. If you can't pin a sentence down to specifics, cross it off. You haven't lost a sentence but *gained* clarity. Notice how wimpy the following sentences are:

- The Saturn is a *good* car.
- We had an *exciting* time!
- Abused children suffer *mentally* as well as *physically.*

The vague words needing pep are so general that a reader has no specific image from them. In revision, choose words that relate to specific details:

- The Saturn is a sporty, economical, reliable car.
- Our blood pressure blasted off, and we screamed ourselves hoarse.
- We see the scars and burn marks on abused children, but a mother screaming, "I wish you were never born!" scars them, too.

Here's a brief list of vague words to watch out for:

good	bad	great
nice	fantastic	beautiful
ugly	cute	sad
happy	success	awesome
awful	terrible	big/little

Their hazy generality poisons vividness. If you try to improve these words with a thesaurus, you may substitute "salubrious" or "benevolent" for "good," or substitute "deplorable" or "grievous" for "sad." Though slightly more specific than the originals, these still don't *define* or *visualize.* In revising for concreteness, re-see the thing described; think in pictures, not in words. Replacing vague words with specific ones will do more than any other technique to make your writing more tangible and clear. Instead of saying, "He's a good man," write, "He'd take in a sick, stray dog," or "He donates 5 percent of his paycheck to the soup kitchen."

■ **PRACTICE 8-7:** Rewrite the following sentences for more concreteness. This requires you to interpret the writer's purpose, because the sentences are vague:

- American foreign policy toward Muslim nations is messed up.
- What an ugly sight a garbage dump is.
- He is really a great friend.
- Halle Berry is beautiful.

Verbs

One key word to examine is the verb, the strongest word in any sentence because it conveys action. Yet when I ask my students to underline all verbs in their papers, 80 percent turn out to be forms of "to be": was, were, are, is, am. "To be" is the dullest English verb. Other colorless, bland verbs include "go," "have," "get," "do," and "become." Some vivid, action verbs are "hack," "spring," "peel," "plow," "flick," "gobble," or "rip." Study this sample sentence from a student draft:

> **Example:** As the rush of people walk through the downtown area, the clanking and shaking of the old train is heard.

This sentence buries its vivid words "clanking" and "shaking." Make them the main verbs and scratch out the weak "is heard" at the end. Also "walk" is a weak verb when the writer has the word "rush." Here's how the writer's peers revised it:

> **Example:** As the people rush downtown, the old train clanks and shakes past.

In the next sentence "is" saps potentially stronger verbs:

> **Example:** To many people a college education is a burning desire.

> **Better:** Many people burn for college educations.

■ **PRACTICE 8-8:** In the next two sentences, first locate the strong words and then restructure the sentence around a stronger verb.

- The question often asked by apartment dwellers is, "How am I going to furnish this place?"
- There was a clashing of negative events that helped me find myself.

Some verbs like "look" or "walk" are so general, I almost always substitute more specific ones. "She looked at me." Boring. Did she stare, leer, examine, peek, glance, or glare? Notice how the substitutes are more specific and visual than "look." Each adds tone and attitude. Many flat sentences spring off the page with new verbs.

■ **PRACTICE 8-9:** List ten substitute words for "walk" that are more visual and more specific.

Adjectives and Adverbs

You may have been told that adjectives and adverbs describe. True. But adverbs (which modify or describe verbs) and adjectives (which modify or describe nouns) are *helpers*. Rely on better nouns and verbs first. Which of these pairs is the sharpest:

- Janet walked very, very slowly.

  Janet dawdled.
- The car moved quickly away.

  The car sped away.
- Jack was an extremely big man.

  Jack was a Goliath.

In each case the second is more precise and visual because a weak adjective-noun or adverb-verb gave way to a strong noun or verb.

One particularly flat type of adjective or adverb is the **intensifier,** a word that says, "yeah, well, even more than the next word." These are the most common ones:

very	-est (ending)	excessively
so	extremely	least
too	definitely	most
really		

Here are a few in action:

- He was the happiest man alive.
- It was a really easy assignment.
- The oil spill was extremely bad.
- Laws for handicapped rights are so very hard to pass.

Intensifiers remind me a little bit of shouting arguments I used to have with my brother: the louder the better. This sentence beats its chest: "It was an extremely, definitely, extra-important, most so very needed event." The problem is, there's no chest to beat, no concrete noun or strong verb to accentuate. Replace intensifiers with more concrete nouns or verbs. For example:

- He was ecstatic.
- The oil spill covered 300 square miles.

■ **PRACTICE 8-10:** Revise the other two examples and these:

- It was very cold that night.
- She was too unprepared for boot camp.

Metaphors

Vivid writing often relies on metaphors. Albert Einstein used the metaphor of riding a light beam to help explain his theory of relativity, and scientists F. H. Crick and J. D. Watson used the metaphor of two snakes wrapped around each other to describe the structure of the DNA molecule. In Chapter 3 you learned to use metaphor as a thinking strategy. In revision, sharpen metaphors for *compactness, coherence,* and *concreteness.*

Metaphors should be compact. Metaphor power comes partly from suggesting a lot in a small space. Don't explain yourself away:

> Cameron was very tall and very thin and has often been compared to Ichabod Crane. His most distinguishing feature would be his long fingers. If you've ever been to a costume shop and put on a pair of phony fingers, you'll know what his look like. Well, maybe not that long, but they are bigger than yours and mine.

This writer had an interesting, vivid comparison, but he diluted it into a thin tea.

Revised: Tall, thin Cameron has been compared to Ichabod Crane. His fingers are like the scrawny, phony fingers in a costume shop.

You can suggest metaphors sometimes with just one word—the ultimate in compactness. Here are some from student papers:

- Sandy chirped a reply.
- This popcorn kernel of a man was a marine?
- Bill's cabbage brain couldn't understand.

■ **PRACTICE 8-11:** Write out a one- or two-sentence metaphor and then rewrite it compactly with one star verb or adjective. For example, "Our economics course is like a maze in which you cannot find your way out, like experimental rats in a psychology experiment" could be reduced to "We groped through the maze of economics all semester."

Metaphors should be **coherent**—everything in the picture should fit together. The following metaphors pull the reader in several directions:

Example: Our household was emotionally *barren,* much like the *deserts* of loneliness people create to save themselves from being *bruised* or *hurt* by someone else. (The writer creates an effective desert image but then stirs in a new metaphor with "bruised." He needed to continue his desert image, perhaps with a reference to being lost, thirsty, or victimized by sun or desert predators.)

Example: Even though James Brown possessed extraordinary potential as a musician, his motivation was like an *abrupt red light* that *faded* in and *slithered* out periodically. (Another good metaphor derailed. The word "slithered" switches images. Red lights can fade but they can't slither. The writer should have stuck with the traffic light imagery.)

■ **PRACTICE 8-12:** Revise the two examples listed above.

Finally, **metaphors must be concrete.** They should appeal to our senses with sharp sights, smells, sounds, tastes, or touches. Notice how the following improves with more specific visualizing:

Example: Her dreams were ruined by fear, like the presence of an ugly pollutant in a clean body of water.

Revised: Her dreams were ruined by fear, like chemicals seeping into a pristine pond.

■ **PRACTICE 8-13:** Rewrite these sentences for sharper metaphors:

- The city fire chief was a tower of strength.
- We are at a crossroads where we must sink or swim.
- His voice was like a lion's. It made a lot of noise and it felt like it was coming after you down a hallway if you tried to get away.
- Peace comes like rain.

STYLISH SENTENCE STRUCTURE

Variety

Glance at your sentences. Do they all follow a subject—verb—modifier format? Are most stubby or are they long, twisted snakes? Readers like variety. Reading many short, choppy sentences is like picking up a handful of beads; help the reader string them together. A page of continuous long sentences is like a jungle to hack through—you want more air and light. Break up a series of straight statements with an occasional question. Mix simple, compound, and complex sentences (for more see Chapter 16).

■ **PRACTICE 8-14:** Find a place in your last paper in which three sentences in a row are nearly the same length or use almost the same structure. (*Hint:* Look for ones using a subject—verb—modifier pattern.) Change the length or pattern for variety.

■ **PRACTICE 8-15:** Just to see what your sentence lengths are, count the number of words in each sentence of your last paper. What is the shortest? What is the longest? What is the average length? In class, compare with your classmates.

Parallel Structure

Parallel structure means matching words or groups of words in a series or on each side of a conjunction:

Example: The president ordered troops, ships, and planes overseas. (*Troops, ships,* and *planes* are all nouns and all ordered by the president.)

Example: She wanted to stop the civil war, unite the American people, and open the harbors for oil tankers. (Three verbs with modifiers and all are things she wants.)

Wrong: The president ordered troops, ships, and bombed the airfield. (The last item is a mismatch.)

Wrong: She wanted to stop the civil war, the votes of Americans, and open the harbors for oil tankers. (The second item, a noun, mismatches.)

You might consider one other aspect of parallel structure when working on a particularly important sentence: the items should build to a climax.

Example: His childhood days were filled with fear, cruelty, and a concealed love. (Because the student contrasted love with negative things, it springs up at the end like a surprise blossom; in the middle of the list, it would lack emphasis.)

Weak: The congressional plan backfired; 2,000 soldiers were killed unnecessarily, Congress was recalled for an extra session, and the plan cost $100,000 more than expected. (The soldiers' deaths are most important and therefore belong last.)

■ **PRACTICE 8-16:** Write two sentences that list parallel items in a series. Each item must be a phrase or clause of at least three words.

CONCISENESS

Essayist and children's book author E. B. White recalled his former writing professor, William Strunk, leaning on the lectern in class, peering over his wire-rimmed spectacles, and barking, "Avoid unnecessary words! Avoid unnecessary words! Avoid unnecessary words!"

I'd like to leave it at that, but we need to make a distinction. I receive a number of papers each semester that are *brief,* say, half the length asked for. They're usually not *concise,* however. Concise writing says *as much as possible in as few words as possible.* This means keeping a reader interested, supplying vivid supporting detail, and emphasizing key points. Many brief papers simply state a thesis without bringing it to life. They may be wordy or vague or simply cover less than a concise longer paper.

Few people could top President Calvin Coolidge for brevity. Once asked by his wife what the Sunday sermon was about, Silent Cal replied, "Sin."

"Well, what did the preacher say about it?" his exasperated wife asked.

"He was against it," Coolidge replied.

This brevity says nothing. However, most great writing is concise. The Lord's Prayer is 56 words; Lincoln's Gettysburg Address is about 200; the Ten Commandments is under 300; and the Declaration of Independence is about 1,500. (Freshman papers run 500 to 1,000 words.) On the other hand, a U.S. Department of Agriculture memo on how to price cabbage weighed in at over 25,000 words!

We all talk around our ideas most of the time. But in revision, average writers can trim 20 to 30 percent of their draft. Much small-scale wordiness takes up space but contributes nothing:

Wordy	*Better*
"He went on to say . . ."	"He added . . ."
"The hat was red in color . . ."	"The red hat . . ."
"We proceeded to depart."	"We departed."
"In my opinion it seems to me . . ."	"I believe . . ."
"Ken was slugged by Joe."	"Joe slugged Ken."
"Due to the fact that . . ."	"Because . . ."

Here's an introduction that spins nothing into empty cotton candy:

Example: It is very interesting to compare what different essay writers have to say about writing essays. In our book we have different essays on writing by E. B. White, Alice Walker, and Joan Didion, who are all famous modern authors today.

Notice the repetition and lack of a clear thesis; the writer may think she's started, but the reader knows she's still clearing her throat.

> **Improved:** E. B. White, Alice Walker, and Joan Didion present three different views on writing essays.

Nothing important is lost; the sentence is improved for being direct. Like watery wine, low-test gasoline, or air-puffed bread, wordy writing doesn't offer enough pop per ounce. Readers expect a certain density of information per paragraph. A high-octane effort means not only using high-intensity concrete words and vivid verbs, but removing the water.

Redundancy: A hat that is "red in color" says it twice; red cannot be a shape or a smell, only a color. Is the "honest truth" more true than just "the truth"? Chop redundancy to strengthen the following sentences:

- The Constitution was totally demolished.
- He is a completely unique artist.
- The railroad was extended a distance of 60 miles.
- I plan to enter the field of nursing.
- In the fall of the year school once again reopens.
- At that point in time, we faced a serious job crisis.

All writers puff up first drafts; good writers condense final drafts. Concentration and practice, not talent, will make your writing concise.

Connecting words such as prepositions, "that" or "which," or anything not carrying the main weight of a sentence may be fluff. Cutting two verbs to one strengthens sentences, especially if you exterminate a "to be" verb:

> **Wordy:** The bureaucrats avoided some *of the* work *they were* assigned.

> **Concise:** The bureaucrats avoided some assigned work.

> **Wordy:** The catalytic converter *is used for the purpose of* reducing air pollution.

> **Concise:** The catalytic converter reduces air pollution.

■ **PRACTICE 8 17:** Make each of these sentences more concise. Save vivid words, and convert hidden strong verbs into active ones.

- At that point in time Lee attacked north for the purpose of scaring the Yankees.
- The Capitol was entirely destroyed by fire.
- He had a long gray beard that had not been trimmed very recently.
- Ike brought tears of laughter to a great number of people with his jokes.
- Those who commit murder are not deserving of the state's mercy.

USING A COMPUTER TO REVISE WORDS

Computers are great for word revision. A thesaurus feature can find synonyms for poor word choices and a word search will tell if you overused one word. You may be able to instruct your computer to beep at suspect words: absolutes like "always," intensifiers like "very," clichés you want to put a lid on (beep!), vague words like "good," or "to be" verbs like "was." Then you scroll through your draft and consider changing each. You don't have to change all of them, but the computer is ruthlessly honest about telling you exactly what's there—if you want to know.

■ **PRACTICE 8-18:** Create a hot list of style words and instruct your computer to alert you when your draft uses absolutes page 145, intensifiers page 151, vague words page 149, and forms of the verb "to be" page 149.

PLAYING WITH LANGUAGE

The best way to improve your style is to play with language. Rearrange words the way you rearrange furniture in a room to see how it looks or the way you try a new batting stance just to see how it feels. Is change always good? Of course not. But you will never be any better than you are right now unless you try new things. Besides, as you play with language, you should find that it stimulates new ideas and details like any other brain teaser. Suppose you were asked to give your opinion on the *Survivor*-type television shows in which people compete to be the last one "alive." You could say:

> The people who are on these shows are freaks and idiots. They give up all their secrets and privacy to be famous for a few weeks. Everybody laughs at them and says what jerks they are.

Commentary: Now, this is direct and bold—but flat. Nothing is supported by concrete detail. All three sentences start with subjects and verbs. Almost all the verbs are bland ("are," "give," "to be," "says," and one action verb "laugh"). It slips into absolutes ("all" and "everybody"), which imply that all contestants fit the stereotype. It does not use crude language exactly, but "freaks," "idiots," and "jerks" come close, making the writer appear snobbish. Am I condemning the writer's idea? No. In fact, I tend to agree. But the style does not convey it well.

■ **PRACTICE 8-19:** Supply concrete details (examples and descriptions) and play with the sentence structure, verbs, absolutes, and labels to improve the paragraph on *Survivor*-type shows. If you disagree with the writer, rewrite the paragraph to fit your opinion.

InfoTrac® College Edition: Reading on Style

For tips on using *InfoTrac®* College Edition, see page 464.

Constance Hale, "7 Secrets of Good Prose: Ways to Pare and Polish Your Work As You Revise." *The Writer.* June 2002.

Concreteness, conciseness, parallelism, and rhythm in your style.

Highlights of Chapter 8

- Revise your draft for words and style by going over it once for *each* aspect listed. A focused reading is more likely to pinpoint problems than just riding the flow to find a bump.

- Revising for *honest word use* means using a vocabulary you control, testing the accuracy of your words, avoiding weasels and absolutes, and getting rid of euphemisms, crude language, and clichés.

- To make your style more *vivid*, revise for more concrete words that visualize, replace "to be" and other dull verbs with action verbs, replace some weak modifier–subject combinations with stronger nouns and verbs, eliminate intensifiers, and flash an occasional metaphor.

- Revising *sentence structure* can improve style, too. Vary your sentence lengths and format and revise for tight, climactic parallel construction.

- *Concise writing* has more impact. Ruthlessly cut wordiness.

- As you read over your draft, anytime you find yourself daydreaming or skimming, stop! Go back. Read the last few sentences with microscope eyes. A reader's attention will be twice as fragile as yours. Sharpen a verb, eliminate a wordy phrase, or be more concrete to keep that reader with you for the rest of the ride.

Writing Suggestions and Class Discussions

Revise the following for honest word use, vividness, parallel structure, and conciseness.

1. It was a blistering June day; the heat could be seen radiating from the pavement.
2. Pete is definitely one of a kind.
3. We must grab the bull by the tail and face the situation.

4. The first time I encountered José, it was in a foreign country.

5. The war with Iraq was filled with a great many human atrocities.

6. Dr. Baikman is a short, dark man who looks as if he's beginning to get old.

7. She has a way of making people feel very special.

8. Alan's superficialities were especially on my bug list.

9. Queen Morena dumped on the count. She declined his matrimonial proposal.

10. A garden is in her face where roses and white lilies grow.

11. Americans must give up drugs if they want to escape the prison of this filthy crutch they use to bury their weaknesses.

12. After returning from the little girl's room, I proceeded to expostulate on the numerous beneficial phenomena of mixed-gender lavatories.

13. When I was at the age of 12, my mom started to become a little better, treating us more like human beings, although the discipline was still there.

14. Upon my arrival, I quickly apprehended the culture change and beheld the New Hampshire accent and idioms embellished by the McCormack family.

15. After the whistle, Sam attacks his opponent with a killer instinct, driving him to the mat and gratifying what he sets out to accomplish.

16. There was a fear of anyone approaching him.

17. His right eye was dangling out of its socket, his lower lip was stretched under his chin, his nose was almost completely torn from his face and hanging facial skin.

18. Her medication was putting weight on her that was visibly noticeable within a few days after it was prescribed.

19. Carolyn's life was like water, moving and shifting with no anchor.

20. It's always too late to straighten a kid out after he's been in jail.

21. There are many different variations in color.

22. Janet lacked a confidence factor.

23. Negotiations will either grind to a halt or be hammered out.

24. At 7 A.M. in the morning, the weatherman predicted major thunderstorm activity.

Make a chart listing "male" and "female" at the top and write the qualities brought out with each reference to gender in these 24 sentences (e.g., fear, purposeful). Then evaluate the overall sexist slant to the first 24 sentences.

Three Ways to Revise Style

1. Exchange rough drafts with another student in class. Do all you can to help each other with honest word choices, vividness, sharp sentences, and conciseness.

2. Your professor will mark one paragraph in your draft or paper needing stylistic pruning and pep. Revise it thoroughly.

3. Find an example for ten of the following in the draft of a paper you're preparing. Then revise. Most people can find at least two of the starred items in drafts:

   - Overly fancy vocabulary
   - *Absolutes
   - *Exaggeration
   - Weasels
   - Euphemism
   - Crude language
   - Clichés
   - Sexist language
   - *Areas needing more concreteness
   - *Dull verbs
   - *Weak adjectives or adverbs
   - *Intensifiers
   - Weak metaphors
   - Monotonous sentence structure
   - Nonparallel sentence structure
   - *Redundancy
   - *General wordiness

Sample Revision for Style

Here is a rough draft of part of a student essay, with suggestions made for style. The author is Mary Updaw, and the comments were made by her and others. Ignore the comments as you read, then go over each of them.

Revised Student Essay and Analysis

Good Intentions

WORDY
and weak verb

I ~~was in urgent need of~~ a tracheotomy operation a year ago.

~~Since then, some difficult situations have occurred.~~ So this is for the

VAGUE not concrete

strangers ~~whom~~ I meet daily and their good intentions.

unnecessary

When you ~~get on~~ an elevator with me, do not suggest I ~~go see~~ my doc-

weak verb - ride? enter?   *weak verb*

tor if I cough. I do not have enough time between floors to explain to a per-

fect stranger my condition. Please do not stare at me with sympathetic

eyes if you notice my trach bib. I am not some poor little lamb you should

Absolute

feel sorry for, and I resent ~~any~~ indication that I am. Please do not ask fool-

ish questions if you see me using my inhaler. I am not a drug addict, and

cut intensifier   *redundant*

wordy   ~~I feel~~ it should be ~~quite~~ obvious I am taking medication ~~for my health.~~ I do

weak verb   *better verb*

not ~~go up to~~ people I see popping aspirin and ~~ask~~ if they have a headache.

stare?

If your child happens to ~~look~~ in my ~~direction,~~ please do not whisper in

used twice - cut one

his ear and steer him in another direction. I am not ~~some kind of~~ freak he

wordy   *a*

should ~~be afraid of.~~ To the strangers who want to swap medical war sto-

ries, I say forget it. I have not been graced with a Purple Heart for my con-

too crude!

dition; they are only for the men who deserve them, ~~and, frankly, it's none~~

harsh + unnecessary

~~of your [#*!%] business.~~ For the well-wishers who secretly are glad it is

me and not you, you are more transparent than you realize, and ~~I don't~~

~~care to be around you.~~ *— redundant — this is obvious*

Commentary

Reviewers knew this draft based on a bug list had strong potential. Honest
and direct, it hit the reader hard. They also liked the style of the sentences,
which are balanced and parallel to make Mary's structure clear. The notes
focus on cutting wordiness, replacing vague words, weak verbs, and sharp-
ening the existing sentence structure. The final draft is 20 percent shorter
but more lively in style.

Final Draft

Good Intentions

I urgently needed a tracheotomy operation a year ago. But the real shock came later—dealing with strangers and their good intentions.

When you ride an elevator with me, do not suggest I rush to my doctor if I cough. I do not have enough time between floors to explain my condition to a perfect stranger. Please do not stare at me with sympathetic eyes if you notice my trach bib. I am not some poor little lamb you should feel sorry for, and I resent indications that I am. Please do not ask foolish questions if you see me using my inhaler. I am not a drug addict; it should be obvious I am taking medication. I do not ask people popping aspirin if they have a headache.

If your child glances at me, please do not whisper in his ear and steer him in another direction. I am not a freak he should fear. To strangers who want to swap medical war stories, forget it. I have not been graced with a Purple Heart for my condition; they are only for the men who deserve them. For the well-wishers who secretly are glad it is me and not you, you are more transparent than you realize.

✓ **PEER REVIEW CHECKLIST FOR STYLE**

Author: _____

Reviewer: _____

The reviewer should read through the rough draft **only** for style. Make suggested changes on the rough draft itself, but please leave the original legible for the author.

1. Find two weak verbs (is, are, has, or get) and suggest more visual action verbs to replace them.

2. Accuracy/honesty: Find an exaggeration or absolute that ought to be modified. Suggest a revision.

3. Concreteness: Find a cliché that needs a fresher image or an unsupported generalization that needs more detail. Suggest a revision.

4. Find an intensifier and suggest a stronger noun or verb to replace the weak one the intensifier tried to build up.

5. Look for an example of sexist language or stereotyping and suggest a revision.

6. Conciseness: Pick one paragraph of the essay and make at least three suggestions to eliminate redundant or empty words.

CHAPTER 9

Description

Making Your Audience See

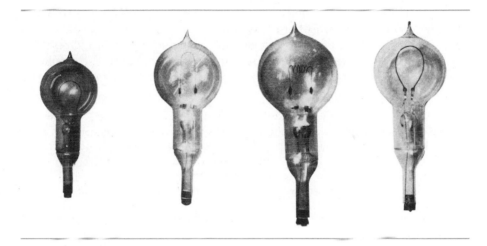

The question is not what you look at, but what you see. . . .
A man has not seen a thing unless he has felt it.

—HENRY DAVID THOREAU

To see takes time—like to have a friend takes time.

—GEORGIA O'KEEFFE

Look! Look!

—COLETTE (HER LAST WORDS)

Which of these statements are true?

- Description is flowery and poetic.
- Description bogs down writing.
- Description belongs in creative essays, not persuasive or informative writing.

None. They all distort the real nature of description. Fancy, gooey descriptive passages can smother ideas and are unacceptable as professional communication. Such passages give description a bad reputation. **Good description doesn't need to be gooey or fancy.** For example, the following passage describes a seizure a student's infant daughter suffered as a result of a DPT vaccine for pertussis:

> Lying in a puddle of vomit, Katelyn's head tilted to her shoulder, her eyes fixated left, looking like quarter moons. When I picked her up, I realized her head was locked to her shoulder. "Katie!" I yelled. She didn't hear me. Once in her father's arms, her legs locked straight out. Her tiny arms pulled tight against her chest, and her head shot back. My husband held down her tongue just as her jaw locked shut. Her eyes rolled upward, then they were gone.

At the hospital, the child's condition is stabilized, and the author goes on to describe her condition:

> There, lying in a crib resembling a cage, clad only in her diaper, was our baby daughter. Her chest was covered with leads monitoring her heart. Her arms, braced with tongue depressors, were violated with tubes and needles. Inches from her body was a "crash kit" equipped with electric paddles should they be needed.
>
> —*Alana J. Lockwood*

This vivid, factual description draws readers into the author's informative critique of the DPT vaccine, which each year causes seizures in thousands of normal children.

Description breathes life into writing—transforms typed words into pictures, sounds, and ideas. *Good* description makes the writer's idea dance in readers' heads, so they forget they're reading words. *Bad* description, by trying to impress readers with lush words, distracts from the idea. It makes us focus on the writer jumping up and down in a purple wedding dress.

Good description is essential for *all* writing, from business reports to personal letters to poems to persuasive essays. **Description commits writers to honesty by pinning down vague statements with concrete details.** Honest description shows the world as it is with all its warts, pimples, and secret beauties. It challenges safe stereotypes and preconceptions by getting down on its knees to scrutinize the topic closer, to find and report what's really there. This tough attitude resists gooey description, making writing lean and hard, as in this student example:

It takes 938 steps to walk from one end of the beat to the other. The air is cold and crisp, the kind that fills my lungs with crystals—like a dagger in my chest. Only an hour and a half left until I'm done. The night is clear, almost too clear. The sound of my boots pounding the frozen turf is the only real thing. Our Air Force bombed Libya two days ago—an act of war. Tonight the lieutenant issued live ammunition. Boring guard duty became relevant.

Step 452, almost to the mid-point, 17 steps away. I can see where I marked the center with a line scratched in the path. The center is an insecure place, where the distance between start and finish is the same. I just hope that the powers that run things have enough sense to go back to the start.

—*Scott Nairy*

This passage makes us *see* as well as understand, which is description's great virtue.

In persuasive or research papers, powerful description can support a thesis in combination with statistics and other facts. In a paper arguing for strong penalties for pregnant women who use drugs, a student's research describes the effects of cocaine on newborns:

Because cocaine causes fetus malnutrition, when the baby is born, its dry, cracked skin resembles the cover of an old, leather-bound book (Fulroth 70). Cocaine babies are almost always underweight. Their heads are 20 percent smaller than average. Their limbs jerk and jitter constantly, and their hands fly periodically to the sides of their heads, eyes startled wide in terror. Cocaine babies' heartbeats soar, and their lungs pump like hyperactive bellows. They cry inconsolably, a creepy, catlike wail that can last hours and which indicates severe neurological damage (Knight 71).

—*Heidi Daniels*

A WRITER'S EYE: SIX WAYS TO VISUALIZE IDEAS

Experience the Subject: Don't Think in Words

When I ask students to describe a place, I often receive an essay that begins: "My room is 10 feet 6 inches by 11 feet and painted blue. I have a bed, a dresser, a stereo, a chair. . . ." This dead thing wants to be buried. Some students who realize it's flat "enliven" it with so-called descriptive words: "My room is robin's-egg blue with beige accents. I have an antique maple dresser, an enormous bed, a four-speaker Dolby-sound stereo cassette player. . . ." Bury this one in a fancy casket; it's just as dead as the first. Both examples fail because of mistaken goals.

- Description is *not* a catalog of everything present.
- Description is *not* created by thinking up picturesque words.

Here's an example of a description of a room that does not fall into these traps:

My room is only a pit stop between the evening and the morning. It has no luxurious, fluffy pillows, no king-sized bed. No extra time is spent in this room. It's get your clothes and out. At sunrise, the light glares off the television in a way that burns your face. In the evening, the coldness sets in, making you pull all the blankets right up to your chin.

—Scott Smith

This sample combines a few sharp details with an angle, a theme. *Both* are needed to make writing vivid.

Description *is* created by mentally reexperiencing what you hope to describe. Thoreau and O'Keeffe must have had this in mind when they wrote the sentences heading this chapter. A catalog may help as a brain teaser, but it won't create *quality* description. For that you must create an *idea* on which the description hangs, and you must concentrate on seeing and feeling your subject, not on choosing descriptive words. Evoke it inside yourself, and only *then* describe it in words. Reexperiencing often leads to vivid words naturally *and* ties description together.

Suppose I was writing about access for the disabled in public buildings. My first brain teaser list of descriptive details might include the following:

- Wide stalls in restrooms
- Interpreters for the deaf in college
- Low water fountains with large handles
- Wheelchair lifts on buses
- Disabled people I've known

I could use this list to compose a paper, perhaps on "Improvements in Public Access in Recent Years," but these descriptive details aren't sharp enough to write a strong paper. I haven't reexperienced them vividly.

Let's take the bathroom stall example. I started to skip this for decency, but I realized that decency allows people to hide many facts about the disabled. Imagine yourself entering that stall in a wheelchair. Experience the bodily movements you need to accomplish this simple act. Go slow: See or feel each moment clearly before going on. Could you do it during ten minutes between class? I picture myself rolling amid the waists of walking people, bumping open the restroom door and scraping past, rocking and turning several times to shut and lock the stall door, spilling books and papers off my wheelchair tray when I hoist myself with the cold bar, my chair sliding nearly out of reach, contorting to flush the knob behind my back and speeding to class late, bumping cluttered chairs to make a space, and wondering if the professor thinks I'm using my disability to get away with something.

I try to experience Carmen—a wheelchaired student in my literature class one summer. A wonderfully smiling young woman, she loved romantic stories. I experience being her —four feet tall, round-faced, back-bent wrists gripping the chair control knob. I imagine someone dressing me, cramming shoes onto my unresponsive feet, straightening my clothes so they feel right. During those hot classes, did she wish she could shift in her seat like others? Using a pen cost her agony during quizzes. Yet she made no complaints, no special requests, no mention of her disability. She seemed to fly, not to roll.

Thinking of Carmen reminds me of Eva, the old blind woman who lived with my family when I was a boy. Eva never bumped walls or furniture as she walked. From memory, she taught me to read, and she taught herself to read Braille and do leather work for pocket money. She sewed and did all the housework my mother or grandmother did, and when she eventually went to a nursing home, she learned its paths within months. Eva "saw" more than any of the seeing people who lived in our house. Her disability gave her special power and authority.

That makes me recall Tom, a disabled student who scoffed angrily when he was named a hospital's "Patient of the Year" for scoring a 4.0 GPA while working full time. "I'm not a patient," he sputtered. "I'm a man."

I've presented my train of thought roughly as it came out. It's a brain teaser in paragraph form, not finished writing, but it shows more life, more intense description than my first list. Most important, it stimulated my mind. I can advocate disabled rights now with vivid detail. If I advocate a hands-off policy, I have three examples of tough, independent people. If I want to inform people about barriers the disabled face, I have better information.

Although it may seem like I thought in words, I really thought in pictures, touches, and sounds, for that's how we experience things. Experience the subject from *inside,* not from outside. **Allow yourself to become your subject, let it speak through you; don't treat it as an object.** At its extreme, this is the mystical experience of poets and fiction writers, when they swear something "wrote itself." But even a restaurant menu writer must see, taste, and smell dishes to describe them well. Business reports and college papers require it, too. The more you re-feel or visualize your topic, the easier vivid description will be.

Some writers can type or write *as* they reexperience, but many writers can't. If words block experiencing, try this: **Sit back, *pen out of reach,* and picture your subject, imagining new details as you expand into it.** Relax. Let the topic talk. Release your subconscious. Censor nothing. Accept everything. Concentrate on seeing ever more sharply as you go on. Push your memory, recall facts, use *all* your senses, daydream. Most people stop when the first shadowy pictures appear. You should continue. Go slower, deeper. After a vivid experience gels, record your sensations on paper, still not paying attention to words. Simply record vivid images, allowing new description to flow too. *Later* you will take control and fine-tune the picture. As W. E. B. Du Bois said, "Produce beautiful things, but stress the things rather than the beauty."

■ **PRACTICE 9-1:** Experience two of these for five minutes, and only afterward record your descriptions. No catalogs, no fancy words.

- Your room
- A machine or tool
- Teenage alcoholism
- Senior citizens
- An experience with the police

■ **PRACTICE 9-2:** Freewrite a page for a descriptive topic you're considering for a paper.

Use Brain Teasers to Train Your Eye

Experiencing concentrates on unrestricted seeing. Brain teasers prod your eye in a more organized way. The two most important descriptive brain teasers from Chapter 3 are **Senses** and **Listing Examples.** If as you reexperience your topic, you only see obvious things, switch senses. Concentrate on hearing your topic or smelling or touching it. Or consciously list examples for your topic. Then experience it.

Suppose you're describing to your boss flaws in the design of the store you work in. Be a customer. Walk through the door. Wait! How does the door open? Is it a pull door people always push because it has a horizontal, long handle, not a small grabber? *Feel* yourself jolt as the door bounces—loose from many bumps, shabby. It angers people. How about the entranceway—cluttered with gumball machines and a kiddie ride? The *sound* of the whirring, whumpy-whump of the horse ride and kids begging mothers for quarters. Angry mothers, worn-down mothers. Nickel–dime robbery. Now into the store. The first *sight* is the line of people and cash registers, instead of a pretty dress, glittering jewelry, or the *scent* of sweet perfumes. Walk through other stores with your senses for *comparison.* Now you're ready to write.

For fresher description, push past the obvious with a **Break Stereotypes** brain teaser. Describe the obvious, then puncture it. Suppose you're describing the wonderful vacation cottage your family rented last year. There's the breathtaking view of lake and mountain, the Fourth of July fireworks display reflected in the water, the fish that beg to be caught, the clean, wholesome country air. Stop! Look closer! Listen harder; didn't you see trash in the stream leading to the lake? Weren't trucks hauling building supplies up that pristine mountain? Didn't motorboats roar past midnight?

Comparisons, alternative viewpoints, and **metaphors** can also stimulate your descriptive eye. If you're describing a local park, for instance, think of alternative viewpoints. Some people might only see broken glass, litter, missing basketball nets, and a rusted fence. Others might never notice the missing net, but just see dunks, layups, spins, passes, the thunk-thunk of dribbling, laughter, and sweaty drama. Yet others might see the park as it was years ago—a bandstand, people in straw hats, and a popcorn wagon. Allowing yourself to experience these other viewpoints makes you see more. We are what we see, so the more you see, the more you become, and the more powerful and alive your description will be.

■ **PRACTICE 9-3:** Do a Senses brain teaser and one other brain teaser to gather sharp description for two of the following topics. *Experience* them for five minutes before you focus on words.

- A childhood place
- An eyesore local authorities should fix or remove
- A commercial product about which you have strong feelings
- Student housing
- The taste of an orange or other fruit

■ **PRACTICE 9-4:** Use a Senses brain teaser and one other to dig up more descriptive detail for your topic from Practice 9-2.

Use the Iceberg Principle

Ernest Hemingway explained his descriptive technique as "the iceberg principle." He said powerful writing only shows the tip of the iceberg, nine-tenths of which rides under water. In essence, he meant that less description is sometimes more because it can suggest more than is visible. When faced with describing a complex or huge topic, *don't feel obligated to cover everything!* You may end up with a shapeless catalog. Instead, **search for a few key details that capture the essence of the larger picture—like a camera close-up.**

In describing a new word processing program, for instance, you'd probably confuse and bore readers by detailing all its features. Anyone who has resolutely begun to read the manual that accompanies a computer knows what I mean. You might illustrate the computer's accessibility by describing how one or two functions operate, such as moving a sentence from one spot to another and reformatting.

The iceberg principle draws readers in close. That perspective creates surprise and drama. It also requires you **to trust your reader. By relying on a small, intimate detail, you hope the reader will infer the larger picture by actively imagining along with you.** If someone writes, "Ralph set fire to the child's kite," there's no need to add, "I think it was cruel."

Describing a red-veined, bulby nose and a sleek, powdered nose suggest quite different things about the noses' owners. Such description can carry the idea of an essay by symbolism or by representation. To describe a group, you don't have to describe every member of the group. Pick *typical* representatives. This applies to describing "Japanese Cars," "Presidential Dirty Tactics," "Robert Frost's Poetry," or "French-Canadian Culture in Maine."

If I wrote about women in their thirties, forties, and fifties returning to college, here are two examples of "iceberg tips." Bernie, a little volcano of a woman, erupted into life after being bottled up for years. She had raised her children and, at fifty-plus, wanted to go into real estate and politics. College started her lava flowing again. She laughs at her mistakes, loves combat in class discussion, and relishes risks. Then there's Alecia, early thirties, petite, and shy under her long hair. She's afraid she'll fail, but is even more afraid of never trying. She knows something creative lives in her, but the world has squashed her before, and she hesitates to risk herself in front of 30 people. She's taking two courses, just dipping a toe into the water to see if sharks will bite.

These two examples don't capture all the problems and feelings of being an "older" woman in college, but as the tip of the iceberg, they stimulate a reader's imagination and memory. Icebergs strike more ships than watery generalities.

■ **PRACTICE 9-5:** Take an iceberg approach to two of these topics to describe the group to which they belong:

- ■ "Older" men in college
- ■ Suburban houses *or* city apartments
- ■ Local election campaigns
- ■ Local weather
- ■ The youngest or oldest child

■ **PRACTICE 9-6:** Take an iceberg approach to your topic from Practice 9-2.

Try Other Eye-Training Tricks

- ■ **Describe your topic as if to an audience unfamiliar with it.** A colleague of mine often asks his students to describe a ballpoint pen and its use (or any other object of modern civilization) to a hermit Tibetan monk. If you imagine your audience knows nothing, you must see freshly.
- ■ **Think of your topic as part of a *process***—not as a thing. A static thing invites dullness, but few things are truly static. The entire earth rockets through space a million miles per day, rotates at 1,000 miles per hour, and its crust rises and falls two feet under us each day. Everything has an origin and an end and is recycled into new life. Open your mind to see your topic as a process in time and space. A simple description of your room, then, connects to all the people who lived there before, how it came to be, and what will happen to it after you're gone. If you're writing about handling customer complaints at work, make your audience picture the process all parties go through before and after confrontations.

- **Describe what's *not* there.** A person who doesn't smile, cry, or become embarrassed may be interesting for that. The fact that my first word processor could not combine single and double spacing was a major drawback. The lack of dorms shapes atmosphere at many community colleges. Here's a brief description of scars, created through what's missing.

> When you touch your scars, they feel like they are not parts of your body. They are numb, as if that area of your body has fallen asleep. You can tell there are nerves under your scars, but, like vague memories, you can't quite reach them.
>
> —*Katy Lancaster*

■ **PRACTICE 9-7:** Look closely at a small natural object, like a moth's antennae, an ant's face, or a few grains of soil. Try two of the "other" techniques to think descriptively. Pull your details together with an idea. Do the same for some overlooked part of your anatomy.

■ **PRACTICE 9-8:** Use one of the "other" techniques to dig up more description for your topic from Practice 9-2.

REVISING FOR VIVID DESCRIPTION

To this point I've suggested ways to *think* descriptively. Now, here are a few tips to sharpen description when you revise *wording*. Be open to change. *All* words describe; we want your description to move from shadowy first-draft description to the kind you can rap your knuckles against.

The Sense Test

Ask if your descriptive passages pass the sense test—can you see, smell, taste, touch, or hear something in every passage?

Example: The accounting procedure is awkward to use.

Revised: The procedure requires flipping back and forth among three pages.

"Awkward" is an abstract word we understand intellectually, but it cannot be experienced by readers' senses. "Flipping back and forth" suggests awkwardness and helps readers experience the procedure more fully, with sound, sight, and touch.

Example: The tenement smelled dirty and rotten.

Revised: The tenement smelled like mildewed shoes.

or The tenement smelled of urine and stale beer.

The revisions create different images, but both are sharp. "Dirty" and "rotten" are not sense oriented.

The Specificity Test

In revising, ask if existing description can be more specific. Test your honesty—how concrete and exact can you be? The broader a description is, the vaguer it reads; the narrower it is, the sharper. Try *several* options for unspecific words before deciding.

Example: Heather walked into the room.

Specify the word "room" as "lecture hall," "kitchen," or "men's room" and the sentence focuses instantly. Also specify "walk" as "strutted," "dashed," or "limped" and the sentence leaps at readers.

Example: Ordinary household lawn chemicals cause harmful side effects on a human being's health, including respiratory, skin, and neurological problems. They also can seriously pollute and deteriorate the quality of nearby watersheds.

Here's how a student made this topic more specific and tangible:

> Lawn chemicals cause headaches, runny noses, rashes, and nausea. Other symptoms may include vomiting, heavy sweating, dizziness, and disorientation. Their nitrogen seeps into groundwater, ending up in streams and ponds. This causes algae buildup, reduction of oxygen, and eventually, dead water.
>
> *—Jeanette Crouse*

Specificity names names. Change "car" to "Lexus" or "Taurus" and change "candy" to "M&Ms" or "Peppermint Patty" to help your writing jump into a reader's eyes.

Specificity enhances your meaning as well as visual appeal. Scan these two phrases:

- A beggar with a cup.
- A beggar with a Burger King cup.

Why describe the cup? It visualizes, but also pinches us with the contrast of "king" and "beggar." Try new descriptive adjectives, but slash those that don't carry meaning as well as visual appeal. Don't describe just for more words.

■ **PRACTICE 9-9:** In the following sentences, first mark words that could be more specific or appeal to our senses and then suggest three alternatives for each. *Don't* limit yourself to one-word replacements.

- Bill ate his lunch noisily.
- The union leadership called for a protest.
- The summer breeze off the water is lovely at night.

■ **PRACTICE 9-10:** Revise one of your practice writings on your own topic by applying the sense or specificity test.

The Freshness Test

For fresher description:

- Replace clichés with original expressions. (See Chapter 8 for more.)

    Cliché: The 100-foot canyon walls stood over us.

    Fresher: The canyon thrust out its 100-foot chest.

- Create a **metaphor** to improve dull description.

    Example: He had scary eyes.

    Revised: He had eyes like half-peeled grapes.

    or His eyes tightened around my neck.

- Cut flat details. If you can't improve a dull spot, leave it out—see if anything's really lost. If you wanted to sell a head of lettuce, would you leave on the brown, wilted leaves?
- Do a mini-brain teaser for weak descriptions. Freewrite until something vivid emerges. Select the best for the revised description.

■ **PRACTICE 9-11:** Create a fresh metaphor for two of these sentences:

- The funeral parlor was so quiet.
- She looked angrily into the car at her boyfriend and Marsha.
- The old alcoholic fell down the railroad embankment.

The Theme Test

You may not have a clear theme when you begin a descriptive essay, but in revising, be sure you do. Beautiful description without a purpose is like a glittering speedboat without an engine or a whiz-bang new computer without an electric plug. Themes make description move and live. Read through your draft one more time to ask if each descriptive detail helps point to one central concept, even if you don't directly state it. If not, consider cutting the irrelevant details. Build up details that do support your theme.

■ **PRACTICE 9-12:** In a short paragraph, describe the food you hate the most. Strive for vividness and creative detail, but also work toward a theme beyond "I hate this stuff." How is the food symbolic of some other issue?

InfoTrac® College Edition: Readings on Description

For tips on using *InfoTrac*® College Edition, see page 464.

> Barnaby Conrad. "The Four Deadly Sins of Description." *The Writer.* May 1993.
> *What not to do when you describe.*

> Nancy Kress. "Don't Say It!" *Writer's Digest.* March 1994.
> *How to visualize more with fewer words.*

Highlights of Chapter 9

- Vivid description is appropriate for *all* writing—whether a business report, technical manual, paper on global poverty, or letter telling Uncle Moneybags about the poverty of modern students. Description breathes life into your words.

- A sharp descriptive eye helps writers appreciate and understand life more intensely, for description is the art of experiencing the world honestly. It is *not* fancy word painting.

- The most important part of writing good description is to experience your subject.

- You can also use brain teasers to stimulate concrete thinking or use the iceberg principle to find the representative detail.

- Other eye-training tricks are to describe the topic to a naive audience, see your topic as a process, or describe what's missing.

- Review "Steps to Writing a Paper" inside this book's front cover to be sure you cover all steps of revision.

Writing Suggestions and Class Discussions

1. Write one long descriptive sentence about the greatest meal you ever ate, your favorite childhood toy, or your favorite piece of clothing. Use as many senses as you can. Pack in details without writing it as a list.

2. Write your own abstract, dictionary-like definition of love, hate, or madness. In a separate paragraph, *show* the definition in action. Experience an incident or example. Use picture words, no abstractions.

3. Describe the youngest person you know who is pregnant, homeless, on drugs, in college, dead, or rich.

4. Describe a hospital room. Find four *overlooked* details that, like the tip of an iceberg, represent the hospital experience.

5. Bring a music recording, photograph, or reproduction of an art work to class. Before playing or showing it, read aloud a one-paragraph description you wrote of it. Use experiencing, brain teasers, and the iceberg theory to write your description.

6. Blind writers like Homer, Jose Luis Borges, John Milton, and Helen Keller rely on other senses. Sit in an unfamiliar setting like a bus stop or mall, close your eyes, and *experience* only through your other senses. Spend 15 to 20 minutes. Then write a vivid description.

7. Describe a technical process you know better than most people (developing photographs, tuning a car, or doing a company payroll, for example). Describe this process clearly and vividly for a reader with average knowledge. Use experiencing, brain teasers, and the iceberg theory to start.

8. Describe a common object like a button, key, scar, or can opener. Discover details others might overlook. Write one paragraph.

9. **Descriptive Challenge:** Describe three of these:
   - The sound of an engine stalling
   - The way your feet feel standing in the surf
   - The sound of a dog shaking water off itself
   - Eating a submarine sandwich
   - The face of a famous person (as if telling a blind person)
   - The smell of turpentine, mushrooms, or rain
   - A soap bubble

10. I Spy Assignment: To develop your descriptive eye, *discreetly* observe a stranger for 10 minutes, learning all you can. Study clothes, habits, quirks, speech patterns, as well as physical features. Write several paragraphs. **Warnings:** Don't intrude on the person, and do this in a public place. One student of a colleague of mine got carried away (literally!) when he hotly followed his subject for an hour, and the man turned out to be a detective who arrested him and phoned the professor to verify the "weird alibi."

11. Write a descriptive paper on a place. Vivid detail should support a theme or idea. Write two to three pages. Use experiencing, brain teasers, and the iceberg theory to start.

12. Describe a group you belong to—a company, church, club, team, or clique. Describe it vividly and develop a theme. Use experiencing, brain teasers, and the iceberg theory to start.

13. Peer groups will reexperience areas of the college you're familiar with: bookstore, library, or cafeteria, for example. Dig up creative, vivid descriptions, not through fancy words but by discovering sharp details. The groups will spend part of the period observing and writing, then reassemble to share their notes. Strive to find overlooked details.

14. Describe your worst fear in bone-chilling, graphic detail. Scare yourself!

15. Expand any practice exercise that turned out well into a two- to three-page paper.

Student Essay and Analysis

The Model

Nell Kuitems

As I hurry toward the brick building, I am the only one who isn't carrying a large black portfolio bag. The wind is cold and bitter, stings my skin through layers of sweat pants and coat. I wave hello to a few students struggling against the ripping wind. I will see them in class, but I am not a student, and I am not the teacher. I am the subject studied—their model for figure drawing class, where they study the body in its natural, naked form.

As we enter the room, the lights are off except for two spotlights that shine on a platform in the center. The platform is covered with paint-spattered drop cloths, and a humming space heater blows hot air across them. This is my stage. But for now I wait in the corner while the students line up at their easels and pull out large, crisp sheets of white paper, charcoals and pencils. The professor enters, shuts the door and locks it so prying eyes don't wander where they don't belong.

I open my bag and pull out my dark, green blanket, then slip off my shoes and socks. When the professor nods, I doff my shirt and bra, then my remaining clothing. My skin leaps into goose bumps, and I wrap myself into the rough blanket. I wander from my corner through the students toward the platform where the professor waits. He offers a gentlemanly hand to help me step up; as I take it, the blanket slips from my shoulder, exposing my right breast. Oh, well. It's too late to think of hiding myself now. Off comes the blanket, and I spread it and sit, fully exposed.

I glance at the professor, and he nods again, so I create a position for my body. I lie on my right side, legs bent back so my feet nearly touch my butt. My head rests on my right arm, which is bent into a pillow. I tuck my chin close to my chest, hiding my face. My left, upper arm molds against my body, then bends at elbow to rest under my breasts. I will have to stay in this position for the next hour and then find it again perfectly after I take my stretch break, so I make mental notes of where all my parts are.

Students wander the room studying me from different angles, seeking new curves and shapes. Do they want me from the back, front or side? Top down or bottom up? They study me as they would a ripe bowl of oranges. I have lost all control; I am only an object to be studied. But when they look at me, I wonder if they think about how the glow of my skin changes the closer it is to the heater. My feet and butt must be red with warmth. Do they notice how my breasts are white and taut, my nipples hard when they pass by on the cold side and create a breeze? What do they see when they study me?

continues

Oh, yes. I watch them back. I see their looks of fierce concentration, eyebrows bent together, lips pulled taut, eyes darting to find every one of my hidden details. I would love to be able to transfer my body to canvas, but I can't. Maybe this is why I lend them my body, to let someone with talent do what I cannot. I am not embarrassed any more—not in the usual sense a naked woman would be. They see me every day. Yet little worries nag me. Do they see the mud under my thumbnail? Do they see the bright red, pulsing zit on my back? Out of these imperfections, they must find beauty. This is why I choose to display myself.

I fall asleep, waking at the end of class when someone tickles my feet. I reach out, pull the rough blanket around me, and stretch away the stiffness. I rise, return to my corner, pull on my clothes and become a person again. The professor unlocks the door, and I am through with work. But before everyone packs up, I hurry around the room to take in what they have drawn, proud of the magic created. I devour their work with my eyes, then leave quietly with everyone else.

Outside, the bitter wind nips at my face, but I don't feel it. I am still warm from the space heater and something else. As I wander through the cold, I wonder what form my body will take next time.

Commentary Based on Peer Review Sheet

What point does the essay make? It seems to be about exposure and the mystery of how nakedness becomes art. How do you allow others to see you that way? She knows she's "giving" herself to them and the essay ultimately decides such exposure is not a humiliation, but a transformation, a way a person can take on many forms. Art changes her imperfections into beauty. An intriguing idea and an unusual topic.

Are there any symbolic messages here? Yes. The author uses the iceberg principle in comparing herself to a bowl of oranges, evoking the whole world of art by suggestion. The interplay between cold and heat, outside and inside, all suggest the conflict between two ways of seeing yourself—as art and as a person. The locked door suggests there must be a boundary line carefully kept between these. I like the way she hides her face in her pose—symbolic of hiding as a person while exposed as an object of art.

Organization? It moves through time, but it's more like a "slice of life" from a typical day on the job than a true narrative. She starts out in the cold, moves behind the locked door to the heat (but still has one cold side to her), then back to the cold. The organization beautifully reinforces the message.

Give the essay the sense test. The best descriptive details are almost exclusively visual and tactile sensations (temperature, body placement, the tickle, the professor's hand, the zit). I wonder if there could have been some sounds—scratching charcoal, rustling paper, people's comments—but I have mixed feelings about whether she ought to have included this. Her essay has a very self-enclosed feel to it, and that may be right for the emotion she wants to convey.

Where can it be more specific? I'd ask the author to consider doing a bit more describing the drawings the students did of her. I wanted to see how they interpreted her (fatter, prettier, shyer than she thinks she is?) and her reaction to the art. That would complete the theme by making her see her "real" self differently through art.

Where can the description be fresher? The zit was a great, tiny detail, especially the use of "pulsing," which conveys several senses in one word. I think she might have made the cold wind description fresher. "Bitter" and "nips" are okay, but not creative. She uses "wander" four times and "taut" twice. Both are strongly visual, but lose punch with repetition. Normally, using a word twice is no problem, but "taut" appears again within three lines to describe something else. This essay nicely combines an idea with details in a short space; it is economical, vivid, symbolic. The language is simple and direct, not strained by false, picturesque words.

Sample Student Descriptive Essay for Analysis

Simple Life

Debbie Geen

It's a cool, brisk day in November when the air bites your skin. The sun is out, but the sky looks gray and confused as if it might rain, but the air

continues

smells of snow. The vegetables have been picked, and everything worth harvesting is already canned or stored. All the potatoes and apples, packed neatly in their wooden crates, fill the root cellar.

All that is left are the meat chickens—Cornish-Rock Giants—that had been growing fat for the last eight weeks. Now they're a plump cooking weight—four to five pounds. The process starts when we collect eggs from the nests and bring them into the house where we keep the incubator. An insulated electric heating coil runs through the inside of the unit to maintain a 99.5 degree temperature. A small dish of water inside keeps the humidity up. An acorn-shaped 15-watt light bulb gives just enough light to see that the incubator is working. Thirty to forty eggs are placed on a tray with a screen bottom and wooden dowels keep the eggs in rows. We pull the tray out to turn the eggs a minimum of four times a day to ensure that the embryos develop correctly. After all, a mother hen turns her eggs in the nest 90–95 times in one day.

After 21 days of this careful attention, a faint peeping announces that the chicks are pecking themselves free. They wear bright, innocent yellow fur that doesn't really resemble feathers yet and are so damp that they stick to your palms.

Once dry and able to stand, they're all put in the chicken house to gain weight. They need to eat constantly to gain weight fast. A timed light in their house turns on every four hours to wake them to eat. Little do they know what part the constant gorging will play in their fate.

A short eight weeks later, it's time. My Dad stokes up a fire to boil water. The fire crackles, the black smoke twisting and rising toward the clouds. It's chilly and feels good to warm your hands by the flames. Dad made his own cooking pot from a 55-gallon metal drum which he places on top of the fire. A spoonful of dish detergent added to the water helps penetrate the chickens' natural oils so the hot water can loosen the feathers. This homemade cauldron holds twenty gallons, and once it boils, we head for the chickens.

To capture chickens, we use a four-foot wooden handle with a metal hook on the end. The hook's just big enough to get around the birds' legs and small enough so their feet can't slip out. This is the only way to catch them once the fear sets in—and it always does. The first few are naïve and easy to grab. After the rest smell blood, they squawk and fly wildly, running each other over and scrabbling into walls to escape. Sometimes half their feathers fall off.

Not wanting to waste time, my parents catch two chickens at a time and carry them behind the woodshed. There it is, the old, tattered ash stump, about two feet high and nearly as wide. Since ash is hard wood, it lasts many years and shows signs of the work done on it. Old feathers, dried blood and chips of missing wood tell its story. A rusty nail protrudes from one side. Dangling from it are pieces of old baling twine, some shredded from being accidentally chopped during the beheadings. But one intact piece is looped at the exact length so the chicken's neck will be held in the middle of the stump.

Since two chickens are caught, Dad holds one between his knees, seizes the other by its clawed feet, and slips the noose over its head. By pulling on the scaly legs, the neck is stretched out and centered on the stump. Dad swings his trusty hatchet—freshly sharpened—straight down. With a "whack," the blade cuts through and embeds itself in the stump.

continues

The lifeless head falls, the beak opening and closing a few times as if trying to get a final gasp of air. The beheaded body is cast aside as Dad positions the next victim on the stump. These headless bodies sometimes run around for two minutes, as if they don't know they're dead and don't know which way to go first. Sometimes headless chickens even lift themselves off the ground as if to fly away before lying down for good. Chickens are the only bird granted this final run. Larger birds like geese are hung from the tree by their webbed feet to bleed out.

The chicken bodies are now dunked in the boiling water for thirty seconds to loosen the feathers. Then we pluck, gut, and carry them into the house for their final preparation. After a thorough cleaning, we seal them in plastic bags and lay them to rest in the freezer. And we're ready for another day of simple farm life.

Discussion/Writing

Write an evaluation of "Simple Life" as if you were reviewing it for class, using the "Peer Review Checklist for Description" as your guide.

InfoTrac® **College Edition: Readings that Use Description**

For tips on using *InfoTrac*® College Edition, see page 464.

Melissa Stewart. "Something's Fishy! (unique traits of seahorses)" *National Geographic World*. July–Aug. 2002.

How much can a writer see in a tiny seahorse?

Andre Bernard. "Commonplace Book: Bugs." *American Scholar*. Autumn 2002.

The beauty and beast in bugs.

James Pethokoukis. "Not for the Faint of Heart." *US News and World Report.* 11 Nov. 2002.

What happens at a murder scene after the police are through.

"And a Child Shall Lead Them." *Sports Illustrated.* 18 Nov. 2002.

An athlete without legs.

Edie Clark. "The Flock." *Yankee.* Dec. 1993.

Real sheep and a writer's imagination.

InfoTrac® **College Edition Discussion/Writing**

1. Topic Development: write half to one page on one of these topics:
   A. Read the essays on seahorses and bugs and write a description of some other overlooked, tiny creature or object. Look closely until you can see it freshly.
   B. Read "The Flock" and then describe something that comforts you.
   C. Read "And a Child Shall Lead Them" and then describe someone who is an unknown hero or who displays quiet courage.
   D. Read "Not for the Faint of Heart" and then describe something you normally would find disgusting. Let go of your disgust to see the topic as it is, without judgment.

2. Analysis: Find two of the descriptive techniques discussed in Chapter 9 in one of the readings. Quote a few lines and explain how they demonstrate a descriptive method.

3. Coauthor: Imagine you are the author and your editor has asked you to add a short paragraph to any one of the works listed above—either a comment or more descriptive details. Write the paragraph and say exactly where you would put it.

4. Evaluate one of the pieces using the Peer Review Checklist on page 184 to help you cover important issues.

✓ **PEER REVIEW CHECKLIST FOR DESCRIPTION**

Author: _____

Reviewer: _____

Answer the questions as specifically as possible and discuss the essay with the author.

Ideas: What point do you think the essay makes?

Are there any symbolic messages here? Explain.

Organization: Describe this essay's organization. Highlight the main pattern, don't evaluate.

Would the essay be improved by rearranging, combining, or cutting some sections? Which? Why? Is anything important missing?

Descriptive Details: Give this essay The Sense Test. Where does it do the best, where poorly?

Which section(s) could be more specific? What are the most specific details?

Find a place where the description could be fresher.

CHAPTER 10

Narration

Telling Your Audience a Story

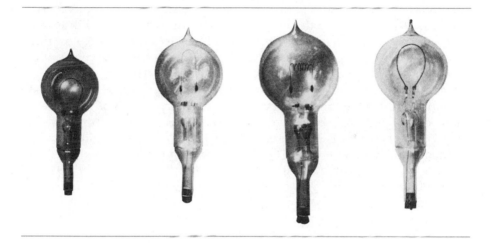

God made man because He loves stories.

—ELIE WIESEL

Real suspense comes from moral dilemma and the courage to make and act upon choices.

—JOHN GARDNER

The earliest writers in every civilization have told stories to convey their messages. Homer's tales of Cyclops, the one-eyed monster, and Circe, whose spells transformed humans into animals, not only entertained but informed and persuaded the ancient Greeks about geography, the gods, humanity's place in the universe, and other things as Homer knew them. The ancient myth of Sisyphus, for example, tells of a greedy king who is condemned in Hell to roll a huge boulder to the top of a hill. Just before Sisyphus reaches the peak, the gods make the boulder roll back down, and Sisyphus must start all over again. Up and down the hill he chases the rock for all time. Over the centuries the story has been a parable about the empty lives of the greedy and also about the futility of much human effort.

Jesus frequently told stories to make his message stronger. "The Good Samaritan" and "The Prodigal Son" seem to stick in our minds much better than, say, a typical sermon on charity. When Jesus told a crowd, "Love thy neighbor," a lawyer asked, "Who is my neighbor?" Jesus, realizing the man wanted to put a limit on whom he was required to love, did not directly define the word "neighbor." Instead he told the story of a man beaten and robbed by thieves in his own country. The victim's neighbors, a priest and local official, walked by without helping. Then a Samaritan, a stranger in the victim's country, stopped, washed the man's wounds, took him to an inn, and paid for his lodging. When Jesus finished, the lawyer knew the meaning of the word "neighbor," not from definition, but from the actions in the story.

Why have these stories lasted so long? Because stories are more visual, more easily remembered than abstractions. When we recall Sisyphus groaning behind his boulder or the supposedly "good" men passing the injured man before the Samaritan stops to help, the writer's abstract message flows along with the story.

Successful speakers from corporation executives to U.S. presidents know that telling a vivid story can be more effective than facts alone. People view a storyteller as creative and smart, as one who commands attention with powerful images.

CONFLICT

The heart of a good story is conflict: forces in tension with each other. The four common types are person vs. person, person vs. society, person vs. nature, and person vs. self. A saleswoman struggling against an employer who cheats clients is person vs. person; a social worker battling the city to hire more disabled people is person vs. society; a young man struggling to find the ski lodge after a sudden squall separates him from the group is person vs. nature; a woman trying to decide whether she should have an abortion is person vs. self.

■ **PRACTICE 10-1:** Take a moment now to recall examples from your own life to illustrate each of these conflicts. One of them may become your next paper. I will refer to this "practice" during the rest of this chapter. Write a few lines for each.

- You vs. another person
- You vs. society
- You vs. nature
- You vs. yourself

Let's look closer at what makes a good conflict and why it helps your story absorb readers' attention. First, only real sparks make real fires. **Conflicts that don't deeply affect us won't make strong stories.** A story about a mother forbidding her daughter to date a certain boy does not sound very promising, no matter how it upset the writer. However, if the daughter learns that her mother has deeper motives—if, for instance, the boy reminds the mother of a boy who jilted her or of one she always wished she married instead of the daughter's father—then we have more hope for this conflict. Or perhaps we will discover the mother is envious of the daughter's social success. Or perhaps the daughter is dating a wild boy because she doesn't like the relationship her parents have. Here we have something more meaningful. The best conflicts draw out some **deeper significance in the characters or the action.** If a conflict in your life really stirred you, there's probably more to it under the surface. Peek under the rug.

Readers want conflict so they can care about the outcome, so they can cheer and fear and doubt with the narrator. They also want **conflicts** *difficult* **to solve.** Wrong vs. right or strong vs. weak doesn't grip readers as much as conflicts in which wrong and right are murky or in which the forces opposed are equal.

Our lives are full of both inner and outer conflicts, but sometimes we don't recognize them. Here are three almost sure ways to find a strong conflict to write about.

Think about the most intense turning points in your life. These have changed not only the *outer* course of your life but the *inner* course as well by developing your philosophy or identity. Readers want a story to matter to the writer, or it won't matter to them. For this reason it is sometimes harder to write about a personal triumph—winning the big race or election—than about a defeat or a tragedy. Winning tends to keep our beliefs intact; often we learn more in losing. However, I can recall an excellent story a student wrote about winning a state wrestling match, because in his moment of triumph he stared into the eyes of the slumped man he'd defeated. Nor do big tragedies necessarily mean a person has grown. As Isaac Bashevis Singer said, "A wise man gets wiser by suffering. A person without wisdom may suffer 100 years and die a fool." The moments that make us grow, that tear away the predictable boundaries of our lives, are the ones that make good papers.

One of my students, a woman who worked at a chemical dependency center, wrote about her conflict with her brother, who was a cocaine addict. Despite what she knew from dealing with addicts, she allowed him to "violate" her with a "merry-go-round of anger, shame, guilt, and fear." Her turning point occurred when she realized that she was "addicted to an addict," that she was "a codependent" even though she never used drugs, because she supported and cared for her brother. Her emotional investment was destroying her, and she learned to let go—to stop feeling responsible for where he was at night, who he was with, what was happening to his body and mind. She still took him for treatment, but she learned she had to break her own emotional addiction.

Are there moments from your life that are too intense to write about? Sure. If you write a paragraph or two and find you really hate dealing with this material, it may be too fresh to see clearly or too raw a wound to reopen. But give it a few paragraphs to see. You may find that something you thought you didn't want to deal with really sets your mind seething with powerful ideas and images. If it wants to pour out of you, keep going.

■ **PRACTICE 10-2:** List three turning points that changed your outlook on life.

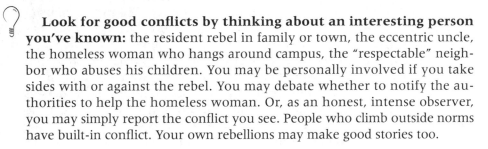

Look for good conflicts by thinking about an interesting person you've known: the resident rebel in family or town, the eccentric uncle, the homeless woman who hangs around campus, the "respectable" neighbor who abuses his children. You may be personally involved if you take sides with or against the rebel. You may debate whether to notify the authorities to help the homeless woman. Or, as an honest, intense observer, you may simply report the conflict you see. People who climb outside norms have built-in conflict. Your own rebellions may make good stories too.

■ **PRACTICE 10-3:** Describe one of the most interesting people you've known and sketch out a conflict that focuses on this person.

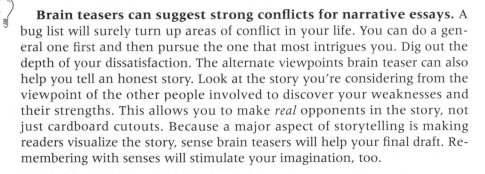

Brain teasers can suggest strong conflicts for narrative essays. A bug list will surely turn up areas of conflict in your life. You can do a general one first and then pursue the one that most intrigues you. Dig out the depth of your dissatisfaction. The alternate viewpoints brain teaser can also help you tell an honest story. Look at the story you're considering from the viewpoint of the other people involved to discover your weaknesses and their strengths. This allows you to make *real* opponents in the story, not just cardboard cutouts. Because a major aspect of storytelling is making readers visualize the story, sense brain teasers will help your final draft. Remembering with senses will stimulate your imagination, too.

■ **PRACTICE 10-4:** Use a bug list, alternate viewpoints, or sense brain teaser to create more notes for one of the stories you sketched in Practice 10-1, 10-2, or 10-3.

COMPLICATION

After finding a powerful conflict, you must make it grow more complicated as the story continues. The novelist E. M. Forster said he always imagined one of his readers to be a person who only cared about what happened next, who wanted to be surprised by new twists, new angles, new insights in each paragraph. **If the story stagnates, it's usually because it has ceased to convey new information.** This does not mean you must have continuous action as many television shows do. Moving forward can be a matter of mental twists and insights as well:

> The new doctor doesn't seem to care about my infected ear. He makes me do all the talking, stares at me when he thinks I'm not looking. Is he nervous? His hand seems to shake a lot. Is that booze I smell on his breath? Or just medicines? He leaves the room and returns after a long time. Maybe I have some horrible sickness and he's afraid to tell me. He even sends the nurse in to tell me I can go.
>
> When I pay the receptionist and get my prescription, I notice a photograph of the doctor and a girl who looks like me—we could be sisters. "His daughter died last month," the receptionist whispers.

What gives this little story some life is not the surprise ending—that's always too late to interest the reader. What gets it going is the initial conflict—the doctor doesn't like the narrator (person vs. person)—and what keeps it going are the competing explanations for this thought that flash through the narrator's mind. Each sentence searches for facts and ideas to explain this behavior; each complicates the story. Without *them*, the ending would have been flat.

Creating complex conflict often means discovering competing ideas in yourself; at each turn in your essay ask if you really felt 100 percent as you wrote. The spots where you waver or doubt need to be in the essay to lead the reader through your honest decision making. Making choices creates conflict and reveals your character and theme. Stories in which things happen *to* a passive narrator lack this element. We *are* often victims of fate, accidents, and bad luck, but the key moments in our lives are the ones we can do something about, the ones in which we **choose our destiny.** This is what John Gardner meant in the opening quote to this chapter.

I once had a student, Bill, who was in his late forties. He wrote a gruesome narrative about what happened to his wife when they decided to commit her temporarily to a mental hospital. Once Bill's wife was signed in, the authorities could keep her there until *they* thought she was cured. They began chemical and electric shock treatments that hurt and scared Bill's wife. She begged to be released. Bill began to doubt her and believe the medical authorities that she was far gone, because each time he visited her she was wilder, more rumpled, more "crazy looking." Some friends and family even told Bill to "detach" himself from his wife. But something deeper in the relationship drew him back. He believed the authorities were more disturbed than his wife, and he eventually fought in court to release her.

This powerful conflict has a number of twists that keep a reader involved. The most interesting is the inner conflict in Bill—whether to believe "sane experts" or the "crazy" wife he loves. The only major flaw in Bill's rough draft was his portrayal of the orderlies and nurses as snarling sadists with dripping fangs. It's easy to see why Bill felt this way, but he portrayed them in descriptions and dialogue that were too exaggerated. He projected his feelings for them instead of seeing them as they were. We worked together using alternative viewpoints and discovered the "enemy" was not cruelty, but indifference. Most employees simply wanted to slide through tough workdays a little easier. People like Bill and his poor wife who asked questions were "troublemakers." The workers were not devils, but people who'd grown calluses over their feelings. Bill didn't release them from their responsibility for his wife's pain, but in looking closer at the orderlies and nurses, Bill discovered the real problem in his wife's mental health care. He believed the employees inflicted pain on patients like his wife to make them act more deranged and therefore less human. If they could feel they were dealing with crazy people, it made their disturbing job easier. It's a powerful, honest insight because it's not oversimplified. The lesson: **be skeptical of any angels or devils you create.**

■ **PRACTICE 10-5:** Using one of your practice notes in this chapter, list some complications in the conflict.

HOW TO RUIN A STORY

Teachers and textbooks don't often advise students how to mess up; but if you're interested in ruining a story, here are three ways to do it. First, **give a lot of background in the opening.** If you're going to tell the story of your great fishing adventure, start the story with getting ready the night before, your restless sleep, waking, breakfast, packing the car, driving to the dock, and casting off. This is boring in one sentence. Imagine how boring it can be stretched out to a full page! If you want an exciting start, begin the essay like this: "I was rebaiting my hook when I realized that a squall had just blocked off the sun and was heading straight for our boat." Or start when your buddy spills the lantern fuel into the campfire. If the story is about meeting a wonderful person during a vacation, start with the moment the wonderful person bumps into you with his cotton candy and tangles it in your hair. *Don't* start with packing, travel, unpacking, and setting up on the beach.

The Romans used the expression *in medias res* (in the middle) to describe starting where real conflict begins. Have your characters begin *in motion*, not preparing to move. Do this and you'll be surprised how busy you'll be telling the real story and how little time you need spend on that story killer—background.

Here are some openings from student papers that hook a reader:

I was hunched over my crying baby brother when I heard Joe's footsteps behind me. "He fell," I tried to explain, "he was on the bed but he rolled and I . . . I . . . ." Pain shot through my spine like a freight train had burst through the floor straight into my rear end. As he cocked his boot again, my mother dashed into the room and screamed.

—*Raquel E. Torres*

Night falls by the time we reach the inn. The crisp, country air, ten degrees colder than the city, makes us shiver. Moths flutter around the lanterns that light our passage, and the only sound is the crunching of gravel beneath our feet. Sumie hurries ahead, sliding open the heavy wooden door.

—*Bernadette Verrone*

She was gone—again. I watched her red Trans Am disappear up the gradual grade, then turned to see my bus round the corner, creeping toward me like a bug in the cool, moist dawn. The breeze was cold, and faraway thunder drummed summer out of service. The bus groaned to a halt in a diesel haze. The driver opened the door, and I was sucked off the street.

—*James Babcock*

All three start with something happening. The first uses dialogue and action, the second mystery, the third symbolic description.

    A second way to ruin a story is to give away the ending. If the following sentence began a story, you wouldn't want to read the rest: "Little did I know the first time Bob approached me after class to borrow a pen that in seven months we'd be married." It's dramatic but kills the rest of the story. Compare that to this opening: "There was absolutely nothing special about Bob that first day he approached me after class to borrow a pen. I would have completely forgotten him except the next day he handed me a dozen pens with a bow around them. Now I've got a nerd after me, I thought." The second version lets us know something is going to happen, but not what.

Giving away the ending applies not only to events, but to the theme. Good readers enjoy figuring out the significance of the events, and an opening sentence like the following can ruin that: "I don't know if I'll ever marry again, but if I do I'll put my wife ahead of my friends." The writer of narratives must tease readers a bit, give them new events and ideas and also leave them a bit unsatisfied so they'll keep reading.

Another way to ruin a reader's enjoyment is to summarize events. Don't bother with details—just cover big chunks of the story in a few words. Now it may seem like you can tell a bigger story by summarizing, but what you're really doing is denying readers the pleasure of watching events unfold in front of them—smelling the air, hearing what the people say, and figuring out how events will turn out. When you summarize, it's like someone rushing from the window to tell about the exciting events happening outside instead of letting you look for yourself.

So how do you make a reader feel "there"? Through scenes and moments seen up close. This means you probably shouldn't write about three years of your life, about your entire football season, or about your entire relationship with a friend. Pick one sunset, one encounter on the team bus, one hour in the hospital's cancer ward. Then you can **give us the rich detail of the moment.** When you think about it, that's how we live—one moment at a time, and nearly all of them lost as soon as they pass. After they're gone, we put a label on them—a summary. Summary says, "Working as a painter of dorm rooms made a lousy, sweltering summer." It may be true, but the real-life moment was more like this: "The sweat dripped off my nose and into the paint can as I followed Bill Kratzberg's massive, paint-encrusted butt around dorm rooms." Summary says, "Grandma shot down my plan." The real moment says, "Grandma told me, 'I never figured someone with my DNA could be so stupid.'"

■ **PRACTICE 10-6:** Pick two potential places where you could begin one of the narrative conflicts you developed earlier in this chapter. Which place seems best and why?

DESCRIBING PEOPLE

If conflict is the heart of a narrative, its body is the characters—the physical presence that moves the conflict. This is where your description must be sharpest, to make the people in your story jump off the page. We tend to make people in our stories reflect our own ideas, habits, and values instead of presenting them as *they* are. Using an alternate viewpoint brain teaser is the best way to overcome this. Give each main character—*especially those with whom you disagree*—a few minutes of rough notes. Think as they do. See as they see. What motivates them? What do they care about? This is essential for *honest, vivid conflict.* If you've been cheated by a salesperson, you must try to convey what she believes, perhaps her anxiousness to succeed, or you will create her as a fake cardboard figure.

 Besides understanding how your characters think, you must help the reader *see* them. Here are some of the things that create a picture of a person in words:

- Physical description
- Habits
- The way they talk
- Their possessions
- What others say about them
- Gestures

The man who empties an ashtray three times during an evening communicates character through this habit. If he also picks threads from his sleeve and rearranges the couch pillow continually, his character will be dominated by neatness in a reader's eyes. Gestures—like poking a listener with a forefinger while speaking, or wrapping a sweaty arm around your shoulder—also create character. In preparing to write about people, **use the preceding list as a brain teaser,** making a list of details for each item.

How do you know which details to actually include in the draft? Let's take **physical description** as an example. Simple, factual description adds detail, but will rarely light up a page. The following is accurate and specific: "Gregory Bates has brown hair and brown eyes and is 5'10" tall and weighs 165 pounds." But these words do not bring the unknown Mr. Bates to life; they should stay on the brain-teaser page. A reader *assumes* a person is of average build unless told otherwise. Brown hair and eyes are so common they only narrow Bates down to several billion people. Instead, search for and choose **unique, distinguishing details:** Bates's Mohawk haircut, the wart on his chin, his gangly arms. The reader will automatically fill in the rest as "average."

Here's another trick to describe people: You want not just the unique features of the person but also those details that convey *more* than simple description. When choosing details from your brain-teaser lists, pick ones that suggest deeper aspects of the person, **ones that capture personality or beliefs.**

Take eyes as an example. No other part of the human body is described so often. Yet "the windows of the soul" attract more flies than fresh air, more clichés than fresh description. Soft, brown eyes, sky blue eyes, and sparkling eyes are dead eyes. A writer needs to find a twist: cow-brown eyes, winter-blue eyes, eyes sparkling like razors. Or are those eyes dung brown, chocolate brown, peanut-butter brown, sooty, muddy, or walnut? Make a list of all the kinds of brown you can think of and then choose the best one for your person's eyes. This will give the reader something specific for *better visualization*. It will *also convey more of the person's character*. Muddy eyes, for example, suggest vagueness, confusion, or even dirtiness of the personality. All of these browns are equally suggestive.

■ **PRACTICE 10-7:** What do these descriptors say about the person?

- Lizard-green eyes
- Moss-green eyes
- Faded-green eyes
- Cash-green eyes

■ **PRACTICE 10-8:** Take a moment to list several vivid substitutes for these bland descriptions:

- Sparkling teeth
- Rosy cheeks
- Dark hair

Possessions reveal character because they represent choices we make. True, most of us own many things unthinkingly—toothbrushes, pens, underwear. But our unique possessions represent conscious choice—the 20 boxes full of baseball cards or chest of grandmother's lace doilies, the pink flamingo or religious shrine in our front yard, the Harley or Honda in our driveway. Gestures, habits, and what others say about someone also reveal character. A one-page brain teaser listing details should result in plenty to bring a person to life in words. If you can't fill a page of notes, you don't know enough about the person to write him or her into the story.

■ **PRACTICE 10-9:** Write a descriptive brain teaser for one person in the story you've been developing during this chapter.

■ **PRACTICE 10-10:** Here's part of a student's narrative essay that describes a person. As you read, mark the six descriptive techniques and look for unique details that also symbolize Lish's personality or beliefs.

Student Essay

The Red Heart

Lisa Neal

I first saw Lish the first day of classes my freshman year at Fredonia. Her parents dumped her at the back door of the brick dormitory like a bag of garbage and then roared off in a black Cadillac.

I was shocked that the left side of her head was shaved and displayed a small tattoo of a black heart. Her hair on the other side was carrot colored and braided like an Indian squaw's. With her head held high, she sauntered in with two leopard skin bags.

Her arrival sent shock waves throughout the dorm. I'm not sure if Lish felt the rocky movement or just ignored it, for minutes after arriving she invaded the bathroom with an old green toothbrush with yellowed bristles and a worn box of Arm and Hammer Baking Soda. I was dismayed she was living in the single room across the hall from me. She left her door wide open as she unpacked her sparse belongings, which included posters of puppies and a Paddington Bear with matted fur and a tattered blue coat. Her night table and dresser were left empty except for a glass incense candle and a fluorescent pink tape recorder.

As the days passed, I deliberately ignored Lish, but her presence oozed under my closed door, and I soon watched her with the curiosity of a child at the circus. At first, though, I only noticed her hair changing from carrot to watermelon pink, the way she dragged hard on her Virginia Slims cigarettes, and the addition of an earring in her nose.

Her parents whizzed in once more that semester, this time in a gray Rolls Royce, to bring her winter clothes. For the fifteen minutes they stayed, the entire hall was pierced by yelling. I heard a few snatches of her father's growled words, calling Lish a "humiliation" and a "disgrace to the family." Her mother whined how Lish should be more like her older sister who was going to become a "respectable and wealthy lawyer" instead of a social worker. The barrage of voices ceased with the sound of shattering glass, and her parents burst out of the room like two tourists fleeing a bear's cave. After a few moments, Lish emerged wearing her usual crooked smile. I was amazed! I would have been in tears. The only reminder that her parents had come was the disappearance of the incense candle holder—reduced to glass shards—and the lingering stench of Macy's perfume.

The next night, while I lay on my pink comforter watching *The Cosby Show* re-runs, my phone buzzed. It was my parents giving me the usual razor-sharp threats to do well in my classes. After our yelling match, I slammed the phone down, pounced on my bed, and smothered my face in my pillow.

continues

> Immediately there was a timid knock, and I was amazed and a bit frightened to see Lish. She wore Mickey Mouse slippers and a pink flannel nightgown as she shuffled onto my robin-egg blue carpet.

DIALOGUE

Like other aspects of describing people, **dialogue must be distinctive—** your characters shouldn't sound like *you* but like themselves. If you use real people in your story, listen for their **unique speech patterns and quirks of language.** If you live in the northern states and have a person from the South in your story, he may use the words "polecat" instead of "skunk," "sack" instead of "bag," or "depot" instead of "station." To a southerner, a Bostonian forgets r's, as in "A bahbah cut my heyuh," but adds r's as in "That's a good idear." When I moved to Rochester, New York, I had to learn that asking for a "red hot" and a "pop" was not provoking a brawl but a request for a "frankfurter and a soft drink" (or is it a "wiener and a soda"?). Be careful of stereotypes, however. Few Californians really use Valley-talk ("like, gag me with a spoon, dude"); few southerners say, "Y'all come back fo' grits, dahling"; and few people from New Jersey refer to their state as "New Joysee."

More important are **individual speech characteristics:** the person who says "hey" or "ain't" or "prevarication" or who addresses people as "honey" or "pal" or "sir." **Education levels** show up in dialogue, too. "You ain't puttin' nothin' ovah on me" and "I'm inclined to disbelieve that assertion" come from two different people saying the same thing. **Age, use of slang, environment, and hobbies all influence our choice of words.** People who are into computers, cars, television, or the military use vocabulary that reflects their interest, no matter what they talk about. Take a minute to think of a friend or relative who has a unique vocabulary or style of speaking.

A storyteller must try to **capture the speaker's voice.** As you see, it's legitimate to break spelling and grammar rules in dialogue for realistic effect. A street punk may not say, "We had quite a blast last night" but, "Freakin' blast last night." Describe these speakers based on their style:

"Isn't that the cat's pajamas, honey? We sat on the same stoop and I didn't recognize him! Mr. Mahoney, the grocer! He could have been the man in the moon!"

"We can say with firm assurance that no such knowledge of any event could proceed without the bureau chief's tacit or at least implied consent."

"It's time for lunch, right? So I get him, right? We meet at the mall, right?"

"Ice it, pops. You beat up your chops too much."

Someone once said, "Dialogue is what people *do* to each other." In stories, you shouldn't pass the time of day in small talk. Skip hello, introductions, goodbyes, and "please-pass-the-butter" talk. Concentrate on the meaningful scenes. **Each piece of dialogue must move the story along.** Dialogue can carry scenes in which important revelations are made about a character, the action, or the theme. For example:

The father rumbled into my office. "Why the hell didn't you put her on the goddamned bus if she ain't sick? I got work."

"Your daughter has several bruises on her lower rib cage," I said, "and I suspect she may also suffer—"

"I feel fine, Daddy," Rachel whispered.

The man stared at her, his thumb working in his belt loop. "Yeah," he said. "You look awright."

How does the dialogue reveal all three characters in a short time?

Here's an example of how dialogue and brief description create an intense scene:

Everyone from the hood had come up to the court to watch the homies play some b-ball. We were soaking up rays when a gold metal-flaked Honda pulled up with Speed and Little Man and a Puerto Rican girl, Blue Eyes. Blue Eyes remained in the car. Speed and Little Man's pants hung off their butts and showed their boxers. Blue bandannas were tied around their heads. Little Man grabbed a 16-year-old boy named Angel.

"Yo, man! Why you be dissing my home boy? What's up with tha? You best chill 'fore I pop a cap in yo ass!"

Angel pulled away and tried to reason with Little Man. "Bro, I don't even know your home boy."

Little Man pulled a small silver hand gun from his boot, held his arms out straight, legs spread apart. His arms shook as he pointed it with two hands at Angel's chest. Angel stepped back, hands up, and pleaded, "Yo! Yo, ain't nobody dissing your homie, Bro. It ain't like that."

People ran from the line of fire. Speed yelled, "Do him! Do him!" Little Man stood, arms shaking the gun pointed at Angel's chest. "You ain't got no props if you don't do him!" Speed yelled. The gun jerked. Again! Smoke rolled from the barrel.

Angel's eyes opened wide. "No!" he mouthed. "No." His head bounced as it hit the ground and his blue tee turned deep red.

Speed cried, "Snap! Snap! Let's be chillin' 'fore five-oh gets here."

—*Dawn M. Schranck*

What parts seem most realistic? How does the dialogue advance the action? Are there any word choices you question?

■ **PRACTICE 10-11:** Create four or five lines of dialogue for the people in your story. Work on realistic style and reveal character.

ENDING A STORY

It's tough to wrap up loose ends, make a point and still have a kick ending when the conflict and action of the story are over. But don't make it harder on yourself than it already is. Rather than trying to explain everything, **it's often better to suggest the conclusion.** If you wrote about your bitter confrontations with your sister, you could end with the doorbell ringing and your hope (or would it be fear?) that it is her. Less can sometimes stimulate a reader's imagination more.

Symbols suggest conclusions without stating a message openly. If you wrote about running away from home and were taken to a juvenile detention center, you might end by staring out the window at the road winding away toward the city to hint at the future.

A third option is to echo the opening. This rounds off a story, helps the reader recognize it as a whole. If you began with weather, why not end with weather? Rain could give way to sun—or sharper rain. An opening that begins with a letter from your dying grandmother could end when you find the letter you mailed her on the table beside her bed. Your father's hand steadying your bicycle in the opening can be echoed as you notice his hand as he takes your arm down the aisle to be married.

■ **PRACTICE 10-12:** You go to the beach and see your lover/spouse with someone else. Write the last line of the story using suggestion or symbolism.

HOW TO SAY SOMETHING WORTH SAYING

How can you make a story convey a good theme?

Tell the truth. Now that sounds simple, but the fact is that the most difficult lies to brush away from the truth are the ones we tell ourselves. Does the theme of your story sound too simple because you've given yourself a candy-coated cliché or a safe, predictable message? You must *re-feel* the events; ask yourself at every turn if you missed something or closed your eyes to something. Use the brain teasers on unquestioned ideas and clichés and alternative viewpoints to help break into new truths. But don't worry at the outline stage if your theme isn't outstanding. Theme requires drafting and revision to emerge.

Question your own motives along with everyone else's. Be honest about aspects of the story that contradict your main idea. If the ending was basically good or optimistic, look for darker meanings lurking there. If it was a sad ending, look for positive aspects. Doing this will separate the superficial paper from the one that's probing. The poet Coleridge once said, "No man does anything from a single motive." Look for multiple causes for your actions and the actions of others.

Why have a theme? Why not just tell what happened? Because how you feel about what you did or what happened to you is more important than the act itself. A reader may make up his mind on his own, but he also wants to know how you interpret it. Working on theme also makes us learn something new.

Here's how one student handled theme in a story about a car crash that horribly maims a young man. Steve's girlfriend, Amanda, helps to nurse him despite his disfigurement and brain damage. Months later, the narrator accompanies Amanda to visit Steve at the care facility for the final scene:

> We wheeled Steve out to the sunporch, a place where we often spent our time. Amanda could barely stand to look at him. Steve was paralyzed from the neck down. He had permanent facial scars and was completely deaf, and both his eyes were damaged. His brain was severely injured. Although he could mutter a few sounds, he seemed to comprehend little of what he said. Amanda said, "I don't look forward to this. I'd like to stop visiting him. It hurts me too much."
>
> "How can you abandon him, Amanda?" I said. "I thought you loved him."
>
> "The person I fell in love with is dead, damn it! All that's left is a pile of mush, some *thing* that can't move, hear, see, or talk. Or even understand who I am or was to him! It's not fair!"
>
> Would it have been better if Steve died in the accident? Maybe Amanda was right. As we walked out of the center that afternoon, I noticed Amanda gently embracing her stomach with both her tiny hands. She rubbed her swollen belly delicately and then smiled slightly. She had lost the most important person in her life. But Steve was still a part of her.
>
> —*Christine D. Reber*

Commentary

The author shows life in its honest complexity. Amanda is neither a saint nor an ogre, but an honest woman who gives what she can. I might wish life were different; it would be so much neater if she would devote her life to Steve and be an angel—or run off thoughtlessly to another man and be a devil. Do you like the last paragraph and what it implies?

■ **PRACTICE 10-13:** Make a rough statement of what you learned from one conflict you've had—perhaps from a previous practice exercise. Now look for a contradiction or opposite message that you could have drawn from the same experience.

Revising Narrative Essays: In addition to specific suggestions made in this chapter, review "Steps to Writing a Paper" inside the front cover of this book.

InfoTrac® College Edition: Readings on Narration

For tips on using *InfoTrac*® College Edition, see page 464.

Sol Stein. "The Power of Dialogue." *The Writer.* Feb. 2000.

Ten guidelines for great dialogue in narratives.

Leon Rooke. "How to Write a Successful Short Story." *The Antioch Review.* Summer 2002.

A fictional and humorous account of breaking the "rules" of narration.

Highlights of Chapter 10

- Telling stories is a powerfully visual way to convey a point and to explore personal experiences more deeply.

- Conflict is the heart of narration; it focuses your story and makes readers turn the page.

- Stories are most often spoiled by not getting to the conflict soon enough, by giving away the outcome too soon, or by continuing after the conflict has ended.

- Stories should begin in the middle of conflict, complicate the initial conflict, and force the people in the story to make tough decisions.

- Create breathing, walking people in stories through their physical appearance, habits, dialogue, possessions, and gestures. Details that symbolize their beliefs or personality will be the most powerful.

- As with all other types of writing, honesty—a questioning attitude—will lead to a theme that tells the truth about some segment of life and will guard you from predictable clichés.

Writing Suggestions and Class Discussions

1. Tell your best family story.

2. Tell a story of a run-in you had with a relative, but tell the story with the relative as the narrator and you as his or her antagonist.

3. Write a narrative essay about an intense event in your life that changed your philosophy or way of seeing the world. Be honest.

4. Dialogue Practice: Write how *you* would ask where the restroom is at a restaurant. Now, ask as an Englishman, a Texan, a New Yorker, an elderly schoolteacher, a street kid, and a construction worker might ask. Choose words and style carefully.

5. Fun with dialogue: Play a videotape of a section of a film you have not seen—with the sound off. Write the dialogue you imagine the actors might be saying until you have a page.

6. You are 85 years old, and your friends are gathered around your hospital bed. Before you die, you want to tell them one story of the many you've experienced, a story that will reveal to them who you really were and what your life meant. Tell that story. (It should be something that has not yet happened to you.)

7. Description Practice: Describe the eyes, mouth, and one other feature of someone close to you. Make a list of potential descriptions, then choose the most revealing for character. Turn in one finished paragraph, and also turn in your brain teaser.

8. You are a drug rehabilitation counselor and have been asked to address a group of high school students on the dangers of drug use. You're afraid they'll be bored if you start out preaching, so you decide to tell a dramatic story to lead in to your point. Write this speech.

9. Tell a story that brings an abstract idea to life. It may be true or fictional. Use one of these topics:

   ■ Courage
   ■ Prejudice
   ■ Failure
   ■ Cheating

10. Alternate Viewpoint Practice: A mother (or father) aged 39, daughter (or son) aged 18, and a grandmother (or grandfather) age unknown, live together. The grandparent wants to remarry. Break the class into groups of four—one for each part and one to record notes. Present possible ideas each character would have.

11. Describing People Practice: Use the list of character features on page 192 to create a page of details to describe either yourself or a close friend. Go beyond the obvious.

12. List five conflicts in your life that could be potential narrative essays. Under each specify the opposing forces and mention a key incident in which the conflict came to a head.

13. Do several brain teasers on the best conflict in number 11 and write a two- or three-page essay.

14. Tell your peer group a story you're thinking of writing. Then ask each peer to express the ideas and feelings of one person in the story.

15. Read and discuss the student narrative essays "Pa's Secret," "Midnight Diner," and "Bastard" in Chapter 15, and "Spring Break 1989" in Chapter 3.

Sample Student Narrative Essay

Live Abortion

Beatriz Valle

opening conflict

Cooky's baby was born fourteen weeks premature. She was on a venti-lator and losing ground. The Hospital, Centro Medico de Mayaguez in Is-abella, Puerto Rico, was supposed to have an advanced neonatal intensive

flashback

care unit. That's why Cooky chose it. My sister had had two miscarriages.

adds a new complication

Her doctor had even performed a cerclage, tying her cervix shut to pre-vent one miscarriage that happened anyway. This time the baby was alive, but she weighed only one pound, ten ounces.

Jessie, Cooky's husband, and I left the tattered furniture in the lobby and rode the elevator to the sixth-floor nursery area. Its dreary yellow curtains were closed. I rang a bell, and a long while later a nurse appeared. "May I help you?" she asked. Jessie couldn't utter a word. His face was drained.

dialogue raises new conflict and complications

"Yes," I said. "We are here to see Rebecca Rivera's baby. This is the fa-ther." As I touched Jessie's arm, my voice broke.

"It isn't visiting hours yet," the nurse answered, pointing at the sign on the door.

"He's her father! What if she dies before visiting hours?" I snapped back.

"She is considered a live abortion," the nurse replied, but she signaled us to move to the window.

description draws us in

I could never have prepared myself for what I was about to see. Her head was no bigger than a tangerine. Her eyes were horizontal slits. She had no eyebrows, eyelashes, or hair. Her hands were no bigger than the tip of my finger. Hoses and tubes jammed into every orifice of her frail body. If I could pick her up, she would easily fit into the palm of one hand. I hugged Jessie and we cried.

Later we were told if the baby survived 24 hours and then died, the family would have to make the funeral arrangements. If she died prior to then, the hospital would not release the body. Which was better? I wondered.

more complications and inner conflict

Cooky was anxiously awaiting us so she could see her baby for the first time. Jessie wrapped his arms around her as we shuffled to the nursery. Cooky pressed her face against the window and waited for the curtain to open. When it did, she whimpered. Jessie embraced her and she sobbed.

That evening Dr. Gomez said, "Don't expect to take her home. Don't expect her to leave the hospital alive."

new conflict complication

Cooky turned on him. "You are _not_ God. I _will_ take her home alive."

Months later, four-pound Rebecca Beatriz Rivera left the hospital. During that time she survived two heart attacks, fought for each ounce she gained, and was scarred all over from the tube insertions. But we were elated.

complications

Chicky, as she's now called, celebrated her sixth birthday last Sunday. Her vision is very poor and only recently did glasses give her a clear picture of the world. She walks on tippy-toes and often stumbles and falls.

complication

The hospital is not being held accountable for what happened. We found out later that after the birth, Chicky had been placed on a paper-lined tray to be disposed of. After several minutes, she cried. A nurse scooped her up and ran her to the neonatal intensive care unit. Only then did she receive adequate care. Because she suffered from lack of oxygen, she now has a mild case of cerebral palsy.

complication

Commentary

Opening: The opening establishes immediate conflict.

Ideas: Complications build quickly. Cooky has already lost two babies. The nurse's coldness, and later the doctor's, add person vs. person conflict to the baby's battle against nature. When the narrator worries what's best, we have some inner conflict, too. The conflict is directly related to the theme. This child was given no chance to live and was treated as if she were already dead, yet life can beat the odds. In the end the author seems to suggest that although the hospital was not held legally accountable, its presumption of death led to Chicky's cerebral palsy. I like the honest inner battle the author wages: part horror, part love, part anger.

Details: The description of Chicky is powerfully honest and vivid. Comparing her to a tangerine and suggesting what's missing ("no eyebrows . . .") demonstrate that the baby is not visibly human. Yet the family refuses to accept the appearances. The sharp one-word descriptions of the hospital furniture and curtain are enough for background. More could be done with Chicky's description at age six; we need to see her in full humanity now to prove the theme.

Dialogue: The "live abortion" comment and Cooky's defiance of the doctor are strong. I'd like to hear Cooky say something when she first sees her baby. It seems like an important moment. Punctuation and paragraphing are fine.

Ending: The author did not give away the ending, but a new conflict is raised and left dangling. Although I favor short endings, I'd like the author to tell us how she feels about the hospital's responsibility. Another possibility is to give this information earlier—perhaps as a complication occurring before she leaves the hospital.

Student Essay

Holy Hell: Religion Can Be Our Salvation or Our Destruction

Sherri White

My family's Apostolic Pentecostal religion was fanatical, consuming and oppressive. I attended church Wednesday, Friday and twice on Sunday. Saturday was spent cleaning the church, working the bake sales and spreading witness. Services began at 6 P.M. and ended around midnight. And everyone was expected at fellowship after most services. Each member was to give at least 10% of all earnings to the church, even if that meant the family would need to stand in the government's free cheese line.

One particular service stuck out more than others. The evening began with an hour prayer. Then things began to move. The cold, tan, cinder block walls seemed to warm once we sang the sweet, soulful gospel hymns. The organ bellowed, the piano chimed, and tambourines beat the familiar rat-a-tat-tat as the voices sang one memorized hymn after another to "make a joyful noise unto the Lord." Hands clapped, then feet stomped and bodies swayed. Just as you thought things could not be livelier, one person stepped from his pew and began walking around the church's perimeter. Others joined him until a train of faith marched around the sanctuary. Around and around they went, young and old, men and women, surrounding the evil in their midst. People began to run, then faster. The Bible says, "David danced before the Lord with all his might." So people began rolling on the floor, screaming, dancing, jumping and whirling in circles.

Somehow my pastor halted this frenzy for his sermon. His subject was the Black Walnut Festival that our town was hosting—with its parade, exhibits and carnival. At that moment, the carnival was no more than 200 yards from us, just across a creek. From church, we could hear people's laughing, screams of delight, gasps of fear and the hissing of hydraulics for the rides. Brother Willis shook his head in disgust and pointed a vibrating finger toward the carnival. It was the work of Lucifer himself to interrupt the Lord's service. He was soon enraged and yelling. Finally, he slammed his fist on the pulpit and shouted, "All those people frolicking at carnival will surely perish in the fiery lake of hell!"

continues

Someone in the congregation answered, "Amen!" and someone else exclaimed, "Preach it!"

For two hours, Brother Willis did preach, assuring us that none of the sinners at the carnival would enjoy paradise unless they converted to our religion and a thousand other things. The wooden pew was so hard my back felt like two-week-old bread. Finally, he made the familiar call to sinners and backsliders within our midst to come to the altar. "If you are not ready when our Lord calls us home, you will burn for an eternity." That night he called us by name, many of us children. He pleaded, "Come forward, little ones! Mommy won't be able to help you in hell!"

This fear had been instilled in me since birth. It was so deep that escape was impossible. The lump in my throat swelled, my palms sweat, my knees buckled. I filled with pure terror. Cautiously, I glanced around—my friends shook with fear as well. Then he called my name. My body rose without me telling it to. I reluctantly shuffled the fifteen feet to the altar, each step an excruciating fight to understand what was happening to me. My mind reeled in confusion. I had been primed for this moment every day of my six years of life, but what now? What was I supposed to feel?

Once at the altar, not knowing what else to do, I prayed. In a flash, I was swarmed by my family like mosquitoes attracted to a porch light. I prayed and prayed and prayed some more. Nothing happened. Something should have happened. I didn't know what, but something. That scared me even worse. Was I so bad that even God didn't think I was worth saving, that He wouldn't come to me? I found out later that I prayed up there like that for an hour. I was exhausted, and finally my speech began to slur. I started to mumble.

"Hallelujah!" screamed my aunt.

"Praise the Lord!" my father said. "Praise Him!"

People said I spoke in tongues, that I had the Holy Ghost in me. People shook in their seats. I don't remember much after that. Some hymns of thanksgiving were sung on behalf of those of us who had been saved that night. Prayers were said and we were dismissed. The lost sheep were saved!

Yet it was all false. I did not speak in tongues. I was mumbling, drugged with exhaustion and confusion. I was no different than I was seven hours earlier. Somehow I found the courage to confess this to my father. He said, "Your Aunt is your elder. You cannot question her." For me that was the beginning of the end. I left the church six years later and did not return to any religion until I was married. It took thirteen years to get the bitter, rancid taste out of my mouth. I am now Episcopalian. Like my former religion, there are financial, time and talent obligations, but it's not an environment of fear but of love. One thing I know: I will not raise my children to be respectful drones.

Discussion/Writing

1. Evaluate this essay as a narrative, using the Peer Review Checklist for Narration that follows as a guideline.
2. Write about a moment of revelation you had about religion

InfoTrac® College Edition: Readings that Use Narration

For tips on using *InfoTrac*® College Edition, see page 464.

Rudy Giuliani, *et al.* "We're Under Attack." *Time.* 31 Dec. 2001.

The mayor of New York and others tell the story of terrorist attacks on the city.

Beth La Barre, as told to Ruth G. Davis. "The Day I Thought I was Going to Die." *Cosmopolitan.* Dec. 2001.

One woman's experience on 9/11.

Andrew X. Pham. "Gifts." *American Scholar.* Summer 2002.

Vietnam haunts a man until he returns years later.

Karen Dammann. "Called Out of the Closet." *The Advocate.* 1 Oct. 2002.

The story of a lesbian pastor and her partner.

Steve Nadis. "I'm a Believer." *Skeptical Inquirer.* March–April 1997.

A very personal conflict between belief and skepticism.

Asha Parekh. "The Dancer." *Prairie Schooner.* Summer 2002.

Two lonely girls begin life's dances. (Fiction)

Mitch Allsom. "Misguided Drug War Has Taken a Ridiculous Turn." *Los Angeles Business Journal.* Nov. 2002.

A drug raid on a hospice filled with sick people.

InfoTrac® College Edition Discussion/Writing

1. Topic Development:

   A. Read Giuliani and LaBarre's stories and then freewrite your own memories of the 2001 terrorist attacks.

   B. Read Pham's story of returning "home," and then return to a significant place from your past (a park, school, home, or street). Write the feelings, memories, and sense impressions it evokes. The details with conflicts in them will make the best stories.

   C. Read Nadis and Damman, then tell a story about your faith, uncertainty, or rejection of faith. Since this will be a story, not an editorial, you will need incidents and events to carry the theme.

   D. Read Parekh's story and then tell about an exotic friend you met as a child, someone who opened your eyes as the new girl does in the story.

2. Analysis:

 A. Allsom's story of a drug raid has a strong theme. Does it overpower the story or enhance it? Does the story *prove* medical use of pot should be legal? If one of the police raiders were to tell his story of the same event, what might his feelings and inner conflicts be?

 B. State the theme of one of the other stories and explain, with brief quotations, how the author conveys it.

3. Coauthor: For one of the stories, add another scene of one page in which you—as yourself—appear as a character and add a new twist to the narrative. Specify where you would add this and work it in with a smooth transition. Maintain the viewpoint of the existing story (if someone else is the "I," you must describe yourself as "he" or "she").

4. Evaluate two of these stories using the Peer Review Checklist that follows.

✓ **PEER REVIEW CHECKLIST FOR NARRATION**

Author: _____

A question you have for the reviewer: _____

_____

_____

Reviewer: _____

	Strong	Average	Weak
Opening: Opening Sentence			
Early Conflict			
Ideas: Complications of Conflict			
Honesty/Depth of Theme			
Details: People Are Vividly Described			
Actions Are Vividly Described			
Dialogue: Realistic and Sharp			
Punctuation, Paragraphing			
Ending: Ends with a Punch			

The most vivid aspect of this story is:

Use several adjectives to describe the feel of this essay:

Respond to the author's question. Offer several suggestions if possible:

continues

Make another two or three suggestions about the story and discuss them with the author. Start by helping with areas you marked less strong in the boxes.

 SELF-EVALUATION CHECKLIST FOR NARRATION

Instructions: Evaluate your own narrative essay, rating it for each item. You may rate it "A" through "F" or "Good," "Average," or "Poor." Explain what you might do to improve the weaker areas.

Conflict:

     Impact of Conflict(s)

     The Turning Point or Interesting Character

Complications:

     New Complications

     Competing Explanations or Choices

     Not Giving Away the Ending

Organization:

     Early Conflict

     Smooth Flow

     Concise Ending Resolves Main Issues

Description Of People And Action:

     Vivid

     Some Symbolic Detail

     Dialogue Is Vivid and Realistic

Theme:

     Honesty and Depth

Proofreading/Grammar/Mechanics:

The part of my paper I like best is:

The reason I like it is:

The part of my paper I'm least pleased with is:

One way I might revise it would be to:

Right now this paper deserves an overall grade of _____.

CHAPTER 11

Informative Writing

Telling Your Audience What It Doesn't Know

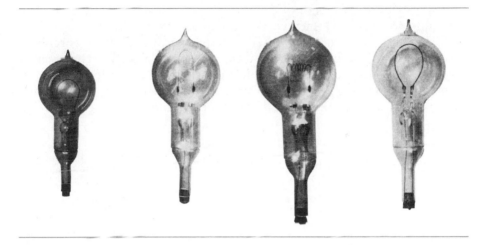

Nothing can be loved or hated unless it is first known.

—LEONARDO DA VINCI

There's something in life that's a curtain, and I keep trying to raise it.

—MAXINE HONG KINGSTON

Men occasionally stumble over the truth, but most of them pick themselves up and hurry off as if nothing had happened.

—WINSTON CHURCHILL

A college student using *Ideas and Details* wrote me a note asking, "Why does a person who is going to be a television technician need to know how to write informative essays?" He'll find out. Most college graduates are surprised by how much writing is required in their careers. Nurses, social workers, police officers, technicians, and businesspeople discover writing fills far more job time than they ever anticipated. One engineer recently estimated that she spends 50 percent of her office time writing, not calculating or sketching plans. And of the writing you will do as a college graduate, more will be informative than any other kind: technical and business reports, memos, brochures, summaries of meetings, letters, speeches, and perhaps research projects or articles for professional journals newsletters in your field. The person who can convey instructions, facts, summaries, and analyses *concisely, clearly,* and *vividly* will have an edge in becoming a valued employee or leader.

AUDIENCE AND TONE

Informative writing strives for *objectivity*. This means a reader must be moved *by your information, not by your opinions*. Using facts to support personal opinions on controversial topics or to make new proposals is persuasive writing—discussed in the next chapter. In informative writing your tone should be unbiased; you should not think of yourself as converting your audience but rather as educating it. **On the most basic level, you can simply report**—as in a research report, a summary of an article your professor asked you to read, or a report of what happened at the student senate meeting. But in college most informative essays you'll be asked to write must **analyze a situation—use your reasoning and interpretive skills to explain.** This kind of informative writing is traditionally called *expository writing*—you expose what might not be obvious. At some point, of course, it can cross a murky line into persuasive writing. This happens all the time in published writing, and it's not wrong as long as you don't try to hide propaganda behind a façade of objectivity.

For example, your *informative report* may explain how an abortion is done or contrast the pro-life and pro-choice positions without any personal opinions. An *analytical informative essay* you write could go further. It might explain the effects abortions have on women or the reasons men tend to lead anti-abortion activities, but you would cross into persuasion if you try to tell the reader to oppose or support abortion laws. In other words, **you should restrain your personal opinions in informative writing.** If in describing the process of an abortion, you write, "the baby is then ripped in agony from his mother's womb," you have loaded the dice with opinion. Likewise, if you write "the reproductive wastage is cleaned from the uterine wall," you load the dice the other way.

Another aspect of objectivity is **your obligation to present all major *legitimate* viewpoints where there is difference of opinion.** Which are legitimate? They must be either widely accepted or verifiable through science or direct observation. Many people believe that a newly conceived fetus has a human soul, so, even though we cannot prove it scientifically, you ought to include that viewpoint somewhere in an informative paper contrasting positions on abortion. However, you do not have to include the supermarket tabloid claim that aborted fetuses are being implanted with computers and grown to be robotic servants of the FBI. The source is untrustworthy and the claim has not been verified by reputable observers. Scientists do disagree, however, about whether a fetus feels pain during an abortion. They debate how developed the nervous system is at various stages, so both theories should be presented.

But don't think of informative writing as dull or boring, a mere reciting of facts. The writer's job—*always*—is to keep the reader awake, no matter what the topic. Unless your audience requires stiff formality—as in a lab or business report, for instance—occasional humor, vivid anecdotes, and lively words are usually welcome.

Writers do adjust their tone in informative writing for the audience. The amount and kind of information you might use writing about an archaeological dig will vary greatly depending on whether you write a paper for your anthropology professor, a letter to your mother, or a section of a job application. The professor will want technical and interpretive information; your mother may find the events of the trip more important; a potential employer may be most interested in the skills you learned and how well you meshed with the rest of the team.

Suppose you are writing an informative paper entitled "The Gift of Life"—donating your organs to sick people when you die. How would your tone and information differ for the following audiences?

- A sociology professor
- Transplant surgeons
- The family of a dying person
- The general public

To illustrate, here are some details about the procedure. Which of the preceding audiences especially would or would not want to know the following?

- In a way organ donation allows the dying person to continue living.
- The donor is usually brain dead (a flat EEG line), but the heart is still beating and a ventilator keeps the person breathing during the removal of transplant organs (organs deteriorate quickly without blood and oxygen).
- A neurologist is consulted to declare the person brain dead.
- The transplant doctor does *not* decide when it's time to save the organs.
- The hospital *does* notify transplant doctors of likely cases so they can prepare ahead of time. They contact the receiving family and wait anxiously with equipment poised for permission to begin removing organs.

- The Uniform Anatomical Gift Act allows your spouse, child over 18, parent, or adult sibling to donate your body even if you have not signed a donor card.

- Doctors refer to these as "organ harvests."

- It is a rapid operation without anesthetics. The body is simply sliced open—"peeled back" as one doctor said in a professional journal—to save time. The desired organs are removed as quickly as possible. Then the breathing machine is turned off and the person dies.

- The body cavity can be packed and stitched up for a funeral.

As you can see from the facts just listed, an informative writer must be sensitive to the intended audience. Even in this list there is obvious slanting of the facts presented. I aimed at a general student/teacher audience, easing back on the technical information.

Failure to consider the intended audience has led to some absurd "informative" writing. In 1919 British prime minister Lloyd George wrote an informative report to the Italian government on the economics of growing bananas, concluding by advising them to plant great banana plantations to reduce their trade deficits. He didn't know that bananas can't grow in Italy.

PACKING IN DETAILS

Here we are again. There's no way to write well without details, and the informative essay should bristle with them. During the prewriting stage, **tease your brain by asking reporters' questions.** You might start with this overall one: "What would *I* want to know about this topic if I could ask any expert?"

Suppose your topic is the effects of a nuclear war. **Ask personal questions:** What would happen to *me* if a nuclear bomb struck a half-mile away, a mile away, 5 miles, 50 miles? Ask for graphic details—what would happen to my skin, bones, hair, eyes, sexual function, and digestion? How would it affect me if I survived? How would I eat? Who would I live with? What would be the odds of finding friends or family? What aspects of society would remain?

Ask fewer personal questions: How would the living deal with all the dead and dying? Would society revert to a primitive cave culture as some people predict? Would the survivors be inspired to deeper comradery? Would there be just a few bombs or would the warring countries let loose hundreds? Would the atmosphere be poisoned for all life on earth as in Nevil Shute's *On the Beach?* How likely is the nuclear winter that Carl Sagan and other experts predicted—should the sun be blocked by billions of tons of dust thrown into the atmosphere? How would we respond if it was terrorism and not war? Can you add three or four questions to this list? Try it now for practice.

It's easier to ask questions, of course, than to answer them, but in asking sometimes answers emerge. In asking you also mark which territory you will be able to handle best when you focus the topic more. So the first step is to ask the honest questions—the ones you really care about. Tough questions require tough, gutsy details. They'll help point you toward a good paper.

■ **PRACTICE 11-1**: Ask four or five tough questions about the topics below. Suspend what you do know about them and ask what you really should know:

- Drug use in junior high school
- Television nature programs
- The value of a college education
- A topic of your choice

SURPRISE VALUE

Good informative reports or essays should *surprise the reader with new information*. If you only tell us what we already know, you are not informing us of anything. For instance, most people know that nuclear bombs generate great heat and do awful things to human flesh. But when you read John Hersey's book *Hiroshima,* you learn that some people caught within a quarter mile of the blast were vaporized so suddenly that they didn't even have time to scream or turn away. How do we know? Because they stood between concrete walls and the blast, and exact, perfect outlines of their bodies are preserved on the concrete—a painter raising his brush, a mother straightening the blanket on her baby. Their bodies shielded the wall from the intense heat just enough to imprint their silhouette.

That is information. Give your reader the same kind of **essential, inside information.** "General" information and "official" information usually tell readers only what they already know, unless you pick exotic topics—such as spelunking (cave exploring), cooking Indonesian food, or teaching sign language to the deaf.

Do you have to do original research to write informative essays? In a sense, yes. However, you don't have to travel to Japan or work ten years in a lab. **Your eyes, ears, fingers, and brain are researching the world every day.** If you can imagine a world without electricity, family, schools, police, hospitals, or law enforcement, you may be able to create a plausible essay on the world after nuclear war. If you can use your human experience to imagine what it might be like to see a dying relative put on a respirator and can honestly picture a doctor asking you to sign over the person's organs, you can write about some of the issues in the "gift of life" topic.

Here's an example of meticulously detailed information based on personal observation. It's from a student essay titled, "Dealing with the Dragon":

When he returned to the car, Mayito pulled out a syringe from its orange and white shrink wrap and a tiny brown cellophane bag with a palm tree stamped on it. His hands shook as he tore the top and poured the brown powder into a tarnished silver spoon. He meticulously drew up 20 cc of water from a puddle he poured in his palm. With the needle, he stirred the water into the powder in the spoon. He then held a lighter to the belly of the spoon until the mixture bubbled. He uncapped the syringe with his teeth, stuck it into a piece of filter from his cigarette, and drew up the amber liquid. He then jabbed the needle into a bulging vein in his arm with the skill of a sharpshooter. As he pulled back on the plunger, blood mixed with the drug. He told me, "turn your head!"

But I couldn't turn away. As he depressed the needle, the fluid returned to his vein, and I felt nauseated. I knew this was how it was done, but to see it! I threw open the car door and stood on the pavement, the sun beating on my head. I was sure I would throw up, but I didn't. Mayito stepped out and stared at me. Tears rolled down his cheeks as he buried his face in his hands.

—Janice Mundorff

Many informative papers you do for college *will* require some outside research without being full-scale research papers. Be sure to document these sources (see Chapter 14). Here's an example by a student who was writing on bulimia, or binge eating. To enhance her personal knowledge, she cited two sources with surprise value in details:

Jessica, a 36-year-old financial analyst from California, gorges herself, then takes three hundred laxatives. She has done this each day for sixteen years. A teenager with bulimia starved herself, gorged herself, and made herself throw up. She died while retching over a toilet bowl (Cauwels 2). Suzanne Abraham recorded one patient's "bad binge": she ate a bag of potato chips, a jar of honey, a jar of anchovies on bread, one pound of rolled oats, two pounds of pancakes, one pound of macaroni, two instant puddings, four ounces of nuts, two pounds of sugar, one box of Rice Crispies, a pound of margarine, two quarts of milk, a gallon of ice cream, a pound of sausage, a pound of onions, twelve eggs, a pound of licorice, a dozen candy bars, and ended with a bottle of orange cordial. This totals 1,071 grams of protein, 1,964 grams of fat, and 14,834 grams of carbohydrates (85). These violent abuses of the body profoundly affect bulimics' social life, self-esteem, and psychological functioning. It may cause death from suicide or cardiac arrhythmia.

—Andrea Macaluso

■ **PRACTICE 11-2:** Write a sense and example brain teaser about a natural disaster you know about: windstorm, earthquake, blizzard, or fire, for example. Be especially alert for details with surprise value—little things that many people might not know.

POOR INFORMATIVE TOPICS

Introductory topics, such as "How to Play the Piano," can lead to disaster. There's so much basic definition and terminology, it is very hard to write an interesting paper. You might do better to focus on "How to Handle Your First Piano Recital" or "What Makes Jazz Piano Sound Different." Another problem with introductory topics is that most educated people will be familiar with the basic information. Picking topics such as "Techniques of Safe Driving" or "Basics of Gardening" will bog you down saying the obvious. Pick an *aspect* of the topic that promises more surprise value: "Why Truck Drivers Are the Safest Drivers" or "Garden Health Hazards."

    Broad topics such as "What Is a Good Marriage?" can also doom your paper. You'll only be able to say the most general and superficial things about this topic because you promised more than you can fulfill in sharp, gutsy detail. Better choices: "How to Handle a Family Argument over Money" or "Six Questions to Ask Your Fiancé Before Walking Down the Aisle." Notice that in both of the narrower topics, the opportunity exists for a definition of a good marriage to emerge.

GOOD TOPICS

Lurking inside all poor topics are potential good topics, and keeping two things in mind will help you recognize which kind you have. First, has it been **limited to an aspect you can cover *in depth*** in your allotted pages? Can you really tell us something fresh and fill the essay with vivid details? Second, do you have **a specific slant or message** to convey—a thesis? To help you arrive at a thesis, let me explain a half-dozen time-tested ways of structuring informative writing. This illustrates an important point that sometimes gets lost: The steps in writing an essay are really interdependent—the thesis helps determine structure; the structure helps create ideas. The four steps of the writing process described in this book—Getting Ideas, Order, Draft, and Revision—in actual practice constantly play back and forth to each other.

■ **PRACTICE 11-3:** List three or four potential topics for your own informative essay. Narrow each so you can cover it in depth in a few pages. You will be building on these topics throughout the chapter.

ORGANIZING INFORMATIVE WRITING

After narrowing your topic somewhat and doing some brain-teaser lists, you can invent your own scratch outline for the material. But here are six common structuring and thinking devices people use to convey information. If you start with one early in your prewriting, focusing and structuring your informative writing will be easier. This is not to say you should always rely on these devices—the most creative topics often break new ground.

- The Process or "How-To"
- The Essentials or "What-Is"
- Causes or "Why"
- Effects or "What's Next?"
- Comparison or Contrast
- Classification

The last two are brain teasers from Chapter 3. The other four are also brain teasers. All not only dig into corners of your brain for ideas, but suggest a focus and structure as well. Let's look at each in some detail.

The Process or "How-To"

One way of focusing and organizing information is to present it as a *process.* Imagine yourself telling the reader *how to do* something: "How to Skydive," "How to Con a Professor," "How to Teach Children Manners." Process can also be used to focus on issues simply for *understanding:* "How Refugees Become Terrorists," "The Stages of Juvenile Delinquency," or "The Fall of Communism in Eastern Europe." Your scratch outline will consist of *chronological steps.* Try several scratch outlines until you're satisfied. If, for instance, you find yourself with three stages that have very little information and one bloated with examples and ideas, you probably need to divide that step and combine the smaller ones. If I were writing on skydiving, for instance, I don't think the following outline would work well:

- Saying goodbye to family
- Arriving at the airport
- Preparing your equipment
- The flight up
- Diving
- Cleaning up

The first, second, and last items don't deserve full steps in the process. They can be brief transitions. Preparing equipment seems reasonable as a main heading, but the dive seems most important and ought to be divided into several stages itself: the (ulp!) leap, the free fall, opening the chute, and the landing. **Organizing chronologically does not imply that you must give equal time to each element. Focus on the key moments.** Slowing time down at a key moment can heighten the informative effect.

The Georgia Paramedics Against Drunk Driving, for instance, published an effective brochure that describes the process of an accident at 55 mph. This brochure describes the one second after a car smashes into a solid object. In the first tenth of the second, the bumper and grille collapse. In the second tenth, the hood crumples and hits the windshield. The car frame stops, but the rest of the car still travels at 55 mph. The driver braces his legs against the crash, and they snap at the knee. In the third tenth of the second, the steering wheel shatters. In the fourth, the front two feet of the car collapse while the rest still moves at 35 mph. The driver is still traveling 55. In the fifth tenth, the driver is impaled on the steering column and blood fills his lungs. In the sixth tenth, the impact can rip his feet out of tightly laced shoes, the brake pedal snaps off, and the driver's head strikes the windshield. In the seventh tenth of the second, hinges pop and seats break free, hitting the driver—who is now dead.

After deciding on your scratch outline, brain-tease again and add details and ideas to each heading. This is true for each of the outline patterns that follow.

■ **PRACTICE 11-4:** Describe a process in slowed-down fashion, as the Georgia paramedics did. Try a kiss, falling down stairs, or your own topic from Practice 11-3.

The Essentials or "What-Is"

This approach informs a reader of *essential* characteristics of your topic. For example: "The Essentials of a Good Photograph," "Problems Children Have When Parents Divorce," "What's Really Bad About Rats," or "What Is Unique About Adrienne Rich's Poetry." Your scratch outline consists of each key element you will explain. For instance, for children involved in divorces, you might have:

- Loss of a father/mother figure
- Dealing with parental sorrow and grief
- Feelings of guilt about causing the parents' divorce
- Often loss of home when property is sold and divided
- New "uncle-daddies"/"aunt-mommies" in the home
- Loss of friends if the family moves

Under each of these you can list the examples, facts, questions, or bug items from your brain teasers. If you find some items have little information, omit them. If one item draws most of your attention, you might focus more exclusively on it. For instance, one common thread I notice in my list of ideas is *loss*. I might decide at this point to focus on "Things Children Lose During Divorce."

■ **PRACTICE 11-5:** Make a list of the essentials of a good relationship with a boss or the essentials of a good shopping mall.

■ **PRACTICE 11-6:** State one of your topics from Practice 11-3 as an "essentials" topic and make a scratch outline of main headings.

Is there one "right pattern" for your essay? The topic on good photographs and the one on divorce would also be possible as process essays, describing the stages of taking a good photo or the stages children go through during a divorce. The organization of the paper changes, but it might be equally effective. On the other hand, the topic on rats might not work so well as process—unless you wanted to tell the story of one incident ("Our Apartment Building's Battle with Rats" or "Chicago's History of Rat Control"). The real point here is having a *plan that does not mix approaches.* That might confuse a reader—and *you.*

Causes or "Why"

Organize the paper by informing the reader of the causes of a particular situation. Here are the same topics from cause perspectives:

- What motivates (causes) a person to skydive?
- What were some less obvious reasons that the United States and its allies sent troops to Iraq?
- What causes a rat infestation?
- Why do children feel guilty during a divorce?
- How are juvenile delinquents created?

List as many causes (reasons or motivations) for the situation. Each may become an outline heading and eventually a paragraph in the paper.

■ **PRACTICE 11-7:** Make a list of possible causes for one of the cause topics.

■ **PRACTICE 11-8:** State one of your topics from Practice 11-3 as a "cause" topic and list three or four headings for an outline.

Effects or "What's Next?"

Instead of looking backward for the source of the situation, look forward to the effects or consequences of a situation. Explaining our topics from this perspective we have:

- Long-term effects of skydiving on your body
- How terrorism affects American foreign policy with other countries
- The psychological effects of rat bites
- When children of divorce marry
- The effects juvenile delinquents have on their peers

To develop one of these, I would list as many effects or consequences as possible. Under each effect, I would list details.

■ **PRACTICE 11-9:** Create an effects approach for each of the following topics. Then list four to five possible effects one of them leads to

- Drunk driving
- The 12-month school year
- A change in your neighborhood
- Dating through the Internet

■ **PRACTICE 11-10:** Create an effects approach for one of your topics from Practice 11-3 and draw up a scratch outline of headings.

Reasonable causes and effects: Suggesting causes and effects for events may be controversial or lead to logical errors. The informative writer must try to avoid arguing and instead suggest all reasonable causes and effects without bias. For instance, the following would be reasonable causes of the computer revolution:

- To improve business efficiency and reduce human errors
- To reduce information storage space
- To speed up communications
- To save money by eliminating jobs

But how about these?

- To bend the minds of children away from religion
- To help government gain secret control of people's finances

The last two demand a lot of arguing to prove they're true and are more appropriate for persuasive papers than informative ones. "But," someone might say, "look how children *are* turning away from religion just as computers became widespread! It's a fact!" No, it's an opinion without the widespread acceptance the first four causes would have.

Here is an objective example of cause analysis that explains what clues tell fire investigators that an arsonist has set a fire. Notice how the student explains the whys behind the causes:

> The color of the flames is a clue that a fire might have been caused by arson. An arson fire burns hotter than a normal fire, creating brighter flames with less smoke. Due to the heat, there is purer combustion and less smoke. Unintentional fires usually start small, so when bright red and yellow flames roll out the windows, firefighters should be suspicious.
>
> When fire spreads, it moves up and away from its origin and leaves a "V" mark on walls. If the floor is burned from one end to the other, this may be a sign that an arsonist spread gasoline or kerosene. If there is a lack of deep char around the point of origin, it indicates a fast-spreading fire that may have been helped by an accelerant.

—*Bruce Teague*

■ **PRACTICE 11-11:** Explain the causes of some social problem today, **or** if you could change one decision you made in the past—at least one year ago—describe the effects a different decision would have had on your life. Be as honest and objective as possible.

Comparison or Contrast

Let's try our topic list for comparative structure:

- Skydiving is safer than hang gliding
- Afghanistan and Iraq: Two ways of handling the media
- Rats vs. cockroaches: If you had to choose
- Is it worse for a parent to die or to divorce?
- Teaching manners to kids in the United States and in Italy
- Gangs today and in 1990

Next you would list your points of comparison as headings and support each point with details.

■ **PRACTICE 11-12:** Develop a brain-teaser list of comparisons or contrasts for one of the topics just listed.

■ **PRACTICE 11-13:** Create a comparison or contrast approach to one of your topics from Practice 11-3 and draw up a scratch outline of headings.

Classification

Here are some of the topics structured by classification (you can refresh your memory on page 51):

- Three types of governments emerging from former communist regimes in Eastern Europe
- Four kinds of excuses to use on your professors
- Five skydiving styles
- Three common reaction patterns for children of divorce
- Types of female gang members

After deciding on your main points, fill in each category with details describing it. In your draft, each heading will become a paragraph.

■ **PRACTICE 11-14:** Create a classification approach to one of your topics from Practice 11-3 and draw up a scratch outline of headings.

■ **PRACTICE 11-15:** Pick one of the following topics and try to see it in five of the six thinking structures. Create a one-sentence statement for each:

- Evolution (or any other scientific concept)
- *Romeo and Juliet* (or any other literary work)
- Schizophrenia (or any other psychological term)

■ **PRACTICE 11-16:** Take your two best topics so far and sketch out how you'd organize each in three of the six informative patterns. Be sure to label each of the six scratch outlines you develop.

■ **PRACTICE 11-17:** Create a brain-teaser page exploring the most promising topic you outlined in Practice 11-16.

Drafting and Revising Informative Writing: Refresh yourself by reviewing "steps to writing a paper" inside the front cover. For an example of a first draft and revised draft of an informative essay, see "How to Get Back the Family You Lost" in Chapter 15.

InfoTrac® College Edition: Readings on Presenting Facts and Interviewing

For tips on using *InfoTrac*® College Edition, see page 464.

William Raspberry. "An Encyclopedia at Your Fingertips." *Newsbytes.* Nov. 1999.

Visualizing facts and their value in informative writing.

Ronald Kovach, "Studs Terkel: On the Art of Interviewing." *The Writer.* May, 2002.

How to get great information—from the master of the interview.

Lynn Alfino, "10 Tips for Top-Notch Interviews." *The Writer.* May 2002.

From preparation to closing question.

Highlights of Chapter 11

- Adjust your approach to audience in informative writing.
- Pack in plenty of details with surprise value. Ask questions and use other brain teasers to stimulate ideas.
- Narrow your topic to one you can handle in your allotted space. Avoid broad, introductory topics and pick ones with a sharp focus.

- Consider several options when organizing an informative essay. Create your own pattern, describe a process, explain the essentials, explain causes, explain effects, compare or contrast, or classify.
- Don't mix organizing patterns in short essays.

Writing Suggestions and Class Discussions

1. List five topics on which you think you can write a nonresearched, informative essay. Highlight the ones you think will offer the most surprise value for a general audience.

2. Write a "Reporter's Questions" brain-teaser list (with answers) and one other brain-teaser list for two of the best topics from number 1.

3. Narrow the best topic further and write three scratch outlines (just main headings). Use three different organizing patterns.

4. Using the same topic, decide which organization plan conveys your message best and fill it in with details from your brain-teaser lists.

5. Write the paper and revise it.

6. Audience and Tone: Suppose you were writing an informative letter entitled "My First Semester at College." How would your tone and information included differ depending on to whom you were writing?
   - The college president
   - Your boss (who reimburses your tuition)
   - Your best friend (who is not attending college)

   Make a list of information for each letter.

7. Rewrite these weak topics into sharper, more interesting ones still related to the originals; give two alternatives for each:
   - How to bowl
   - Today's music
   - How to balance a checkbook
   - Police brutality
   - Smoking is bad for your health

8. Ask five tough questions about each of the following topics, questions that will lead to surprise value information:
   - Teenage marriages
   - The future of gasoline consumption in the United States
   - Community colleges vs. four-year colleges
   - Television satellite dishes or cable television

9. Write a process or how-to essay, packing as much information as you can into one or two pages. Concentrate on vivid details and smooth organization. Topics:

   ■ How to drink with style

   ■ How to meet men or women at college

   ■ How to deal with a sexist (or a racist or homophobic) boss

   ■ How to give an "A" oral report

   ■ Open topic

10. Explain how a process works that you know well, but which most people don't understand—a CD burner, sink trap, spark plug, antibody, therapy for autistic children. No more than 250 words.

11. Class Exercise in Process Writing:

    Create a diagram or doodle of your own of about the same complexity as this one: Write a process description of it so someone else can draw it without seeing the doodle. Proportion is important, but actual size is not. You will have ten minutes. Members of the class will try to draw it only from the read-aloud instructions—no changes allowed from your written text.

    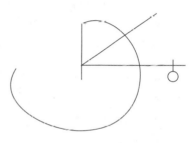

12. Write an Essentials essay on one of the following, packing as much information as possible into one or two pages:

    ■ A good love letter

    ■ A top action film

    ■ The most common clichés of television situation comedies

    ■ Handling being an older adult student in college

    ■ Open topic

13. Create a brochure for an organization or cause you believe in. Explain its essential features in no more than 250 words.

14. Essentials: Invent a contest and write a press release for it. Be as straight or wacky as you like, but explain the contest rules and prizes in clear detail. Aim the contest at a clearly defined, limited audience, not the general public

15. Inform a person you're attracted to of your essential personality features. This should *not* be a sell, but an *honest* appraisal. Offer at least three key aspects about yourself that a future spouse should be aware of. Pack in vivid, supporting detail.

16. Write an informative essay on the essentials of a career you're considering. Interview a person in the field, asking real questions you have. Here are some all-purpose starter questions:

    - What do you like best about your job?
    - What one piece of advice would you give to someone wanting to enter this career?
    - What qualities are most important to be a successful _____?
    - What are you most proud of in your career?
    - What part of your job would you gladly give to someone?
    - What most frustrates or disappoints you about it?

    Before calling for an interview, read page 223 for proper etiquette and techniques of interviews.

    A sample career research paper is on page 389.

17. Write a cause essay on one of these topics. Your job is to consider less obvious reasons as well as ones most people are aware of:

    - Why people get body piercings
    - Why SUVs are so popular
    - Why the drug Ecstasy is popular among younger teens
    - Why divorce is more socially acceptable today
    - Why Physical Education is required in college

18. Write a Causes *or* Effects essay on one of the following, packing in as much information as possible in one or two pages:

    - Loss of wildlife habitat
    - Democratization of Russia
    - High salaries for athletes
    - A recent career change you made
    - Open topic

19. Imagine changing any one historical event and discuss the effects that might have. For examples, suppose the U.S. Supreme Court had decided to give the disputed Florida votes to Al Gore and he won the election instead of George Bush, or suppose cloning human beings was not declared illegal.

20. Imagine altering one "law of nature" (such as eliminating winter or not having to kill to eat). Start by explaining why you might change it (the causes) and then forecast possible effects. Look for both positive and negative effects.

21. Write a one- to two-page informative essay comparing or contrasting two of your current textbooks. Evaluate them based on the standards established in this chapter for conveying information: adaptation to audience, surprise value, and covering the tough questions readers have. Quote examples to support your views.

22. Compare or contrast two competing products, such as DVD versus VHS format for videos or the PC versus the Mac for computers. Your job is not to judge but inform us objectively about similarities and differences.

23. Write a classification essay on one of the following, packing as much information as possible in one or two pages:

    ■ Male attitudes toward women

    ■ Female attitudes toward men

    ■ Levels of racism

    ■ Student clothing styles

    ■ Types of video game players

    ■ Open topic

24. The class will be divided into six groups. Each will apply a different one of the six informative organizing patterns to the same topic. Each group should write a focus sentence, an outline, and some details for each heading.

25. In addition to the informative essay that follows, read the student informative essays on page 372.

Sample Student Informative Essay Using the Classification Pattern

When The Bough Breaks: Black Children In Crisis

Tokeya Young

Millions of black children live in crisis today: crises of violence, poverty, and ill health. Their families, their communities, and their government have failed them. Most people have heard of the failures of some families and communities, but in 1991 the United States was one of only a few nations not to ratify the Rights of the Child Treaty sponsored by the United Nations that would have set standards for "basic safeguards any civilized nation must provide for its children" (Cottman-Becnel 94).

INTRO classifies three crises

Many black children don't live to see their 18th birthday. In 1990, almost two thousand Black youths were killed by guns. Every day in

violence

continues

America, an average of four black men under 19 are murdered (Weathers 70). It saddens me that the value of a young life can be measured by the price of designer sneakers, leather jackets, gold jewelry, or "gang turf." In urban areas, a young black man is more likely to die from violence than a soldier was on a tour of Vietnam (Weathers 70). Inner cities are battle-grounds filled with children armed for war. Sixty percent of all deaths of black boys between 15 and 19 are from guns (Weathers 71).

poverty

ill health

Many black children are growing up poor and in ill health. Almost half of black children live in poverty (Cottman-Becnel 94) and for that reason many are never immunized against childhood diseases and are malnour-ished. Black babies are twice as likely as white babies to die within their first year (Johnson 74). Another health problem is children with AIDS. There are eight in Monroe County who have full-blown AIDS, and in New York State over 1,300 (Machuca). Half of all youngsters nationwide with AIDS are black (Johnson 83). There are also thousands of cocaine babies. Their parents' prenatal use of cocaine causes these innocent victims to suffer withdrawal and often physical and learning disabilities the rest of their lives. In 1991 in Monroe County, there were 197 reported cocaine babies, 84 percent of whom were black (Machuca). Other causes of child-hood ill health are improper nutrition and lack of immunization. If more clinics offered free immunization, underprivileged youth could be protected against childhood diseases. One and a half million American children— many of them black—don't have health insurance (Johnson 74).

con-clusion

Black children live in a crisis not witnessed since slavery. Violence, poverty, and ill health disrupt their lives and threaten society's future.

Works Cited

Cottman-Becnel, Barbara. "Poverty as Policy." *Essence*. Dec. 1993:

92–94.

Johnson, Kirk. "Alive and Well." *Essence*. Dec. 1993: 74–83.

Machuca, Paola. Telephone interview. 2 May 1994.

Weathers, Diane. "Stop the Guns." *Essence*. Dec. 1993: 70–71.

Commentary

Surprise value: Because people know *generally* that African American children often face great stress, the essay's surprise value lies in specific data. People who assume the United States champions child rights would be surprised by the veto of the child rights treaty. I thought the paragraph on violence had the best surprise value in statistics. The fact that the author made a personal call (to AIDS Rochester) to get local facts would appeal to her class audience.

Details: Some were vivid. Comparing children's survival rates to soldiers in Vietnam was powerful. More detail was needed on poverty—the skimpiest of the three sections.

Organization: This is a classification essay. The introduction states three types of crises. Violence is handled cleanly, but poverty and ill health mix in the third paragraph. The poverty section needs more hard detail and its own paragraph. The conclusion is concise.

Tone: Mostly objective. Only "it saddens me" in the second paragraph is personal and her call in the third paragraph for free immunizations verges on argument.

Audience: Her classmates: a local but general audience. The style is clean, nontechnical, and accessible to average readers.

Research: The documentation format is fine, but notice that all three published sources come from the same issue of one magazine. *Essence* is respected, but other sources would strengthen her impartiality. Her sources could also be more up-to-date because they rely on statistics.

Questions the essay should answer but doesn't: Why is poverty such a crisis? We need details. Second, what diseases do African American children suffer from because of lack of immunization?

Strongest aspects: Specific statistics and clean style.

Additional suggestions: I think there's room for examples, perhaps based on the author's observations. Name a child who died in a crossfire or describe a family who lives in poverty. She doesn't have to become opinionated to describe some people up close. The essay's reliance only on statistics keeps the reader at arm's length from the little kids she obviously cares about. Second, she should identify her phone interview source in the body of the paper. Who is Paola Machuca? What's this person's position?

Sample Student Informative Essay Using the Effects Pattern

Going To The Chair

Michele Myers

Soft music whispers as you enter the cheerful waiting room. A coffee table holds the latest *Woman's Day* and *Bass Fisherman* magazines. When you check with the receptionist, she greets you with a sweet smile. Soon your name is called by a masked person in scrubs and a lab coat, and you are waved forward. Down the hall you hear the unmistakable whining whistle of machinery over the mellow tune. You sit in a reclining chair that could have come from the set of an old sci-fi show. The assistant clips a pink bib napkin and cool metal chain around your neck. Your eyes focus on sharp instruments on the tray and the water swirling in the tiny bowl. Does this make your pulse increase? You're not alone. But going to the dentist can affect people in many ways.

I have been a dental assistant for five years, and, contrary to popular belief, not everyone is afraid of the dentist. Take Darrell, for example. He falls asleep as we are working on him. It's as if the drill is the soothing sound of the ocean, and after a few minutes, he starts to snore. I can't imagine being that comfortable in The Chair. He told me once that he wants to buy a dental chair for his home to sleep in on Saturday afternoons.

Other patients react to dentists with fearlessness. My mother actually prefers to have treatment done without anesthetic. She says, "I don't like the after effects of the novocaine. It makes me bite my cheek." When I ask her about the pain, she just says, "Yeah, but it's mind over matter. Besides, it's usually over fast." Mind over matter? Is it possible pain is only how we perceive it, that if you tell yourself it won't hurt, it won't?

But I know from experience that fear of The Chair isn't as simple as physical pain. Sometimes pain is just how people express their feeling of lack of control. They fear depending on someone with a sharp, gleaming instrument entering their body. Otherwise I don't know how to explain the effect dental work has on Anna, a mother of five. She works in a factory and has strong, worn, calloused hands; yet whenever she has dental work done, she says, "I'd rather give birth than have a shot in the mouth." She cringes as the doctor tilts her back, and she squeezed her eyes shut as he reaches for the syringe. Like a mother comforting a child, I must hold her powerful, frightened hand until the injection is over.

Roger has a sister who is a hygienist. Therefore, that makes him an expert on dentistry. He questions everything the dentist does because he suspects the dentist is in on some conspiracy. When the dentist leaves the room, Roger asks me, "Should I really have a filling in this tooth?" or "Is it normal to have novocaine for this size filling?" Recently Roger came in with a formula that he thought could re grow tooth enamel—a mixture of toothpaste and mouth wash. The fact that enamel is 96 percent inorganic doesn't bother him. He says he's going to have the formula patented.

I will never forget the first time I met David. When I called him from the waiting room, he snapped, "It's about time!" I apologized for being

continues

behind, although it was only five minutes. He proceeded to lecture me about how valuable his time was and that I should have told him we were running late. Going to the dentist makes lots of people upset, but when the dentist came in, David turned from the beast Mr. Hyde into Dr. Jekyll. His anger vanished. He smiled and asked nicely about the doctor's family. He released his tension on me, then turned on his charm for the man who was going to drill him.

For pure fear of The Chair, we have John. He spends ten minutes in our bathroom psyching himself up before he will enter the room. Once there, he paces around the chair until the doctor comes in. Perspiration runs down his face and he hyperventilates. When he finally sits, he gets pale and wilts like a cut flower. His feet shake nervously. Even if it's freezing outside, he will beg us to crack open a window. Then the dentist can examine him. It takes John another 15 minutes of settling in before any real work can be done on him. By the time he leaves, John is physically sick and exhausted.

Sometimes dental professionals glimpse the deeper effects dental visits have on patients. On Steve's first visit, he smelled like cigarettes and stale beer and dressed in Harley biker clothes. He was gruff and scary. He had never liked the dentist, so his teeth and gums were in total break down. Now he needed dentures. When told his remaining teeth would be surgically removed, he just shrugged. But at the mention of the impression, he grew agitated and said he had a severe gag reflex. I didn't even get the tray half way to his mouth before he started gagging. In a rush he confessed to me that as a child he had been sexually abused by his father. He told me his father would say to him, "Open up and suck on this." As he spoke, it was as if he suddenly became a little boy again. I felt bad and didn't know what to do. The doctor had to return to take the impression. It was the longest two minutes as Steve coughed and gagged while the material set up.

From my experiences as a dental assistant, I have learned that fear is very real, although it is not always the direct effect of the dentistry. So when David yells at me, I try to remember that he is so nervous, he doesn't know how to deal with it in any other way. And Roger's suspicions are caused by his fear of lack of control. Part of my job as assistant is to recognize patients' nervousness and discomfort and do the best I can to eliminate those fears, even if they are caused by hidden factors. That's ok. I don't mind holding a patient's hand, because I hope I'll have someone's hand to hold when I need it.

Discussion

Evaluate this essay using the guidelines from the peer review sheet and the commentary on "When The Bough Breaks" as a model. Think especially about other possible effects a dental visit has on people.

For samples of student essays using other informative structures, see:

Process: "Simple Life," (page 179); "The Autopsy," (page 375); or "How to Get Back the Family You Lost," (page 380).

Essentials: "Career in Imagination," (page 389).

Contrast: "Food for Thought," (page 372).

InfoTrac® College Edition:
Readings that Convey Information

For tips on using *InfoTrac®* College Edition, see page 464.

Doug Brunk. "Children Are Direct Victims in Families Reported for Violence." *Clinical Psychiatry News.* July 2001.

> *The grim **statistics** about family violence.*

"Children's Nagging Guides Purchases." *About Women and Marketing.* Feb. 1999.

> *This **statistical report** tells how children get parents to buy what the children want.*

Jim Collins. "Close Encounters of the Furred Kind (road kill)." *Yankee.* Dec. 1993.

> *The **essentials** of a dead animal sale—all you didn't need to know.*

"How to Hibernation Rules." *Motorcyclist.* Dec. 2002.

> *The **process** of putting a motorcycle to sleep for the winter season.*

Azadeh Moaveni. "They Didn't Know What Hit Them: How the U.S. Killed a Senior al-Qaeda Leader without Putting a Pilot's Life at Risk." *Time.* 18 Nov. 2002.

> ***Process:*** *attacking an enemy from a distance.*

Cait Murphy. "How Bad Government Feeds Rage." *Fortune.* 24 Dec. 2001.

> *A skeptic examines valid and invalid **causes** for citizen anger at government.*

Michael Renner. "Lessons of Afghanistan: Understanding the Conditions That Give Rise to Extremism." *World Watch.* Mar. 2002.

> *Examines the **causes** of extremism.*

Susan E. James. "The Secret Scar: Evaluating for Sex Abuse." *Addiction and Recovery.* May–June 1993.

> *An **effects** essay about child abusers.*

Dashka Slater. "The Hidden Life of What's Under Your Sink." *Sierra.* May–June 2002.

> *What **effects** do the chemicals stored in our houses have on us and others?*

Dominic Kemps. "Asian Women Read Niche Magazines: So Why Aren't More Mainstream Advertisers Using this Medium?" *Brand Strategy.* Sept. 2001.

Contrasts advertisements aimed at Asian and mainstream British women.

Kevin C. Johnson. "Pop Music Magazines Are Different—Here's How to Tell Them Apart." *Knight Ridder/Tribune News Service.* 18 Nov. 2002.

A detailed comparison of the top five pop music magazines.

Sora Song. "Body of Evidence." *Time.* 21 Oct. 2002.

Classifies types of evidence collected at crime scenes.

InfoTrac® College Edition Discussion/Writing

1. Topic Development:

   A. Think up ten topics you could write using these essays as inspiration. For example, Kemp's essay contrasts how advertisers target two kinds of women—you could write about how advertisers target two kinds of teenagers or senior citizens.

   B. If you could get accurate statistical information on any topic you wanted, what informative essay would you write?

2. Analysis:

   A. Read "Children Often Are Direct Victims . . . " or "Children's Nagging . . . " and study how the authors use **statistics.** Is there any overkill? Any bias in interpretation? Areas not explained well? Point out the most effective numbers or facts used and say why. Were there additional questions the researchers should have asked?

   B. Read any two of the essays labeled by a **structure** discussed in *Ideas and Details.* Write a scratch outline of the essays' main points.

3. Coauthor: Read any of the pattern-structured essays and look for places where you could add information: another essential element, step in the process, cause, effect, contrast, or category that could or should be added. Write a half-page of notes stating what you would add. You may simply say what information you would like to see added if you don't know the facts.

4. Evaluate two of the readings as informative writing. How strong is the surprise value of the ideas? The surprise value of the details? Point out weaknesses in the structure and the tone. Which topics seem most original to you? Use the Peer Review Checklist that follows as a guide.

✓   **PEER REVIEW CHECKLIST FOR INFORMATION**

Author: _____

The organizing pattern I used for this essay is: _____

Describe it if you created your own pattern.

I'd like help with this paper in this area: _____

Reviewer: _____

	Strong	**Average**	**Weak**
Ideas: Surprise Value			
Details: Vivid			
Enough Detail			
Organization: Clear/Easy to Follow Transitions/Paragraphs Mark Major Shifts			
Tone: Unbiased, Informative			
Audience: Style Suits Audience			
Research (if used): Documentation			

Do you agree with the author's assessment of the organizing pattern? Explain where/how it might be strengthened.

Respond to the author's request for advice:

Evaluate the essay's surprise value. What was new; what wasn't?

What questions about the topic should the essay answer that it doesn't?

What is the strongest part of the essay to you?

Give two additional suggestions for revision:

1.

2.

CHAPTER 12

Persuasive Writing

Seeking Agreement from an Audience

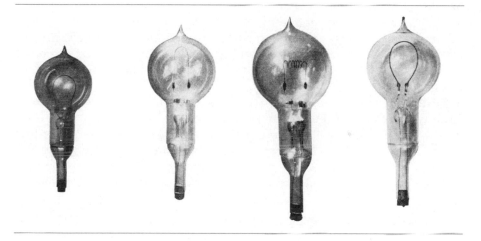

The aim of argument should not be victory but progress.

—JOSEPH JOUBERT

The civilized world represents the victory of persuasion over force.

—PLATO

Persuasive writing has a bad reputation. At its worst we picture a slimy hoodlum twisting someone's arm to "persuade" him to tell where the diamonds are. We think of battleships and bombers hovering off the coast of a tiny country to "persuade" its government to change its policies. Cigarette advertisements in magazines "persuade" men that one brand will make them feel as if they're riding a snorting stallion on the range while another brand will make women feel daring and rebellious. How about empty political campaign speeches or a father screaming at his late, tipsy teenager at 2 A.M.? Persuasion is commonly pictured as forcing, tricking, seducing, or lecturing people to buy or do something not really in their best interests. Too often these tactics work. But that's not the kind of persuasion we're interested in here.

Honest, ethical persuasion means bringing readers—through their own reason and emotions—to believe or act as the writer does. In this sense, readers willingly and *consciously* discover that it is in their best interest to agree. This type of persuasion, which will be required of you in many college assignments and in most persuasive writing done in business, professional, and technical careers, is an *honest appeal to reason and feeling*.

AUDIENCE AND TONE

Advertising, political speeches, and barroom debates often imply the audience is so dumb or so bullheaded that it must be pounded into submission. Reasonable persuasion assumes your audience is uncommitted (unless you know for *sure* you are dealing with supporters or those holding opposite views). It assumes your audience is educated and will weigh your arguments reasonably. This audience wants facts and logic, expects you to be ethical, will be critical of shortcomings in your position, and will not fall for the gimmicks of advertising.

This means that you, as a persuader, must achieve a good persuasive tone. You do not have to be somber or dull. In fact, humor not only enlivens persuasion but can demonstrate the writer is broad-minded. Overall, strive for perspective and common sense. Sentences like "All people who support abortion are murderers!" and "Antiabortionists want to enslave women!" share the same hysterical tone. Wild, undisciplined language usually results from wild or undisciplined thinking, and smart, open-minded readers will be skeptical about such statements and skeptical about writers who lose their tempers. **Assume your readers are intelligent, present many facts and reasons for your position, and trust them to see the logic.** If you try to bully readers into agreement with shouting, they won't be convinced—they'll only want to get away from you.

Several years ago I received an anonymous letter from a student. The fact that it was anonymous made me question the writer's integrity from the start. The student was complaining about the revealing clothes a woman in the class wore, arguing that they were out of place in college. I admit the woman's clothes lacked taste, and if I'd received a reasonable letter, I may have gritted my teeth and spoken to her about it—even though I don't think a teacher should be a police officer. But the student's letter used numerous profanities to describe the woman—"slut" and "bimbo" being among the nicer. It ended: "I want action! Have *YOU* any sense of decency??!!" Me? Me?! The student steamed and frothed so much that he totally lost perspective. He was attacking his reader, and he lost whatever chance he had of persuading me to act as he wished. I felt more inclined to counsel *him* than the woman in question.

Before we agree with an argument, we must trust the arguer. **Give readers reasons to trust you.** Is the persuader ethical? Knowledgeable? Reasonable? Your credibility is damaged by using profanity, bullying, ranting, or threats, by twisting facts or calling rumors "facts," and by relying on slogans, clichés, stereotypes, or other oversimplifications. The writer who calmly *helps* a reader sort through the complexities of a situation, who honestly *shares the difficulties* of right and wrong in the issue, and who *respects the truth* will open doors with a quiet knock. The persuader who approaches with a battering ram or who tries to sneak in a back window is the one against whom readers build barricades.

So before you begin persuading readers, try to put yourself in an honest, helpful frame of mind; open yourself to alternative viewpoints in the early stages especially, so the point you set out to prove is as reasonable and fair as it can be. Keep Joseph Joubert's statement in mind: "The aim of argument should not be victory but progress."

As long as you consider your audience's reactions, are willing to modify your ideas to strengthen them, and use many brain teasers to open the topic, you will make honest progress. If you seek victory over a reader, ignore or hide facts that threaten your idea, or lose control of your emotions, your case will start to crumble.

■ **PRACTICE 12-1:** Recall two persuasive situations you've been in: one that led to hot tempers and anger, one that led to "progress." Think about the attitude of the people involved in each.

To help achieve a good tone, **write to real people for a real reason**—actually send your ideas to someone. My students' persuasive papers have been published in the college newspaper, city newspaper, Humane Society newsletter, Ukrainian Club newsletter, and several magazines. One wrote a proposal to a bank to finance a towing company; another asked a museum curator to reinstate cancelled free art classes for poor children; another used the class paper as an opportunity to answer her supervisor's negative job evaluation of her. One of my students wrote to her town school board to protest a policy against students using calculators during tests. Irene's dyslexic son knew his math, but made simple errors, such as writing "45"

instead of "54," without a calculator. Her letter brought a state assistant secretary of education to a board meeting, and the rule was changed. Irene was later asked to address a convention of 500 educators on the topic and help rewrite the state rules. There's no inspiration like writing to real people for real reasons.

You can write to your student loan service center with suggestions, to your boss at the retail store about changing an exchange policy that costs the store thousands of dollars, to a local high school principal to persuade him to make driver's education a required course, to the campus facilities director to add a bus route for the dorm in the woods, to a father to persuade him not to retire from racing, to the Hallmark Company persuading them to sell Christmas jewelry you designed, to Apple Computer proposing a software registration plan that will keep prices low and prevent others from duplicating the software. These are all recent papers my students wrote—and mailed. **Going "live" can give you some of the best education you will have in college.** But do wait for peer and/or your professor's reactions before sending out your ideas.

PERSUASIVE TOPICS

When choosing a topic for persuasion, **you have basically two choices: to take a stand on an existing controversial issue or to make a proposal to solve a problem.** If you choose to take a stand, you will have the advantage of some preexisting arguments but will need to find additional arguments and examples of your own. Freshness of idea will be difficult with some topics such as pornography, nuclear power, and drug laws because most supporting arguments on *both* sides are well known. If you make a proposal of your own—a new solution to a problem—you will have to invent all your own arguments. But you will have the advantage of freshness. Proposals sound more stimulating:

- "Students with 'A' grades in a course will receive free tuition; those with 'D' or lower will pay double tuition."
- "No politician should serve more than one term in office."
- "Put a $1 per gallon tax on gasoline and use the receipts for solar research."

But proposals require more careful thinking: Can you think of a serious objection to each of these proposals as well as a positive benefit?

In career writing, of course, you will be writing proposals 98 percent of the time. Most employers pay people for new concepts and plans, not rehashing of old issues. Persuasion will be needed to convince your supervisor and colleagues, and more persuasion needed to sell clients, government agencies, customers, and other institutions. The higher you rise in your career, the more persuasive proposals you will write, and in fact, writing proposals for new ideas is one way to rise rapidly. Imagine how an employer would react to receiving proposals like these from you under your own initiative:

- We can draw more customers to the store by providing a shuttle bus service from three locations.
- Bookkeeping at the company can be simplified if we adopt the following plan. . . .
- The summer recreation program can be improved if we stagger the children's nap times and alternate quiet tasks and outdoor activities.

■ **PRACTICE 12-2:** Write a trial proposal for your employer, college, society, or family. List a few details of the plan.

■ **PRACTICE 12-3:** State your stand on three controversial issues today. We'll be developing these throughout the chapter. Try to pick ones about which you have some mixed feelings so you'll have a more honest paper.

RAISING PROBLEMS THAT MATTER

As in the preceding examples, your thesis should be stated in a single sentence, and in most persuasive writing it appears at the end of the introductory paragraph. This is not unalterable law, but it is a pattern that makes reading easier to follow. It's a mini-map for reader *and* writer. Short persuasive essays may defer the thesis until the conclusion, especially in cases when the writer finds both sides appealing. It is used less often simply because it's trickier to bring off successfully. What does the rest of the introduction do? It makes the reader care about the problem. The introduction can also establish your reasonable tone. For example, one might start the essay on "Grades and Tuition" this way:

> Teachers complain many students are unmotivated. Colleges don't figure transfer grades into one's grade-point average—"C" is good enough for credit. Many graduates wonder if working hard for a high cumulative GPA is really worth the effort when they might get a job based on their personality. Many good students just slide through with little effort, and the taxpayers foot much of the bill. Perhaps we can motivate students with something closer to home: cash.

At this point the writer has established a problem and has shown she's considered it from several angles (teachers, transfer colleges, several types of students, and taxpayers), and she probably has the reader saying something like this: "Yes, motivation is poor; what should be done about this?" In other words, **by showing us a serious problem, the writer has made the reader hungry for an answer.** Then the thesis is presented as the last sentence of the paragraph followed by the essay that supports it.

The proposal for the shuttle bus might begin this way:

> A customer who wants our product circles the store three times. Our tiny parking lot is full; street parking is full. Will that customer ever return? Unlikely. No one in the area will sell us space for parking, the city has refused to run a bus route nearby, and we have already made our employees park six blocks away. If we can shuttle them, why not our customers?

One way of starting to think about persuasive writing tasks is to raise all the problems you can about a topic—perhaps by writing a brain-teaser bug list. Much of this may turn up in your introduction.

■ **PRACTICE 12-4:** Take an issue you find important—perhaps one of your topics from Practice 12-2 or Practice 12-3—and write three or four sentences explaining why it is a tough problem. Be fair to all sides. Then, if you think there is a way to solve this problem, write a trial thesis sentence.

■ **PRACTICE 12-5:** Think about a decision you must make, writing three or four sentences explaining why it is a tough problem. At the end write a trial thesis you could defend.

■ **PRACTICE 12-6:** Pick one of the following questions and list three reasons to support a "yes" answer and three reasons to support a "no." Then take a stand, with whatever modifications to the original you need, and write a one-page essay:

- Should a woman adopt her husband's last name?
- Should government authorities have the right to torture known terrorists to get information to prevent future terrorist acts?
- Should countries that have had long religious or ethnic civil wars (such as Northern Ireland, Rwanda, and Israel) be divided into two countries?

SUPPORTING EVIDENCE

A reasonable person expects reasonable evidence before believing something. In the previous examples, you'd want to be convinced that cash motivation would work for grades: that it would be fair, that the specific economics of the plan would fly, and that it would be good for students and teachers.

Can you imagine three or four questions you'd want answered before investing in shuttle buses if you were the store's manager? **Always anticipate your audience's barriers to belief.**

When you argue persuasively, pack in as much supporting evidence as possible. Think of yourself as a lawyer convincing a jury. There are three types of evidence:

- Facts
- Appeals to values
- Logic

These are new brain teasers for persuasive writing. Make a list of all the facts you know (or need to know so you can research them later), all appeals to value you can use, and all logical arguments you can use.

 # FACTS

Statistics are one type of fact you can use to support a thesis. A proverb says, "There are two kinds of lies: regular lies and statistics." It means that statistics can be twisted to bolster weak arguments. Maier's law even says, "If the facts do not conform to the theory, they must be disposed of." This attitude may be held by less reputable advertisers or politicians, but in honest, ethical persuasion, you must be especially careful to **handle your statistics fairly and accurately.** If we say, for instance, "A recent study found that 94 percent of people surveyed believe the ban on television advertising for cigarettes is unfair," our reaction to this statistic changes if we learn it was conducted by a tobacco company in the town where its factory is located. An ethical arguer must reveal such information or not use the statistic.

The source of your fact strengthens or weakens its impact. Generally, your facts will be more credible if they are based on recent research conducted by an expert and published in a reputable journal, web site, or book. Material from *The National Enquirer,* material assembled by astrologers, or work done 30 years ago in fast-changing fields such as psychology or physics is generally not considered reliable. Even experts are not absolutely trustworthy. Lord Kelvin, Leonardo da Vinci, and Sigmund Freud all made whopping errors in their fields.

Another problem with statistics is simply making the reader *see* them clearly. Today we are bombarded with numbers: billions of dollars, millions of highway deaths, thousands of recalled products. Despite our modern sophistication, big numbers seem unreal for most people, and **the writer must help the reader see what the number means in a concrete way.** When the United States went past the $1 trillion mark of indebtedness, for instance, most people simply shrugged until one representative of Congress found a way of visualizing the statistic. He calculated that if we stacked 1 trillion $1 bills on top of each other, the pile would reach the moon! That gave people an image of $1 trillion they could visualize, and it persuaded many people to demand government action, as the representative had hoped.

Here are three facts. Which is the most visual?

- 200 million tons of dirt/rocks were dug to create the Panama Canal.
- A typical hurricane releases 50 times the energy of the first atomic bomb.
- Hoover Dam holds back 10 trillion gallons of water.

I'd pick the second example because we can see 50 atomic bombs (even if we cannot fully comprehend the impact), but without careful calculation I couldn't even tell whether 200 million tons of dirt or 10 trillion gallons of water would be the bigger volume.

■ **PRACTICE 12-7:** Take a minute to creatively visualize in words those other two facts for a reader.

■ **PRACTICE 12-8:** State two facts or statistics you know about a topic you chose for Practice 12-2 or Practice 12-3. Then help a reader creatively visualize them through a concrete comparison.

Plan on doing occasional research for persuasive writing. The facts I just gave took me five minutes to locate in a geology textbook. Statistics give authority to your persuasive voice.

Some statistics can come from your own observations. In a letter to the Vice President for Facilities Management at the State University of New York at Buffalo, a student proposed that the college expand its parking facilities. At one point, she produced her own statistics by driving around campus counting spaces:

> It may also be possible to turn parts of faculty lots into student parking, since faculty lots are seldom full. There are 27,000 students and 4,000 faculty members at UB. All 19,000 commuter students and, I estimate, one quarter of the 8,000 who live on campus drive to class. There are eight student lots on North Campus, three of which hold approximately 300 cars, five of which hold 200 cars, for a total of 1,900 spaces. Yet there are five faculty lots with a total of 1,000 spaces. On the South Campus, there are four student and two faculty lots, each accommodating 200 cars. I calculate the ratio of faculty to parking spaces is three to one and of students to student parking spaces is eight to one. After viewing the parking lots throughout the semester, I believe you can afford to transfer at least several hundred spaces to students.
>
> —*Tina C. Maenza*

There's a second kind of fact, one handy for all of us: **examples.** Use examples from (1) what you've seen; (2) what your friends and families have seen; (3) historical or current events; and (4) hypothetical cases.

If you're writing about the law that forbids those under a certain age from drinking alcohol, for instance, you probably know a dozen cases that could support either side—from firsthand experience, from what others have told you, and from the news. Everyone can dig up a couple of examples of drunken teenagers causing fatal accidents—or of drunken middle-aged people killing sober teenagers; of teenagers bribing an adult to buy illegal liquor—or of responsible teenagers arranging a designated driver who will not touch alcohol during the evening.

Historical and news stories carry more weight with a reader—she can think, "Oh yes, I remember that." It is verifiable. **Personal examples** may make the reader wonder if you've colored the facts; however, your own examples give you the chance to write vividly. You can describe the accident scene, quote dialogue from the beer party, build narrative conflict, and write with a freshness you can't with historical cases—and you should. **Examples you heard from your friends** are less satisfactory because, as lawyers say, it is "hearsay" testimony. It is one step further removed from the reader and hence less reliable. We all know truth has a way of getting watered down (or spiced up!) as it gets passed along.

Hypothetical examples are necessary to fill in gaps when facts are not available or to project future events for which there are no facts. Hypothetical examples are simply made-up cases of things *likely to happen*. In the abortion debate, for instance, several hypothetical cases are usually raised: "Suppose a woman gets pregnant through rape" or "Suppose a pregnant woman discovers the fetus is badly deformed." Both scenarios are likely to happen sometime in our society. We might be able to track down facts about actual women in these cases, but if we can't, a hypothetical example can appeal to the reader's common sense. The reader will test your common sense in explaining the hypothetical case as well. You would be on shaky ground, I think, to portray a woman pregnant through rape as a person who should forget how she became pregnant and within months develop normal maternal tenderness, or look forward to the experience of childbirth the way an intentionally pregnant woman would. There are noble people who can do this—but wouldn't you agree that they are rare? It would be equally unlikely for most normal women, even under such stress as this, to be driven to suicide should they not be allowed to have an abortion.

Facts and examples are important support for most arguments; pack plenty in your essay, and use them fairly and vividly. Rely most on firsthand experience and reliable sources. Secondhand and hypothetical examples should be used as last resorts.

■ **PRACTICE 12-9:** Use a web site to find two strong facts you could use to support your topic from Practice 12-2 or Practice 12-3. Then add three examples—yours, your friends', historical and/or hypothetical.

APPEALS TO THE READER'S VALUES

People are persuaded not only by facts but by realizing that your proposal supports *values* they believe in. Facts without a context of values seem meaningless much of the time. Amory Lovins, an energy expert, calculated in 1980 that if the United States were to take all cars off the road with gas mileage of less than 15 miles per gallon and were to replace them with cars with gas mileage of at least 35 miles per gallon, the United States could reduce its gasoline consumption by 15 percent. Ho-hum, right? Well, it becomes more interesting when Lovins reminds us today that if we reduced oil consumption 15 percent, we would have needed to import no oil from the Mideast, need station no ships in the Persian Gulf, risk no soldiers' deaths, perhaps have fewer diplomats, reporters, or businesspeople there who might be taken hostage. This puts the fact about gas mileage into a values context.

Some values that writers consider in persuasive writing are *economics, fairness, health, safety, love, environmental impact, freedom, beauty.* As Abraham Maslow showed in his hierarchy of needs, certain basic needs must be met before people are willing to consider others. We are, therefore, unlikely to consider an appeal to our sense of beauty (put up a gorgeous city sculpture that will delight our minds) if the project will bankrupt us or be dangerous for children to play on. Maslow said we must have safety and basic physical needs met before we strive for "higher" values such as fairness and freedom. After we achieve *them,* Maslow argued, humans will give priority to love, beauty, and spiritual matters. Here is a simplified list of Maslow's values, starting with the most basic:

- Physiological (food, shelter, water, health)
- Safety (security, order, stability)
- Belongingness and love (family, friends, social groups)
- Esteem (status, power, recognition, money)
- Self-actualization (reaching your *individual* potential; for example, oneness with God, nature, or lover; creativity, justice, beauty, and freedom)

Maslow was being descriptive of how he saw people behave, not how he thought they *ought* to behave. By contrast, most philosophies and religions insist spiritual values are more important than, say, status, recognition, or even safety. People like Martin Luther King, Jr., or Mahatma Gandhi, as well as millions of unknown people, have put justice, freedom, creativity, or love above personal health, safety, and status.

You will have to decide for yourself if Maslow is right about what values motivate people the most. Would *you,* for instance, bulldoze a beautiful neighborhood park for an industrial plant if it meant secure jobs for your family? Would most people? Germany, where most wilderness has been devastated, values nature preserves more than Brazil, which is burning down its vast tropical rain forest for industry in hopes of improving its people's standard of living—what it sees as a higher value. One of the more interesting aspects of persuasive writing is dealing with the changing, conflicting values of people and groups.

A student of mine served several hitches in the U.S. Navy SEALS. This young man had been in Lebanon when a terrorist drove a truck filled with explosives into a Marine barracks, killing nearly 300 men. He vowed revenge. In one paper he announced he was going into counterterrorist activity so he could torture terrorists and kill them. He described in vivid, gory detail what he would do to his country's enemies and concluded by saying, "I'm doing this so my future children can grow up in a decent, moral world." What hierarchy of values does he hold? Do you agree?

■ **PRACTICE 12-10:** Make a list of *your* most important eight to ten values, trying to include several not already listed here. Star the two or three values you think are most important.

In practical terms, the persuasive writer might start thinking about defending a proposal by going down a checklist of values, asking how each value can suggest new arguments to support his position. It's another brain teaser. Suppose I am proposing that my state outlaw legal gambling and close betting parlors. The list of values below is written so you can use it as a brain teaser to think up support for many topics.

- What *economic* benefits will my position have? For whom? How much?
- Will it increase people's *security or satisfy basic needs?*
- Is it *fair* to all parties involved? Think through—one at a time—how various people might see it.
- Will it enhance or limit anyone's *freedom?*
- How will my plan affect *families?*
- Will my plan appeal to the reader's concern for *beauty?*
- Will my plan affect the *environment?*
- Will my plan build *self-esteem or status* for anyone? Who? Why?
- How might this help people *actualize their potential?*
- List *other values* of importance to yourself. How can they be appealed to by your proposal?

■ **PRACTICE 12-11:** Go through this list to see what support it triggers to ban legalized betting. Some questions will lead nowhere; just move on.

For example, let me respond to the first question. Outlawing gambling may prevent some bettors from losing (or winning) money, but I suspect many would then bet illegally. This would actually increase the gambler's odds of economic success because the government keeps a higher percentage of money bet than bookies do. Outlawing gambling would deprive the state of this money and perhaps cause taxes to rise. If other states don't ban gambling, my state may lose some tourist dollars as well. I realize now I need to research how much is spent in my state on the lottery and horse racing and how much the state keeps.

Here's another example. An 18-year-old student of mine wrote to persuade her parents to rent her (at less than half price) one of the apartments they owned. Vera admitted to our class that privacy, freedom, and fun were the values that interested her most in this proposal. But in her letter, she appealed to her *parents'* needs—how her moving out would benefit *them*. She would no longer mess up their apartment. She wouldn't disturb *them* when she came home late or when her friends phoned at one A.M.; it would give *them* more room for their younger children; it would teach Vera self-reliance to give *them* more freedom; life for *them* would be more peaceful when clashes with Vera stopped; and finally Vera would do better in school because the children and television would not interrupt her homework. Thus, she would get her degree sooner, save her parents money, and become a success they'd be proud of. Let's see—she hit status, economics, environment, freedom, and self-actualization. Vera's parents, as you might guess, saw through the "advantages" to them and said "no" anyway. Why? Because they agreed with Maslow that safety is more important. And while I admired Vera's cleverness, it was too obvious a ploy.

■ **PRACTICE 12-12:** Try the same list (and perhaps your own high-ranked values) with these proposals, looking for support:

- The United Nations ought to be given command of a permanent, powerful military force.
- Evolution ought to be the only creation theory taught in public schools.
- Churches should pay property taxes.
- The Internet must be censored for pornography and dangerous information such as bomb instructions.

■ **PRACTICE 12-13:** Use the same list to create more supporting arguments for your topic from Practice 12-2 or Practice 12-3. Try to create at least six arguments that appeal to values on the list.

   A good persuasive letter targets the needs and values of the person you address. It's not enough to show how your idea will benefit you or society. How will it benefit your reader? Vera, who wanted her parents to give her an apartment, tried to do this. She looked at the value list through her readers' eyes. But she needed to look at *all* the list. Can you think of a way of allaying her parents' concern over safety? If you want a more relaxed dress code at the upscale men's clothing store where you work, it's not enough to appeal to the employees' comfort. Your boss cares about profits and a classy atmosphere to attract upscale clientele. Can you appeal to that value? This does not mean you have to be dishonest and pander to your reader. It means you have to see how your reader will see your ideas. You might, for instance, suggest that the salespeople could wear the upscale casual wear sold in the store—modeling it as they work. You might focus on today's more relaxed styles and suggest that old-fashioned white shirts and ties make the store look stodgy. Any other ideas?

LOGIC

Logic alone rarely persuades people, but it draws together facts and appeals to values. In its simplest form logic takes one fact (the minor premise) and one value (the major premise) and shows that if they both are true, a reasonable conclusion drawn from them must also be true. Let's take an example.

Suppose I want to persuade people that abortion is morally wrong and ought to be illegal. To do this I present a value—killing a human being is morally wrong and illegal. Then I present a fact—that a fetus is a human being. If these two are true, then the conclusion is inevitable: Killing a fetus is wrong and should be illegal. Someone who disagreed with me, however, might argue that one or both of these premises are *not* true. With the abortion issue, people usually question whether a fetus is really a human being. Do you see how the logic of my claim disintegrates if that "fact" is proved false? The opposition might also question my other premise by pointing out that killing humans *is* morally or legally acceptable in a number of circumstances. Can you name some?

Logic, then, is rarely perfect. One or both of the premises can be questioned. There are about a dozen common flaws writers fall into when using logic. We call these "logical fallacies" because they make any argument that uses them invalid. They are forms of dishonest persuasion. Here are nine of the **most common logical fallacies.**

1. **Endorsement.** Michael Jordan likes a certain hamburger. The commercial claims you will like it too. A doctor on a TV show recommends a particular kind of coffee. Are you persuaded to buy it? Obviously we suspect that these people's recommendations are strongly influenced by what they are paid. But the endorsement's fallacy isn't really lying, but logic. There is no necessary connection between the tastes of one person and another. Had a genuine doctor recommended a coffee for its health effects, we might have had a stronger case. An athlete endorsing a hamburger is far less effective than an athlete endorsing sneakers. In such cases there should also be an explanation of *why* the product or viewpoint is correct. Does the hamburger use the highest quality meat, cost less, or avoid dangerous preservatives? These are the real issues. This applies to experts you may quote in your papers as well. It's not enough to say Abraham Maslow or Rachel Carson believed something. For the reader's understanding you also need to explain how the theory works or what the facts are.

2. **Hasty Generalization.** I hate Professor Smith. My friends in the class hate him. Therefore, Professor Smith must be an unpopular teacher. Sorry. You need more evidence. Several students from a class of 25 are too few to support such a claim. Perhaps your group is on Professor Smith's bad side because of poor performance or attitude. How about this: The Democrats always start America's big wars—Democrats were presidents when Vietnam, Korea, and World Wars I and II started. This is also hasty generalization—can you explain why? A hasty generalization means you base a conclusion or claim on too few examples or oversimplified evidence. You can overcome this in your essays by deluging your reader with cases and examples.

3. **Bandwagon.** This is similar to the endorsement, except that instead of picking a prominent person who supports your claim, you say your position must be right because many people support it. There's a quick cure for this fallacy: Just remind yourself how many millions of people thought Hitler and Mussolini were saviors. Closer to home, remind yourself how President Richard Nixon won a landslide election and resigned a year later for dishonest and illegal activities. Was his presidency justified because so many people supported him? No. What makes an argument right is that it *is right*, not that millions of people *believe* it's right. Your job is to show how it's right, not how it's popular.

4. **Tradition.** "It's always been done this way" or "My parents taught me to believe. . . ." This is a cop-out from thinking. You're hiding behind someone else's thinking instead of walking the reader through the arguments themselves. There's a quick reminder you can use if you're tempted to rely on this fallacy: Suppose the first human beings one million years ago had latched onto this principle: "We've always eaten our meat raw and slept in trees. No fire, no caves!"

Traditional beliefs prevent people from rushing to each wild, untested idea that floats along, but just because a belief once may have been valid does not mean it still is. Tradition fights new good ideas as well as bad ones.

5. **Unqualified Generalization.** In our enthusiasm for a claim we sometimes exaggerate: "Television game shows are the worst thing for our children's minds today." Really? Worse than pornography? Worse than fighting parents? Worse than an abusive teacher? A statement like the previous one shows the person has simply not thought through the idea. *Qualifying makes it more acceptable.* "Television game shows are bad for children's minds." It is now no longer at the head of a list of *everything* bad. You could also say, "*Some* TV game shows *may* harm a child's mind as badly as pornography." The reader cannot toss these away at first reading—she must first see how you support such a view. Avoid words like "all," "always," "never," "nobody in her right mind," or "everyone." Use considered words like "most people," "usually," or "under normal circumstances."

6. **Faulty Cause and Effect.** This means claiming one thing caused another to happen when the only tangible relationship between the two things is that one preceded the other. You may be able to prove the one did indeed cause the other, but a simple time relationship alone does not. "My parents got divorced after I was born. Therefore, I broke up their marriage." Or, "Every time I get a day off, it rains." Or, "The family has deteriorated in the past 20 years—since feminism became strong. That proves how harmful feminism has been to America." None of these holds water as complete arguments. In the first case you need to prove that your parents' marriage was solid before you came along and that you were the key problem in arguments your parents might have had. In the second, you'd have to establish that meteorological powers

infuse your body on a day off. With the antifeminist statement, think of all the competing explanations for why the family has deteriorated: decline in church-going, increased violence, increased sexual activity outside of marriage, increased drug use, increased materialism, worse public morals, a more highly mobile society. All three cases need to show a *connection* between cause and effect.

7. **Sentimentality.** This means pleading a cause based on your feelings (usually misery) rather than on its merits. "You've got to give me a 'C' in this course or I won't graduate"; "You can't withdraw me for absences; I'll lose my state aid." Sorry. The grade in a course says you have performed at a certain level, and your misery at not doing well should not persuade a professor your merit is greater than it is. Your state aid is given assuming you will attend class; you earn it by attending and performing at an acceptable level. "A promotion will make me so happy!" By itself, not good enough. The logical questions are: Did you earn it? Do you show potential?

8. **Attacking Your Opponent.** Instead of attacking a position, value, or fact to advance your case, you attack the person who made the proposal. "Don't support President Bush's plan to reform business ethics; he did the same corrupt things before he was president." To a fair-minded reader, this is con artistry. The bill and its sponsor are two separate issues, and the plan should be discussed on its own merits. How about these cases; are they valid criticisms?

   - "We should not elect Al Gore president; he was vice president for Bill Clinton."

   - "We shouldn't do business with the Captain Computer Company; its head salesman smokes pot."

9. **Either . . . Or.** "Either we enact the president's plan or the economy will not recover." "We should either marry or break up." The "or" part of these statements *may* happen if we don't do the first part, but there are lots of other possibilities, too. We can compromise on the president's plan and on dating less seriously. The economy (and our love life) may go downhill for a while, then recover on its own. There may be several creative alternatives. "Either . . . or" limits the possibilities to only two choices when there are many. People who want you to be either for or against gun control, drug legalization, or abortion and who refuse to notice gray areas, compromise, and alternatives are falsifying the issue to make it a choice between good and evil. Most of the time, things are just not that way.

■ **PRACTICE 12-14:** Think of two arguments that infuriate you: political, parental, peer, or commercial statements. Now, using the fallacies as a guide, expose the logical flaws in these arguments.

■ **PRACTICE 12-15:** What is one argument supporting your topic from Practice 12-2 or Practice 12-3 that seems to rely on a logical fallacy? It will be easier to find an opposition argument, but be honest enough to look for one on your side.

An Example of Support and Logic

In the following selection from a student essay, Candace Northrup proposes that we ought to allow doctors to prescribe marijuana for medical purposes under strict hospital supervision. Here is one of her support paragraphs:

> Marijuana has been shown to help people with many illnesses. For glaucoma patients, marijuana reduces fluid pressure in the eye that causes the person to lose vision. AIDS patients use marijuana to increase appetite and decrease nausea. Some multiple sclerosis patients claim marijuana improves their motor functions and reduces muscle spasms and pain (Dickinson 135). Healthy people may not realize the pain these patients endure. My aunt, who has multiple sclerosis, can barely walk because the pain eats away at her. If marijuana was legal, she would suffer less.

Commentary: This scores high for packing specifics into a short paragraph. By listing the benefits of pot for three types of sufferers, Candace shows the issue affects many people. If she had mentioned only one of the diseases, it would lack punch. Notice also that Candace explains *how* pot helps each disease–giving her authority as a persuader and educating her audience. She appeals to the **values** of health and fear from pain, but also makes an **emotional appeal** to the reader's pity for the sufferers. The concluding example of her aunt personalizes the medical facts.

Candace's essay next raises several **refutations:**

> How many people already use marijuana for medical purposes? One researcher says, "Six hundred thousand people now have criminal records because marijuana is not legal for medical use"; as a result, California and Arizona have passed initiatives approving the medical use of marijuana (Ziegler 70). So the government has been forced to look at the issue. Yet General Barry McCaffrey, head of drug policy, was quoted as saying, "Just when the nation is trying its hardest to educate teenagers not to use drugs, now they are being told that marijuana is medicine. There could not be a worse message to young people" (Stiefell 9).
>
> This is one argument against legalizing marijuana—that children will see it as medicine and might think it is all right to smoke for recreation. As a teenager, I don't see that threat. Marijuana was around my small town. Legalizing marijuana for medical purposes is not going to cause much increase in teen usage. I don't see where General McCaffrey gets off saying, "The nation is trying its hardest to educate children on drugs . . ." because I haven't seen much education from the government. Even if we were educated, would it really stop the use of marijuana? Teenagers are curious and oblivious to the world. If teens have their minds set on smoking marijuana, then they are going to smoke it. Even though General McCaffrey opposes medical use of marijuana, the government recently agreed to spend $1 million to look into it (Stiefell 10).

Another question often raised is why legalize marijuana if THC, the main ingredient, is already being prescribed? THC is available as a legal pill (Brookhiser 28). Unfortunately, the pill can take hours to begin working. Smoked marijuana is effective within minutes (Dickinson 135). Second, treating nausea with a pill is not the brightest idea because nauseated patients may not be able to keep the pill in the stomach long enough for it to begin working. One report found that "Oral THC is metabolized through the liver, which neutralizes more than 90 percent of the chemical; smoking delivers the THC—as well as sixty other unsynthesized cannabinoids, many of which are therapeutic too—directly to the bloodstream" (Dickinson 135). Marijuana also seems safer than oral THC. The DEA's own administrative judge, Francis L. Young, declared, "Marijuana is one of the safest therapeutically active substances known to man" (Dickinson 135).

Commentary: The first two paragraphs fairly raise an objection based on the consequences to youth of legalizing pot, but Candace falls into three fallacies in responding: unqualified generalization, bandwagon, and attacking one's opponent. The unqualified generalizations occur in her description of teenagers as "oblivious to the world." Qualifiers like "some" or "many" or examples are needed.

■ **PRACTICE 12-16:** Find the bandwagon and attacking one's opponent fallacies.

Candace's third paragraph raises another refutation: Why not prescribe the chemical in pot without legalizing pot? This is a good objection and one many readers may not have heard. An unethical arguer might have ignored it. She does a fine job of responding with facts to refute this objection, providing details of why smoked pot works better for sufferers. At the end of the paragraph—when she quotes a DEA official to contradict the DEA position—is this an endorsement fallacy or a valid point?

Now look at Candace's **sources:**

Works Cited

Brookhiser, Richard. "Pot Luck: Any Sick Person Who Wants to Use Marijuana to Help Himself Has to Break the Law." *National Review* 11 Nov. 1996: 27–28.

Dickinson, Ben. "What If Weed Is Exactly What You Need?" *Esquire* Oct. 1997: 134–35.

Stiefell, Chana Frieman. "Marijuana on the Ballot: Should a Menacing Drug Treat Some Chronically Ill Patients?" *Science World* 21 Feb. 1997: 8–10.

Ziegler, Jan. "Up in Smoke." *Hospitals and Health Networks* 20 June 1997: 70+.

The first source is politically conservative, the second liberal, and the last two scientific/medical. Should we care? Does her list of sources create a stronger image of the writer?

STRUCTURING THE PERSUASIVE ESSAY

If you have the time and creativity to invent your own persuasive structure, do it. But over 2000 years from Roman orators to today's editorialists, one model structure stands out.

Not only does this model help you organize your ideas, but also it generates new ideas and makes sure you cover key aspects of any persuasive presentation. The four-part structure is Introduction, Main Supporting Ideas, Refutation, and Conclusion.

The **introduction** should begin by intriguing us with a concrete problem that is difficult to solve and end with your solution to this problem, your thesis. You establish a reasonable, ethical, knowledgeable tone here by showing the reader your familiarity with several issues involved.

The introduction should also outline in detail exactly what you are proposing. *Explain* how your plan will work, define key terms, who will do what, how it will be funded, what the timetable or stages are. Before you defend it, show the reader exactly what you propose. A complex plan may require several paragraphs to explain. Don't skimp here!

The main supporting evidence should be arranged tightly, one paragraph or perhaps two for each main supporting idea, and the paragraphs filled out with examples, facts, appeals to value, and logic that support the idea. Study how Candace's paper does this. In papers of three to five typed pages, you should have room to develop three to four supporting ideas. In papers of one to two pages, two supporting ideas may be all you can support in depth.

To outline, list the main arguments and fill in support from brain teasers under each. Try several scratch outlines until your main headings are crisp and distinct. The Roman orators believed support should start strong and end strong and that the less strong arguments should be in the middle. Their rule of thumb: Second strongest argument comes first, strongest comes last, and the others in the middle. If you have a flimsy argument, put that in your wastebasket.

■ **PRACTICE 12-17:** Drawing on your notes from other practices, make a scratch outline of your main supporting ideas for your topic in Practice 12-2 or Practice 12-3.

The **refutation** comes next in the paper. After raising your main supporting ideas, take time to **consider one or two major objections someone might have against your views or proposal.** Some people may ask "Why should I attack my own case?" Why indeed? Well, in a written persuasive paper, as contrasted with a debate, you have total control over the presentation of ideas; no one can raise questions about your ideas—*except the reader!* And believe me, when someone is trying to persuade a person, she or he will raise objections. Most people love to find reasons why things cannot be done. Hiding weaknesses in your position won't work with a good reader. So be honest. Also, by considering objections, you can modify and improve your ideas to be more convincing. It's not only honest but in your best interest as an arguer and will help you improve your ideas. As John Locke once observed, "To judge other men's notions before we have looked into them is not to show their darkness, but to put out our own eyes."

In the refutation section, **one strategy is to show how the objection is flawed.** You must state opposition ideas with full honesty—so it would satisfy the opposition. Present these as valid questions, not as pesty troublemakers. Then, pinpoint *fallacies* in the objection, correct *"facts"* the objection may have mistaken, or question the *values* in the objection. In other words, the same brain teasers used to create support can also create refutations to an objection.

Suppose you have written an essay defending television, saying it contributes much to American culture and is a great educational tool. In your refutation section, you must consider objections people might have to your view. One objection would be that television watching has caused a decline in children's ability to read. This contradicts your claim of television's educational value. To be an honest arguer, you might point out that children do seem to watch television more than they read books; perhaps you might acknowledge that reading scores on standard tests have declined steadily in the past 15 years. How do you refute this now? **Begin by seeing if the objection falls into a logical fallacy.** Faulty cause and effect, for instance, seems to apply. Just because a decline in reading scores followed an increase in television watching does not prove one caused another. We have had Republican presidents most of the past 50 years; can we claim *they* caused a decline in reading scores? Of course not. In refuting, you should also suggest possible causes of the decline other than television. Perhaps the schools aren't teaching reading the best way; perhaps school discipline problems disrupt the teaching of reading; perhaps the lack of family togetherness (reading aloud after supper, discussing the newspaper) has contributed. Perhaps today society as a whole values reading less.

Question the facts. Perhaps the reading tests are outdated. Do the lowest test scorers watch the most television, or do the best readers also watch television? You can get examples from your classmates or perhaps do some quick research. You can also **question the values** behind the objection. You might argue it's too easy to blame a machine for our problems as a society when we ought to blame ourselves for not working hard enough to learn, support, and teach reading.

A second way of handling a refutation is to concede some truth to the objection. "Television has probably contributed somewhat to a decline in reading ability. However. . . ." *Then* writers usually say despite this drawback, there are too many good reasons to let this one objection stand in the way. This is often the only solution where there is no compromise possible, usually because of moral issues. If you were in favor of allowing abortions, for instance, you may have to concede that aborting a fetus really is the taking of a human or potentially human life. You might even acknowledge this would be wrong in a perfect world, but that the misery an unwanted or deformed child endures is worse yet.

Another type of concession offers compromises. People who are against abortions, for instance, might reluctantly agree that a woman in danger of dying in childbirth may be granted an abortion. But they should probably add that the principle of the sanctity of human life is still not compromised—that the taking of a life is to save a life.

The refutation section of a persuasive essay is perhaps the most important; it establishes your integrity as a writer, it forces you to consider your thesis more deeply, and it gives you the chance to make your argument even stronger. Refutation may be placed in a separate section of the essay, or you may handle it as objections might be raised against your supporting points.

■ **PRACTICE 12-18:** Raise two objections to one of these proposals (from Practice 12-11) and then see if you can refute the objections through logical fallacies, facts, or values:

- The United Nations ought to command a permanent, powerful military force.
- Evolution should be the only creation theory taught in public schools.
- Churches should pay property taxes.
- The Internet must be censored for pornography and dangerous information.

■ **PRACTICE 12-19:** What two major objections might someone raise to your position in Practice 12-2 or Practice 12-3? Refute them with logic, values, or facts; concede; or compromise.

The **conclusion** in persuasive writing can be a simple reaffirmation of your thesis, but it's usually better to look forward. You might paint a picture of the world in which your plan is enacted, or you might paint a picture of how less effective plans than yours would affect people's lives. Or you might end with a dramatic statistic or example.

Drafting and Revising Persuasive Writing: Refresh yourself by reviewing "Steps in Writing a Paper" inside the front cover and in Chapters 6–7.

InfoTrac® College Edition: Readings on Persuasion

For tips on using *InfoTrac®* College Edition, see page 464.

Philip Vassallo. "Persuading Powerfully: Tips for Writing Persuasive Documents." *ETC.: A Review of General Semantics.* Spring 2002.

Writing business proposals: tips on audience, openings, fallacies, and endings.

Noelle C. Nelson. "Get Your Way Using Lawyers' Techniques." *Executive Female.* July–Aug. 1997.

Persuading like a lawyer.

Highlights of Chapter 12

- To find a persuasive topic, use a bug list, fantasy, or ask questions. To develop your argument, use the special brain teasers for persuasion, making a list of facts (including all the examples, statistics, and hypothetical examples you can think of, as well as from research you do) and making a list of values supporting your proposal. To develop the refutation, you need to see from alternative viewpoints and then use fallacies, facts, and values to break down the objections.

- The traditional order for persuasive writing is introduction, support, refutation, and conclusion.

- While drafting your persuasive paper, write a concrete, problem-solving introduction, adopt a reasonable, honest tone (be a host, not a preacher), speak to your audience, and visualize statistics and examples.

- In revising your persuasive paper, ask if the thesis is clear, if there is sufficient support, if you fall into any logical fallacies, if your audience would object to anything, and if you are being fair and reasonable. Test your word use to qualify generalizations and eliminate extremist language.

Writing Suggestions and Class Discussions

1. a. Make a list of five topics you could develop into persuasive essays. Try for a mix of personal, career, and social issues. Choose topics that matter to you.

   b. Develop one of these into a proposal, explaining your plan.

   c. Use several brain-teaser lists to develop supporting ideas and details. Begin developing a refutation idea.

   d. Order the essay in a scratch outline.

   e. Draft and revise the essay.

2. Complete the following, and bring it to a peer review workshop or conference with your professor:

Quick Guide to Creating Persuasive Writing

Identify a Problem You'd Like Solved (Try a Bug List Brain Teaser)

List 3–4 Possible Solutions for the Problem
   1.
   2.
   3.
   4.

Choose One (Your Trial Thesis)

List Three Reasons to Agree with Your Proposal:
   1.
   2.
   3.

List Two Possible Objections to Your Proposal That Someone Might Raise:
   1.
   2.

How Might You Answer These Objections or How Can You Modify Your Proposal to Satisfy These Objections?

Why Is One Other Possible Solution Inferior to the One You Chose?

---

3. Read the letters-to-the-editor section of several papers and pick out an example of a letter with an appealing tone and a letter whose tone put you off. Explain why one works and why the other doesn't. Bring the letters to class.

4. Write a tell-off letter to someone you know or to a person in the news about an idea they hold that you don't accept. Be sarcastic, abusive, snotty, and personal to attack this person's idea. Let it rip! Be a nightmare. *Then,* rewrite the letter as good argument, as though hundreds of calm, unbiased, decent people have come to listen respectfully to you.

5. Write an introductory paragraph for a paper on teenage sex. Your job is to show the reader how difficult the problem is to solve and also how important it is to solve. Establish a tentative thesis by the end of the paragraph.

6. List a page of statistics, examples, and hypothetical examples that could be used to support one of these theses:

   - Baseball is America's most exciting game.
   - Most white people have little idea what subtle discrimination most minorities suffer in an average day.
   - The rules of normal life are suspended once you enlist in the armed services.
   - Raising a child isn't as sweet as many people believe.
   - High school is a time of continual humiliation for many students.
   - Old age can be the best time of a person's life.

7. a   Make a list of the *ten* values you hold highest. This will be a brain-teaser resource for persuasive papers.

   b.   Use this list to support or refute the following proposals:

   "The CIA should assassinate known terrorist leaders."

   "Gay or lesbian teachers should not be hired in elementary schools."

   "Public television stations ought to be supported by a special tax of $50 on all television sets sold."

8. What *values* would you use to support these two statements?

   "I am a citizen of the world."

   —Socrates, Greek philosopher

   "I have no responsibility to save the world."

   —Richard Feynman, Nobel Prize winner in physics

9. Write examples to illustrate five fallacies. These can be real or made up. Label each example with the fallacy it demonstrates.

10. Pick out a magazine or newspaper advertisement, and write a paragraph explaining a fallacy in logic in the ad.

11. If you could change one historical event, what would it be? For examples, have Jesus not be crucified or warn the United States of the surprise attack on Pearl Harbor. Speculate on the hypothetical effects this change would have; then defend your change by appeals to value.

12. Write a response to an editorial in the local or college newspaper. Respectfully disagree with the author. In your introductory paragraph, accurately and fairly present the author's views; then work on refuting logic, facts, and/or values.

13. Write a one-paragraph letter to persuade your mother you really are working hard at college. Help her visualize the amount of work you're doing by making the statistics (number of pages read, papers done, hours studying, and so on) more visual.

14. Write a personal letter to a family member or friend to persuade that person to change his or her mind about a personal issue. See the sample student letter on page 261.

15. Write a one-page letter to yourself, persuading yourself to reform some habit or trait you know is wrong. Be sure to consider a refutation.

16. Write a one-page persuasive essay on some subject of college policy. You will be expected to send a copy to the student newspaper.

17. Write a letter persuading a company to change its television advertisement that you find offensive. Address it to the Public Relations Department and provide a stamped envelope so your professor can mail it.

18. Write a newspaper or Internet advertisement to sell a product you like. Use facts, values, and logic, and be ethical.

19. Write a letter to any bureaucratic official, persuading him or her to change some policy or activity you don't like.

20. Write a proposal to your employer to solve a company problem. After revision, send it to your supervisor.

21. Write a proposal of your own—some new idea that would solve a current problem—and defend it.

22. The United States has just discovered a $100 billion vein of gold on federal property and Congress is debating whether to use the money (1) for increased antiterrorist units; (2) to lower the national debt; (3) for space exploration; or (4) to feed starving people in developing nations. Use Maslow's list of needs/values and make up a *list of arguments* based on those values for the plan you would support.

23. Read and discuss the sample student persuasive writings in Chapter 15.

24. Write a job application letter for yourself. Apply for an actual job you want now or imagine one you will want after graduation. Honestly sell yourself by referring to your main accomplishments, skills, experience, and personal qualities. If there is an obvious refutation (your lack of experience, for instance), answer it.

25. Group Activity: Open Hearing. The class will be divided into four groups. Each will develop its own proposal to solve a local or college problem, doing research and brain teasing for supporting facts, values, and logical arguments. Each group will present its plan to the rest of the class in an open hearing for feedback: refutations, suggestions for additional research, new ideas. Then each student will write a persuasive paper on the topic.

26. Group Activity: Bring to your peer group a thesis and two or three main supporting ideas for a persuasive paper. Each member of your group will role-play a person or group who is likely to have a strong view about your proposal and express how that person or group might argue for or against your thesis.

27. Group Activity: Predict the arguments the following groups would make about this proposal: "The Internet must not be censored in any way."

   - A parent of school-age children
   - A Chinese pro-democracy leader
   - A white supremacist militia man
   - An FBI official
   - A wheelchair-confined person

Sample Student Persuasive Letter

22 Anyplace Road

Rushville, NY 14544

June 14, 2003

Eileen N. Iannuzi

Director of Student Loans

Sallie Mae Corporation

Loan Servicing Center

Box 352

Waltham, MA 12534

Dear Ms. Iannuzi:

Recently while contacting your agency concerning the status of my loan, I was told by several unknown voices, "No, I'm sorry. We have no record of that conversation taking place that day. . . . We can't release any information to you unless you are the authorized party. . . . I'll send you another form immediately." These nameless voices who know little about my account create a frustrating communication barrier almost every time I call.

anecdote to draw interest

continues

thesis

I would like to suggest three changes to increase cooperation and communication between the loan holder and the Loan Servicing Center.

point 1

First, please consider documenting all calls concerning an account, so your representatives will know more about the callers. I have called the center many times to inquire about changes in my loan since Chase Manhattan transferred my loans to Sallie Mae. Consistently being told there was no record of any previous conversations with your agents irritates me. Documenting the date, time, and matter of each call could eliminate further confusion and frustration for both your agents and the loan holders.

point 2

refutation 1

Second, you should establish *joint accounts* for loan holders so other family members can receive information. For example, I have called several times to check on my parents' loan, since I will be the one to pay it back. But I am often told no one except my father can receive certain account information. Your representatives have an obligation to keep financial information private; yet the loan holder could sign a release of information to other parties. The company would benefit by not having to wait so long to receive important papers when other parties are involved.

point 3

Finally, why not assign one agent to each account? Having one agent follow an account would decrease mix-ups and lost information. Within the past six months, I have spoken with a dozen different agents concerning my loans. Frequently, because these agents know little about my account, they just send me another form to fill out. One authorized agent with knowledge could check his or her records for definite answers.

refutation 2

I recognize Sallie Mae handles a tremendous number of loans and can see how easy it might be to confuse, misplace, or lose valuable information. These ideas might help. The cost would be minimal to activate these ideas. You would lower mailing costs since there would be fewer forms sent out, and hours spent on the phone would be drastically reduced.

The growing cost of higher education continues to astound college students, and loan agencies like Sallie Mae that relieve the pressure need to be more efficient. Open lines of communication between agents and loan holders, joint information request forms and recorded conversations could help eliminate confusion and frustration and give peace of mind to worried college students. Thank you for your time and consideration.   *conclusion*

Sincerely,

Amy Meritt

Amy Meritt

Commentary

Introduction: The anonymous, bureaucratic voices draw us into the paper. The thesis in paragraph 2 is direct, but unspecific. We must read the entire letter to learn her three points. So I'm glad she uses clear markers like "second" to keep us on track Her plan could be more specific in point 1—how would these calls be documented? Tapes? Notes written by the agent?

Tone: The author is "irritated," yet avoids abuse or sarcasm. She makes "suggestions," not demands.

Ideas: Is it a fresh idea? I'd never heard of this problem. But as a topic, I wonder how many people aside from students with loans will be interested.

The audience: It is directly targeted and several times she shows sympathy for the corporation.

The number of arguments: Three points and a refutation are fine for a short letter. The power of the arguments was good, but not highly creative. Why not computer access?

Details: Supporting facts: Her support needs more "oomph." Perhaps add an example from a friend's experience?

Visualization of facts: Recreating actual conversations makes her reader see better.

Values appealed to: Cooperation, communication, efficiency, accuracy, economics, and peace of mind. I particularly like the way she stressed that the loan company and students' interests are linked through shared values.

Logic: I saw no blatant fallacies. She might have fallen into sentiment (parading her suffering), but doesn't. She avoids unqualified generalizations by saying *"almost* every time I call" (not "every time") and "voices who know *little* about my account" (not *"nothing* about my account"). I'd ask her to specify how often she received the run-around—to prove it's not hasty generalization.

Refutation: The essay raises two refutations, but only the first is well answered. In paragraph 4 she concedes that "your representatives have an obligation to keep financial information private." She breaks this objection by suggesting her father be allowed to sign a release and by appealing to efficiency (the corporation would receive forms faster if the author could fill them out).

The next-to-last paragraph acknowledges the "tremendous number" of loans the corporation handles. She's polite, but has not deeply visualized an agent's job. Could one agent remember details of several thousand loans? I suspect these telephone agents don't stay long on this job—would she be dealing with new people anyway just from turnover? Wouldn't delays be longer if you had to get to just one agent instead of the first open line?

The strongest aspects of this essay are its tone and organization.

I'd suggest building up the details and going deeper into the second refutation.

Sample Persuasive Essay

Homosexuals Adopting Children

Kerry Burton

In some states gays and lesbians are allowed to marry legally. In this country, homosexuals should be free to live as they choose, but children should not be involved. Homosexual couples, married or not, should not be allowed to adopt children.

Even in our modern age, homosexuality is still taboo. People laugh and say, "God created Adam and Eve, not Adam and Adam." When Ellen Degeneres, the sitcom actress, came out of the closet, it was a big deal, a TV "event." But homosexuals adopting kids is more serious. A study was done by British researchers to see if there was a significant difference in the sexual orientation of kids raised by homosexual versus heterosexual parents. They monitored 46 young people over 16 years. Among the lesbian mothers, 23 kids were straight and 2 gay. Among heterosexual mothers, 21 kids were straight, none gay (Dunlap 15). This could be interpreted two ways. If you do not support homosexuals as parents, those two kids who turned out gay are significant. When kids are raised with gay parents, that's what they see and what becomes normal to them. But in our society, homosexuality is not normal. If you support homosexuals adopting kids, you might think two kids out of 46 is not significant and may be what you'd find if all the kids were raised by heterosexual parents.

Everywhere you turn, people are saying how wrong homosexuality is. One of the biggest reasons I think it is wrong is that kids need a mother and a father. Sometimes it can't be helped if kids grow up without a mother or father, but with homosexuals adopting kids, it can be helped. Times are hard enough with the social issues today's kids must cope with: popularity, peer pressure, drugs, alcohol, and violence. Why would any homosexual adult add to a child's pressure by adopting him or her? Imagine the ridicule that kid will endure in school. In one story I read, a mother had to give up her son for adoption. But when she discovered that her son was going to be adopted by a gay couple, she tried to reverse the adoption. She said, "Every child needs a mother and a father" ("Mother" 8). For this

continues

reason and others, adoptions by homosexuals are prohibited in Florida and New Hampshire ("Mother" 8).

This issue is difficult and controversial. Many studies prove that you do not have a choice to be gay; it is already built into your DNA when you are born. It would not matter if you are raised by straight parents, gay parents, or a pack of wolves—there would be no influence on your sexual orientation. One might also ask if it really matters if a kid has a mother and a father as long as the kid is truly loved. If a homosexual couple loves a child unconditionally and wants it strongly, they should make excellent parents. Many kids today do not have two parents who love them like that. Perhaps a homosexual couple could substitute a friend or family member to supply the missing role of the opposite sex. Of course those homosexuals who do get pregnant or get someone pregnant should be permitted to raise their biological children.

But only heterosexuals should adopt kids. A kid's life is tough these days. Why should we make it harder on them? It's not fair to do it for the selfish reason of wanting a child.

Works Cited

Dunlap, David W. "Homosexual Parents Raising Children." *New York Times*. 7 Jan. 1996, Sec. 1: 15.

"Mother Fights Son's Adoption by Homosexuals." *New York Times*. 1 Jan. 1994, Sec. 1: 8.

Discussion

Evaluate this essay as persuasion, using the **Peer Review Checklist** on page 269 as your guide. Other student persuasive writings can be found on pages 261–266.

InfoTrac® **College Edition:**
Readings that Persuade

For tips on using *InfoTrac*® College Edition, see page 464.

Jim Wallis. "Hard Questions for Peacemakers." *Sojourner.*
Jan.–Feb. 2002.

A religious viewpoint on resisting terrorism.

Eduardo Galeano. "The Theater of Good and Evil." *New Internationalist.* Nov. 2001.

Argues that the United States provoked the terrorist attacks.

Alison Hornstein. "The Question That We Should Be Asking: Is Terrorism Wrong?" *Newsweek.* 17 Dec. 2001.

Why Americans shouldn't blame themselves for terrorism.

Marian Wright Edelman. "Mr. President, We Want Our Slogan Back: Bush's Welfare Plan Belies His Promises to 'Leave No Child Behind'." *National Catholic Reporter.* 2 Aug. 2002.

An editorial criticizing administration policy.

Jennifer Hattam. "No Habitat? No Problem. Aiding Industry, the Bush Administration Abandons Endangered Species." *Sierra.* July–Aug. 2002.

An argument against administration environmental policy.

Luke Fisher. "Marijuana as Medicine: the Government Lets me Legally Smoke Pot. So Why Can't I Legally Buy it?" *Macleans.* Oct. 2002.

A Canadian perspective on the hypocrisy of laws regulating drugs.

Terrence Wells. "Biased and Intolerant." *The Other Side.* Nov.–Dec. 2002.

Where does the tone of this letter-to-the-editor go out of control?

Frank H. Wu. "Affirmative-Action Debate a False One." *Knight Ridder/Tribune News Service.* 23 July 1999.

Challenges the way we talk about affirmative action.

continues

Rich Devos. "The Power of Faith: Without Faith, We Are Lost, Adrift in the World Without an Anchor." *Saturday Evening Post.* July–Aug. 2002.

An argument for faith.

David Darling. "Supposing Something Different: Reconciling Science and the Afterlife." *Omni.* Winter 1995.

Science and soul are not mutually exclusive.

InfoTrac® **College Edition Discussion/Writing**

1. Topic Development: Read several essays that interest you and then write an introduction to your own position on one of the topics. Use a quote, paraphrase, or fact from the original essay as a "grabber" opening to get you started. Write your opening paragraph, and list some main points in scratch outline form under it.

2. Analysis:
   A. Read the first three essays (on terrorism) and discuss how any one of the authors would refute the other two's views if he/she had the chance to respond.
   B. Write a letter to Wells, Wu, or Fisher commenting on the author's tone and making suggestions for how he/she might be more persuasive. If you disagree with the author's position so strongly that you cannot see a way to help, suggest a major refutation someone might raise, but do it in a respectful manner.

3. Co-Author:
   A. Add a refutation paragraph to one of the essays. Writing as if you were the author, create a new objection that should be considered and then do your best to answer it. Tell exactly where in the original essay you would insert your new paragraph.
   B. If you were in President Bush's administration, how would you refute the arguments made by Hattam or Edelman? Respond in a one-page "press release" as if you were a spokesperson.

4. Evaluate any two of the readings as persuasive writing. Cover all the elements listed in the Peer Review Checklist.

✓ **PEER REVIEW CHECKLIST FOR PERSUASION**

Author: _____

Author's intended audience (explain background if necessary):

One concern or problem the author has with the paper is: _____

_____

Reviewer: _____

	Strong	Average	Weak
Introduction: Grabs my attention			
Raises problem			
Thesis proposal is clear			
Plan is detailed			
Tone: Respectful, open-minded			
Ideas: Thesis is a fresh idea			
Ideas target the audience			
Number and power of arguments			
Details: Supporting facts			
Visualization of facts			
Appeal to values			
Logic			
Refutation: A major objection is raised and answered			
Documentation: Sources are credited			

Respond to the author's concern:

The strongest part of this paper is:

Here are two things you might work on in revision:

  1.

  2.

Here's another reason or example to support your idea:

Here's a possible objection someone might raise to your idea:

CHAPTER 13

The Literary Essay and Review

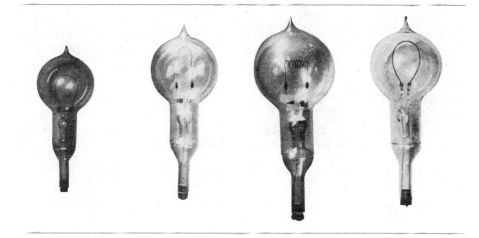

In every work of genius we recognize our own rejected thoughts.

—RALPH WALDO EMERSON

Men take possession of art as a means of covering their nakedness a little.

—PABLO PICASSO

During college you will probably be asked to write papers about literature—poems, plays, fiction, or essays. Why? Partly to practice critical thinking and writing. But also because literature's great works often fully express our own unborn or rejected ideas. Writing about literature not only teaches us how the best writers write; it also helps develop thoughts we have not been able to ripen alone. Literature's compact intensity often reveals patterns, emotions, and ideas more clearly than in real life—which is watered down with trivia.

Exactly what is a literary essay? What does it do? First, it is *persuasive,* for you must convince a reader with evidence that your analysis is valid. It's *informative* as well, because most literary essays strive for an objective tone and reveal something about the work, not just your feelings. Some require *research.*

 At heart, the literary essay *explains* **or** *analyzes* **a literary work. It is** *not a summary.* Analysis seeks the *why* under the surface of a literary work. It discovers not-so-obvious organization, style, or ideas. **Analysis creates a** *thesis* **to be proved about the work:**

"*Moby Dick* is a book about hunting the God who runs this world, not about hunting whales."

"In Frost's poem 'Stopping by Woods on a Snowy Evening,' the horse represents civilization and order."

"*The Glass Menagerie* uses music and lighting to create a mood of fantasy."

Notice that each thesis requires supporting evidence from the literary work, and each says something *about* the work that the work's author does not state; it does not simply retell the story.

Here are the same three theses stated as vague summaries—theses that will lead you to "D" papers or worse:

"*Moby Dick* is about a man obsessed with killing a white whale."

"'Stopping by Woods on a Snowy Evening'" tells how a man is tempted to enter a beautiful woods instead of going home."

"*The Glass Menagerie*'s main character is a frustrated young man who lives with a bossy mother and a fragile sister."

A good thesis may also compare or classify several works:

"Modern detective stories still use Poe's tricks."

"Marlowe's *Dr. Faustus* and Goethe's *Faust* portray two very different men who sell their souls to the devil."

"We can see Sylvia Plath's changing view of death if we compare one early and one late poem."

■ **PRACTICE 13-1:** Explain what a writer would have to do to prove each of the six good theses listed above.

HOW MUCH CAN YOU SEE?

Here are some preliminaries: **Read the literary work** *slowly* (fast reading is for newspapers). Allow the story or poem to lead you into its world. **Suspend judgment at first.** Say to yourself, "Maybe what's going on here is . . . ." rather than committing yourself to one idea. **Read it again, marking passages** that strike you as important or meaningful. These may not always be something you understand; in fact, sections that seem irrelevant or puzzling may be the most fruitful because you hope to explain the not-so-obvious.

Your job as a serious reader of literature—and as someone who wants to enjoy it—is to see how much you can see. There's no one right answer the author has hid behind door number one, two, or three. You will succeed if you patiently explore the literary work by crawling around inside it without preconceptions and without labeling, noticing as much as you can—the odd words and unexpected twists, the smells and images the work creates in your own head. How does it make you feel? Billy Collins, Poet Laureate of the United States, says a reader should "drop a mouse into a poem/ and watch him poke his way out" to understand the poem. Think of that mouse as your own feelings and thoughts. Experience the poem or story with your imagination, emotion, and physical senses. Leave the abstracting until a little later. First, sniff the story, nibble it, check out the interesting debris in the corners and the little holes in the wall. How does it make you feel? What pictures does it bring to your mind?

■ **PRACTICE 13-2:** Read one of the poems starting on page 285 and mark lines that grab your attention, then finish these sentences:

"When reading this, pictures of . . . came into my mind."

"When I was reading, I experienced feelings of . . . ."

"Maybe what's going on here is . . . . "

At this point, an *idea* for a thesis may occur to you. The marked passages will be handy *details* for evidence. But if no thesis pops up automatically, common ways of thinking about literature can be applied as brain teasers. I'm going to suggest **four major approaches to get ideas about literature**:

- Use your own gut reactions.
- Try to discover the author's intention.
- Use a critical perspective.
- Explicate or analyze the words in the work.

Like most literary critics today, I lean toward the last approach and will spend more time focusing on that, but all four have virtues and in fact often combine in one paper.

BRAIN TEASERS FOR LITERATURE

1. **Use your own gut reactions.** Reading requires *collaboration* between writer and reader. Writers are helpless without readers' imaginations. They rely on readers to catch suggestions, to feel sad or afraid. Your response is part of the literature. You're not simply a visitor looking at an object, but a vital part of an experience, and your presence alters its meaning. In fact, your gut feelings help create all literary works, for they are incomplete without a reader's interaction. This is the philosophy of **reader-response interpretation.**

   Start by listing your thoughts on a literary work. Simply **freewrite your impressions and observations.** Begin by describing the emotions the literature made you feel, what you thought about after reading it, or how you might behave if you had been in the same situation as the main character. Reread the work's significant passages to restart the flow when you stall. If an idea sizzles, continue in paragraph form until the spell cools; then start new ideas.

   The drawback to gut feelings is that they may not be in the work. If you enjoyed pet garter snakes as a child, for instance, you may allow this personal experience to misread a poem like Emily Dickinson's "A Narrow Fellow in the Grass." Dickinson's comment that snakes make her feel "zero at the bone" does not allow a cuddly snake interpretation. *You* may write such a poem, but Dickinson didn't. As I will point out in the fourth brain teaser, you must be able to *support* your gut reactions with evidence from the work.

2. **Explain the author's intentions.** One person who should know what a literary work means is its creator. So to understand the work, we might try to discover the author's intentions in creating it. This involves researching what authors have said about their work or biographical events that relate to the work. Poet T. S. Eliot attached more than 50 notes to "The Wasteland"—most readers need these comments and explanations to understand the poem. Another example is poet and novelist Thomas Hardy, who often wrote about chance and fate. Two biographical incidents may explain why. Doctors pronounced Hardy stillborn at birth, but he was revived by a skeptical nurse. Weeks later, he was found with a poisonous snake sleeping beside him. These stories, vividly told to young Hardy, gave him a sense of his mythology as a person and may have influenced the accidents and twists of fate that afflict his characters.

   There are dangers in biographical analysis. A book does not necessarily reflect an author's life. Writers often disguise their personal lives, create purely from fantasy, or build a mythical public image of themselves. Robert Frost cultivated the kindly, simple New England farmer image, but his poetry was cynical and elegant. Ernest Hemingway's books are tough and antireligious, yet we know he was a soft touch for friends in need and often slipped into churches to pray. Robert Browning raised another problem. A popular English poet, Browning was asked late in life to interpret one of his first poems, "Sordello," because no one had ever understood it. Browning stared hard. "When I wrote 'Sordello,'" he said, "only God and I knew what it meant. Now only God knows." He could no longer explain his own poem! The point is that authors aren't omniscient about their writing. Their intentions—if we can really discover them—may strike readers quite differently. It's perfectly reasonable to disagree with an author's interpretation of her own work— *if* you can prove the words support your view. If you do find an author's life or philosophy relevant to the work, you must also show evidence from the work. Most professors will be uneasy with a totally biographical interpretation of a literary work, but some connections may help develop your ideas.

3. **Consider critical perspectives on literature.** Like biographical interpretations, these ways of thinking step outside the strict boundaries of the text. They relate the literary work to ideology or social issues and give you new ways to think about the writing. Here are some common ones:

- **Political perspective.** You can interpret literary works as expressions of common social problems. John Steinbeck's *The Grapes of Wrath* or *In Dubious Battle,* for instance, can be interpreted as attacks on capitalism during the Depression and as portraits of the struggle to establish labor unions. Your paper could discuss the accuracy of Steinbeck's portrayals of history or the new ideas he created for social justice. Edward Abbey's novel *The Monkey-Wrench Gang,* which advocates sabotaging bulldozers, driving spikes into trees (to ruin saw blades), and blowing up dams, inspired the "Earth First!" group that actually does some of these things. A historical approach could compare Abbey's ideas and Earth First's or debate the ethics of his philosophy as expressed in the book.

- **Feminist perspective.** You can evaluate literary works' portrayal of women and of sex roles of both sexes. Shakespeare often gets credit for creating smart, witty, independent, strong women like Portia, but is criticized for paper dolls like Ophelia, who falls apart, or for shrews like Kate, who is "tamed" into meek obedience by her loud-mouthed oaf husband. Or, as some critics suggest, has Kate learned to play along with male egos in public so she can be free in private? Your paper can evaluate or define how women and gender roles are handled in the work.

- **Ethnic perspective.** Mark Twain's *Huckleberry Finn* has come under attack lately for its portrayal of African Americans. After an explosion, someone asks if anyone was killed. A boy replies, "No . . . only a nigger." Was Twain a racist or using irony to attack racism? Twain's life, we are fairly sure, showed respect and love for African Americans, and most critics believe he wanted to make white readers feel the ugly horror of racism. To write a paper on this topic, you would have to dig up ethnic references from the book and use them to support a thesis. Shakespeare's portrayal of the Jew Shylock in *The Merchant of Venice* has been considered anti-Semitic. Your paper could gather references in the play, research the way Jews were seen and treated in Shakespeare's day, and draw comparisons to current literature.

- **Other perspectives.** Any belief system can be a brain teaser, a window through which you see the text. And each perspective alters what ideas will be let loose in your head. You can analyze any literary work from a Christian, Hebrew, Hindu, or Muslim perspective. Or from a psychological, mythological, or sociological perspective. For example, John Barzelay's student paper in Chapter 15 looks at the ancient Greek epic, the *Odyssey,* through the perspective of the psychology of Attention Deficit Disorder.

The danger of critical perspectives is that you may distort the literary work to make it fit your idea. Is Freud's Oedipal theory applied to Hamlet—a latent sexual attraction toward his mother—a brilliant idea or an exaggeration? As with biographical interpretations, you must return to the words in the text for supporting evidence.

4. **Focus on the words.** Most literary critics today stress the work itself—the words and form. They say an author's atheism or comments made to friends and the work's connection to politics are secondary. They say because words create meaning, the analysis should focus on them. This school has convinced most other critics that *any* analysis should include some *explication of the text.* This means a close reading of the text in detail. Your entire paper may be a line-by-line interpretation of a poem or a selection from a short story or, more often, may explicate several short sections to show how the literary work supports your thesis. At the brain-teaser stage, work through key passages, explaining lines and tying ideas together. Here's an example from Thoreau's *Walden:*

> Time is but the stream I go a-fishing in. I drink at it; but while I drink I see the sandy bottom and detect how shallow it is. Its thin current slides away, but eternity remains. I would drink deeper; fish in the sky, whose bottom is pebbly with stars.

Brain Teaser: Time is like a stream. Okay. What are the fish? He also drinks from time—we all do. Time nourishes us—like food and water. But Thoreau sees through time and realizes it is "shallow" and "sandy." These aren't really negative words, but they do show how small and impermanent time is—which is ironic because time seems immense to most people. Time flows away and is thin because the present moment is all we can ever grasp and that's gone as soon as it comes. He compares time with eternity. He wants to be nourished by something deeper than time. The sky is like a giant stream, or ocean and stars like pebbles. Magnificent—the cosmic beach. This contrasts with the shallow, sandy stream of time. The sky at night does resemble a giant ocean, but he's talking about it on a deeper level, about the soul or heavens perhaps, finding nourishment from things that do not change and slide away but which are permanent. How do we grasp that, find it? Thoreau's two years at Walden, then, may have been a kind of fishing in time. Self and even nature are incredibly tiny fish.

A few observations on this process: My rough brain teaser opens up potential ideas but must be focused when I develop a trial thesis. Second, notice how long the explication is compared to the original. That's normal—works of genius compress much into a small space. Third, notice that a rough explication moves backward and outward for connections; you cannot simply plod through line by line. Tie ideas together.

■ **PRACTICE 13-3:** Quote a few favorite lines from a song you like. Explain the meaning based on your gut feelings, then explain them again using one of the other brain teasers to see if you can either add to what you've said or see the lines freshly enough to get a new perspective or possibility.

BRAIN TEASERS FOR EXPLICATION

1. **Theme.** Look for the message in the text, but don't settle for the first idea you see. Make a list of possible themes. Very few literary works have one underlined purpose. And often the first ideas that occur to you, as with any brain-teaser list, will be superficial. You should be especially suspicious if your theme sounds like a cliché: "What goes around, comes around" or "You can't judge a book by its cover" are probably too obvious for a serious literary work. Also, don't think of theme as the ultimate point of a literary work. Literature is not a sermon in rhyme or dialogue, but an experience of life. There's more to it than a moral.

   In its proper form a theme must be:

   ■ A complete statement, not just a single word

   ■ Stated in terms outside the literary work—stated in universal terms

      Example: The theme of *Romeo and Juliet* is that romantic love cannot exist in this corrupt world.

      Weak: The theme of *Romeo and Juliet* is love. (What *about* love?)

      Weak: The theme is that Romeo loves Juliet too much when their families are fighting. (This is not universal.)

   How do you figure out what a theme is? There's no formula, but you might start by putting into words what the main character learns or why the work ends as it does. **Start with a topic word like *jealousy* or *freedom* and try to say what the story or poem demonstrates about the topic.**

2. **Conflict.** List the forces in tension in the work. In the quote from Thoreau, "time vs. eternity" is most obvious, but you could also list "earth vs. heaven" or "permanence vs. impermanence." In a short story or play, conflict occurs between characters, in a character's mind, or between a character and society or nature. List all the conflicts and fill them out with examples or evidence from the story. Then draw a conclusion about the conflict, and you have your thesis:

   ■ In *Walden*, Thoreau struggles toward heaven but is unwilling to let go of earth.

   ■ In *The Sun Also Rises,* the conflict between the matador and bull in the bullfighting scenes reflects the conflicts among Jake, Brett, and Robert Cohn.

   Your paper must then illustrate and prove its thesis with detailed evidence.

3. **Character.** Drama, fiction, and some essays and poems can be approached by thinking about character. Start with gut reactions, but also apply these questions:

   ■ What *consistent* qualities does a character have?

   ■ What *motivates* the character?

   ■ What *complexities* does the character show?

   ■ Does the character *change,* and how?

   To discover ideas, comment on each question and note details from the work for support. In *The Great Gatsby,* for example, Jay Gatsby is *consistently* polite, gentle, a big spender, mysterious, and somehow detached from real life. He's *motivated* most obviously by wealth and the desire for Daisy, the rich girl he loves but who married someone else. Underneath, there's also his motive of wanting to live in the past. He's *complex* because he has contradictions and inner conflicts: He has gangster pals and a poverty-stricken past and yet can be naive and gallant and really doesn't care about money except to attract Daisy. Does he *change?* Scholars have debated this point since the book was published. This brain teaser can supply ideas and details for any paper on fiction or drama.

4. **Images.** Most literature can be analyzed through its images and symbols—pictures and other sense details. Scan the work, listing images, searching for patterns and repetitions. In *Romeo and Juliet,* for instance, Shakespeare uses religious images (saints, prayer books, a shrine) to refer to Juliet. This suggests both love's holiness and Romeo's melodramatic excess in Act I. In *The Great Gatsby,* the author repeatedly mentions the green light on Daisy's dock across the bay. Perhaps Gatsby wants a green "go" light from Daisy to pursue his romance, but this hazy, uncertain light may represent Daisy, who likes the youth and fun Gatsby brings her settled life but who is too selfish to risk herself. Like the light, she is a tease. There's usually something significant behind a repeated image. Write down page references and your first interpretations. Look for a pattern.

5. **Form/Style**. Each genre or type of literature has its own principles of style and form. *Poetry* can be analyzed by looking at the rhyme, rhythm, sound devices, and format (sonnet, ballad, and so on). But you can't just *describe* rhyme pattern, for instance. Show how it relates to the overall meaning of the poem by having a *thesis* about the rhyme.

> **Sample Thesis:** e. e. cummings uses rhyme that doesn't quite match (off-rhyme) in "when serpents bargain for the right to squirm" to show that humans are not in harmony with nature.

Fiction can be analyzed through narrative point of view (who the speaker is and how much he or she knows of characters' thoughts) or by explaining how the time sequence is constructed. As with poetry, show how the form or style contributes to the story's overall effect:

> **Sample Thesis:** Nick narrates *The Great Gatsby* because Gatsby is too ignorant of himself and too blind to Daisy to tell the story honestly.

Drama's unique element is staging—the props, actors' gestures, lighting, the set, and visual effects. Show how these elements contribute to the overall themes/conflicts:

> **Sample Thesis:** The main sets in *Romeo and Juliet*—the street, bedroom, and tomb—set up the three main conflicts in the play.

All literature can be analyzed for word choice and "tone" or "mood"—what we might call the writer's *attitude* toward the subject:

> **Sample Thesis:** When e. e. cummings distorts ordinary, simple English words, he is showing his real theme: That people should pay such close attention to the simple, basic things in life that they become strange and new to us again.

■ **PRACTICE 13-4:** To illustrate how these concepts work together, read this poem by Robert Browning:

Meeting at Night

The grey sea and the long black land;
And the yellow half-moon large and low;
And the startled little waves that leap
In fiery ringlets from their sleep,
As I gain the cove with pushing prow,
And quench its speed i' the slushy sand.

Then a mile of warm sea-scented beach;
Three fields to cross till a farm appears;
A tap at the pane, the quick sharp scratch
And blue spurt of a lighted match,
And a voice less loud, through its joys and fears,
Than the two hearts beating each to each!

First reading: What's going on? Is a character or the author telling the poem? Any vocabulary you need to look up? First reactions?

> **Brain teasers:** List the conflicts. Who is meeting and why is it so secret? List the images—what pattern emerges? Is there meaning in this? Regarding form, how do the two stanzas mirror each other? Listen to the sounds by reading the poem aloud, especially the end of stanza one and the middle of two. Does this poem have a theme?

After answering some of these, formulate a thesis you can defend in discussion with supporting evidence from the poem. Is it possible our close reading and interpretation will create ideas an author did not intend? Of course—although we are far more likely to underestimate a professional's rich use of words. **The point of literary interpretation is not to hit exactly what an author meant to say, but to exercise and develop our minds to see and think more deeply and to help a reader see new possibilities of meaning in the literary work. Your interpretations will be legitimate as long as you can support your ideas with details from the literature.**

ORGANIZING LITERARY ESSAYS

After you turn the story or poem over a few times and examine different parts, you're ready to focus on an aspect of the work—to create a *thesis* like those shown already. In developing a thesis, examine your notes for an idea *worth* proving—one with some complexity. In literature this often means recognizing *multiple truths*. Good vs. evil rarely occurs cleanly in life or good literature. More often we face a choice between two partial goods or two partial evils. Gatsby, Hamlet, Ahab, and Hester Prynne interest people because good and evil mix in them. **An honest thesis embraces ambiguity.** A categorical thesis suggests that either the poem or the interpretation is superficial.

> **Weak:** Daisy in *The Great Gatsby* is an evil woman who doesn't care what harm she causes.
>
> **Better:** Daisy causes much evil from weakness, fear, naïveté, and selfishness (specific, and outlines the four points that will organize the essay).
>
> **Weak:** Ahab in *Moby Dick* is a lunatic, pure and simple.
>
> **Better:** Ahab may be crazy, but it's a magnificent, sane madness.

After focusing your thesis, assemble evidence from the literary work—quotes, incidents, details of character—whatever interesting, relevant bits you have combed from reading, brain teasers, or research. Place like material together until you have solid outline headings.

DRAFTING LITERARY ESSAYS

A good way to start a literary essay is to explain why your topic is important or puzzling. Why does it matter to you? How does what you're about to prove add to a reader's understanding of the entire work? Your introduction should probably also let the reader know which three or four main issues will be covered to prove your one overall thesis.

As you draft, assume your audience has read the story, play, or poem carefully, so there's no need to retell the plot or identify the characters. You should focus entirely on proving your thesis. Look for all the evidence in the work that bears on your point, and don't get drawn into other issues. You will need to constantly clarify and support your ideas by quoting relevant passages. Think of yourself as a lawyer building an argument in court. So look deeply into each quotation you present, picking apart the words. As a general rule of thumb, **your explanation of a quotation should be twice as long as the original.** Why? Because you must point out *why* and *how* it proves your thesis.

The following is a nice example of a student assembling evidence to build a point. "Revelation," a story by Flannery O'Connor, is about an older woman, Mrs. Turpin, who feels morally superior to other people. While in a doctor's office, a young woman, Mary Grace, grows upset with Mrs. Turpin and finally throws a book at her and calls her "an ugly old wart hog from hell." The girl has a seizure, so Mrs. Turpin tells herself the girl was crazy and the ugly one. But Mrs. Turpin's superiority is shaken, and the story ends with her having a vision of being one of the last summoned to heaven. The student's introduction asserts that Mary Grace is not a lunatic but "a manifestation of a supernatural being representing goodness or oppressed suffering," and that Mrs. Turpin, although she represents herself as a charitable, God-fearing woman, may be evil. In this section, the student supports her idea of Mary Grace as supernatural force:

> The most obvious clue that something supernatural is going on is the end when Mrs. Turpin watches the parade of souls going to heaven. However, the whole work is peppered with symbols representing supernatural things, beginning with the title, "Revelation." The "Grace" in the girl's name could be religious imagery suggesting goodness. Then there's this description of Mary Grace: "She was looking at [Mrs. Turpin] as she had known and disliked her all of her life—all of Mrs. Turpin's life, it seemed too, not just the girl's life" (121). The idea that the girl's hate goes back before her mortal life began hints that Mary Grace is not simply a mortal, sensitive teenager. An examination of the waiting-room scene shows that Mary Grace flares up angrily when Mrs. Turpin merely thinks evil thoughts. An example is when Mrs. Turpin is thinking about how white trash are beyond help:

> > All at once the ugly girl turned her lips inside out once again, her eyes fixed like two drills on Mrs. Turpin. This time there was no mistaking that there was something urgent behind them. (123)

If Mary Grace were mortal, her flare-ups, dirty looks, and scowls would be limited to those times that Mrs. Turpin glares at someone or says something nasty. But if she represents the spirit of God's intention that we live in harmony, her anger would rise against the oppression and ridicule in Mrs. Turpin's mind.

—*Marjorie Pixley-Ketzak*

Copy **quotations** accurately. If three lines or less, incorporate them into your paragraphs. Should you quote poetry this way, you must use a slash to indicate the actual line ending, as in this example from Marvell's "To His Coy Mistress": "Had we but world enough, and time, / This coyness, lady, were no crime." If a quote is more than three lines, set it off like this selection from Tennyson's "Ulysses":

> The lights begin to twinkle from the rocks;
> The long day wanes; the slow moon climbs; the deep
> Moans round with many voices. Come my friends,
> 'Tis not too late to seek a newer world.

The lines are *indented* ten spaces for both poetry and prose, and *no quotation marks* are used. Some people double-space all indented quotes, and others stick to the older practice of single spacing. See Chapter 16 for punctuation of tag lines for quotations. Try not to pour on quote after quote. Quote the best, paraphrase the rest. (For documentation of quotations, see Chapter 14.)

REVISING LITERARY ESSAYS

Refresh yourself by reviewing "Steps in Writing a Paper" inside the front cover of this book. But pay special attention to your thesis. Does it still fit what you wrote? Some parts may have to go, or the thesis may need to be rewritten. Have you wrenched the literary work's main idea out of line to make your point? Cut where you dwell on the obvious. Beef up interesting ideas treated too briefly.

Revise details. Too little support? Too many quotes? Are your explanations sharp and vivid?

Revise mechanics and style. Literary essays use the present tense to describe the work (after all, literature is immortal), so you would say, "Flannery O'Connor says . . ." even though she is dead and "said" it years ago.

THE REVIEW

Related to the literary essay is the review—of books, restaurants, plays, concerts, art shows, speeches, films, or any other event or work that can be judged by *standards of performance*. Like literary essays, reviews persuade readers through supporting details. If it was a bad dinner followed by a worse speech, describe the limp green beans and mushy potatoes as well as the speaker's bad jokes. Like a literary essay, a review can interpret the purpose or themes of its subject.

Reviews differ from literary essays, however, in several regards. First, **descriptive summary *is expected*.** Up to half of a review may inform readers accurately about the topic. Assume readers of literary essays are already familiar with the work being discussed, but a review must help readers sample the unknown. Teach us! Second, the **review emphasizes *evaluation*.** Your purpose is to make a judgment of value and then support that judgment with evidence. If your professor wants a **critical review,** go heavier on evaluation and lighter on summary. As with any persuasion, **make your standards of judgment clear.** Specify what you mean by "good service" at a restaurant. Some people like a server to check on their needs every few minutes; others consider that pesky. In an art review, does "old-fashioned" art mean the red barn school of painting or anything that does not use lasers or computers?

Chances are good you will write reviews in your career and in college. In your career, you may be asked to review a new product your boss is considering buying or to review another employee's job performance. You will need to set up standards of performance and interpret how well they have been reached, supported by specific, descriptive details. For a product, some standards might be:

- Efficiency
- Ease of use
- Price
- How necessary it is
- Safety

You might outline your review by using these headings, then comment on each with details. Under safety, for instance, you might point out that the new computer tends to give employees a tan after a week's use. For a job evaluation, common standards of performance are:

- Amount of work done
- Quality of work
- Reliability
- Ability to work with others
- Initiative

What else would you add?

You will likely review books or theories for college courses. Your psychology professor may ask you to contrast how behaviorist and humanist psychologists would deal with a teenage alcoholic and then evaluate which will succeed best. What should be the standards of success?

Although people don't usually write reviews of dates or parenting style, in your private life you can use the techniques of a review to help decide what car you want to buy or which college you want to attend. Prioritizing standards and a sharp eye for supporting detail can help you evaluate with more depth and clarity.

■ **PRACTICE 13-5:** Make a list of *your* top five standards of performance for one of the following: art, restaurant, book, film, or theatrical event. Now apply these standards to one specific painting, concert, work, or performance.

Highlights of Chapter 13

- A literary essay explains or analyzes a literary work. It is *not* a summary. You aren't ready to begin until you have a thesis to be proved about the literary work.

- Four brain teasers can help you to form a thesis:

  Freewrite or list your own gut reactions.

  Discover the author's intention through biographical research.

  Use a common perspective: politics, history, feminism, ethnic perspective, religion, psychology, and myth.

  Explicate the text itself. Most literary analysis today closely examines individual passages. You might limit yourself to one aspect: theme, conflict, character, images, or form.

- During the drafting of a literary essay, you must continually *prove* your thesis with evidence, so before starting, assemble a list of quotations and significant incidents from the work that support your idea. As you draft, explain these passages in detail.

- The review, like the literary essay, supports a judgment about someone else's work with evidence. It both summarizes *and* evaluates.

Writing Suggestions and Class Discussions

1. Write a review of a restaurant, film, art show, or other subject with performance standards. Make your standards clear, and support your opinion with specific details.

2. Write a review of your essays written so far for this course. Establish standards of performance and evaluate your work, quoting from past papers to support your points.

3. Write a job evaluation review of someone who works with you. Fairly and specifically evaluate their work, with supporting details. Conclude with a recommendation.

4. Read the sample student review in Chapter 15.

5. A peer group will research and analyze a literary work. One person each will (a) research the author's life and connect it to the work; (b) apply critical perspectives to the work, doing necessary research; (c) explicate theme; (d) explicate conflict or character; (e) explicate images and symbols; and (f) explicate style. The group will discuss and combine ideas and then report to the class.

6. Choose a literary work. Do preliminary brain teasers and turn in three possible thesis statements you might defend. After review with peer groups or professor, organize, draft, and revise the paper.

7. Compare and contrast works by two authors on the same topic (Gaines and Walker on racism, Millay and cummings on love, for examples).

8. Study how one poet or fiction writer deals with a narrow topic (Yeats on escape, Lawrence on love, Hopkins on nature). Support your thesis with explication of several works and any other evidence you can find.

9. Five poems follow. Although from different historical ages and using different forms, all deal with the idea of time. Here are several ways you can use these poems to improve your ability to analyze literature.

   - Pick one poem and come to class with ideas to discuss about it. Formulate a tentative thesis.

   - Look for similarities and differences among the poems. Consider theme, imagery used, and form. Have specific evidence from each poem to support your ideas.

   - Research the author's life for one poem and see if you can draw some connections to the poem. Does the poem alone support your biographical interpretation?

Poems for Explication and Discussion

Sonnet 73

That time of year thou mayst in me behold
When yellow leaves, or none, or few, do hang
Upon those boughs which shake against the cold,
Bare ruined choirs, where late the sweet birds sang.
In me thou see'st the twilight of such day
As after sunset fadeth in the west;
Which by and by black night doth take away,
Death's second self, that seals up all in rest.
In me thou see'st the glowing of such fire,
That on the ashes of his youth doth lie,
As on the death-bed whereon it must expire,
Consumed with that which it was nourished by.
    This thou perceiv'st, which makes thy love more strong,
    To love that well which thou must leave ere long.

—*William Shakespeare*

Vocabulary: *thou:* you; *mayst:* may; *boughs:* branches; *fadeth:* fades; *doth:* does; *perceiv'st:* understand; *ere:* before.

To the Virgins, to Make Much of Time

Gather ye rosebuds while ye may,
    Old time is still a-flying;
And this same flower that smiles today
    Tomorrow will be dying.

The glorious lamp of heaven, the sun,
    The higher he's a-getting,
The sooner will his race be won,
    And nearer he's to setting.

That age is best which is the first,
    When youth and blood are warmer;
But being spent, the worse, and worst
    Times still succeed the former.

Then be not coy, but use your time,
    And, while ye may, go marry;
For, having once but lost your prime,
    You may forever tarry.

—Robert Herrick

Vocabulary: *ye:* your; *succeed:* follow; *coy:* shy or flirtatious; *tarry:* linger behind.

Ozymandias

I met a traveller from an antique land
Who said: "Two vast and trunkless legs of stone
Stand in the desert . . . Near them, on the sand,
Half sunk, a shattered visage lies, whose frown,
And wrinkled lip, and sneer of cold command,
Tell that its sculptor well those passions read
Which yet survive, stamped on these lifeless things,
The hand that mocked them, and the heart that fed:
And on the pedestal these words appear:
"My name is Ozymandias, king of kings:
Look on my works, ye Mighty, and despair!"
Nothing beside remains. Round the decay
Of that colossal wreck, boundless and bare
The lone and level sands stretch far away.

—Percy Bysshe Shelley

Vocabulary: *antique:* ancient; *visage:* face.

A Noiseless Patient Spider

A noiseless patient spider,
I marked where on a little promontory it stood isolated,
Marked how to explore the vacant vast surrounding,
It launched forth filament, filament, filament, out of itself,
Ever unreeling them, ever tirelessly speeding them.
And you O my soul where you stand,
Surrounded, detached, in measureless oceans of space,
Ceaselessly musing, venturing, throwing, seeking the spheres to connect them,
Till the bridge you will need be formed, till the ductile
    anchor hold,
Till the gossamer thread you fling catch somewhere, O my soul.

—*Walt Whitman*

Vocabulary: *promontory:* a peak of high land overlooking the sea; *spheres:* planets or stars; *ductile:* plastic or stretchable.

Childhood Is the Kingdom Where Nobody Dies

Childhood is not from birth to a certain age and at a certain age
The child is grown, and puts away childish things.
Childhood is the kingdom where nobody dies.
Nobody that matters, that is. Distant relatives of course
Die, whom one never has seen or has seen for an hour,
And they gave one candy in a pink-and-green striped bag, or a
    jack-knife,
And went away, and cannot really be said to have lived at all.

And cats die. They lie on the floor and lash their tails,
And their reticent fur is suddenly all in motion
With fleas that one never knew were there,
Polished and brown, knowing all there is to know,
Trekking off into the living world.
You fetch a shoe-box, but it's much too small, because she won't
    curl up now:
So you find a bigger box, and bury her in the yard, and weep.

But you do not wake up a month from then, two months,
A year from then, two years, in the middle of the night
And weep, with your knuckles in your mouth, and say Oh, God!
    Oh, God!
Childhood is the kingdom where nobody dies that matters,—
    mothers and fathers don't die.
And if you have said, "For heaven's sake, must you always be
    kissing a person?"
Or, "I do wish to gracious you'd stop tapping on the window
    with your thimble!"
Tomorrow, or even the day after tomorrow if you're busy having
    fun,
Is plenty of time to say, "I'm sorry, mother."

To be grown up is to sit at the table with people who have died,
    who neither listen nor speak;
Who do not drink their tea, though they always said
Tea was such a comfort.

Run down into the cellar and bring up the last jar of raspberries;
    they are not tempted.

Flatter them, ask them what was it they said exactly
That time, to the bishop, or to the overseer, or to Mrs. Mason;
They are not taken in.
Shout at them, get red in the face, rise,
Drag them up out of their chairs by their stiff shoulders and shake
    them and yell at them;
They are not startled, they are not even embarrassed; they slide
    back into their chairs.

Your tea is cold now.
You drink it standing up,
And leave the house.

—Edna St. Vincent Millay

(From *Collected Poems,* Harper & Row. Copyright [copyright] 1934, 1962 by Edna St. Vincent Millay and Norma Millay Ellis. Reprinted by permission of Elizabeth Barnett, Literary Executor.)

InfoTrac® College Edition: Readings on Poems and Fiction for Discussion

Your professor may ask you to print copies of some of these to discuss in class. For tips on using *InfoTrac*® College Edition, scc page 464.

Poems

C. K. Williams. "Dissections." *The Atlantic Monthly.* Nov. 2002.

    An ancient man is dissected for modern people to contemplate.

Jonathan Musgrove. "Her Last Night at Home." *The Atlantic Monthly.* Oct. 2002.

    The narrator looks behind the curtain for symbols, and there's nothing there.

Marilyn Krysl. "Skipping the State." *The Atlantic Monthly.* Oct. 2002.

    Is this really a poem about child support payments?

Alison Pelegrin. "The Recently Sober Woman Tries for Grace at a Roadside Motel in North Louisiana." *Prairie Schooner.* Fall 2002.

    Fighting the addiction.

Jeff Dolvin. "Someone to Watch Over Me." *Southwest Review.* Winter 2002.

The child-angel who sits on our shoulder.

Sue Owen. "The Devil in the Details." *Southwest Review.* Winter 2002.

A devil to sit on our other shoulder.

Aimee Nezhukumatathil. *Prairie Schooner.* Fall 2002.

Guilt on a date.

Look up *Poetry* magazine on *InfoTrac®* College Edition (use power search and limit by journal) and look through it until you find a poem you like. Print a copy. The other journals listed above also carry many poems.

Fiction

Rotimi Ogunjobi. "Brain Surgery on the Highway." *Queen's Quarterly.* Spring 2002.

Is the man on this bus a mystic, a con artist, or something else?

Sondra Spatt. "A Loaf of Bread, a Jug of Wine." *Antioch Review.* Summer 2001.

How a lover gets pushed over the edge.

Susanna Moore. "Just Like a Woman." *Harper's.* Aug. 2002.

In a strangely ritualistic story, a girl and her mother swim into an underwater cave.

Michael Kelly. "Comes a Cool Rain." *Canadian Fiction Magazine.* Annual 2000.

A car crash that leaves his father paralyzed makes a boy consider the unthinkable.

You can find more literary fiction in the magazines listed above as well as in *Southwest Review, Prairie Schooner, The New Yorker, Yankee,* and others carried on *InfoTrac®* College Edition.

InfoTrac® College Edition Discussion/Writing

1. Choose one poem or story, read it carefully, then freewrite a one- to two-page response to it. Just write what comes to you, how it might relate to things you've seen or thought, what it says to you.

2. Pick out the key moment for you—the image or scene that seems most important—and write just about that. Why is it significant?

3. Apply one of the principles of the chapter to the literary work: examine its imagery, conflict, or characters, for instance. Write a page explaining what you see.

Sample Student Literary Essay

Structure and Feeling in

"Childhood Is the Kingdom Where Nobody Dies"

Carrie Gaynor

why she chose topic

"Childhood is the Kingdom Where Nobody Dies" by Edna St. Vincent Millay captivated me with its vivid images and emotional confessions. It defines what it means to grow up. Childhood is a vast place, a kingdom wrapped in the innocence that allows us to act as though time were on our side. But that all changes when the people who matter most to us are

thesis

snatched away, along with the deception of security. When you grow up, you realize how exposed and vulnerable life is. In order to convey these feelings, Millay blends images with various structures.

outline overall approach in paper

The poem is presented in two parts. The first deals with what it means to live in the kingdom of childhood. Millay then creates visual images that intensify to an emotional climax. To support this progression, she starts with distant relatives, then comes closer to home with the family cat. In describing the distant relatives, Millay speaks in third person in a long, rambling structure. This makes it go fast and seem insignificant:

supporting quote

Distant relatives of course

Die, whom one never has seen or has seen for an hour,

And they gave one candy in a pink-and-green striped

  bag, or a jack-knife,

And went away, and cannot really be said to have lived

page reference

  at all. (286)

Notice the matter-of-factness of the words and the lack of emotion. A family gathers and one's great uncle brings a piece of candy. He has nothing to do with your life, and his death is no event.

In the next stanza, Millay begins to draw the reader into a comparison of sorts. You are home, and your cat, full of life and fleas, lies on the floor, dead. And you place the cat, now in rigor mortis, into a box and bury it under a tree. You weep. Millay creates a personal sense of loss by switching from third-person to second-person narrative, directing the image at the reader:

> You fetch a shoe-box, but it's much too small,
>> because she won't curl up now:
> So you find a bigger box, and bury her in the yard, and
>> weep. (286)

The use of the box symbolizes the child's need to expand her view of the world to match her experience.

The next stanza continues to make you feel words in your belly. The rambling sentence plays with your adrenaline. There is no ambiguity about what now defines childhood:

> But you do not wake up a month from then, two months,
> A year from then, two years in the middle of the night
> And weep, with your knuckles in your mouth, and say
>> Oh, God! Oh, God!
> Childhood is the kingdom where nobody dies that
>> matters,—mothers and fathers don't die. (287)

explication

style analyzed by comparison

explication of quote

quote needs explication

continues

transition to last section

At this point, the poem switches to dialogue, signaling the turning point. The reader gets a last glimpse of the child's sense of timelessness while at the same time touched by an awareness that tomorrow may never come.

The final section deals with images and emotions of grieving. This process starts with numb unwillingness to accept loss:

> To be grown up is to sit at the table with people who
> > have died, who neither listen nor speak;
> Who do not drink their tea, though they always said
> Tea was such a comfort. (287)

explication

This passage brings to mind a child conducting a tea party for her make-believe friends: the dead. The child continues, despite the dead people's ("they") lack of response. All adults are haunted by the dead, and the desperate child tries to trick her "guests" into participating, returning:

> Run down into the cellar and bring up that last jar
> > of raspberries; they are not tempted.
> Flatter them, ask them what it was they said
> > exactly. . . .
> They are not taken in. (288)

These passive, rational attempts abruptly change to aggression:

quotes need explication

> Shout at them, get red in the face, rise,
> Drag them up out of their chairs by their stiff
> > shoulders and shake them and yell at them;
> They are not startled, they are not even embarrassed. (288)

conclusion

The final act of growing up is learning to accept what is. The last stanza reflects the change from the absence of any control to very careful control. Millay switches back to a matter-of-fact tone as she ends the tea party. Time has passed, the tea grown cold. The child stands. She is no longer part of the delusion and leaves the house. Leaving the house suggests what being grown is: when one is completely exposed, deprived of all security. The last words are small, the last lines short, and they make the reader feel that way—exposed at the end of the page.

Work Cited

Millay, Edna St. Vincent. *Collected Poems*. New York: Harper & Row, 1956.

Commentary Based on Peer Review Sheet

Ideas: Insight. This essay has some wonderful depth of interpretation. Her last paragraph asserts potent truths about childhood. Although the author does not raise her personal experience, I sense the poem touched her.

Sticks to thesis: The opening prepares us for analysis of theme, but the second paragraph announces she will use a section-by-section analysis that combines structure and imagery. How about a sentence telling us that the structure and imagery support the theme she's discussing?

Details/Amount of support: Plenty. Every section is supported with several direct quotes and other references.

In-depth interpretation of quotes: At times the quotes fly too thick without explication. Just before the concluding paragraph there are eight lines of poem with only one line of explanation. In those quotes I'd like to know if the "cellar" and "raspberries" have deeper significance. A cellar is like a grave, and raspberries, once juicy live fruits, are now preserved there. Since she's been discussing living, dead, or dead-while-alive relatives, this must mean something. Generally, her paper has fine depth. For instance, she perceptively lays out the switch from the impersonal "one" to "you" and ties it to her thesis.

Organization: It's smooth with nice transitional markers ("In the next stanza," "At this point," and "The final section . . .") to help the reader.

Format: A fine model for handling quotes/citations.

Most creative interpretation: I'm impressed with how she blends idea and style. She shows how the relaxed, rambling sentences give way to abrupt, hysterical ones, reflecting the change in the child from calm to shock.

What else ought the writer explain? She ignores the scene in which the dead people sit at the table with the child. It's the boldest, most puzzling part of the poem to me. Are they memories? Ghosts? Living people who act dead? Wishful thinking?

Poem and Sample Student Literary Essay

Batter My Heart, Three-Personed God

Batter my heart, three-personed God; for You
As yet but knock, breathe, shine, and seek to mend;
That I may rise and stand, o'erthrow me, and bend
Your force to break, blow, burn, and make me new.
I, like a usurped town, to another due,
Labor to admit You, but O! to no end;
Reason, Your viceroy in me, me should defend,
But is captived, and proves weak or untrue.
Yet dearly I love You, and would be loved fain,
But am betrothed unto Your enemy.
Divorce me, untie, or break that knot again;
Take me to You, imprison me, for I,
Except You enthrall me, never shall be free,
Nor ever chaste, except You ravish me.

—John Donne

Vocabulary: *o'erthrow:* overthrow; *usurped:* taken by force or trickery; *fain:* gladly; *betrothed:* engaged; *enthrall:* enslave.

Three-Personed God

Nancy L. Galleher

In "Batter My Heart, Three-Personed God," the narrator addresses the three facets of God's Trinity: Father, Son, and Holy Ghost. The poem uses images relating to battle and capture to describe man's heart. For the narrator—like all men—has been captured by God's enemy, Satan. The line, "I, like an usurped town to another due" (5), describes this surrender. The word "usurped" means seized or taken possession of by force, wrongfully.

The poem separates the Trinity or "Three-personed God" (1) into three intertwined entities that struggle to redeem man's heart. Whenever God is mentioned in the poem, the words "You" or "Your" are capitalized. The line, "for You/As yet but knock, breathe, shine, and seek to mend" (1–2) describes the Son sent by God the Father to redeem man with tenderness and love. The words all suggest a gentleness embodied by the lamb of God. The word "knock" reminds me of a mural behind the altar in the church I attended as a child. It is a picture of Christ gently knocking on a gate to a lovely garden—which symbolizes the door to man's heart. "Breathe" and "shine" are words of life. "Seek to mend" suggests the care and concern God the father has for man, which is why he sent his son. Man instinctively recognizes and loves his heavenly father in whose image he was created: "Yet dearly I love You" (9) and is desperate that God love him: "and would be loved fain" (9). He works hard to give God access to his heart: "I . . . Labor to admit You" (6), but he fails:

> . . . but O! to no end;
>
> Reason, Your viceroy in me, me should defend,
>
> But is captived, and proves weak or untrue. (6–8)

Man's heart is a prisoner of war, "captived" by the enemy. "Proves weak or untrue" suggests betrayal under the pressure of captivity. Man has been given reason by his creator to govern his actions, just as a viceroy who

continues

represents a king is expected to rule and carry out his king's wishes. God expects man's reason to defend him better.

In scripture, Jesus is compared to a bridegroom at a wedding feast. He lived among men, died, and was resurrected by God to prepare the wedding feast at God's table in heaven. Man's heart is often referred to as Jesus' beloved or bride. With this in mind, the poet effectively uses the image of marriage in these lines:

But am betrothed unto Your enemy.

Divorce me, untie or break that knot again; (10–11)

"Betrothed unto Your enemy" means promised in marriage to Satan, which occurred when man first sinned in the Garden of Eden. Man knows the only way this unholy relationship can be severed is by divorce, which will "untie" or "break the knot." Marriage is symbolized by the knot, an intertwining of two souls. The word "again" refers to the time when man's heart belonged to God alone, before it was captured by Satan.

Man has been given the Holy Spirit to empower him to wage war against Satan. The lines:

That I may rise and stand, o'erthrow me, and bend

Your force to break, blow, burn, and make me new. (3–4)

describe the bestowing of this gift. When Jesus ascended to heaven, he promised his disciples a power to enable them to carry on his battle against evil. At the Feast of Pentecost, the force of the Holy Spirit sounded like a strong wind blowing ("blow"); tongues of fire appeared and touched every person there ("burn") and filled them with the Holy Spirit ("make me new"). This empowers man to do God's work and resist evil. Man's will must be broken and the wall surrounding his heart penetrated. This is suggested in the plea: "Batter my heart, three-personed God" (1). "Batter" suggests ramming down barriers by repeated attacks that overwhelm and subdue. When God "batter[s] my heart," He breaks those walls that have kept Him out. The force increases in intensity from lines two to four: "Knock" becomes "break," "breathe" becomes "blow," "shine" becomes "burn," and "mend" becomes "make me new." The narrator wants to be recreated, not just repaired.

Man must be a servant—but to which master, God or Satan? He pleads:

Take me to You, imprison me, for I
Except You enthrall me, never shall be free,
Nor ever chaste, except You ravish me. (12–14)

He recognizes that even though he knows which master he wants to serve, the only way he can be certain to serve God is to have his free will taken away and his soul captured. "Enthrall" means to hold or reduce to slavery, as well as to spellbind. However, man has been given free will and is continually asked to make choices about which master he will serve. The last line, "Nor ever chaste, except You ravish me" (14) creates two contrasting images. "Chaste" means pure, holy, and without sin. A person who is chaste is in control of his impulses and actions. The word "ravish," in contrast, implies being overcome by force or rape. How can a person become pure by such an act? The poet seems to suggest that the only way a man's heart can become pure is if his will becomes subdued. Then, and only then, will he be truly free of Satan's grip on his soul.

Discussion

Using the Peer Review Checklist for ideas, comment on the strengths and weaknesses of Nancy's analysis. What else did you see in the poem that she does not mention? What words or phrases might be taken in a different sense?

InfoTrac® College Edition: Readings that Interpret Literary Work

Professional literary essays are written for people with extensive background in literature and may be tough reading if you do not know the literary work. I've chosen two essays on well-known works and subjects touched on in *Ideas and Details* to help you. Since *InfoTrac®* College Edition contains thousands of reviews, I'll let you find a review on a work you know. For tips on using *InfoTrac®* College Edition, see page 464.

> Hyejin Kim. "Black, White and *Huckleberry Finn:* Re-imagining the American Dream." *College Literature.* Summer 2002.
>
> *Is this American classic a racist work or not?*

> Kevin Rea. "The Colour of Meaning in *The Great Gatsby.*" *The English Review.* Apr. 2000.
>
> *The imagery and symbolism of colors in the greatest novel about the roaring twenties.*

Look up a film, CD, or book review on *InfoTrac®* College Edition for a work you know. Print a copy.

InfoTrac® College Edition Discussion/Writing

1. Topic Development: Look for issues of race or the use of colors in a story, poem, play, or novel you know. List incidents or lines that are relevant.

2. Analysis:

    A. List the main points Kim or Rea make in their essays. Find the thesis that holds the essay together. Locate a place where the author explains a passage from the original text and paraphrase the point made about it.

    B. List the standards the reviewer used in rating the film, CD, or book you looked up. Does the reviewer make his/her standards clear? Are they fair? What else might you suggest for rating this work or others like it that the reviewer does not consider?

3. Co-Author: Write a paragraph adding a new facet to the review you read— some aspect of the work the professional reviewer did not mention. If you strongly disagree with the reviewer, write as if your comments will be in a separate article responding to the original.

4. Evaluate one of the literary essays or the review you chose using the Peer Review Checklists at the end of this chapter.

✓ **PEER REVIEW CHECKLIST FOR LITERARY ESSAYS**

Author: _____

I would especially like the reviewer to comment on:_____

_____

Reviewer: _____

State the author's thesis as you see it. Author and reviewer should discuss the accuracy of this statement:

	Strong	Average	Weak
Ideas: Insight into literary work			
Sticks to thesis			
Details: Plenty of supporting evidence			
In-depth interpretation of quotes			
Organization: Smooth and logical			
Transitions: Mark idea shifts			
Format: Page citations for quotes			
Punctuation of quotations			

What was the most creative interpretation the paper made?

Respond to the author's request:

What else about the literary work ought the writer explain to prove the thesis or to dig out its complexity? What questions do you have that are still unanswered after reading the paper?

What lines or events in the literary work might tend to *disprove* the author's thesis? Discuss.

✓   **PEER REVIEW CHECKLIST FOR REVIEWS**

Author: _____

Question or problem for reviewer: _____

_____

Reviewer: _____

	Strong	Average	Weak
Ideas: Standards of performance are clear			
Depth/creativity of analysis			
Details: Support for evaluation			
Visualization (vivid description)			
Organization: Clear and logical			
Transitions: Mark idea shifts			
Tone: Reasonable			

Respond to the author's question:

What do you think is the best part of the paper?

What standards does the author seem to value most? What others might be used?

Is there anything the author ought to cover in more depth or to cut? Explain:

Offer a possible refutation to the author's evaluation (Hint: See the evaluation from the viewpoint of the person being evaluated):

Offer two other suggestions for the paper:

CHAPTER 14

Research

Written with Christopher Otero-Piersante

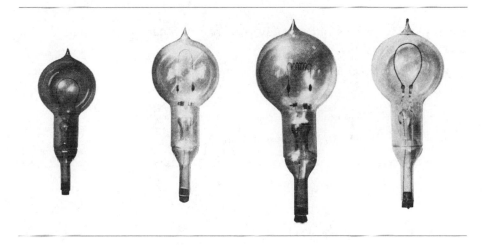

When I slept, armies of footnotes marched across my dreams.

—TED MORGAN

Do not complain about the truth.

—I CHING

It's 2 A.M. Books are piled on the desk and floor. A thousand scraps of paper snow you in. Blank, fanned-out 3 × 5 note cards await entries. You've quoted so much, your paper will be one long citation. You've been waiting for someone to return your most important book to the library. You forgot to copy a source's publication date and pray to the demon god of the Internet that the link will still be there tomorrow. In 12 hours your finished copy is due.

or

It's 2 A.M. Five weeks ago, the day your research paper was assigned, you created this schedule:

Week One:	Do general reading—reference section
	Narrow chosen topic
Week Two:	Assemble books, magazines, and web sites
	Join an online newsgroup
Week Three:	Read sources and take notes
	Conduct personal interview
	Record bibliographic information
Week Four:	Weigh all evidence
	Decide on thesis
	Create outline
	Write rough draft
	Bring draft to peer group
Week Five:	Revise paper
	Type Works Cited list
	Print extra copy for security
	Send thank-you note for personal interview

Beside each item, as relentless as marching soldiers, checks appeared as weeks passed. *You* snagged the library books first and had time to contact the web site to update your missing link. Notes neatly stacked, you're about to proof the paper. The only thing wrong, really, just nagging the back of your mind, is that your paper seems bland, lifeless.

The first scenario is full of chaos, and the second is idealized, but overly mechanical. If you balance these two extremes, you might be able to enjoy research. Use deadlines to keep on track, but allow yourself a little chaos to be creative. Let's start by looking at what research really entails and how you'll use it in your life.

PRACTICAL RESEARCH FOR YOUR PROFESSIONAL, ACADEMIC, AND PERSONAL LIFE

Think of your career goals. If you become a financial advisor, you might research investment trends for clients. As a civil engineer paving the courtyard of an apartment complex, you might need to learn about water drainage systems. As a nurse, you might have to study new laws about barcoding medications, so the right patients are administered the correct drugs. It's important to enter the work force ready with information, but it's just as important to be able to discover information you don't know.

Think of your academic studies. Use your research paper to learn more about a topic introduced in class. Choose something your professors *didn't* cover, and you may stun them! If you have an interest in some aspect of your major not discussed in class, this is your chance to educate yourself. If your course doesn't directly relate to your major, create a connection. For example, if you're a computer science major taking a literature class, link technology issues to the poems you're studying. If you're a psychology major in a history class, apply a theory of aggression to politics.

Think of your personal life. A friend of mine suffered from labored breathing, sharp eye pains, and kidney stones. After five referrals, she was finally diagnosed with sarcoidosis, a disease with no real cure except for time—up to 20 years, the doctors told her. Lillian searched the web to learn more about what she could do to ease her symptoms and even provided her doctors with new information about the disease.

A student who rented an apartment from her sister thought her sister was taking advantage of her by charging excessive rent, barging in without knocking, and not maintaining the place (it had broken windows, a loose door lock, and a mouse scuttling in the ceiling at night). Isabelle researched current housing regulations and wrote a formal complaint letter. She also used personal arguments—an appeal to sisterly love and a hint she would inform Mom and Dad, who lived in another city. The sight of the written facts and ideas prodded Isabelle's sister to action. "Now she knocks! She actually knocks!" Isabelle told the class.

RESEARCH AND THE WRITING PROCESS

Research papers usually follow the same writing process as any other writing:

- Thinking (Chapter 3)
- Organizing (Chapter 5)
- Writing (Chapter 6)
- Revising (Chapter 7)

GREAT RESEARCH TOPICS

Choose a topic you care about. If your only purpose is to get a grade, you've missed an opportunity to empower yourself. Professors assign research papers to encourage creativity—so seek it. Find the exciting angle within the broad, bland topic. Remember this: In most cases, readers care about your topic only half as much as you do. So you must be enthusiastic about your topic to keep them reading.

Seek connections between your personal experiences and your class requirements. If your assigned topic for a history course is World War II and you're interested in automobiles, research transportation technology during this era. If you love sports, study the Nazi Olympics or games soldiers played. If your boyfriend is in the military, research how wives and girlfriends handled loneliness or grief. Or you might research the way female military aides were treated. If you fear you're narrowing the topic outside your professor's guidelines, simply ask.

Thinking is messy and redundant. Narrowing your topic and creating a thesis is not a one-step process. Before, during, and after your research, refine your topic and improve your thesis. Keep separate notepaper to record new ideas that surface.

■ **PRACTICE 14-1:** This exercise will be referred to throughout the chapter. Inside two of these subjects, find at least two research topics that interest you (four topics total):

- Your own topic
- Criminal psychology
- Chemical warfare
- Blues music
- Children's literature
- Advertising

ESTABLISHING KEY RESEARCH QUESTIONS

Before you begin to research, ask questions you want answered. Finding the answers will be your research. They will also keep your focus on the important issues. For instance, suppose one of my ideas from Practice 14-1 under "blues music" was "the African roots of the blues." These questions occur to me:

- How did slavery contribute to the blues?
- What stages did African music go through before becoming the blues?
- Which African tribes had the most impact on the blues?

Raise new questions and scrap ones that grow stale or seem obvious. For example, as I begin my research, a new question might ask if the blues has any connection to grunge, hardcore, and rap—musical styles that often vent frustration.

Use other brain teasers to identify what you already know. On the blues topic, a *sense details* brain teaser could record your impression of the music. Get African music and *contrast* it to the blues. Listen for similar riffs and refrains. *List* the different instruments used in each. *Classify* the African music into spiritual, festive, and folklore. *Compare* them to the different types of blues (e.g., Delta, Texas, and Chicago). *Break stereotypes* about who listens to the blues and how it appeals to many ethnicities and economic classes.

Think actively. Figure out what's important. Keep asking "why" and "how" at each step. Thinking about the effect of blues on contemporary music, I might ask, "Why are there no riots at blues concerts? Why do the blues and hardcore music express frustration, but cause different behaviors from the audience?" Questions like these might uncover more than my original questions—or might change the focus of my research topic.

■ **PRACTICE 14-2:** For one of your topics in Practice 14-1, ask four key research questions, and do a half-page brain teaser to clarify what you already know.

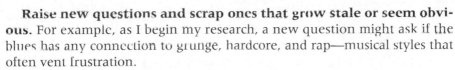

LIBRARY RESOURCES: LIBRARIANS, BOOKS, JOURNALS, AND COMPUTERS

Librarians

When you begin your search for answers, keep in mind that librarians know how information is organized. They can guide you through pamphlet files, computer indexes, microfilm, and the web. To keep these wonderful people on your side, come prepared with your key questions as well as your homework assignment, and they'll be happier to work with you. If you only bring a general topic such as "war" or "music," librarians might think that you expect them to do your work. The more specific you are, the better information you'll get. Do the obvious research *before* asking for help—check out basic references, electronic catalogs, and periodical indexes.

The Reference Section

The reference section includes dictionaries, encyclopedias, almanacs, and other books that summarize large bodies of information and provide raw facts and statistics. If you want to write on the dangers of importing Mideast oil to the United States, the *Information Please Almanac* will tell how many billions of barrels of oil the U.S. imports.

Because I needed to know more about the general history the blues, I first read an encyclopedia entry which answered one of my key research questions. I discovered that the blues were nonreligious forms of spirituals. Although the encyclopedia was a good place to start, I won't use it as a main reference source—it is too superficial for a college paper.

The reference section can help refine your key research questions and topic. During this initial research, I discovered lots on how the blues affected early rock and roll, but hardly anything on how the blues evolved into today's musical styles. If I write about blues history, there's so much information that I will have to narrow my topic sharply. If I focus on the effects of blues on today's music, I will have to draw my own conclusions, possibly making my essay more original than anything currently published.

Here are some recommended reference books. Most can also be accessed through the web (some provide free trial memberships):

General Background

- *Encyclopædia Britannica* (www.eb.com)
- *Van Nostrand's Scientific Encyclopedia*
- *Encyclopedia of World Biography*
- *Occupational Outlook Handbook* (stats.bls.gov/ocohome.htm)

Facts and Statistics

- *Information Please Almanac* (United States, world facts; www.infoplease.com)
- *The Statistical Abstract of the United States* (www.census.gov?stat_abstract)
- *Rand McNally Commercial Atlas and Marketing Guide* (business statistics)
- *CIA World Fact Book* (www.bls.gov/oco/home.htm)

I recommend browsing such books as *The Statistical Abstract of the United States.* **Curiosity and a few minutes can dig up strong facts on almost any topic.** For my music topic, I found that 26 percent of African Americans, 8 percent of whites, 7 percent of American Indians, and 9 percent of Asians sang in a group at least once in 1997 ("No. 441. Participation in Various Activities: 1997"). I don't know how or if I'll use this fact, but the differences intrigue me. If I were writing on gun control, I'd find these 1999 facts powerful: 65.2 percent of all murders in the United States are caused by guns; 6.8 percent are caused by "personal weapons" such as hands, fists, and feet ("No. 295. Murder Victims—Circumstances and Weapons Used..." 185). If I were writing on the death penalty, I would include that of the 272 people sentenced to death in 1999, 36 percent percent were actually executed—more than double the number in 1996 ("No. 337. Movement of Prisoners Under Sentence of Death..." 203).

■ **PRACTICE 14-3:** What conclusions might you draw from these facts?

■ **PRACTICE 14-4:** For your practice topic from 14-2, list the reference works you'd use, the specific subjects you'd search under, and the specific facts/statistics you'd like to find.

Books

Electronic card catalogs allow you to locate books at your library and other libraries. Examine the following online catalog card found under the subject of blues music:

Author	Elmer, Howard
Title	**Blues:** its birth and growth/Howard Elmer.
Publisher	Rosen Pub. Group, 1999.
Paging	64 p.: ill (some col.); 25 cm.
Series	The library of African American arts and culture.
Notes	Discography. pp. 58–59
	Includes bibliographical references (pp. 60–61) and index.
Summary	Traces the origins of blues music, its evolution in the United States, and its influence on jazz and rock and roll.
Subjects	**Blues** (Music) History and criticism; Juvenile literature.
Format	Child.

How reliable will this book be? Answering this question can help you think more deeply about your topic and spend less time on weak sources. Here are tips to help you decide.

- **Ask how closely the title relates to your topic.** This title looks good, but makes no direct connection to hardcore rap or grunge.

- **Compare the book's length with the size of the topic suggested by its title.** A history of music in 400 pages will be more superficial than a history of the blues in 200 pages. This book is only 64 pages long, so it's bound to be superficial—strike one against the book.

- **Consider the author's credibility.** Is this author an expert? I searched Amazon, an Internet bookstore, and the OCLC, an online reference to books in print, and found nothing else by Elmer—strike two.

- **Check the date.** How important this is depends on your topic. Scientific and technological topics often must be published within the last five years to be up to date. Psychology considers ten years old to be out of date. In books about historical events or music, "recent" can mean something published 25 years ago. Elmer's book, published in 1999, might include something on the blues and today's music. This book is still in the game.

- **Evaluate the book's format.** This book is formatted for a child, so it's probably oversimplified. I would have to be desperate to give it a quick look.

- **Check the source for an index.** An index helps you scan the book's subjects before you read the entire work. This book does have one.

- **Use the book to help you find more sources.** This book includes a discography (a list of popular musicians and titles) and a bibliography (a list of works the author used to write the book). Published in 1999, it might include some newer titles.

- **Use the subject line to learn how the book is categorized.** By checking the subject, you might discover new phrases to help refine your searches. This book tells me that I can find more books under the subject "blues history and criticism."

Should I use this book? I probably won't cite it in my essay, but it could lead me to better ones. Besides, I always gather more books than I'll need, so I can choose from the best.

For books worth reviewing, write down the title and call number. If you're working online, print the bibliographic information—and use the back of the sheet for note taking.

When you find good books in the library stacks, scan adjacent books. Related books are shelved next to each other.

To locate books not in your library, check *Books in Print,* which lists all books currently being sold, or visit the Online Computer Library Center (OCLC), a worldwide card catalog that connects 11,000 institutions with access to 22 million volumes. You can call up complete books and articles from more than 800 popular magazines published since 1994. Or search online bookstores such as Amazon (www.amazon.com) or Barnes and Noble (www.barnesandnoble.com). Write down the publisher and date, so you can ask the librarian to request an interlibrary loan from another college. Books usually take a week to arrive.

■ **PRACTICE 14-5:** Find a book title for your topic from your library's card catalog and another from *Books in Print,* the OCLC, or an online bookstore. You do not have to read the books, but do record complete bibliographic information. Then evaluate the likely reliability of the books.

Magazines and Newspapers

Why would you want magazine and newspaper articles if you have a book? Most new books are already one to five years old the minute they reach the bookstore because of lag time in writing, editing, and publishing. Magazines and newspapers cover current topics too small for books; for my blues topic, I might find many articles on musician Bo Diddley but no book. You can read many writers' ideas in magazine articles in the time it takes to read one book.

Periodical Indexes

Periodical indexes are hardbound catalogs for magazines and newspapers. They list articles written on a topic, giving the author, magazine, date, and, sometimes, brief summaries. Because thousands of magazines exist, there are many indexes, each covering up to 400 magazines.

Choose the appropriate index for your topic. Here are some major indexes and the dates they started:

- *Applied Science and Technology Index* (1958)
- *Art Index* (1929)
- *Business Periodicals Index* (1958)
- *Computer Literature Index* (1971)
- *Criminal Justice Abstracts* (1968)
- *Education Index* (1929)
- *Environmental Index* (1971)
- *Hospital Literature Index* (1944)
- *The Humanities Index* (1974)
- *The New York Times Index* (1913)
- *The Reader's Guide to Periodical Literature* (1900)
- *The Social Science Index* (1974)

Use general indexes for basic information. The most commonly used general indexes are *The Reader's Guide* and *The New York Times Index*. *The Reader's Guide* lists articles written in more than 200 magazines with the largest circulations, such as *Redbook, Time,* and *People.* Many of these magazines are thought-provoking and carefully researched, but some are too lightweight for college research.

Use specialized indexes for more high-powered information. In-depth research on Michelangelo's paintings, for example, will more likely turn up in magazines listed in *Art Index* than in those listed in *The Reader's Guide*. *Hospital Literature Index* will provide stronger sources on natural childbirth procedures than *The Reader's Guide*. In freshman English, *The Reader's Guide* and *The New York Times Index* may do quite well, but as you take upper-level courses, you'll need to know how to use specialized indexes. Here is a sample entry in the 1999 *New York Times Index* for the topic "The Blues."

Peter Watrous tribute to BlueNote Records, jazz label that marks its 60th Anniversary; Bruce Lundvall, who revived label in 1984, comments, interview; Photo. Jan. 10, II, 37:1.

Although this source might provide historical information that covers 60 years, it does not immediately focus on the African roots of blues or the impact of blues on today's music. For now, it would be a low-priority source.

■ **PRACTICE 14-6:** Which periodical index listed above would you use to find articles on these topics?

- Your topic from Practice 14-2
- Holes in the ozone layer of the atmosphere
- Welfare fraud

- Aristotle's philosophy
- Junior- and high-school violence
- End-of-time prophecies

COMPUTER INDEXES FOR MAGAZINES AND NEWSPAPERS

Computer indexes are rapidly replacing hardbound indexes. This textbook gives you a pass code to a premier periodical index called *InfoTrac*® College Edition (infotrac.thomsonlearning.com), which contains full-text articles. It has all the convenience of the Internet and is more reliable than the web for college research. For tips on using *InfoTrac*® College Edition, see page 464. I will use *InfoTrac*® College Edition to demonstrate how to use computer indexes for research.

Like many other computer indexes, *InfoTrac*® College Edition's first screen is where you enter search information. I started with "blues music," which gave me more than 1,000 hits: way too many! To focus, I entered "history of blues," and 70 citations popped up. Much better! To narrow even more, I combined "blues music" with words like "grunge," "hardcore,"and "hip-hop." Eight citations came up, but none were promising. Finally, I searched "blues music and rap," which turned over 73 hits. Scanning some of these hits helped me decide on my focus: the effect of blues music on hardcore rap.

Below is one *InfoTrac*® College Edition screen for my subject search: "blues music and rap."

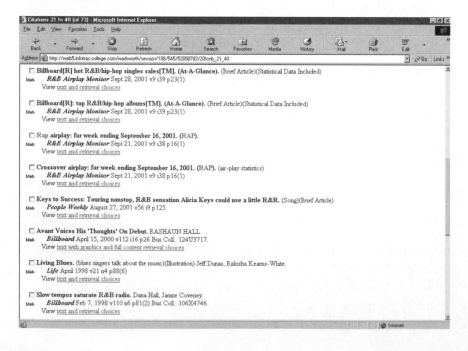

■ **PRACTICE 14-7**: Which of the articles shown on the screen (on the previous page) promises to be most useful for the topic "blues music and its effects on hardcore rap"?

I clicked on the seventh article, "Living Blues." Below is the start of the full-text article on *InfoTrac®* College Edition. I printed out the full-text article as well as e-mailed it to myself.

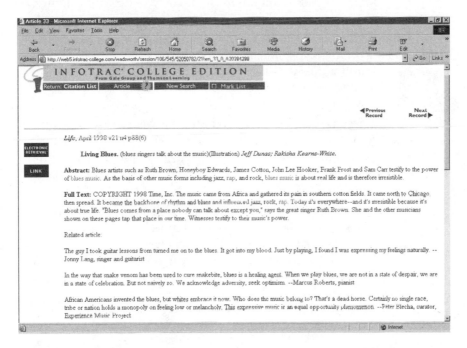

■ **PRACTICE 14-8**: Research your own topic on *infoTrac®* College Edition. Find at least two articles that seem worthy of review. For log-on information and tips, see page 464.

Your library may also provide these other common computer indexes:

- *ArticleFirst!* (full-text articles from sources similar to those in *The Reader's Guide to Periodical Literature*)

- *Expanded Academic Index* (full-text articles and sources from magazines and Internet sources)

- *First Search* (humanities, business, and science indexes)

- *NetFirst* (resources for web pages, listservs, and newsgroups)

- *ProQuest* (*New York Times* and hundreds of periodicals)

- *Wilsonselect* (*The Reader's Guide, Business Periodicals Index,* and other indexes; provides full-text articles)

Hints for Using Computer Indexes

- **Use indexes before you search the web.** They're as easy to use, better organized, and more reliable than Internet sources.

- **Start specific, and then broaden searches.** Type in your most specific topic first ("Blues"). If your results are minimal, try broader categories ("Music"), then scroll the list to discover better subheadings.

- **Use a variety of words to shorten the list of hits.** Many indexes provide a thesaurus topic list related to your search. If you get 361 hits as I did on *InfoTrac*® College Edition under "Blues Music," combine words and phrases ("Blues History" or "Roots of Blues") to reduce the number of hits. Using the words "The Blues and Africa," I landed 21 articles.

- **Limit your searches by date.** When I narrowed my *InfoTrac*® College Edition search for articles between 1999 and 2002, I found nine.

- **Change your search options.** *InfoTrac*® College Edition's opening page allows you to search by subject or keywords. A subject search gave me 1,231 hits, but a keyword search turned up 23.

- **Divide your subject into subcategories.** When I did a subject search on "rap music," *InfoTrac*® College Edition provided me with 97 subdivisions. One subcategory called "demographic aspects" listed four articles on who enjoys rap and why. Each database is like a door in a house. You need to look in all the rooms to find the best information.

WEB SOURCES

The web is the preferred means of research among college students, but it can be risky because many sites are unreliable. Here's how you can become a smarter Internet user.

Reliable and Unreliable Web Sites

- **The Internet is unregulated.** No official verifies the web's validity. Although published authors make mistakes and distort facts at times, editors try to correct them. Readers cancel unreliable publications. After bad reviews crush weak books, the library staff picks only the survivors to shelve. Your odds of reading trustworthy information in a college library are a lot better than when you plug in to Smokin' Billy's web site.

- **Knowing the type of web site you're viewing will help you evaluate it.** For example, the National Rifle Association (www.nra.org) and Green Peace (www.greenpeace.org) are nonprofit organizations, yet their commitment to causes means they often provide biased information. Educational institutions (edu) usually are the most objective. Commercial sites (com) are bound to slant information, but some list resource-filled links associated with their product. For example, a company that sells toddler car seats might provide articles on car safety. Government (gov), organization (org), and military (mil) sites are as reliable as the groups that create them.

- **Avoid web sites with advertising banners and pop-up windows.** These sites want your money, not your mind.

- **Web sites with their own search engines tend to be the best organized and most reliable.**

- **Check for the site's last update.** If the page hasn't been updated for six months, forget it. The page's creator is too lazy or uninterested to be reliable.

- **Review the site's "Links" page.** Click on a few links to learn more about the person who maintains the page.

- **Personal web pages often contain a tilde (~) within the web site address.** For example, the *BluesWEB* address is www.island.net/~blues. This page might reflect its owner's biases.

■ **PRACTICE 14-9:** Find one reliable and one unreliable web site for your topic from Practice 14-2. Explain why one is weak and the other promising for academic essays.

Searching the Web

The smart online researcher works efficiently, targeting prime sites and browsing before devoting hours of intense reading.

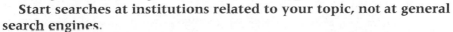

Start searches at institutions related to your topic, not at general search engines.

- For social or economic topics, visit the U.S. Department of Justice (www.usdoj.gov/02organizations/index.html).

- For historical topics, try the Smithsonian Institute (www.si.edu).

- For health and human services topics, visit the Food and Drug Administration (www.fda.org).

- For vital statistics and population growth, visit the U.S. Census Bureau (www.census.gov).

Visit major news sites. For up-to-the-minute information, try these:

- *CNN News* (www.cnn.com)

- *National Public Radio Online* (www.npr.org)

- *New York Times Online* (www.nytimes.com)

Use search engines *after* **trying computer indexes and institutional sites.** While search engines attempt to categorize the entire world's web sites, new sites emerge each minute! And their creators report their presence to only *some* search engines. So which is the best to use?

Your search engine should provide current information. To learn which engine is best and whether new ones are available, I visit *Search Engine Showdown* (www.searchengineshowdown.com). *Yahoo!* has been a favorite, but *Google* has been taking the web by storm since 2002.

Your engine should categorize searches. A site like *Yahoo!* organizes information by subject. I learned that "blues music" was subcategorized like this: Arts > Music > Styles > Blues. I clicked on "Styles" to retrieve information on "hip hop" music. By reading the categories, I learned new phrases to refine my search.

Your engine should provide an advanced search link. A site like *Altavista* lets you search with exact phrases, such as "hardcore rap" or "history of the blues music."

Your engine should retrieve images and audio. *Alltheweb*, like many engines, lets you limit searches by photographs, streamlined video, and sound files. This was useful for my blues topic when I wanted to know what B. B. King, a famous rhythm and blues musician, looked and sounded like. Using *Alltheweb* connected me to Broadcast.com (www.broadcast.com), which stores free online videos.

Your engine should search through other engines. Meta-search engines report only the top hits of other engines, saving you the hassle of going to each one. *Dogpile* lives up to its slogan: "All results. No mess." Another favorite is *Metacrawler:* It "crawls" through other engines.

Here are addresses for the search engines mentioned:

- *Alltheweb* (www.alltheweb.com)
- *Altavista* (www.altavista.com)
- *Dogpile* (www.dogpile.com)
- *Google* (www.google.com)
- *Metacrawler* (www.metacrawler.com)
- *Yahoo!* (www.yahoo.com)

■ **PRACTICE 14-10:** Search two engines listed above using the same word or phrases for your topic from Practice 14-2. Which engine gave you the better results? Explain.

Electronic Mail and Newsgroups

E-mail an author and request a virtual interview. During my literature class, one presentation group stunned us with a letter from Ron Carlson, a short-story fiction author. They located him at a Midwest university and e-mailed questions about his story. Within a day, they received a two-page response!

Visit college web sites to find e-mail addresses of professors who might share expertise. Because e-mail is essentially an interview, be professional. Do some homework to avoid asking obvious questions. Let the person know in advance what your assignment entails, where you are located, and what class you're taking. This openness will likely lead to a conversation. As a kind gesture, send the person a copy of your paper, along with a thank-you note.

Post a question at an "Ask an Expert" web site. These sites allow you for free to ask experts specific questions related to your topic. Usually within three days, you receive a response e-mail with links to more information. Check out Allexperts.com (www.allexperts.com).

■ **PRACTICE 14-11:** Post a question related to your topic at *Allexperts.com*, and bring the response to class.

Register your e-mail address with an online newsgroup that discusses specific topics. Whenever articles or responses are posted, they are automatically e-mailed to you. *InterBulletin* (news.interbulletin.com) lets you search through 30,000 newsgroups. I found several groups related to blues and rap. I also visited MTV (www.mtv.com) and joined one of its online communities. I asked, "In what ways is rap like traditional blues? Is rap a real outlet to frustration or is it just fake music?" Within a day, 30 people responded. Many knew less about the topic than I did, but a few gave me great leads to artists and song lyrics I could use in my essay. Because responses may take a week, join a newsgroup as soon as your research paper is assigned.

■ **PRACTICE 14-12:** Go to *Interbulletin*. Find at least two newsgroups related to your paper topic.

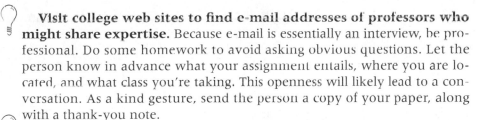

OVERLOOKED RESOURCES: LOCAL COMMUNITIES, SMART FRIENDS, PERSONAL EXPERIENCE

Use the Yellow Pages telephone directory to contact local organizations or businesses related to your topic. One of my students concerned about pollution in the lake near his home discovered specific information by calling local conservation departments. They told him which species of fish and turtle were dying, the specific sources of water deterioration, and current pollution levels. Another student researching funeral rituals interviewed several undertakers and was given a very detailed tour of the facilities. She learned far more than books would have taught her. Food, sports, housing, technology, child care, and a host of other topics have local experts. Most will give information over the phone to courteous callers.

Ask friends, family, bosses, and professors for leads. For my topic, I called a friend who sings in a blues band. He named several famous blues women to research. A student of mine wrote a proposal to reduce crime among inner-city youth. I gave her a contact to a program in which teens manage four acres of inner-city land and sell the produce. My student interviewed them about how the program helped build positive futures.

Create your own good sources for research. A student who wanted our college to offer more televised courses called the regional public broadcasting station to find out how many were offered locally and nationally. To project how popular telecourses might be, she conducted an informal survey in several of her classes. She also used an almanac to discover that 88 percent of American homes with television sets now have VCRs, so she concluded that colleges could offer telecourses at unpopular time slots because most people can tape programs. She found no books, but located a few magazine articles. Her own brain-teasing ideas were that telecourses might relieve our college's classroom shortage, attract students with irregular schedules, and reduce traffic and parking congestion. She sent her proposal to the college curriculum committee.

Collect your own research firsthand. Here's an example of a student gathering her own research simply by counting. This paragraph comes from a letter Jennifer Wheeler sent to her employer's retail clothing store. She wanted the store to recycle or eliminate plastic wrapping to "do its part in saving our planet":

> During a typical week in the Ladies Sportswear Department at my store, we receive approximately fifteen rolling racks of hung clothing and between five and ten racks of boxed clothing. Each individual piece of merchandise is needlessly prepackaged in plastic that is thrown away. Weekly, we throw away approximately 3,000 plastic bags and 2,250 plastic hangers. This is only Ladies Sportswear. My manager informed me that monthly our store discards one ton of plastic. Many of these bags can be reused, and all the hangers can be used in the store instead of switching the clothes to our store hangers. This would save salesclerks six hours of work in our department each week.

Tips for Soliciting Research in Person

- *Ask* for the person's time a week ahead, and explain exactly why you want it. Suggest a few sample questions and how much time you'll need. (I recommend 30 minutes.)
- Do your preliminary reading first. Your awareness will encourage your source to provide better information.
- Prepare questions, but be open to new ideas during the interview.
- Come with paper and pen. If you want to tape a formal interview, ask permission.
- Dress professionally—you will get better information.

- Start with an easy question to loosen things up, but move to the key research questions quickly, so you don't run out of time before asking them.

- *Immediately* after an interview, fill out your notes and record your reactions before they go cold. Be sure to indicate which are quotes, paraphrases, and personal reactions.

- Send a typed thank-you note, along with a copy of your paper.

■ **PRACTICE 14-13:** Make a list of three people or organizations that can give you information for your topic from Practice 14-2. List at least five questions you'd ask.

NOTE-TAKING STRATEGIES

There is no one "right" way to take notes, but here are some suggestions:

- **Skim your list of sources before reading any.** Read only the most recent, expert, or relevant to your topic. Scan the headings, index, or table of contents to find the best information quickly.

- **Use Post-it notes as tabs in the margins of books and journals.** Label tabs with topic headings, and write down questions and reactions on them.

- **3 × 5 note cards provide two advantages.** They're neater than a mess of papers. Also, cards can be easily rearranged when you organize the paper—provided you limit yourself to one fact or one idea per note card. With two ideas on one card wanting to go different places in the essay, you'd be like Solomon, debating how to divide the brainchild.

- **Loose-leaf paper provides space to write reactions, but will tempt you to put too many ideas on one page**. To keep yourself organized, label your first sheet of paper, "Bibliography." On it, record only each source's bibliographic information. Number each one. Next, label a second sheet of paper "Notes." This is where you quote, paraphrase, and comment on your sources. Instead of rewriting all of the titles, use only their numbers from your first page. You can also use color highlighters to identify related ideas or facts.

- **Paraphrase instead of copying long quotations.** Condense the original, and quote only key sentences or phrases. Try not to look at the original as you paraphrase so you don't risk plagiarism. This will help *your* voice control the draft. After reading the source, ask yourself, "What is the one key point I need from this source?" Then write. Of course, if you unearth an absolutely sparkling paragraph, take it whole. In your notes, always quote accurately: Use quotation marks and record page numbers.

- **Comment on and analyze source material while reading.** Be an active thinker, not just a copier, when you take notes. Raise an objection to the author, add a personal anecdote, or connect sources. This is easy on full-size notebook paper. For note cards, use a separate card to react to sources. In either case, be sure to label "My Ideas" or "My Comment" at the top so you never confuse your ideas with those borrowed from research. Staple or clip comment cards to the source cards. The following example on blues music shows actual notes that I wrote. The first two cards separate source material and commentary:

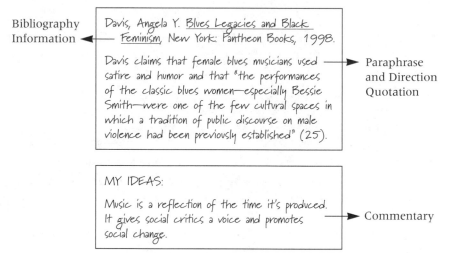

Bibliography Information ◄——

Davis, Angela Y. *Blues Legacies and Black Feminism*, New York: Pantheon Books, 1998.

Davis claims that female blues musicians used ——► satire and humor and that "the performances of the classic blues women—especially Bessie Smith—were one of the few cultural spaces in which a tradition of public discourse on male violence had been previously established" (25).

Paraphrase and Direction Quotation

MY IDEAS:

Music is a reflection of the time it's produced. It gives social critics a voice and promotes ——► social change.

Commentary

Here's an example that combines source and commentary on one card:

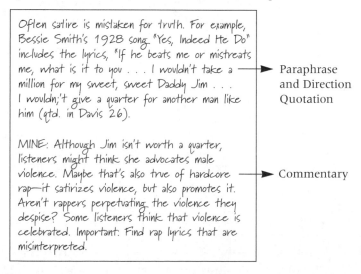

Often satire is mistaken for truth. For example, Bessie Smith's 1928 song "Yes, Indeed He Do" includes the lyrics, "If he beats me or mistreats me, what is it to you . . . I wouldn't take a ——► million for my sweet, sweet Daddy Jim . . . I wouldn;'t give a quarter for another man like him (qtd. in Davis 26).

Paraphrase and Direction Quotation

MINE: Although Jim isn't worth a quarter, listeners might think she advocates male violence. Maybe that's also true of hardcore ——► rap—it satirizes violence, but also promotes it. Aren't rappers perpetuating the violence they despise? Some listeners think that violence is celebrated. Important: Find rap lyrics that are misinterpreted.

Commentary

■ **Record the complete bibliographic information with your notes.**
Write page numbers after each paraphrase or quotation. You don't want
to lack a publisher or date after the library closes for the weekend or discover the web site you've used has been removed.

■ **PRACTICE 14-14:** Fill a note card or sheet of paper on your topic from
Practice 14-2 based on a source you found. Paraphrase most of your source
but include a short quotation.

ORGANIZING RESEARCH PAPERS

Identify patterns. To organize your research notes, start by looking for
patterns of ideas and details. If you used note cards, place them into related
piles and create headings. If you used loose-leafs, spread them out on a table
to create main headings. Read through your notes and put them aside. On
a separate sheet, list the main points you want to cover. Then go back to
your notes and put the paraphrases or quotations under the headings. For
the blues, these are my tentative headings:

- Origins of blues/rap
- Blues and the black experience
- Blues and the human experience
- Blues' influence on hardcore/grunge

Formulate a thesis statement *before* **creating a detailed outline.**
Especially with long papers, a working thesis helps to create structure for
your piles of notes. Read through your notes, marking ones that relate to
the thesis, and write several trial thesis sentences from them. Remember:
Make your thesis a statement, not a question. One sentence is preferred.
Here are three possible thesis statements for my blues topic:

- Despite the negative stereotypes of rap and hardcore, they connect with
  traditional blues music.
- Like the blues in its early days, rap and hardcore express human frustration.
- Because American cities have become more violent, the evolution of the
  blues into hardcore rap is natural.

Instant self-analysis: My first two seem obvious and bland. My last
thesis statement is edgier. I can compare blues and rap as outlets of frustration, yet explore how hardcore rap, unlike the blues, often promotes the violence it despises.

Work in bold stray facts or quotations. If good statistics or quotations
don't fit into one of your headings, you might use them in your introduction or conclusion.

Expect to do more research. Now is a good time to look for gaps. Write
a list of missing information that you'll need to improve your essay.

Write an outline or abstract. Many professors require students to submit parts of their research papers in stages for approval. Try not to think of this as an extra chore, but as an aid in writing: It forces you to think and organize early, stimulating your subconscious to incubate, and it provides feedback before a grade is at stake. Get used to preliminary reports. Often business and professional research requires an "abstract"—a thesis and a paragraph summary of the main points. This is usually submitted for approval before the paper is written and may accompany the final draft. Here is my paper's very rough outline. Notice how much more specific it is than my first list of tentative headings on page 319.

- The blues reflects early 1,900 frustrations
- Hardcore rap reflects today's frustrations
- How blues helped people
- How hardcore rap helps people
- How blues kept people downtrodden
- How hardcore rap perpetuates victimization

■ **PRACTICE 14-15:** Formulate a thesis statement and main headings for your topic from Practice 14-2.

WRITING RESEARCH PAPERS

Drafting a research paper involves the same process discussed in Chapter 6. An **introduction** should grab the reader with key research questions, an anecdote, or a strong fact, which smoothly leads to a clear thesis statement. Often introductions preview what you will cover and explain why you will not cover others. In my blues topic, I probably would not cover the obvious connection to rock and roll, but instead explore the less studied "blues and hardcore rap." **Work quickly on the first draft,** so you aren't sidetracked by little problems. Your main goals are to clarify your sketchy ideas and to support them with sharp details.

What's unique and complicated about research papers is using sources, which will be the focus of the rest of this chapter. Incorporating research into essays requires four parts: the tag line; paraphrase or quotation of the material; commentary; and citation.

Use Tag Lines

Tag lines make quotations, paraphrases, and facts flow with your paper. Tag lines introduce the source before you present the quotation or paraphrase: "As one social researcher says . . ." or "After 30 years as a judge, Kristin Landon believes . . ." Tag lines prepare readers for a new voice and tell *what authority* your source carries.

Paraphrase or Quote Directly?

Paraphrase all but the most important sentences. You cover ground faster with paraphrases. Strings of quotations frustrate readers, who assume correctly that the real message is in your voice. If two or three writers agree on one point, quote or paraphrase only the best one; don't drag readers through redundant quotations. Here's an example of a good student paraphrase mixed with bits of quotation from a clinical description of an animal test by Mindy Reynolds:

> The Draize Test involves testing cosmetics for eye damage that might occur to *Tagline* humans. Reports describe how researchers smear mascara, for example, over the eyeballs of rabbits. Unlike humans, rabbits have no tear glands to wash it off. The *Paraphrase and Quotation* animals are "immobilized" in a stockade device. In some cases their eyes are held open with clips. As a result, they cannot blink to get even a moment's relief and ultimately suffer "eye ulcers, bleeding, and blindness" (O'Connor 94). And for *Citation Author* what purpose? The tests do not even resemble how humans use the product. *commentary*

Block-format quotations that are four lines or more. Indent the entire passage five spaces. The quotation's font and line spacing remain the same as the rest of your essay. No quotation marks are needed. Use block quotations sparingly. Here's a sample block format I took from an article written by singer Ruth Brown in the April 1998 issue of *Live* entitled "Living Blues":

> As black Americans, we naturally have the greatest feel for [the blues]. We have the reasons. But the blues itself knows no color line. It is about people—old people, young people as well—learning how to go inside themselves and touch something. The blues is like vocal crying. It is a way for a man to cry with dignity. Usually, society doesn't allow a man to cry. But look at B.B., Bobby "Blue" Bland, T-Bone, John Lee Hooker. Dignity (98).

■ **PRACTICE 14-16:** Paraphrase the above quotation in your own words. Be prepared to read and compare the source's words to your paraphrase during class.

Comment on Sources

Interpret your source material. Your commentary ties the source to your essay—makes everything fit smoothly. Agree, disagree, expand, or clarify the idea of the source when you comment. If you don't comment, readers might misinterpret your information or simply not understand how it supports your thesis.

Here's an example from an essay against the banning of handguns. It's from the student's refutation section, where Barbara Collins considers arguments opposing her thesis. Notice how she leads us back to her thesis:

Tagline
Paraphrase
and
Citation

Commentary

According to a *U.S. News and World Report* study, police argue that a gun is six times more likely to be shot at a family member or a friend than at an intruder (Baer, Gest, and Anderson 35). This, however, does not justify banning guns. Let's take the husband who goes mad and wants to kill his family. He goes to the gun case and notices his gun is missing. Does he change his mind and decide to let them live? No. People in a rage use knives, clubs, or their bare hands. The weapon isn't the gun; it's hatred and insanity.

Handling and Interpreting Statistics

Like quotations and paraphrases, you must comment on statistics or you will lose your reader. Imagine reading a political science essay on voting, and in the middle of a page you run into this table lifted from *The Statistical Abstract of the United States*.

No. 401. Voting-Age Population, Percent Voted, 2000

Characteristic	Voting Age Population	Percent Voting
Total	202.6 million	54.7
18–20 years old	11.9 million	28.4
21–24 years old	14.9 million	24.2
25–34 years old	37.3 million	43.7
35–44 years old	44.5 million	55.0
45–64 years old	61.4 million	64.1
65+	32.8 million	67.6
White	168.7 million	56.4
Black	24.1 million	53.5
Hispanic	21.6 million	27.5
School Years Completed		
8 or less	12.9 million	26.8
9–11	20.1 million	33.6
12	66.3 million	49.4
1–3 years of college	55.3 million	60.3
4 years of college	48.0 million	72.0
Employed	133.4 million	55.5
Unemployed	4.9 million	35.1

If you're like me, you skimmed this table. It's just too much to absorb. In the middle of a research paper, it'll have the same zero effect. To make it count, you must **draw conclusions about the statistics.** Here's my point as it might appear in a draft (without the table):

> Research shows that older, better-educated Americans vote more and consequently have more power getting their candidate in office. People more likely to be poor—the young, minorities, the less educated and the unemployed—all vote less than their counterparts. For example, in the 2000 presidential elections, only 28.4% of 18- to 20-year-olds voted, while people over 65 voted at a 67.6% rate ("No. 401. Voting Age Population" 251). Is it any wonder that Congress makes Social Security a priority while it cuts college loans and job programs?
>
> Likewise, while 56.4% of whites and 53.5% of blacks voted, only 27.5% of Hispanics voted (251). Of course, the language and cultural barrier may keep many Hispanics home, but which came first? Do they not vote because the politicians ignore them, or do the politicians ignore them because they don't vote? The unemployed voter—who should have high stakes in electing people to create jobs—only voted at a 35.1% rate compared to 55.5% for the employed. And those with college degrees were more than twice as likely to vote as those who never finished high school (251). The young, minorities, less educated, and unemployed should be better motivated to have their voices heard. Yet it is the "haves" who vote most often. Perhaps because they are "haves," they believe in the system and keep it going. Those who are alienated may feel the system will not listen to them anyway and don't vote because it best expresses how they feel.

[Margin annotations: Author's idea; Statistic supports idea; Commentary; Statistic; Commentary; Statistics; Conclusions]

Notice how my commentary alternates with hard statistics—ideas alternating with details. But two flaws in my paragraph must be dealt with. First, I did not mention that the voting age population includes noncitizens—a footnote in *The Statistical Abstract*. This affects my interpretation of the Hispanic voter, since large numbers of Mexican and Cuban immigrants in the United States cannot vote. Perhaps if noncitizens were left out, the statistics would show that Hispanics vote at much higher rates. I need to find out! To be an honest researcher, you must present and account for all factors in the statistics that might affect your conclusions. The second flaw is an unstated assumption that groups vote as a block in their own self-interest. But a grandmother may want students to have loans, and an employed person may want better job-training programs. Can you think of any other issues the statistics and my conclusions raise?

Use Parenthetical Citations

- **Always use citations in the body of your essay to document sources.** A citation is the material in parentheses that follows any ideas taken from a source. For your English papers, use the **Modern Language Association (MLA)** format.

- **Citation format:** List the author's last name and the page number where the material was found, like this: (Toutelli 52). Notice there are no commas or abbreviations for page numbers. The reader can locate the entire source at the end of your essay in the Works Cited list—arranged alphabetically by the authors' last names. The Works Cited list will be discussed later in this chapter on page 326.

- **Author's name used in tag line:** If you use the author's name in the tag line of your quotation or paraphrase, as in "Professor Toutelli declares . . ." then the parentheses would only include a page number, like this: (52).

- **Source with no page number:** When a source such as an Internet article or pamphlet doesn't provide a page number, use "n.pag." in place of the page number: (O'Shea n. pag.).

- **Two sources by one author:** If you use two or more sources by the same author, you must indicate in the parentheses which one the material came from, like this: (Toutelli, *Demon Data* 52). Use ellipsis points to shorten long titles (Toutelli, "Finding . . ." 12). The first citation is from a book (it's italicized) and the second from an article in a magazine or newspaper (the title is enclosed in quotation marks).

- **No author is named:** Use the title of the work in the citation: ("Internet Excess" 31).

- **A source within a source:** Suppose you're using Richland's idea quoted in Toutelli's work. Include both names like this: (Richland qtd. in Toutelli 30).

- **American Psychological Association (APA) variation:** Social and natural sciences papers require the date of the publication just after the author's name and a "p." or "pp." before the page number(s): (Toutelli, 1999, p. 226). The APA requires a page reference only if you give a direct quotation or statistic; general summary needs only a name and date, like this: (Toutelli, 1990). Use this format for citations in papers you write for psychology, sociology, and science courses. To study how a sample research paper uses APA citations (on *InfoTrac®* College Edition), see page 346.

■ **PRACTICE 14-17:** For your note card or sheet from Practice 14-14, write a brief paragraph that introduces the source smoothly and uses a proper MLA citation.

AVOIDING PLAGIARISM

Under current copyright law everything anyone writes, including student essays, is copyrighted—that is, protected by law from being used by anyone else without written permission. Copyright laws protect authors and publishers from other people profiting from their efforts. However, this would create havoc if millions of college students needed publishers' permissions to quote sources in papers. So all have agreed that proper documentation will substitute for written permission to use copyrighted material for scholarship. Documenta tion proves your material comes from reputable sources, and also "pays" an author and publisher by acknowledging them for using their work.

Use introductory tag lines to tell readers where source material begins, and use the citation parentheses to mark the end of source material. Anything else you are claiming as your idea. Quotations or para phrases without citations create doubts and may result in a teacher accus ing you of plagiarism—academic theft. Although it's easy to steal or buy papers on the Internet, it's also much easier for professors to catch plagia rism with today's smart search engines and detection software. Don't risk your college education! The following must have citations:

- Quotations
- Paraphrases or summaries in your words
- Statistics or facts

Rewriting does not make an *idea* yours; it only makes the *words* yours. A citation credits the *idea* to someone else. Quotation marks credit the *exact wording* to someone else.

Common knowledge does not need citation. The core of knowledge possessed by most educated people is called "common knowledge" and does not require citations or Works Cited entries: It is considered the common property of society. This includes **famous quotations** like these:

- "I have a dream."—Martin Luther King, Jr.
- "Oh that this too, too solid flesh would melt."—Shakespeare
- "I am not a crook."—Richard Nixon

Common knowledge also includes ideas:

- The First Amendment to the U.S. Constitution protects the right of free speech.
- Capitalism stresses individual rights, while socialism stresses group rights.
- Most religions say death is a release from the pain of life, not a dreaded event.

Common knowledge can be facts and statistics as well:

- Shakespeare lived in England 400 years ago and wrote the plays *Hamlet* and *The Tempest*.
- DDT spraying 40 years ago still pollutes water today and kills fish and birds.
- Michelangelo painted the Sistine Chapel.
- The speed of light is more than 186,000 miles per second.

Expert knowledge requires citation. Higher degrees of specific knowledge cease to be common knowledge. If, for instance, you quoted the rest of Hamlet's speech, or discussed the debate over the approval of the First Amendment that took place in 1790, or described the specific chemi cal reaction DDT causes in bald eagle eggs, it would cease to be common knowledge for the public. Among *experts,* this information may still be considered common knowledge, but until you establish yourself as an expert, you must document.

Anything you learn from reading specifically for a paper must be documented. If you read something at least three times in different sources, you can suspect it is common knowledge. Ask your professor if you're not sure.

■ **PRACTICE 14-18:** Which of the following is common knowledge? Which is expert knowledge?

- Tupak Amaru Shakur, a famous rap artist, was murdered in Las Vegas, Nevada.

- Shakur's parents were Black Panthers; his mother was pregnant with Shakur while imprisoned in New York.

- "Tupak Amaru" means "Thankful to God" in Arabic.

WORKS CITED

MLA Format

MLA Works Cited Format

- The entire *list is alphabetized* by the author's last name, so citations are easy to locate.

- If there is no author named, alphabetical order is determined by the first main word of the title.

- Indent second and third lines five spaces to keep the author's name visible.

- Double-space.

- Follow punctuation and order of items exactly.

- Title the list "Works Cited" on a separate page at the end of the paper (but don't use quotation marks around it).

- Include only works you actually cite (not everything you read for the paper).

Here's how an MLA Works Cited list of three sources might look at the end of your paper:

Works Cited

"Fatherhood in America." <u>Fathers and Families: Advocacy for the Father Child Bond</u>. 22 Mar. 1999. 27 Aug. 1999
    <http://www.fathersandfamilies.org/about/fathers.htm>.

Price, Margaret. "Beyond 'Gotcha!': Situating Plagiarism in Policy and
Pedagogy." College Composition and Communication
Sept. 2002: 88–115.

Reeve, Christopher. Nothing is Impossible: Reflections on a New Life.
New York: Random House, 2002.

The first is from the web, the second from a journal, and the third from a
book. When you create your own Works Cited list, find the proper format
for each source and follow it exactly.

Works Cited Formats

Basic book format—author, title, place of publication, publisher, and date
published. Use the latest date listed on the copyright page. You may use a
short form for publishers ("Thomson" instead of "Thomson Heinle").

Feynman, Richard. The Pleasure of Finding Things Out. Cambridge,
Massachusetts: Perseus, 1999.

Book with editor, but no author—title, editor name(s) in normal order,
place of publication, publisher, and date published.

The Whole World Book of Quotations. Eds. Kathryn Petras and Ross Petras.
New York: Addison-Wesley, 1994.

Book with two or three authors—second and third authors' names are
in normal order.

Brody, Marjorie, and Shawn Kent. Power Presentations: How to Connect with
Your Audience & Sell Your Ideas. New York: Wiley and Sons, 1993.

Book with more than three authors—"et al." means "and others."

Axon, Pamela, et al. Juggernaut. New York: Smith, 2000.

Book not in first edition—after title, insert edition.

Botwinick, Rita Steinhardt. A History of the Holocaust: From Ideology to
Annihilation. 2nd ed. New Jersey: Prentice-Hall, 2001.

Book that collects the works of various authors—list the author of the
work you cited, the title of that work, then information on the book. Page
numbers are needed.

Bambara, Toni Cade. "The Lesson." American Mosaic: Multicultural Readings in
Context. 2nd ed. Eds. Barbara Roche Rico and Sandra Mano. Boston:
Houghton Mifflin, 1995. 417–23.

Book in more than one volume—insert volume before place of publication.

Journey into China's Antiquity. Ed. Yu Weichoa. Vol. 1. New York: Art Media
Resources, 1998. 39–44.

Common reference books—complete publishing information not needed. Edition date only. List the entry under the heading where your information was found.

"Fauvism." <u>Encyclopædia Britannica</u>. 2003 ed.

Lecture—speaker, title of lecture, sponsoring group, location, and specific date.

Gould, Steven Jay. "Wonderful Life." Rochester Arts and Lectures, Rochester, NY. 26 Apr. 1990.

Monthly magazine—author, title of article, magazine, and date. Abbreviate months except for May, June, and July. Pages of entire article listed. If the article skips pages, use a "+" instead of listing all pages.

Burka, Paul. "Spare the A-Rod." <u>Natural History</u> Feb. 2001: 7+.

Weekly magazine—specific date included.

Zunes, Stephen. "A Case Against War." <u>The Nation</u> 30 Sept. 2002: 11–14.

Quarterly magazine—volume number and issue after magazine title, then the year in parentheses followed by page number. If magazine pages are numbered continuously throughout the year, do not include the season in parentheses. The "25.1" here means it is in volume 25 and the first issue of the year.

McDougall, Walter. "Why Geography Matters." <u>American Educator</u> 25.1 (2001): 10.

Newspaper—include section with page number. If the section here had been a number instead of a letter, you would write "sec 5: 25."

Quindlen, Anna. "Forward March." <u>New York Times</u> 7 Jan. 1990: E25.

Newspaper without city in title—include after title in brackets.

"Archer Drawn to Art of Making Bows." <u>Democrat and Chronicle</u> [Rochester, NY]. 29 Sept. 2002: D8.

No author listed—with any source not naming an author, start with the next item needed, alphabetized by its first letter. The following example would be listed under "R" in the "Works Cited."

"Rating Desktop Computers." <u>Consumer Reports</u>. Sept. 1996: 22–24.

Interview—use book or magazine format if you read the interview, but use the following if you conducted the interview yourself.

Raines, Tim. Personal interview. 18 May 2002.

Corporate or group author—specific unit listed as author and larger company or group listed after title.

Microsoft Product Support Services. <u>Getting Started with Works 2000</u>. Microsoft, 1999.

Pamphlet—author, title, place of publication, publisher, and date, if available. Try to follow the book format. In the following entry, the city of publication was not named.

> Forestry Office. <u>Trees and Shrubs in New York</u>. New York State Department of Environmental Conservation, 1999.

Television program—program title, director ("Dir."), narrator ("Narr.") or writers ("By"), station name, location, and date.

> <u>CBS Evening News</u>. Narr. Dan Rather. KTVT, Fort Worth, TX. 4 Jan. 2000.

Videotape, no author—episode (if any), title, format, producing company, date.

> "Part I." <u>Thomas Jefferson: A Film by Ken Burns</u>. Videotape. By Turner Home Entertainment, 1996.

Audiocassette—composer or author, title, volume (if any), format, producing company, identifying number (if any), date.

> Missler, Chuck. <u>Cosmic Codes</u>. Vol. 1. Audiocassette. Koinonia House, BPZ07, 1998.

Electronic Sources

There are so many ways to access electronic sources that it's difficult to standardize their Works Cited formats. But the first step is to categorize your source as previously unpublished or previously published.

Previously Unpublished Electronic Sources

"Previously unpublished" means that the material has not been printed in a newspaper or magazine before appearing electronically. Although some of the information below may not be provided on the Internet, give whatever is listed.

Article that is only available on the web: Author. Title. Place of publication. Date published. Date of your access <complete Internet address>.

> Galewitz, Phil. "Milestone for America's Richest: Group Passes $1 Trillion Mark." <u>ABCnews.com</u>. 23 Sept. 1999. 24 Sept. 1999 <http://www.abcnews.go.com/sections/business/DailyNews/forbes990923.html>.

Professional or personal web site: Author. Title of article. Name of web site. Date of your access <complete Internet address>.

> Smith, Gary. "King of the Delta Blues." <u>BluesWeb</u>. 29 Aug. 1999 <http://www.island.net/~blues>.

Newsgroup or bulletin board posting: Author. Title taken from subject line in quotation marks. Online posting. Date material was posted. Name of forum. Date of access <Online address of newsgroup or bulletin board>.

> Sanchez, Ramon. "This Too Shall Pass." Online posting. 19 Oct. 1999. True
>   Freedom. 30 Oct. 1999 <www.truefreedom.com>.

Sound recording or clip: Author. Title of file. Name of record or audio label. Name of web site. Date submitted to Internet. Date of access <complete Internet address>.

> Lanegan, Mark. "Little Sadie." Sub Pop Records. <u>RealGuide Jukebox</u>. Sept. 1999.
>   10 Oct. 1999 <http:/realguide.real.com/category.rxml?category_uid=
>   405&artist=Mark_Laneg>.

E-mail communication: Author of e-mail. Title of message taken from subject line. Recipient of e-mail. Date received. (Note on etiquette: Request permission from the e-mail's author.)

> Rock, Sarah M. "Blues History." E-mail to Jason O. Tollers. 14 Sept. 2002.

Previously Published Electronic Sources

"Previously published" means the source was originally printed on paper, then later converted to electronic form. Usually, these types of sources are from CD-ROMs or computerized indexes like *InfoTrac*® College Edition. Typically, you can tell if works have been previously published if the site includes periodical titles, volume numbers, page numbers, and dates.

These formats are tedious, but here's a hint: **Use the traditional MLA format first, and then tack on the following electronic information (when a computer service is not listed, skip it and go to the next item):**

- Name of computerized index underlined (*InfoTrac*® College Edition, *ProQuest, ERIC, NY Times Online*, etc.)
- Publication medium (when source is from a CD-ROM or diskette)
- Name of computer service or producer (Nexis, BRS, Prodigy, AOL, etc.)
- Date you looked it up if online or date of electronic publication to CD-ROM
- Complete web site or file transfer address (be exact—one missing letter will create an incorrect link)

Article from a CD-ROM or CD-ROM database: Traditional MLA citation for the article (in this case, a weekly newspaper). Computerized index title. Publication medium. Date when CD-ROM was produced.

> Clines, Francis. "An Ode to the Typewriter." <u>New York Times</u> 10 July 1995: A3.
>   <u>ProQuest</u>. CD-ROM. Jan. 1996.

Articles from a computerized index or web site: Traditional MLA citation for the article (in this case, a monthly journal). The name of the computerized index. Date you viewed the Internet article <complete web address>.

Johnson, Kate. "Stop giving antibiotics for the common cold." Pediatric News 36.6 (June 2002). InfoTrac. 29 Sept. 2002 <http://web5.infotrac-college.com/wadsworth/session/607/753/24359636/37!xrn_14_0_A88128247>.

Book on the Internet that was previously published: Traditional MLA citation for the book. The name of the computer service or producer. Date you viewed the Internet book <complete web address>.

Mandela, Nelson. Long Walk to Freedom: The Autobiography of Nelson Mandela. New York: Little, Brown, 1995. Open Book Systems. 10 Sept. 1999 <http://www.obs-us.com/obs/english/books/Mandela/Mandela.html>.

Missing Works Cited Information

Substitute these abbreviations for missing information in your sources:

- n.d. (no date of publication)
- n. p. (no place of publication; no publisher)
- n. pag. (no pagination)

To see MLA format demonstrated, look at the sample student essays "Pigs as Pets" and "Quakers: America's First Feminists" at the end of this chapter. Consult the current *MLA Handbook for Writers of Research Papers* for further information. John Barzelay's paper on page 420 illustrates electronic sources. Two professional research papers using MLA format are listed from *InfoTrac®* College Edition on page 346.

■ **PRACTICE 14-19:** Arrange the following bibliographic information using the appropriate MLA works cited formula:

- Date accessed online: September 29, 2002
- Magazine title: U.S. News & World Report
- Author: Boyce, Nell
- Internet service provider: Earthlink
- Original publication date: September 16, 2002
- Page: 62
- Number of paragraphs: 6

- Computerized index used: *InfoTrac®* College Edition
- Web site: http://web5.infotrac college.com/wadsworth/session/607/753/
  24359636/42!xrn_9_0_A91257269
- Article title: "West Nile Worries"

■ **PRACTICE 14-20:** Bring to class a book, a magazine or newspaper, and an Internet article. Be prepared to use them to create a Works Cited.

APA Format

The American Psychological Association (APA) prefers a slightly different format. In your social or natural science papers, observe the following changes from MLA format:

APA Reference List Format

- Only initials are used for first names.
- "Works Cited" is called "References."
- Capitalize only the first letter of all titles of articles and books.
- The date appears immediately after the author's name.
- The year always appears first in any dates used.
- Quotation marks are not used around the titles of articles from magazines or newspapers.
- "p." or "pp." is used before all page numbers; "p." is for single pages, "pp." for consecutive multiple pages.

Here is a sample Reference List in APA format:

References

Hanson, D. (1999, Dec. 13) EPA struggles with human testing issue.
    Chemical & Engineering News, 34.

Sobel, D. (1999) Galileo's daughter: A historical memoir. New York: Walker.

Yarris, L. (2002). Honoring the 2002 Nobelists. Retrieved October 31, 2002, from
    Berkely Lab Currents web site: http://www.lbl.gov/Publications/
    Currents/Archive/Oct-18-2002.html#Nobelists

The first is from a weekly magazine, the second from a book, and the third from the web. For additional formats, consult the current edition of *Publication Manual of the American Psychological Association*. To see a sample research paper using APA format on *InfoTrac®* College Edition, see page 346.

Note to Students: Yes, colleges ought to have one simple, logical form of documentation for all areas of study, so researchers can concentrate on ideas and evidence, not on format. Perhaps the APA and MLA will cooperate one day. For now, check with your professors to see which system you should use.

■ **PRACTICE 14-21:** Create a Works Cited page using all the sources you found in researching your topic from Practice 14-2.

REVISING RESEARCH WRITING

Revising research papers proceeds as any other revision. Start with the big things first. **Reread only the introduction and the topic sentences to make sure that ideas support your thesis statement.** Then move to paragraphs, sentences, and word choice, and finally proof for mechanics. See Chapters 7, 8, and 16. Here are specific items for revising research papers:

- Edit long-winded quotations or paraphrases. Pick the most vivid or relevant; eliminate the rest.

- Make sure each source has a smooth introductory tag line, citation with page numbers at the end, and your own commentary tying it to the thesis.

- Research papers usually restate the thesis in the conclusion.

InfoTrac® College Edition: Readings on Research

For tips on using *InfoTrac*® College Edition, see page 464.

> Michele Green. "Turnitin' Snares Online Cheaters." *NEA Today* April 2000.
>
> *Who cheats in college and how often, and ways professors are catching them.*

> Moira Allen. "Fact or Fiction? The Internet is Brimming with Information, but It Isn't Always Accurate." *The Writer* July 2002.
>
> *How to verify your source's reliability.*

Writing Suggestions and Class Discussions

1. Ten years from now—in your chosen career—what two research projects might likely come your way?

2. What research does your employer need done now?

3. List three topics you'd like to research in college for personal use— consumer, health, or hobby topics, for instance. See page 303 for more ideas.

4. Take one topic from 3 and do a brain-teaser list of key research questions. What do you want to know?

5. Narrow two of these topics until they interest you:
   - Changing family patterns
   - Natural disasters
   - Skyscrapers
   - Religious principles

6. Make a list of key research questions, and do a brain-teaser list on one narrowed topic from 5.

7. Suppose you had to write a research report on one of the following. Without actually doing the research, make up a list of places to go for information—in the library and elsewhere.
   - Violent patients in hospitals
   - Abstract art
   - Solar-heated houses
   - Students' rights in college

8. Research Scavenger Hunt: Pick any one topic created in 1 through 7 and find information on it from each of these sources:
   - A computer index such as *InfoTrac*® College Edition
   - The *New York Times* or your library's card catalog
   - The Internet

   List the source in proper works cited format and then write—in note card form—several lines paraphrasing what you learned.

9. Pick any famous historical event that happened since 1920: the stock market crash of 1929, the bombing of Pearl Harbor, the first moon landing, for examples. Use *The New York Times Index* to locate an article written on the topic, and use *The Reader's Guide to Periodical Literature* to locate a second article. Or use *InfoTrac*® College Edition to find two articles. Find and read the articles, summarizing both and quoting one strong sentence from each. Turn in your notes with complete works cited information attached.

10. Do the same as 9, but use the Internet to find two sources.

11. Do the same as 9, but use a book and a reference section book as sources. You need to only read enough to fill out one note card for each.

12. Look up *The New York Times* for the day you were born. What were the main headlines for the day? For fun, name a headline that secretly "announced" your birth ("Budget Deficit Again" or "Madman Holds Bank at Bay" for example). Explain why it fits you.

13. Do the same as 12 for a weekly magazine such as *Time*.

14. Using *The Statistical Abstract of the United States* or another almanac, find an interesting fact about two of these topics. Be sure to include complete bibliographic information and page numbers. Comment on the significance of each statistic:

   - Crime
   - Marriage
   - Sports
   - Ecology
   - Your own topic

15. Peer groups will develop research questions for one of the following topics and establish a list of sources to contact or read:

   - Overcrowded national parks
   - Laws protecting homosexuals from discrimination
   - Illegal immigrants
   - AIDS testing confidentiality
   - Single fathers
   - Self-defense murders of abusive spouses/parents
   - Pregnant drug addicts
   - Crime victims' rights

16. Works Cited Exercise: Find ten sources on a topic on which you might write a research paper. Try for a mix of books, reference works, magazines, newspapers, and Internet sources. Assemble it in proper bibliographic form.

17. Find two reviews of a book you loved or hated. Try *Book Review Digest* (which includes abstracts of the reviews) or *The New York Times Index*. Write a one-page paper summarizing the reception the book had, citing each source, giving a proper bibliography, and also commenting on the reviews.

18. Write a career research paper to investigate thoroughly a career you're considering. Combine library and nonlibrary resources, including one formal interview with a person who holds the kind of job you want. Your list of key research questions should include all the hard information you want to know about the career—the gutsy truth about its ecstasies and agonies. Finally, evaluate your research and decide if this career fits your interests and abilities.

   A student who interviewed a lawyer found there was "no gavel-pounding or cries of 'order! order!' but simple, solemn procedure." The lawyer admitted liking pinstripe suits and shiny black briefcases from "the horn of plenty." A student interviewing a special education teacher for emotionally disturbed children was taken to a developmental center for half a day where "it is a major accomplishment to have a kid say 'hi' to you."

A student interviewing a reporter was quickly disillusioned about the job's status, glamour, and danger. The working reporter noticed only low pay, stress, dull hours in police stations, and editorial interference.

For more ideas about this topic, see page 223 and the sample essay on page 389.

For more research projects using *InfoTrac*® College Edition, see Chapter 17, page 467.

Student Essay Using MLA Documentation

Pigs as Pets

Annette McFarland

Thesis

Pigs should be pets, not sandwiches. These animals are not the smelly beasts most people think. In fact, pigs are clean, intelligent animals that make great household pets.

Scientist quoted

According to Tony J. Cunha, chairman of the Department of Animal Science at the University of Florida, "People who see pigs wallowing in mud often consider them dirty and stupid. But hogs keep themselves cleaner than most farm animals. Hogs are also intelligent" (250). Although it's time to shatter anti-pig prejudice, few publications are dedicated to this animal. However, there are personal accounts. Singer Belinda Carlisle

Personal story

admits to having two pet pigs. Does she wallow with them in mud or rearrange the silk pillows on her Henredon sofa for her pink pals?

Not so glamorous an owner was Buddy Thorne, an ex-rodeo rider. He found a baby javelina pig in the Texas brush. It was alone, starving, and so young its umbilical cord was still attached. Buddy took the baby home to his wife and teenage daughters, who nursed it to health. Bubba slept in a doll carriage under blankets, with his forearm wrapped protectively around

Anecdote

an orange teddy bear. The family fell in love with him. Bubba watched TV and butted Buddy's mattress each morning to wake him for breakfast. A single scolding taught Bubba not to jump on the bed. Bubba would sit beside the girls every morning as they brushed their teeth, waiting for *his* daily brushing. It took just 24 hours to paper-train Bubba (it took weeks to train our dog, a supposedly smart seeing-eye breed). Buddy claims Bubba was smarter than any dog or horse he'd ever known. Bubba ate from spoons, loved beer poured down his throat, and chewed slowly to savor his food. He'd place his head in a lap and fall asleep if his ears were scratched. "I'm sure other families have loved an animal like we love Bubba," Thorne says, but I'll be darned if I know any. . . . He was like one of our kids" (Coudert 144–48).

This should be our image when we think of pigs. All too often we picture pigs in a sty or lying appetizingly between two slices of bread. But this endearing creature was never meant to be food. Deuteronomy says, "Of their flesh ye shall not eat, and their carcass shall ye not touch; they are unclean to you" (14:8).

Author's Commentary

For those who like the scientific stamp of approval, modern science verifies this biblical law. In the Bible, animals listed as clean to eat were cud-chewing vegetarians with divided hooves like deer and cows. Their sacculated alimentary canal and secondary cud receptacle (basically three stomachs) purify their food—which takes over 24 hours to be converted into flesh. Swine, on the other hand, will eat anything. The pig has a single badly constructed stomach and limited excretory organs. In about four hours, its foul digested food becomes flesh, which humans eat (Josephson 45–46).

Religion and science

The hog was created as a scavenger to clean the earth, like a vulture or a maggot. He eats anything dead and decaying on the ground (Josephson

Health Issues- toxins

continues

46). If you think farm pigs raised for human consumption don't have access to repulsive matter, you're mistaken. Farm pigs eat and drink the excretions of other animals. They chew the cancers growing on other pigs (Josephson 48–49).

Pigs have running sores under their hooves. With a little squeeze, green matter oozes from outlets designed to rid the pig of poisons he ingests. Sometimes this artery clogs, so toxins back up inside the pig, forming internal green growths. A meat packer testified, "We're instructed to just trim them off, and when the meat inspector comes, he puts his stamp on" (Josephson 50). Considering that humans eat what was cancer and fecal matter only hours before, it's no wonder God ordered men not to eat pigs.

Health Issues – fat

Here's another thought: 40 percent of all Americans are 20 pounds overweight (Avon 100). Almost 50 percent of American women are trying to lose weight ("Watching Our Weight" 530). *Mademoiselle* magazine points out that "everyone knows ham is fattening" ("The Most Unwanted List" 244). In fact, the meat with the most calories is cured pork (bacon) at 750 calories per 4 ounces. In comparison, barbecued chicken has only 225 (A to Z 82–83). The solution to America's weight problem may be the porkless diet. It's been around for centuries.

Health Issues – sickness

Let's look at other health problems. Many authorities accuse pork of causing blood disease, weakness of the stomach, liver troubles, eczema, consumption, tumors, and cancer (Josephson 47). Dr. Laird Goldborough writes, "In the pork Americans eat there too often lurk myriads of baffling and sinister parasites . . . minute spiral worms called Trichinella spiralis. . . . A single serving of infected pork—even a single mouthful—can kill or cripple or condemn the victim to a lifetime of aches and pains. . . . The trichinae are often so minute and so nearly transparent that to find them,

even with a microscope, is a task for expert scientific inspectors. 'US

Government inspected' does not mean that any official inspection

whatsoever has been made as to whether this pork is trichinous or not. It

has merely passed the routine inspection" (Josephson 58).

[margin note: Quotation shortened with elipses]

Many think cooking prevents trichinosis. But a university lab tested in-

fected hog flesh. Even when heated to incredibly high temperatures,

worms still lived (Josephson 59). Anyway, who wants to eat dead worms?

The butcher/owner of a supermarket adds, "When pork begins to get

bad, it spoils from the inside out, where it is noticed last. On the other

hand, when beef breaks down it starts on the outside" where it can be de-

tected at once (Josephson 55).

[margin note: Health Issues- spoilage]

There is no profit for anyone persuading you not to eat pork. But the

pork industry has billions of dollars at stake to persuade you to eat it, even

at the expense of your health. And, if by chance you don't care about your

health, don't you even at least want to look svelte in a bikini in the few

years before you develop a serious disease?

[margin note: Conclusion]

As an alternative, make pigs into pets. If you can't eat 'em, join 'em.

Works Cited

A to Z Diet Guide Calorie Counter. Miami: Merit Publications, 1977.

Avon Products, Inc. Looking Good, Feeling Beautiful. New York: Simon &
     Schuster, 1981.

Coudert, Joseph. "Where's Bubba?" Woman's Day 27 Oct. 1987: 144+.

Cunha, Tony. "Hog." World Encyclopedia. 1970 ed.

continues

Josephson, Elmer. <u>God's Key to Health and Happiness</u>. Newark: Fleming,

1976.

"The Most Unwanted List." <u>Mademoiselle</u> Aug. 1986: 244.

"Watching Our Weight." <u>Vogue</u> Oct. 1986: 530.

Commentary

Introduction: The thesis seems clear and sharp, but it's contradicted later when the writer describes how filthy pigs are.

Ideas: It's fresh and insightful. It's a topic few students write on and makes a serious point. It's also creative to combine scientific and religious evidence. Third, she uses humor—although it fades about halfway through, then returns at the end.

Details: The number of details is good: We learn a lot about pigs. The vividness is excellent. Several students each year tell me after reading this essay that they will never eat pork again. Most vivid were the pigs' hooves, spoilage, and trichinosis. Notice, she doesn't just say pork is bad for our health; the gory details teach us why.

Organization: It's easy to follow because she divides it into three main parts: personal, biblical, and health reasons not to eat pigs. Transitional expressions like, "Let's look at other health problems" keep us on track.

The logic is flawed, however. Her biblical and meat-packing facts contradict her thesis that pigs are clean.

Citations: Proper format: Yes. Page references in parentheses follow each paraphrase or quote. The author's name is included if it didn't appear in the tag line. Anonymous articles are listed by the first item in the Works Cited for easy cross-reference.

The sources are smoothly worked in. Tag lines prepare us for source material, and notice how she begins paragraphs with an overall point of view of her own. She summarizes most sources or, as in the third paragraph, combines a few direct quotes with summary. The one long quote (in paragraph 9) has been condensed by using ellipses. These features keep it from being drawn out.

Works Cited format: This is a fine model to follow.

Strength of sources: Her first source is reputable—and she lets us know it through her tag line—but Buddy Throne and Avon's credibility are weak. The three popular magazines have only average authority for a college paper. She relies too heavily on one source—Josephson—but by quoting Dr. Goldborough in Josephson (and letting us know in the tag line he's a doctor), she tries to overcome this. The sources (and the paper) are from the 1980s. But I have seen no newer evidence to refute her claims.

Strongest part of the paper: The vivid details.

Suggestions: To straighten out the contradiction about pigs' cleanliness, she might suggest that when pigs are treated individually as pets they are clean, but the overcrowding caused by raising them for food drives them to filthy habits. A second suggestion is to get at least one more strong source. College papers should show more in-depth research. A student wrote to me with another suggestion about this essay. Akilah Stevens said, "One thing Annette failed to speak about. In Timothy, God says to Peter, 'Do not call anything I make unclean.' As long as you bless the food, it will be all right." Do you agree?

Sample Student Informative Research Paper Using MLA Documentation

Quakers: America's First Feminists

Carol Nobles

Quakers, or the Society of Friends, are quiet rebels whose tireless humanitarian efforts have led to reforms protecting the rights of slaves, Native Americans, the poor, the insane, prisoners and women. In fact, they were the first American feminists.

European Quakers brought to the New World their fundamental belief in the spiritual equality of men and women. Three hundred years ago when women were traditionally denied so many rights accepted today, Quaker women were allowed—even encouraged—to preach, prophesize and share responsibility. Because of this reputation, in 1655 Boston Puri-

continues

tans lay in wait for Mary Fisher and Ann Austin—the first Quaker women to arrive from England—believing they were "dangerous heretics and unsubmissive women." These women were stripped, searched for signs of witchcraft, imprisoned for five weeks, then shipped back to England (Bacon, *Mothers* 25).

Puritan belief in male domination contrasted with Quaker ways and set the stage for 40 years of persecution. But Quaker leader William Penn was far more accepting of feminism. In the only witch trial held in Pennsylvania, Penn is said to have asked the accused woman, "Art thou a witch? Hast thou ridden through the air on a broomstick?" When she replied she had, Penn simply said that he knew no law against that. She was found guilty of "the common fame of a witch, but not of being one" and was released, not burned at the stake (Bacon, *Mothers* 29).

When not polishing their public speaking skills by preaching, Quaker women held business meetings which further developed early feminist ideas. One researcher notes that Quaker women were leaders in the women's rights movement in the 19th Century and credits "the women's training in business meetings with providing the necessary experience" for that leadership (Bacon, *Mothers* 42).

In addition, couples wishing to marry had to appear twice before the women's as well as the men's meetings. Parental permission was needed, but Quakers were not supposed to force a daughter to marry without her consent. During the ceremony, no legalistic vows were repeated, but declarations of love and faithfulness were made by both bride and groom. The following guideline for marriage appeared in the *Pennsylvania Chronicle* on January 8, 1770:

They were so one, that none could say,

Which of them rul'd or whether did obey.

He ruled, because she would obey; and she

In so obeying, rul'd as well as he (Frost 172).

Quaker feminism grew from their belief that God exists inside every person. Because of this, a Quaker cannot manipulate or exploit any person without offending God. One member says, "Nor can you give their opinion, beliefs or feelings less regard than your own" (Hubbard 86). This was nearly 300 years before women could vote, an equal rights amendment was defeated, and women demanded equal pay for equal work. A paper from *Women's Studies* discusses the dilemma feminism has with Christianity, which has traditionally oppressed women: "Feminist theologians debate whether or not Christianity can possibly empower women. Some say that since Christianity is rooted in a patriarchal past, it can never shed patriarchal values; others argue that Christ's teachings are anti-authoritarian and, in some cases, feminist. For the Quakers, therefore, feminism was a necessary consequence of religious belief" (Michaelson n.pag.).

Modern feminism, of course, defends the rights of many oppressed people, not just women. Here too, the Quakers are feminists ahead of their time. While other European settlers regarded the Indians as "heathen savages, the Quakers saw them as children of God and treated them with consequent respect" (Bacon, *Quiet* 46). They also deplored the plight of slaves. In 1770, the sect encouraged its members to release their slaves, making it a disciplinary matter (Trueblood 162). Quaker minister and mother of ten, Sarah Harrison of Philadelphia, traveled throughout the

continues

southern states preaching emancipation and is credited with the freeing of some 200 slaves (Bacon, *Mothers* 78).

These early feminists used tactics still successful today. Members boycotted cotton and sugar—slave labor products. Women conducted schools for poor and black children and published anti-slavery articles in newspapers. In 1865, Baltimore Quakers opened a normal school, four industrial schools and over 70 elementary schools for Negroes. During and after the Civil War, women Friends nursed and clothed blacks in newly freed slave settlements (Bacon, *Quiet* 111).

Quaker Elizabeth Fry was an influential leader in prison reform. She succeeded in separating men and women prisoners and hardened criminals from first offenders (West 301). One observer's journal entry from June 11, 1842 stated:

> Elizabeth Fry took us to Coldbath Fields Prison. It is, on the whole, the best of our houses of correction, thou[gh] a severe one, as whipping and the treadmill are still allowed. It was sad to see the poor exhausted women ever toiling upward without a chance of progress (West 321).

Did this early feminist realize the significance of her last sentence? Could she imagine the "glass ceiling" many women today bump against?

Although one can see the origins of American feminism with the arrival of the Quakers, Puritan anti-women values continued dominating the culture; yet these early Quaker women were the prelude. One historian estimates that Quaker women "comprised 30% of the pioneers in prison

reform, 40% of the women abolitionists and 15% of suffragists born before 1830" (Bacon, *Mothers* 1).

Social change is a slow process, and today's Quakers continue their
humanitarian efforts, active in such issues as human rights abuses in
Africa and Central America and nuclear weapons. And women's rights remains a central concern. The title of a newsletter at their last meeting locally sums them up best: "The Friendly Nuisance."

Works Cited

Bacon, Margaret. <u>Mothers of Feminism</u>. San Francisco: Harper and Row,
1966.

Bacon, Margaret. <u>The Quiet Rebels</u>. Philadelphia: New Society
Publishers, 1985.

Frost, J. William. <u>The Quaker Family in Colonial America</u>. New York: St.
Martins Press, 1973.

Hubbard, Geoffrey. <u>Quaker by Convincement</u>. London: Penguin Books, 1974.

Michaelson, Patricia. "Religious Bases of 18th Century Feminism."
<u>Women's Studies</u> June 1993: 281. *InfoTrac.* 15 August 2002.
<www.infotrac-college.com>.

Trueblood, D. Elton. <u>The People Called Quakers</u>. New York: Harper and
Row, 1966.

West, Jessamyn. <u>The Quaker Reader</u>. New York: Viking Press, 1962.

Discussion

Evaluate this essay as a research report, using the Peer Review Checklist at
the end of this chapter and the commentary on "Pigs as Pets" as guides.

InfoTrac® College Edition: Readings that Use Research

Professional research papers are usually long and difficult to read since they target experts in the field. Even if you cannot follow all the details of these papers, you can study how writers introduce their topics, support ideas with outside material, cite their sources, and conclude their articles. Skim when the subject becomes dense or lengthy.

For tips on using *InfoTrac®* College Edition, see page 464.

Steve Nadis. "Utter Amorality: Can Psychopaths Feel Emotions?" *Omni* Winter 1995.

*An inside look at how psychologists devise tests to learn what psychopaths feel. This short research essay is **journalism based on interviews** and does not use a Works Cited format.*

George Feldhamer, *et al.* "Charismatic Mammalian Megafauna: Public Empathy and Marketing Strategy." *Journal of Popular Culture* Summer 2002.

*Despite the intimidating title, this is really a look at how beer advertisements use animals to sell their products. Based on original research by the authors and outside sources. **APA format.** Long reading.*

Hiram Hall. "From Down South to Up South: An Examination of Geography in the Blues." *The Midwest Quarterly* Spring 2001.

*How the Blues evolved as African Americans moved north. **MLA format.** Long reading.*

Michele Scalise Sugiyama. "Of Woman Bondage: The Eroticism of Feet in *The House on Mango Street.*" *The Midwest Quarterly* Autumn 1999.

*This literary essay is a feminist take on the symbolism of feet in general and then in one work of literature. **MLA format.** Long reading.*

InfoTrac® **College Edition**
Discussion/Writing

1. Topic Development: Think of new topics you might want to research, based on these essay ideas.

2. Analysis: Read one of these essays and pick out the thesis and main issues the author covers.

3. Evaluate one of the essays using the Peer Review Checklist for Chapter 14.

✓   **PEER REVIEW CHECKLIST FOR RESEARCH**

Author: _____

One aspect of this draft I'd like the reviewer to comment on is:

Reviewer: _____

	Strong	Average	Weak
Introduction: Purpose is clear			
Ideas: Freshness, insight			
Details: Plenty of them			
Vividness			
Organization: Logical/easy to follow			
Citations: Proper format			
Research smoothly worked in			
Works Cited: Format			
Strength of sources			

My response to the author's question:

The strongest part of this paper is:

Two suggestions I have are:

CHAPTER 15

A Collection of Student Essays

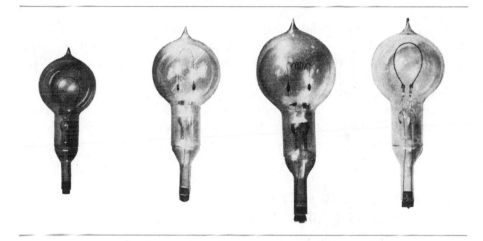

Go into yourself.

—RAINER MARIA RILKE

Look the world straight in the eye.

—HELEN KELLER

JOURNALS

Journals preserve our thoughts, give us a place to be brutally honest without committing ourselves publicly, and remove the pressure of grammar and spelling. You write journals freestyle, not to create a finished product, but to stir up your mind. Journals help us realize how much there really is to our lives. Journals should closely record sights, sounds, facts, and conversation—the hard details of life. They preserve the history of your life. But they should also search for meaning behind those details. A diary records what you did and when and superficially tells how you felt. A journal explains the significance of what happened. It seeks intense moments, insights, conflicting feelings. You can reflect on events in your life or the news, describe a person, place, or thing, remember your past, react to books or films, or record ideas for papers.

InfoTrac® College Edition: Readings on Journal Writing

For tips on using *InfoTrac*® College Edition, see page 464.

Miriam Sagan, "Exercise Your Writing Muscle." *The Writer.* July 2002.
Great tips and exercises.

Debra Allen. "All About Journalizing: Sites That Instruct and Inspire Writers of Various Types of Diaries." *Link-Up.* May 2002.
Resources and more ideas.

Selections from Journal

Richard L. Shields

Nov. 2

I'm sitting on a wooden bench in a holding cell. It's 7 A.M. I'm writing this on toilet paper. It's Monday. If I were home the TV would be on. My orange back pack would be lying on the carpet beside the couch. My homework would be strewn across the coffee table. If I didn't crawl out &

clean up pretty soon I'd be late for KW's math class. I'd feel good about being fifty and going to college—if I was home.

A deputy turns the lock and gestures with his finger. "Time for prints Mister Shields," he says as he holds the cell door open. I follow him to the printing area. There are cells on either side of the main corridor. Arms and hands hang out. Black, white, old & withered, restless & youthful. Faceless with one bond in common. We've all been accused.

My life is spinning backward, like reverse English on a cue ball. Slowly at first—then gaining momentum. Faster and faster. Left hand corner pocket. Scratch! You lose.

Dec. 12

Grandpa was a little guy. He wore a black derby, a gray overcoat with a black velvet collar and high-top black broughams that shone like ice in moonlight. And the old man strutted like a rooster. My mom claimed I was his spitting image, but I couldn't see it. Going on 6, I was almost up to him. He was bald, but I was nappy-headed. I was skinny as a rail in my knickers and sockless PF Keds, and he was a short and stocky fashion plate.

"What have those two sisters of yours been up to since I was here last?" he'd ask when he got off the bus in front of Critie's Ice Cream Parlor. I'd hesitate then because I knew I'd have to make up some exciting gossip for him. He'd reach way down into his pants pocket and drag out that long leather change purse with silver clasps. He'd rummage around until my lips puckered up a story and then go into Critie's Ice Cream Parlor—and my lying ass right behind him.

continues

Feb. 20

The minute I saw the words "Highland Park" in the news-paper head-line, I found myself standing in a bygone era. I was 10 and blazing a trail through Highland Park. My knapsack was filled—rib-sticking peanut butter and jelly sandwich, Oreos, Milk Duds, and Black Crows. Also 2 creme donuts, licorice twists, and Mary Janes I'd been stashing in a shoebox under my bed. I even had Daddy's thermos brimmed with life-saving lemonade. Oh, I remember.

My ears were finely tuned to autumn leaves as they crunched and knuckled under each trail-blazing step. I was on a mission. No longer was I Dickie Shields. I was Crispus Atticus. I was Nat Turner. I was Harriet Tubman. Leading a band of rag-tag runaway slaves through the dense underbrush along the park perimeter.

"Look out boy!" I'd shout. "Dontcha get too close to de edge! Goodman Road out yonder. Ol' massa's men be comin' long dat road afore long. Y'll keep up now."

I crawled along the hill, stopping only to put my ear to the ground to listen for horse hooves. Steam fogged my coke-bottle glasses. My hands sweat. Weak from exposure, I began to hear the howl of bloodhounds. "You got to go on!" I whispered through clenched teeth. I groped feverishly in my empty knapsack, curling around one last melting Milk Dud. It was mangled, fuzzy from knapsack innards. My face squinched as I thought of typhus, gangrene, and TB.

What would ol' Frederick Douglass do? What would Harriet Tubman do? Die on the underground trail and leave her runaways to fend for themselves, their dream of Canada shattered? Or would she risk disease by eating a fuzzy, melted Milk Dud? I broke into whispered song: "Go down Moses, way down in Egypt Land, Tell ol' Pharaoh, let my people go!" I knew what I must do. I blew hard on the Milk Dud, kissed it to God, and plunged it into my mouth. And my strength returned. "C'mon, y'all," I shouted. "Canada!"

Discussion

1. If you were advising Richard to develop one of these journal entries into an essay, which would you push hardest? Why?
2. Write your own journal entries on a low point in your life, a family member, or a childhood fantasy.

Selections from Journal

Tina Thompson

1.

I can't forget the things my mother did to me and move on with life. I want to forgive and forget but don't know how. Maybe if I write it all down, I can get it out of my system, stop feeling sorry for myself and begin to have a normal relationship with my mother.

2.

My sister and I had torn a pair of stockings. "Do you think I am made out of money?" my mother said. "Do you think I can go stand on my head and spit money to replace everything you ruin?" In her hand was the belt! It dangled, quivering like a snake having an epileptic seizure. My stomach lurched. I scurried on hands and knees to reach my sister. We had to hide!

continues

She put her hands over her head, pleaded with Mom not to. But nothing could stop her in a rage. The strap swooshed and the heavy buckle jingled. Then WHACK! WHACK! Leather and metal against my back. The air rushed from my lungs and it hurt breathing again. My sister's eyes bulged. We scratched and clawed our way onto the bed as the belt stung us. My back throbbed like a thumb hit with a hammer. When we were driven against the wall, we scaled it like rock climbers for the window ledge above us. Somehow we scrambled on the two and a half-inch sill.

Mom laughed at our climbing, her round body shaking like Santa Claus. Then she turned and stalked out. My sister and I fell from our perch onto the mattress. Our backs were bruised and bleeding. Our hearts pounded like scared rabbits. We grabbed our blankets and dove under the bed. Maybe we would be safe in the dark for a while.

3.

When I turned 18, my boyfriend gave me a puppy. He was gray with white specks but had a face swollen like a blowfish. He was so bloated that his ears stuck out like Yoda's in Star Wars, so I named him Yoda. He was big, wild, and slightly retarded, but he was all mine! He slept with me every night. I even got him his own pillow and blanket. When I came home from school, Yoda would be waiting by the door, his whole body wagging.

One day my mother thrust my brother's glasses into my hand. The lenses were gone and the frame was mangled. It looked like someone had them for lunch. "Do you know how much these glasses cost me? 170 bucks! Your brother found Yoda eating them."

"Where is he?" I knew something was wrong, horrible.

"Hah! I took him to the pound." She gloated.

"You fat, ugly witch!" I know I was in trouble as soon as I said the words, and ran into the dining room. She bounded after me like a crazed elephant on the warpath. She didn't bother going around the table, but scrambled right across it and dug her nails into my shoulder. But I was so furious it didn't hurt. She'd beaten so much hatred into me, I had plenty to spill out. I dug my nails back into her. She screamed at me and threw me into the wall and yanked my hair, throwing me on my back onto the dining room table. She punched me, each blow like a sledgehammer to my ribs. My legs kicked to keep her off, so she pinned me under her 300 pounds. The old table cracked. My brother screamed. When the table collapsed, I was pinned between the splintered wood and her body. My sister tugged at Mom, yelling, "Are you crazy? You'll kill Tina!" Then Mom took after my sister. Then all of us jumped our mother, writhing and thrashing around the room, stumbling over broken table legs, crashing chairs and pictures to the floor. "This'll be the last time you ever lay a hand on us," we vowed. And she never did again. After the police broke it up, I left home for good. I could no longer take her rage and I realized I could no longer contain my own.

To this day I don't know how to act around her. She owes us an explanation and an apology we've never gotten. Maybe someday, if she can't find the courage to talk about it, I will.

Discussion

1. Tina was willing to share this personal journal with others because she wanted to go one more step. What would you say to her if you could write her a letter in response to this journal?

2. Write your own series of journal entries focused on exploring your memories of a close relative. Don't worry about making it all stick together yet.

3. Describe a pet and what it meant to you.

NARRATIVE/DESCRIPTIVE ESSAYS

Pa's Secret

Carol Nobles

My great-grandfather died on a Monday—which upset my grandma's schedule. On Mondays, Grandma changed the bedding, hung up the week's wash, and sliced Sunday's leftover roast beef. But this Monday there were arrangements to make.

Actually, she'd already begun preparations the day after Pa (my great-grandfather) was taken to the nursing home. Grandma had wedged open his bedroom door and hammered at the sealed windows. Pa was forever cold, even in summer, so they hadn't been opened in years. Panting from the exertion, Grandma said to me, "We've got to air this room out. God knows it needs it."

I only half listened, for I'd never been in Pa's bedroom even though he lived with us two years. I was eight when his second wife died and he moved in. His bedroom door was always shut, but occasionally I'd pass through the hall as he emerged, and a warm, spicy odor sneaked out behind him. The scent reminded me of an old crumpled tobacco pouch I once found hidden in the barn. Maybe Pa had something like that hidden in his room. Why else would he lock his door? If something was in there, now Grandma would find it. She never missed anything.

Grandma watched Pa closely during his last year because he began losing his mind. Today we call it Alzheimer's disease, but back then Grandma only saw it as another chore thrust on her. Pa spent mornings reading the newspaper while huddled next to the kitchen stove, occasionally puffing a cigar suspended from his mouth. Some days he'd forget to flick the ashes, and when they'd drop to the floor Grandma dove on him like a hovering hawk. She'd shriek, "Pa, put that thing out. One of these days you'll start the house afire. You shouldn't smoke those filthy things anyway." Pa never answered, never. He'd just puff and read and reread.

One Sunday, I sat at the table sticking Silly Putty against the comics, imprinting and then stretching Dagwood into all sorts of disproportions, when some live ashes must have embedded in Pa's sweater. Grandma yelled, "Pa! You're on fire!" He just sat there, little smoke streams lifting off his sleeve, while Grandma poured water on him. Only when he felt the wetness did he finally look up with a confused expression. I laughed so hard.

Once, a neighbor called to announce that Pa was "going pee" under the maple tree. Grandma was so mad she must have forgot I was only 10. "That old man's lucky I took him in," she sputtered. "He never cared for me when he was supposed to. My mother died when I was 13, and he took to drink and stayed away nights. Left me all alone for days. But when he asked to live here, I never said a word, just took him in. Not a word! And what gratitude do I get? That dirty old man!"

What angered Grandma most was when he got a girlfriend who lived in the old people's home. Grandma would whisper, "Just watch now. That old fool's in the bathroom sprucin' himself up for that old biddy up at the home. At his age!"

continues

One afternoon, Grandma and I stood in a crowd at the bus stop when she spied Pa strolling down the street with his lady friend. As the bus arrived, she pushed our way to the front and dragged me to a seat so she could watch them pass. "Look at that now, will you? She's got a corsage pinned to her dress. So that's what he's doing with his money. The old fool."

The courtship was short-lived because within months Pa began to shuffle to breakfast unshaven and soon lost his appetite completely. So Grandma called the doctor. A few weeks later I awoke to strange voices on the stairs. Peeking out the door, I spotted two men in white jackets maneuvering a cot around a corner of the hall—headed for Pa's room. Muffled voices were drowned by Pa's "No, no. Don't take me. No." Pleading cracked his voice. Grandma tried calming him, but he wasn't listening, and he moaned steadily.

Later I heard Grandma on the phone saying they'd taken him to St. Mary's Nursing Home: "He's all swollen up down there. The doctor said he only had a few days, but it was going to get messy and this was the best way. I hated to do it, Rose, but I just couldn't handle him anymore."

The next afternoon, Grandma took me to see Pa because it might be for the last time. I asked her, didn't she think I was too young, but she said it was the right thing. At the front desk, a nun glided to us. Tucked into her waist, her rosary beads clicked together as we wordlessly followed her to the room.

It had three other beds. You couldn't see the sick people in them, but you knew they were there by the bulges. They lay flat, motionless, sunken under sheets. I didn't look. I didn't want to see their faces.

"He's in the corner," whispered the nun. She tugged a wooden dowel, opening curtains that hid his bed. It didn't look like Pa, but more like a bunch of bones jutting at funny angles. His pale, wrinkled nightshirt was pulled above his waist, his knees tucked into a fetal position. His legs seemed forced apart by a bulging, angry purplish-red swelling that he fingered.

"Pa! Stop that! Don't do that," Grandma hissed. She tugged at his nightshirt, trying to cover him, but it only made him moan. She grabbed at his hands to stop him from touching himself, but it only made him try harder. The nun whipped up the sheet wadded at the bottom of the bed and covered him, but then he wailed. That's when I left.

On the way home, curled in the back seat of the bus, I tried to remember Pa rocking in his chair, Pa playing cards with me, Pa any way but how I'd just seen him. If he had any more secrets in his bedroom, I hoped Grandma wouldn't tell me.

Discussion

1. What aspect of this essay seems strongest to you? If you could suggest changes to the author in a workshop, what would you say?

2. Study how the author creates conflict. Does the essay start *in medias res*? Point out all conflicts. Describe how the conflict grows more complicated.

3. Study character. There are three vivid people here; how are they made distinct through dialogue and descriptive details? Discuss Grandma's motivation and complexity.

4. The young girl takes little direct part in the action. What does she contribute to the story?

5. Outline the time sequence in the essay. Can you explain why the author might have arranged some parts as she did? Is it too complicated?

6. Study some of the little telling details: Pa's locked room getting aired out and its "spicy" odor; the Dagwood and Silly Putty; and one other you found significant. What do they add to the story?

7. Comment on the last line of the essay. How has the author grown or changed? Why?

8. What is the essay's message or theme?

9. Free write a page about a family secret or an eccentric relative in your family.

Revised Narrative Essay (Original in Chapter 7)

Bastard

Miguel Martinez

A child born out of wedlock is called bastard, illegitimate, or lust child. I know. I am a bastard. When I was five, I asked my mother where Daddy was. I only had a vague idea of what a daddy was. I had heard the word used in kindergarten, but didn't understand the principle behind it. Among the many misconceptions about one-parent children is that we feel as though something is missing. We don't. There is no instinct telling us there should be another. We just accept the one parent we have.

My mother told me the best lie she could. She explained that my father had died shortly after I was born. He was supposed to have been a college professor. I accepted this. But her uneasiness about him kept me from asking more.

I have always been gentle with my mother. When she was young, her mother abandoned her, her three sisters, and a brother. They were all placed in a Catholic orphanage. Two of her sisters found good foster homes, and had decent chances at life. Not my mother.

Earlier this year I was required to get a copy of my birth certificate. I learned there were two kinds. The common one states that you were indeed born. The actual file copy, however, is loaded with information. I examined this one carefully. No father was listed. I had given up on learning anything new about my life when I caught a glimpse of the previous children section. It tells how many times the mother has carried to term, how many were born alive or stillborn prior to the birth certificate. I found out my mother had a child before me.

When I first saw that, things clicked into place. My mother had always vowed she was going to keep me. She struggled raising me, working as a waitress, and keeping odd hours. She was paranoid about someone finding me left by myself. I can look back now and see why.

As I won't ask her what really happened in her youth, I can only guess. I think she used sex as a love substitute, looking to men to give her the love she was not getting at the orphanage. I assume she got pregnant while living there and was forced to give the child up for adoption. This would explain why she would always tell me, "No one is going to take you away from me." By 18, she was probably defiant, and went out and lived. I can see a wild streak in her now, when she refers cryptically to New York City bars and roller skates or firecrackers in birthday cakes. I guess she met my father there, and on a fateful November evening, I came into being.

She tells me that shortly after I was born, she moved to North Rose, where she took a job as a live-in care-taker for an elderly couple. I am told that she wasn't allowed in her mother's house with me, and my grandmother once refused to loan my mother money for a needed hospital visit. It makes you wonder about family.

continues

As for me, I grew up basically alone, as my mother would either be working or sleeping when I was at home. I don't resent that, if the alternative was an orphanage. My mother protected me with her lie about my father being dead; imagine what school would have been like for me if it was known I was a bastard. As it was, my friends sympathized.

Looking back, I think I should have realized something was amiss earlier than I did. A certain conversation always haunted me. It took place with a school administrator, who asked, "What was your mother's maiden name?"

I replied, "Martinez."

"No," he'd say, "I want your mother's maiden name."

"Martinez."

"That's her married name. I need her name before she was married."

Again, I would respond "Martinez" and get flustered. I suppose I didn't want to know.

I never really thought of my father. It seemed silly to wonder about someone who had no influence on my life. Nor can he ever. If I do wonder, maybe it's just a selfish desire to know if I have any inherited health problems.

I finally found out that I was a bastard when I joined the Navy. I had quit school and traveled around the country for a year, with no direction in my life. My mother despaired—pleaded with me to enlist. This was the only time she admitted I needed a male influence in my life. While I didn't agree, I felt that I had failed her by quitting high school and I agreed to join.

As I glanced through the mound of government forms before me, I saw a paper that my mother had signed stating that I had been born out of wedlock, and that my father did not support me. I think she had to submit this to allow me to join the service as a minor. When I saw the paper, I was surprised, but didn't care. What influence did this man have on my life? Didn't he just supply the raw material? To acknowledge that he had any claim on me would be just as absurd as saying a marble stonecutter can lay claim to an artist's sculpture.

The night before I left for boot camp, before I went out for my last fling with the guys, my mother sat me down and told me that my father was still alive. She told me his name and the city he lived in. She said she was telling me in case I wanted to contact him. I remember my mother was nervous, and I sensed it was a sort of loyalty test, for if I did seek him out, it would have been a slap in her face. I responded that I didn't want to contact him; there was no need. She smiled. I had kept her fragile world intact.

In time, I did get curious enough to look up his phone number, but not to call him. I think I just wanted to affirm that he was. The only thing about fathers I really wonder about is what kind I will make.

Discussion

1. You may want to read the early draft of this essay in Chapter 7. How has the writer responded to peer comments and suggestions? What has the essay gained in revision? Has it lost anything you liked about the early draft?

2. What suggestions would you make if the writer were to revise this draft?

3. The author says his grandmother abandoned his mother and then refers to the grandmother refusing to lend money to his mother. Should he explain how they met again later in life or would it pull the essay off track?

4. Free write a page starting a story about a label people have put on you and the conflict it created. How do you deal with it?

5. Write a letter to the author of this essay, explaining what the concept of "bastard" means to you.

Narrative/Descriptive Essay

Midnight Diner

Michael Y. Rodgers

Diners always seem to be warm, busy, friendly, happy places. That's why on a recent Friday night, returning from a long day's work and needing something to help me through the last ten miles, I stopped at a diner for a cup of soup. A diner at midnight, however, is not a diner at noon. I stopped in front of the dreary gray aluminum building that resembled an old railroad car. A half-lit neon sign blinked, "Fresh Barbecue Ribs," and the colors reflected on the puddled parking lot. An empty wine bottle scraped as it rolled back and forth on the cement entrance step. I pulled the door and walked through, but it slammed shut so fast behind me, it almost snapped on my fingers.

The diner was clean and too quiet. Customers slouched over their plates, but there was no waitress on duty. I smelt stale grease and heard only the slight hum of the empty refrigerated pastry case. Most of the booths were empty, sitting back to back in their black, crushed velvet upholstery. On each black and white checkered table were glass salt and peppershakers, a ketchup bottle and sugar packets waiting for the sunrise crowd. I peeked through the round window of the swinging door that led to the kitchen. All I saw were a shiny stainless-steel range, blackened pans, long steel knives and forks hanging on hooks.

I slid onto a wooden seat at the counter. Three men in wrinkled work shirts and with stubbled faces sat near me, smoking cigars and staring into their coffees as if lost in space. I guessed they were shift workers who didn't want to go home yet. Then I noticed a thin young man with a mop of curly black braids. He wore stiff, new jeans with a black, Ralph Lauren polo shirt unbuttoned at the neck, exposing his black, hairless chest. He wore a blank expression as he picked at a plate of limp French fries. For a second I wondered if he was watching me like I was watching him. He looked like he might have just ended a disappointing date.

At the other occupied booth sat a middle-aged black couple. They hadn't gotten any food yet. The guy was staring off into space, tapping his spoon against his palm while the woman drew lines on her napkin with a fork. I felt the loneliness rising around me like water. Why would this couple stop here? There were no candlelight dinners on the menu. This was a diner for the lonely. Not me, of course. I just wanted a cup of soup. Hot soup, that's all.

The young man with the braids left without finishing his fries. I glanced down at his table. A phone number was written on a napkin and the words, "Call me!!" Whew. There's a lot of it around. I wondered if I looked as lonely as everyone else.

Finally a tired waitress with deep black, round eyes and a grease-stained pink uniform approached me with her pad. Under her fake red hair, I noticed black roots. She said, "Can I take your order?"

"A cup of soup," I said, wanting to eat fast and get out.

After gulping it down, I rushed to pay and exit into the night. As I reached the wet parking lot, I realized that the young man with the braids and who left the number behind was standing beside my car. Strange that he'd still be here. "Hey, you need a ride or something?" I said. He just stared at me, and I noticed the way the pale moonlight sculpted the curves

continues

of his face. Outside, he looked healthy and young. Hmm, I thought. What should I do with this one?

When I was at my door, he said, "Can you drop me off uptown?"

I stared him dead in the eyes. "I'll take you, but no hanky panky."

"I can't promise you that," he said. "I'm lonely."

We slid into my car, and I knew the long miles ahead would still be lonely and not easy. But that night, I'd rather have temporary company than be stuck in a midnight diner.

Discussion

1. Look for how Michael uses sense details in this essay. How many senses are used and where?
2. How do contrasts between dark and light contribute to the effect?
3. What seems to be the theme he's working with?
4. List a dozen details about diners he could have used but didn't. See if you can insert a couple into the essay that will add something to it.
5. Write a list of details about an eerie place you once visited, then write a short essay that tries to capture the mood.

Narrative/Descriptive Essay

Daddy Dearest

Christina Kennison

In the doorway with an ear-to-ear grin, my father's face shows creases and pain lines as he gathers his strength to raise a hand in hello. Although he's forty-three, his jet black hair is as wispy as a new-born baby's. Black framed glasses slide down his nose, and he stares blankly, lips parted, droplets of drool forming in the corners of his lips. The drops pool, then run down and off his chin, landing on a towel he wears as a bib. As we go inside, my father's jerky limp from childhood polio resembles a rubber band that snaps at each step. His Old Spice aftershave stings my nose as I trail after.

The apartment could be Blockbuster with its shelves filled with videos. Hundreds. "Dad, did you get more movies?"

He breathes heavily, gurgling rising from his throat as he gathers enough air to reply. He chokes on his saliva, then gives up and just nods. As I sit, I hear "Hi, Chrissy!" from my father's wife, my stepmother, who is calling from the kitchen where she hides out. Sharon is a few fries short of a Happy Meal. "I hope you don't mind spaghetti," she says.

I tell my father the spaghetti better be as good as he claims. At this he laughs, but it looks as though he's choking. Then there's nothing but silence, dead air that makes my ears ring. I do not know what to say to break it, but luckily, the sizzle of water hitting a burner in the kitchen does the job, followed by Sharon's little girl giggle and an "oops!" That and Dad trying to slur directions to Sharon for how to boil water ease my nerves.

Dad turns to me and gathers himself. "UUGHT OOMY U AAN AACH?" This takes him two minutes to say, and as he talks, the image of a falling down drunk comes to mind. I have to ask him to repeat this three times before I understand.

"What movie do I want to watch?" I guess finally.

"Yah." He puffs in relief that I got it.

I walk to the video shelves. He stands and almost falls. After he snaps himself to balance, he joins me, stumbling and dragging his elastic leg. I

continues

remind myself that my father had a brain tumor and has been on medication for seizures since he had surgery. In November he suffered his second stroke and has not fully recovered. "How about this one?" I hold up *Sleepy Hollow.* My father nods and shoves it into the VCR. The volume is so high, my ears scream. A nervous tick makes me tap my foot so my shoelace beats against my shoe. Just as the previews end and the film is about to start, my stepmother announces that dinner is ready. More like a nurse than a daughter, I help my father to the table. I sit across from him, forgetting that I will have to watch him eat. Sharon gives him plenty of napkins and tightens his bib. As I eat, I soon stare past my father at the television. Almost all the food he manages to get on his fork is shaken onto his bib and face, and when he opens his mouth to get the little that's left, drool flies out. It's been nearly four years since I last saw him, and even though I knew he was sick, I did not understand how hard it would be to see him this way. I pity his suffering and humiliation, and it also hurts just because he is my Dad and I have to see him deteriorate.

"UUGT OO U INK?" he slobbers between bites of food.

I shake my head. "Spell it," I say, not wanting him to waste so much energy when he could use the American Sign Language he knows. Only after he spells it twice with shaky hands do I understand. "The spaghetti is very good," I smile. *Sleepy Hollow*—the horror movie—has become background noise.

After dinner, I start toward the kitchen to help with the dishes. "No!" my father says, motioning me to the couch. He plops down, and I sit. The movie is nothing, just a bright blue screen. The horror is here. I stay only another 15 minutes, although it feels like an eternity. When I say my goodbyes, I promise to call later in the week. As I hug my father, he falls into me, and a tear rolls down his cheek.

Driving home, I know I helped cheer him up. It was a tear of joy, I tell myself. But my satisfaction in cheering him fades. I feel bad he is this way, but also that I am related to him. Before his sickness, he didn't visit me, saying he did not have time. I wonder if I would bother to visit him if he were not the way he is, if I didn't pity him. I don't know. As I drive, I plan my week. He will wait for my call. And now that I have the upper hand, I wonder if I will.

Discussion

1. What is the main conflict in this story? How does Christina keep us guessing about what's going on?
2. What roles do the video, the stepmother, and the spaghetti play? How are they symbolic details?
3. What are the best descriptive details here?
4. How do you feel about the father at the end? Then try to state the theme of this story (think especially about the last line).

A Night in the Life of a Bartender

Adam Stevens

Blurry eyed and my head hazy, I finally make out the glowing red numbers beside my bed. Three in the afternoon. I make my way to the refrigerator, grab the cold container of orange juice and gulp down as much as my throat allows between gasps of air. I zone out in front of the television

continues

with a hot cup of coffee and cold slice of pizza. The caffeine starts my blood pumping, and the fog slowly lifts—just in time for work again.

I reach Jazzberry's half an hour early for another injection of coffee. Jack, the door person (we don't call them bouncers any more), greets me with his usual phony Kung Foo moves and sound effects. Once inside, garlic and spices engulf me. Every meal here is made from scratch. Jeremy, the other bartender, yells my name from behind the smiling, chatty, well-dressed business people gathered at the bar for happy hour. The dining room brims with guests, wait staff shuffle busily among crowded tables, and the roadies are setting up stands and drums for tonight's gig. I weave to the bar through it all, exchanging high fives with regulars whose names I don't remember.

Jeremy fills me in on what we need for back up, so I flip through the CDs for what we call "transition time"—when we switch from mellow, jazzy dinner music to rocking nightclub music. The stage, centered against the brick wall beside the bar, is where bands from all over the world have played—jazz, funk, African and punk.

I slip under the bar and am suddenly center stage. My hands start flying—serving drinks to throngs of people competing for my attention. They press against the slab of wood and shout drink orders into my face to be heard above the pounding music. You learn how to read lips and the inventive sign language thirsty people create to keep from spitting in your face. One roars, "Give me three shots of Cuervo, a gin and tonic and two drafts!" I swing around to grab the shot glasses and just miss crashing into Jeremy as he rushes by with four full glasses and the Cuervo. I grab the drafts first, so by the time I'm done with those, Jeremy will be done with the Cuervo. It's all about timing when it's this busy. You live in blocks of five seconds.

The crowd heaves against the bar, hands waving dollars like flags of distress. Jeremy and I spot an attractive woman at the same time, but he jumps in first. That's OK. There are plenty more to meet tonight. The phone rings and I can barely hear the caller over the roar of the music and crowd. He wants to know who's playing tonight. Gimme a break. I duck, as ice thrown by an impatient server whizzes past my head. She wants to serve the last of her orders and be free. I remind her that I am the ruler of her destiny.

To which, she says, "I'll have sex with you if you make my drink order."

"How do I know you're worth it?" I mouth back.

"Ask Jeremy," she says with a big smile. We both laugh at the surprised expressions of the patrons who overhear our harmless banter. We flirt more outrageously as the evening goes on, just to entertain them.

As the last dinner guests filter out, I turn up the music's volume to keep pace with the more intense crowd pushing in for the show. The temperature rises from the sweaty bodies packed into our little world, and the crowd grows thirstier. The floor behind the bar becomes a swamp of stale beer and sticky soda, and our feet are soaked and squishy. The overflowing tip jar helps brush away my discomfort. Three shots bought by admiring fans in the last thirty minutes don't hurt either.

After hours of this furious pace—at three A.M.—the last thirsty patrons trickle and wobble out. I'm still in a daze as I restock the washed glasses and wipe down the bar. Kevin, our bar back, lugs up the rubber mats and mops up the pond of slop on the floor behind the bar. Jack sweeps the main room and collects the last stray glasses and bottles hiding under tables and behind trash cans. Then the band trails out, dragging the

continues

road-worn metal crates covered with stickers of places they have rocked and places they have flopped.

Finally, Jeremy and I sit back with cold beers. I press the wet bottle to my head. Not a bad job for two young, single guys, helping to create a community in our little corner of civilization.

Discussion

1. What new information about bars or bartending did you learn from this essay?

2. Think of four or five secret or overlooked details about a bar, restaurant, or cinema that might help make a reader feel "there."

3. How meaningful is that last line of the essay? Is the idea of community or civilization apparent in other parts of the essay?

4. What advantages or disadvantages are there in starting where the author did?

INFORMATIVE ESSAYS

Informative Contrast Essay

Food for Thought

Yeou-jih Yang

Mr. Chen took a short break from the steamy kitchen. Even though he was sweaty, he had a sense of accomplishment and satisfaction. He ducked out of the kitchen and scanned the dining room. Most tables were full. He watched a man shaking something vigorously into his food.

"What's that, Daddy?" asked a little girl who sat beside him.

"Soy sauce; you're supposed to put it on Chinese food."

Chen's heart sank. He retreated into the kitchen. "You should see what they do to my dishes!" he exclaimed. "After I spend so much time blending just the right seasoning, plup! It's all gone!"

Welcome to the West, or conversely, to the East. Dining experience is often a gate through which we can peek into a different culture. By examining it, you can not only enjoy food better, but also understand another culture and people, maybe even getting along better and promoting peace.

In Chef Chen's case, he had cut the meat and vegetables into bite-size pieces. He had chosen bright orange or red carrots, thick round scallops, curly pink shrimps, tender beef, green tree-shaped broccoli, yellow bamboo shoots, mixed them and gave a quick stir in the wok over intense flames. Then he blended in the sauce that he created. His masterpiece! Its smell provoked the gastric glands. Its appearance had a master painter's color and composition. Its taste made the tongue sing. It was a culture communicator inviting the eater to examine it and appreciate it. Just like tasting fine wines or desserts, we shouldn't just flush or gulp it down the throat. The stomach may be filled, but the head will stay empty and the senses idle.

Chinese dining is filled with loud greetings, bright lights, and crowded seating. In contrast, American dining appears quite harmonious—candlelight, soft, soothing music, and well-matched tableware. Peeling off this superficial appearance, we will find a different philosophy underneath.

To understand, first you must know that the Chinese believe the universe consists of two opposite forces: yin, a negative force, and yang, a positive force. Only if these two are balanced can there be harmony and peace. This applies to food too. Meat is usually yang and vegetables are

continues

yin. A balance produces a peaceful dish. The Chinese avoid extremities. For example, they don't drink icy cold water while eating a hot dish. They avoid conflict. For the same reason there are no knives at the table. Everything needing cutting is already done in the kitchen. The Chinese can't understand the western style of cutting meat at the dinner table, nor the swing from ice water to hot soup back to cold salad followed by a hot entrée and ending with a cold dessert. To Chinese, this causes conflict and unbalance.

"Would you pass the mashed potatoes, please?" someone may politely request at the end of an American rectangular table. With these interruptions, cutting food with two hands and switching the fork from one hand to the other, it can get pretty busy. The Chinese prefer a round table so everyone has equal access to the food. The use of chopsticks with precut food doesn't require switching, so everything is more direct and peaceful.

One day last summer while visiting from Taiwan, my in-laws, armed with a dictionary, local map, some basic sentences, and a lot of curiosity, ventured into town by themselves. When they returned, my father-in-law said, "When I order a steak, the waiter bombed me with a chain of questions: 'How would you like your steak, sir: well done, medium, or rare? What kind of dressing would you prefer? We have French, Italian, Thousand Island, and house. Potato? Baked, mashed, or fried?' There! I thought steak was a simple American food."

My mother-in-law nodded. "All I wanted was an American hamburger, but they asked me how do I want my burger done, do I want lettuce or tomato on it or both? Leave out onion? Keep pickle in? Do I want ketchup, mayonnaise, or mustard in it?" She continued, "Like a tailor, they will make exactly what you want. The problem is, I don't know what an American burger should be. A Chinese chef doesn't make you make all these choices to enjoy it."

When we go to different restaurants, we have the chance to fill our stomachs, but also to fill our thoughts.

Discussion

1. Rate this essay for surprise value in ideas and detail. What do you know now that you didn't before?
2. How does the author enliven this comparison of Chinese and American eating habits?
3. How is the essay structured?
4. Think of two types of food or eating styles from different cultures. Draw up a list of comparisons or contrasts, looking for some "food for thought" behind the surface differences.
5. If you read this essay in a class workshop, what suggestions would you offer the author?

Informative Process Essay

The Autopsy

Gregory F. Matula

The county hospital. People come here to mend broken bodies, but it's also where those whose time has been cut short are sent to find out why. In the back, almost like an embarrassing family member kept out of sight, is the medical examiner's office. This is where the fine art of forensic medicine is practiced.

Above the door a sign reads, "What you see, what you hear, when you leave, leave it here!" A reminder of the sensitive investigations conducted

continues

here. There is complete silence except for a constantly ringing telephone. Three walls in the holding room are covered with tile and the fourth with what appear to be metal refrigeration doors.

This is the world of Dr. Nicholas Forbes, the medical examiner who will be performing today's autopsy. When he enters, his assistant briefs him about the corpse's death. She was a 59-year-old woman whose automobile struck a tree during good driving conditions with clear visibility.

I follow Dr. Forbes into the examining room, and I'm given a gown and mask to protect myself and my clothes from flying debris and blood. In the center are two metal beds that work like draining boards. Holes in the top layer allow water running beneath to wash away the blood that spills. There are instruments, wash basins, and hoses placed around the room for easy access.

On one metal bed lies the naked body of the dead woman. Stitches stretch from the navel to rib cage and continue under each breast almost to the armpit. This is from a brief preautopsy exam performed just after the accident. Abrasions cover her body. Dr. Forbes's job is to determine what might have caused the car accident.

As he disappears to scrub up, his two assistants diligently reopen the cuts made the night before, and the room fills with an aroma best described as that of menstrual blood. One inserts a long needle into the woman's eyes to draw fluid. From this fluid they can determine if there was alcohol in her system. After exposing the rib cage by moving the breasts up and to the side, the gentlemen use a plier-like tool to cut the ribs and remove them. Now the lungs are visible.

With the precision and delicacy of a butcher, one assistant lifts and cuts out organs. The lungs and heart are plopped on the table. A hose suctions out a pool of dark blood from the cavity. From a brief inspection, the man notices that her liver is badly mangled and adds it to the vital body parts. When the pile of organs grows too large for the table, he pulls out a metal bin and dumps them in.

Is this what life is to become? A bunch of scraps thrown in a pile, like giblets for the gravy? It's been said we are "food for worms." I wonder if worms like giblets. Humans tend to think "It won't happen to me," "I can handle it," or "Only old people die." However, the Bible says in James 4:14, "whereas ye know not what shall be on the morrow. For what is life? It is even a vapor, that appeareth for a little time, and vanisheth away." How fragile we really are.

My thoughts are interrupted by a high-pitched whizzing sound. The man has completely gutted the corpse. All that remains is the empty cavity of the woman's torso with her head and appendages. The sound comes from a saw that looks like a drill with a disk. In the empty cavity the man saws the woman's backbone. After a moment he pulls out what looks like a flat oval-shaped dog biscuit. He explains it's a vertebra—to be used for a bone marrow specimen. He points out the spinal cord. It's thin and flimsy, like thick thread.

Next, the man walks to the head of the table, and without a word about what's next, grabs her scalp at the center of her head and folds it over her face. There, directly before me emerges a human skull. Not a picture, not a movie, not a computer replica, but a real skull fresh from its fleshy cage. He wipes it so it almost shines, as if gloating about its ability to protect its

continues

cargo. The saw resumes, and its pitch drops under the strain. Then the man uses a small prying instrument to pop the cap he'd just cut.

I'm privileged to see firsthand the most perplexing organ of the human body. The brain is creamy with black-etched grooves. It's so powerful yet so delicate that it indents like a sponge when the man takes hold and removes it. This magnificent piece of flesh isn't just thrown into the bin like the rest. It's treated royally, set apart on the examining tray. It will be saved for last.

After scrubbing up, the doctor reappears, steps to the table, and makes a visual inspection. He presses a foot pedal and talks into a microphone. In his foreign accent, he announces the time, then picks through the organs in the bin for the heart. He weighs it and announces the result into the microphone. He cuts the heart open for an internal examination and records a few observations. Then, like a butcher discarding excess fat, he drops the organ into a pail lined with a plastic bag.

One by one, the doctor examines each organ externally and internally in the same manner. He has obviously conducted this procedure more often than he might care to calculate.

Dr. Forbes pauses for a moment. In deep thought, he taps a tune on the examining tray with an instrument. For the first time I realize there's an actual person behind that surgical mask. He calls me over to see something unusual in the lung. He explains how he determined she had sclerosis. I'm lost in the medical terms, but it doesn't stop him. He jokes about the red lungs with black tobacco spots having beautiful color just before he throws them into the pail.

Next is the trachea. He explains how it changes as a woman ages and causes her voice to deepen. He cuts intricate samples of each piece of flesh. He begins to quiz me on my knowledge of bodily organs and, like a game show host, he gongs me when I'm wrong.

Dr. Forbes appears to be surprised, when examining the stomach and liver, to see there is no gallbladder. He checks the bin and motions an assistant to look for a scar on the woman to see if it had been removed by surgery. No scar. The doctor notes this into the microphone. He then makes an incision into the stomach to empty its contents into a sample cup. "Well, look what we have here!" he says, as about thirty little yellow pills appear.

At this point, Dr. Forbes realizes this is a suicide. So far, he's determined she did not die on impact, because pieces of her liver were found in her lungs, proving aspiration after the accident. The pills in the stomach weren't even slightly digested, suggesting that she took them just before getting into her car. Due to her frenzied state, she must have driven her car into the tree because she couldn't wait for the pills to take effect. The doctor briefs me on the mental state of suicides.

While Dr. Forbes turns over the pills to the toxicologist for further examination, his assistant returns the skull cap and sews the scalp back together. After inspecting all the organs, Dr. Forbes cuts into the brain as easily as slicing pat[é]. I cringe at the thought of all the memories it once held. It's almost as if with each cut, 59 years of history are erased bit by bit. To me, the inside of the brain is the most beautiful part of the body. The white portions are distinct, highlighted with a creamy layer and graceful lines. If one glance at it doesn't cause you to believe in Creation and the miracle of humankind, then nothing ever will.

Done, Dr. Forbes presses the microphone pedal and announces, "Cause of death, pending toxicology report. Autopsy complete at 11:32."

continues

Discussion

1. What are the steps in the process described? Which steps does the author dwell on and which skim over? Say why you agree or disagree with his emphasis.

2. This is mostly an objective, unemotional informative essay. Do the passages in which the author muses on the meaning of what he witnesses fit? Defend your position.

3. For most people, this essay rates high in surprise value. Think of how you could use firsthand witness to write a great informative essay. List three processes you think readers and you would be interested in, and a few notes about how you would go about it. Greg received permission to observe the autopsy simply so he could write a college paper.

Revised Informative Process Essay

How to Get Back the Family You Lost

Gwen Gardner Brown

Original Essay
lst Draft
[PROFESSOR'S COMMENTS IN BOLD]

This is an essay that I am going to write based on my own experience. It occurred at a point in my life when I thought I had things together. It was back in 1994 when my whole world fell apart and I lost the family that I cherished very deeply, my children. **See Chapter 6 for intro tips.**

It was March of 1994; I had just celebrated my birthday with about 30 friends at a huge party. My children were still sleeping when I heard the sound of knuckles hitting my front door. I was trying to maneuver around the house with a severe hangover from the night of partying. When I opened the door, there stood a social worker telling me I had to go to Family Court because the county was taking my children away. I could not imagine why. ~~for what reason they were going to do this.~~ **Awkward.** I felt I had done nothing wrong. I managed to get myself together and go down to the courthouse to ~~so I can~~ tell the social workers and the judge that there had been a big mistake. Needless to say, you could still smell the alcohol I had been drinking the night before, and I looked like hell. ~~though (even though I thought I looked ok)~~. **Conciseness**

The judge let the social workers take my children away from me based on the fact that I was drinking and getting high too much. I pleaded with them on the grounds that my children were always clean, always had food, were never hit and that they were being well taken care of. But that was not the case, they were suffering more than I could have ever imagined. Not only physically they suffered but emotionally as well. **Strong honesty!**

Losing my children took a major toll on everything I believed in. I went through drastic changes over the fact that I had lost the most important people in my life, the people that I would have done anything for regardless of the outcome. I would have given my life for them, but instead they were taken from my life, and I was lost without them and had no idea of where I was going or what I was going to do. I fell into a deep pit that took me almost two years to come out of. When I was ready to pull myself together and fight for what I lost, there was no stopping me.

In the process of getting the family back that I lost, I had to go through some therapy classes, parenting classes, and I had to attend AA and NA groups. I hated it to no end and did not want to be there. I felt that I had no reason to be there, but the more I listened to everyone in the groups the more I realized that this is exactly the place I needed. Attending these different meetings and groups for almost two years, I was able to stand on my own two feet and hold my head up high with respect and pride. Now it

continues

was time to address the courts on getting my family back. I was in court—it seemed—every other day, fighting and listening to them tear me down but I was determined not to let that happen again. I had gotten strong in my healing process, and I wanted them to see that they could not deter me from what I had set out to do. These were children I brought into this world and they were going to be raised and loved by me and I was not about to let anyone change my views on that.

It took me a long time to prove to the courts and social workers that I was ready to have my family back, but I did it, I won my fight with them and got my children back. The fight was over, but the battle just began. I had to show my children that things were going to be different and that I truly did love them and wanted them in my life. It has been a hard road but one that I will never forget nor forgive myself for.

I want to touch base on both aspects of the addiction problems that we are seeing in our communities. Alcohol and drug addictions are a serious thing not just in our communities but in our families as well. The person who has the addiction could possibly be suffering from a number of different problems, which is what drove them to this point in their life, but the people who suffer the most are the children that live in families with addicted parents. According to the adoption agency that I had spoken with (which requested to remain anonymous), stated that this is the second highest reason children are placed in foster care. The highest is abandonment and abuse. In nine out of ten cases, abuse stems from a parent using alcohol or drugs. **Reference needed here.** This is what has caused our countries **country's** high rate of unadopted children in the states systems. There are so many children of all ages being taken away from their parents, and then these parents are not fighting back to get back the family they have lost. These children then sit in foster care going from foster home to foster home and never really getting the love and stability they deserve. So my question is who suffers the most—the abuser or those lost to the system because of abuse? In my opinion it is those that are lost to the system. **Too persuasive. Your essay is about the process, not cause/effect-keep focused.**

I had spoken several times to a woman named Teresa who works with Monroe County Chapter of MADD **Personal interview citation needed and also the last name.** on the education that is available on the subject of alcohol and drug abuse. She stated that they educate children in elementary schools about the effects of alcohol until they reach the middle school age. I feel that if the education of alcohol addiction went beyond the elementary or even middle school level, we could possibly make a change in the future of our children and those around us. Parents that have alcohol or drug addictions need to take a real look at what is more important to them, the drug or their family. I didn't realize what I was doing until it was to late, but I never gave up hope for my family to be together again. This is what it should be about, family. If we can educate children who have par ents with addictions, maybe we can break the chain of events that are likely to follow later in life.

We need to put our families first. They say our children are the future, but what type of future do these children have that are lost to the system and forgotten in foster care. With proper education we can change what society has become accustomed to.

Professor Christopher Otero-Piersante's evaluation of assignment:

Gwen, this sounds like a very intense circumstance to have endured. It sounds like you're really eager to help people. And this, I think, is the key to your next draft. As an informative essay, there are some things you need to keep in mind as you REPORT information based upon personal experience with objectivity.

Remember—With informative essays almost always avoid the word "I;" it's too biased and, in most cases, when you use it to relay a sequence of events, your essay sounds like a narrative. Use "people" or "you" instead.

The informative essay lets you generalize your experience to others, even though AA and NA say never to do this: "You can only speak about yourself," they say—and they're right in that circumstance because most people have a hard time admitting the first step—which begins with the word "I". But as one gets healthier and stronger, it becomes more okay to generalize. An informative essay must reach out beyond the purely personal to tell us about how other people might do what you have done.

You need a thesis statement that acknowledges the audience. Something like this could work: "When the State takes your children away, there are five steps you can take to get them back into your custody." This will take the essay off of the "I." Using the word "you" helps you talk directly to audiences who have had their kids taken away. It will also help you to be more organized.

Start each paragraph with the "The first step is . . .,"the second step is . . .," etc. These transitions will improve the flow of your essay. Your reader will always know when you're moving from one idea to the next. Also, it'll help you stick to the focus of your thesis statement.

You express your feelings clearly, but you need to work harder on run-on sentences, commas, apostrophes, "that" vs "who" and "too." I've marked some of them for you, but there are more.

Revise this essay if you want a higher grade so that it's less about your story and more about helping someone know the process of getting her kids back.

How to Get Back the Family You Lost

Gwen Gardner Brown

Revised Essay
2nd Draft

When you lose something as precious as your children to the State, there are steps that you need to take to get them back into your custody. This informative essay will help show you how to get back the family that you lost.

The first step is to admit that you have done something wrong for the State to come in and take your children. You may not feel that you have done something wrong; this is called denial. While in this step of the process, you will feel that everyone else is wrong but you. You have done nothing wrong, yet your children are not with you, where they should be. This is the hardest step to take, but once you admit that something is wrong, you can begin working on bringing your life and your family's life back together.

The second step is to meet with the family counselor assigned through Child Protective Services and the courts. She will sit down with you to create a "care plan," a list of things you have to accomplish to get your children back. The items on this list will all be accompanied by a date when you must complete this task. If you do not complete the list, the county can take you back to court and either hold you in contempt or try to take away your parental rights for good. If you lose your parental rights, you lose all chance of getting your children back, and they are placed into adoption.

The third step is to seek some type of help, whether it is a group meeting or one-on-one counseling with a professional therapist. This is where you work out why you have done the things you have done, and think of ways to correct the problems. You will learn things about yourself that you

continues

never knew or things you have hidden somewhere deep within. Once you start to learn more about yourself and your feelings, you can pinpoint things that make you turn to your addiction. You may be required to go through a counseling program, usually lasting thirty-two weeks. Once you have successfully completed the program (this means going to all meetings, participating in group discussions, and doing assignments), you will receive a certificate of completion. You take this certificate to the social worker in charge of your case and work plan.

The fourth step is to attend parenting classes. These classes usually run about six weeks, one meeting per week. The counselor who teaches the class will notify the social worker if you do not show up. You have to participate in class, do homework, and write papers on discipline and general parenting skills. If you have a special needs child, there are extra things you must do. You will have to show the counselor that you are informed on the type of disability your child has and the special needs the child should be receiving. If you go to all the classes and complete all the assignments, you will receive a certificate at the end of the sixth week to prove you are on task on your care plan.

The fifth step is to find appropriate housing for you and your family (even though they are not with you, you must maintain adequate housing as if they were) if you do not already have it. If the social worker feels that you are in a suitable apartment or house, then you may be required to stay away from some of the people that you have been associating with in the past. You will be required to keep a clean and safe living environment for your family to live in. If you fail to do this, they will not let your children come home to stay and may even refuse to let them visit you.

The sixth step is to get adequate and steady employment. You have to prove that you can pay your rent on time every month and pay your bills for six months before they will let your children home for overnight visitation. If you are working hard to accomplish your goals, six months will be over before you even realize it.

The seventh step is to go back to court to show the judge the accomplishments you have made in the time they gave you. You must prove you are worthy of your family and deserve a second chance at having a happy family life, and that you can give your children what they need. Even if you get your children back, you may have stipulations put upon you. You may have to continue with some type of counseling or group sessions, and you may have to continue dealing with Family Services until they feel comfortable with you being on your own again with your children.

If you have not lost your children yet, but are on the verge of losing your family, you can stop this from happening by getting the help that you need before it is too late. There are all types of help out there; however, you must seek it out and ask for it. Don't be afraid to admit that you need help if you are not sure where to turn or what to do. Don't let your family suffer for the bad choices you made. Give them a chance at a good life, as well as yourself. Being a parent is a wonderful and beautiful thing, but some of us just get overwhelmed and make our children pay the price.

Fighting to get your family back once you have lost them is a hard and long fight. Not just against yourself, but against the county, the social workers, and the courts. If you stick to the care plan the social workers set down and do everything within the time frame specified, you and your family can get back together. It will not be easy starting over, but it will def-

continues

initely be beneficial to you and your children. The battle just begins with you trying to win back your children's trust and faith in you. They will question why you let this happen, why they were taken away and if you will let it happen again. This is something they may never forget, but you can hope they will forgive you in time. Time is supposed to heal all wounds, and they will heal if you give them a proper chance. Take your second opportunity to show your children how much they mean to you and how much you love them. Just keep reminding yourself every day that you are worthy of having this family and that they are worth the fight to keep them. You have to stick it out and fight for what you believe in and for those you love. I did, and I got back the family I lost.

Professor Christopher Otero-Piersante's evaluation of assignment:

Wow! I'm really proud of your work, Gwen. A much tighter essay, no doubt! It reads completely different now, much more professional! It's nice to see the extra effort put into a revision. Many aren't so daring, dedicated. Superb.

Discussion

1. How is the first draft persuasive as well as narrative?

2. In the second draft, the episode of the knocking on the door and party are omitted. Should some of this be included in the second draft? Could she do it without making an informative essay into her personal story? How?

3. Find and correct other errors in mechanics and grammar in the first draft.

4. What suggestions can you offer the writer for a third possible draft?

CAREER RESEARCH PAPER: USING THE INTERVIEW AND MLA-STYLE DOCUMENTATION

Career in Imagination

Rob Banwar

When *Star Wars* first came out in 1977, audiences were amazed at the effects: huge ships exploding in space, swords made of light, and laser blasts that defied reality. Yet special effects from such multi-million dollar movies are common now in $50 video games. I was raised on those movies and video games, and I want to be the person to create these awesome effects in 3-D design. But I wondered about three things when I started exploring this as a possible career: How much schooling is needed? How do you apply for a job like this and what salary would I earn? Last, and maybe most important, is it really as much fun as it seems to be, or does being in entertainment ruin it for a person?

When I interviewed John Romero of Ion Storm Entertainment in an online conversation, he told me, "Gaming is a metaphor for reality. In games we can live lives we can't normally have." Mr. Romero was the founder of the gaming company ID Software, which started the first-person perspective gaming with *Doom*. Using a primitive gaming engine and simple eight-bit textures, this game became a benchmark and is still widely played. This game embodies the graphical design career world (Romero n. pag.).

In my research I learned that computer and console games such as *Nintendo* and *PlayStation* are made using 3-D technology. First, CAD (Computer Aided Design) editors use wire frames to construct a model for

continues

a character, a level, or even an entire scene. They then use textures created by a desktop publisher or graphics artist to bring these lines to life. The rock that passes by as mere glitter in a game is, in fact, an individually modeled polygon that has been texturized using a series of texture maps. This requires three people: a programmer, a 3-D modeler and a texture artist (Activision n. pag.). The aspect that interests me the most is the texture art work.

This field is often ignored. 3-D modeling generally pays more and has a larger market since it is used more often in movies. But 3-D creates just the skeleton of an image. Texture is what a gamer remembers. Not the shape of the rock, but how it looks. Was it dark gray? Light green? Wet? Pitted? (Wilmore 112).

Texturing and graphic design salaries typically start at $70,000 a year and can rise into the millions in some markets. Usually an associate's degree in graphic design is all that is needed, but those with master's degrees often start at the higher salaries and work the industry's better jobs (Heckbert n. pag.).

Blizzard Entertainment uses the standard method of hire for these jobs. Applicants send in a demo tape showcasing their best graphics: still frame animation, special effects, or video and code for a game. This way, it is not just credentials that get a person a job; it is talent. For this reason, many people in the field are often college dropouts or fresh out of high school working beside experienced artists with college educations (Blizzard n. pag.).

I wonder about the long-term effects of such a career. Would a career in special effects ruin my imagination? So many games and movies mimic the popular ones to rip off their success. Look at how *Scream* failed so badly to recreate *Psycho*. The masterful effects were just tired and overused. How can the industry stay fresh enough to keep new ideas constantly flowing? When I wonder about growing stale, I think of the president of the United States Patent Office who once declared "All that can be invented, has been invented"; but he said this in 1899! (Wilmore 371).

But even Mr. Romero mentioned burnout. People who draw from their imaginations each day may just run out of ideas. The fun, the entertainment, is sometimes lost in the job's repetition (Romero n. pag.). I don't see this. I love working with my imagination. My job would be crafting imagination and provoking thought. How could creating the impossible ever grow stale?

One last reason I am interested in this career is because it influences culture. People grow up on television, computers, games, and movies. Having influence in shaping young people's minds intrigues me.

Works Cited

Activision Entertainment. "Jobs." Activision. September 1999. 10 Dec.
     1999. www.activision.com.

Adobe Systems Incorporated. "Print Center." Adobe Systems. 1999.
     3 Dec. 1999. www.adobe.com/print/ main.html.

Blizzard Entertainment. "Blizzard Entertainment Employment
     Opportunities—Tips for Game Artist's Resume Submission."
     Blizzard Entertainment News. October 1998. 30 Nov. 1999.
     www.blizzard,com/jobopp/tips-gameartists.html.

continues

Heckbert, Paul. "Jobs and Scholarships in Computer Graphics."

Heckbert's Homepage. November 1999. 30 Nov. 1999

www.lb.cs.xmu.cmu.edu/~ph/job.html.

Romero, John. Internet Relay Chat Interview. 29 Nov. 1999.

Willmore, Ben. Adobe Photoshop 5.0 Studio Techniques. Indianapolis:

Adobe Press, 1998.

Discussion

1. What is your personal evaluation of this career after reading this essay? Why would you be interested or not in a career as a game designer?
2. What aspects of this career does Rob not discuss that you think are key issues?
3. Make a list of the top five things you want from a job. How does your present job or the one you are pursuing through college match up?
4. Create a list of 10 questions to ask someone who has the kind of career you want.
5. Evaluate the concluding paragraph.

THE PROFESSIONAL PERSUASIVE LETTER

You will write many business or professional letters in your life: cover letters for job applications, letters of recommendation, letters to co-workers, bosses, employees, government agencies, and clients. You will write letters to lawyers, banks, medical organizations, and credit card companies disputing charges or asking for information or help. Your writing must look professional to be taken seriously. The professional letter follows a strict format, and you can model yours on the first two included here.

- Single space with double spaces between paragraphs.
- Do not indent paragraphs.
- Your address in the upper-left corner.

- Skip a line and write the date.
- Skip a line and write your audience's name, title, and address on the left.
- Skip another line and write the salutation ("Dear Ms. Lesser:" for example).
- The letter should state its purpose in the opening paragraph and say exactly what you want your reader to do.
- The closing ("Sincerely," for example) goes on the left side of the page. Skip several lines where you will sign your name with pen, then type your name.

PROFESSIONAL E-MAIL

Your style can relax when you e-mail friends or family. But professional e-mail substitutes for a business letter or memorandum and should be as formal as one.

- Check spelling and punctuation.
- Spell out contractions.
- Avoid e-moticons such as the happy face ☺ or frown ☹.
- Spell out e-mail acronyms ("BTW" should be "By the way," and "TIA" should be "Thanks in advance").
- Change cutesy or weird addresses like "Goofygirl@AOL.com" or "Spaced-out@cs.com" to something that will make an employer more confident about hiring you.
- Use the "subject" box at the top to let your reader know this is not a virus or spam.
- Do not use a heading, salutation, or closing because e-mail is in memorandum format. If you want a heading so the reader will have your home address, write in professional letter format and send it as an attachment to a brief e-mail that announces what is in the attachment.
- Choose a common font like New Times Roman or Courier because some fancy fonts do not travel well by e-mail and arrive in Martian.
- Your message should be as concise and direct as other professional communication.
- Do not dash off quick replies to upsetting or professionally important e-mails. Draft a reply, but do not mail it until you have had time to rethink ideas and revise the writing carefully.

Persuasion Using Description

Hanson Street ICF
Newton Area NYDA

June 13, 2003

Brad A. Walker
Director of Employee Relations
New York Developmental Association
Newton, NY 14620

Dear Mr. Walker:

At 6:03 as I enter the group home I am bombarded by screaming and banging. Don, a co-worker, is slumped against the door of the time-out room, hand diligently on the doorlock. Dark circles hang under his eyes. He is utterly exhausted. "Long night?" I ask. He can't hear me. Inside the room, G. L. pounds her fists against the metal door.

As a residential treatment specialist at the Developmental Association, I experience stress on many levels. I have begun to pop Rolaids like candy, and my body is bruised and scratched. I deeply enjoy most aspects of my job: helping residents use a toothbrush, participate in sensory stimulation, or practice sign language. I am part physical therapist, part social worker. Working with the retarded is both important and inspiring.

But every two years we have a 75 percent turnover rate of employees. The house is in a constant state of retraining, which detracts from the quality and amount of goal work with residents. Someone hired a month ago cannot relate well to residents or implement programs. We need to make changes to prevent the burnout caused by unnecessary stress.

One cause of stress is the time-out room used by three of the ten residents at my house. According to G. L.'s plan, for instance, when she becomes disruptive or assaultive, she will be "escorted" to the time-out room. The escort requires two staff members trained in SCIP (strategies in crisis intervention and prevention) to physically relocate G. L. Her arms are held, SCIP staff secure her between them with their hips, and she is forcibly moved. In her agitated state, she lashes and thrashes feet, arms, and head to cause damage. This occurs daily, up to five times in a single afternoon. She is kept in the time-out room for up to an hour where she will yell and bang the electromagnetically locked door. Staff must hold the button at all times or she can exit.

H. T. also exhibits violent behavior. He becomes impatient and disruptive if forced to wait—for dinner, for instance. If ignored, he hurls anything within reach at staff, engages in SIB (self-injurious behavior), breaks windows or furniture, and assaults staff members. He is strong enough to dislocate arms and snap wrists.

Here are some strategies to reduce these stresses.

We could introduce a more dynamic program to vent staff frustration. Our present biweekly meetings deal with modification-to-behavior plans. We could devote more time to good old-fashioned gripe sessions. These would be confidential, nothing would be taken personally, and nothing would be exempt from discussion. Empathy from administration during these meetings is crucial. I have observed that older NYDA administrative members tend to dismiss our grievances—when we do voice them—by saying, "Boy, you should have been here ten years ago. *That* was stress." Maybe so, but it is exhausting now, and they should be more receptive to our suggestions.

We should have access to stress management courses designed for our specific work problems, as well as to teach us how to catch up on sleep after an overnight and manage time better. A group membership at the local YMCA could vent pent-up anxiety and frustration. Ideally, we should have access to deprogramming sessions with a psychologist after particularly bad episodes. We are expected to fulfill our responsibilities regardless of how angry we are at getting spit on, slapped, scratched, bitten, and pulled by the hair. We're frustrated having a behavior plan work successfully one day and blowing up the next. We know each resident has potential; when this potential is not realized, we blame ourselves. We need to know our supervisors support our efforts and understand; we often feel they do not. Making available *any* of these suggestions will show we are taken seriously, respected and appreciated.

My duties at NYDA are not without rewards, but it is increasingly difficult to feel the enthusiasm I once did. Walking into the Hanson Street ICF is like entering a pro wrestling match that does not let up until my ten-hour shift is over. My ears often ring on the drive home.

These stresses detract from my goal: to do something positive and learn about myself and the human condition, not just turn a profit with my head in the sand. I do not regret working with the mentally retarded, but at the current stress level, I do not think I will continue after finishing my educa-

continues

tion. I don't want to be a coffee-gulping, chain-smoking burnout by the time I'm twenty-five. Please consider these proposals for the good of all of us.

Sincerely,

Craig Lammes

Craig Lammes
Residential Treatment Specialist

Discussion

1. What are the main ideas of this letter? What are the best supporting details?
2. The author is writing for an audience who knows something of the subject. If you are not familiar with the operation of group homes, you may feel a bit left out as an audience. Find some word choices that indicate this.
3. What does the author say to avoid sounding like a mere complainer?
4. Write a formal letter to your employer or a public official to suggest a policy change (one page maximum, single spaced).

Persuasive Letters

84 Somewhere Drive
Brighton, NY 14623

April 25, 2003

John D. Perry
New York State Senate
506 Legislative Office Building
Albany, NY 12247

Dear Senator Perry:

I am a registered Democrat residing in your 54th Senate District. I am writing this letter to seek your help in stopping antiabortion demonstrations that block access to doctors' offices, clinics, or hospitals. These demonstrations not only inconvenience medical professionals and patients trapped in a facility invaded by antiabortionists, but they threaten the health of women there for medical attention. Please help by sponsoring legislation that would classify trespassing which prevents administering health care to any patient as an offense punishable by up to one year in prison and up to a $1,000 fine.

I am sure you are aware of the increasing number of antiabortion demon-strations around the state and nation where demonstrators occupy obste-trician-gynecologists' offices, hospitals, or abortion clinics. The demonstrators call these invasions "rescue missions" and justify them on the grounds that they are rescuing "unborn children" from "death." There have been three such demonstrations in Monroe County since the end of December. These resulted in 28 arrests, mostly for trespassing. In all three incidents, women waiting for doctor appointments were prevented from receiving needed medical care. A *Democrat and Chronicle* article about a December 28 "rescue" reported that one patient fainted while detained by the demonstrators; *Democrat and Chronicle* reports of a March 29 demon stration indicated one patient became hysterical because demonstrators would not allow her to leave the office.

Although some demonstrators were arrested for more serious charges such as resisting arrest or obstructing a police officer, most were charged with either third-degree or second-degree trespassing. Third-degree tres-passing carries a maximum sentence of 15 days in jail; second-degree trespassing, a class B misdemeanor, carries a maximum three months. If previous experience holds true, most of those arrested will receive mini-mal punishment such as a suspended sentence, a small fine, or an alter-native penalty such as writing an essay on civil disobedience (the essay was actually imposed by a Rochester City Court judge on antiabortion demonstrators at Highland Hospital last year!). Those jailed will spend a month at most behind bars.

While the punishments fall within sentencing guidelines, they are too le-nient to deter demonstrators. We require a law matching the punishment with the gravity of the offense. New York needs a statute that makes it un-lawful for anyone to deny a person access to health care as a result of tres-passing. While this will not eliminate all "rescue missions," it will make demonstrators weigh the consequences before occupying a doctor's of-fice, clinic, or hospital.

Denying access to a medical facility is not the same offense as refusing to leave someone's yard when requested by the owner (third-degree

continues

trespassing). It threatens the health of patients trapped in the facility or who are outside and need medical care. Although antiabortion demonstrators insist that the only patients inconvenienced are those seeking abortions, both the trapped doctors and patients stated in the newspaper that there were no scheduled abortions those days. The occupied offices are obstetrician-gynecologists' offices, not "abortion clinics" as claimed. As such, many or most of the women there were seeking medical care ranging from regular examinations to prenatal care to emergency treatment. Even if the offices had been abortion clinics, the demonstrators would have prevented women from receiving legal medical treatment.

Denying access to a doctor's office violates the inalienable rights of life and liberty. Newspaper accounts indicate that patients are often detained against their will. Indeed, the March 29 demonstrators refused police access to the hysterical woman. Most patients are innocent bystanders. In addition, these demonstrations threaten the delicate confidentiality of doctor/patient relationship by exposing it to public confusion and chaos. Finally, the minimal punishments given convicted demonstrators weaken respect for the law and encourage others.

Some people may argue that denying access to a medical facility warrants penalties no harsher than trespassing, since these are acts of political free speech. Although no reasonable person would deny antiabortion advocates the right to speak against abortion through picketing, public forums, advertising, and lobbying elected officials, these acts differ from occupying a doctor's office. Genuine acts of speech do not violate the lawful rights of other people.

Antiabortionists may also justify doctors' office occupations on the grounds that they are saving lives of unborn innocents; the inconvenience patients experience is justified by the higher value of life if abortions are prevented. However, the news media in Rochester have never indicated that any abortions have been prevented.

Health worker unions may wonder if harsher penalties against demonstrators blocking health care facilities might be used against their members in a strike at a hospital. These fears can be eased by drafting the law so that nondisruptive political speech, such as informational picket lines, would be permitted.

Harsher laws against denying access to health care are not unlike laws that prohibit disruption of a religious service. Such an act is classified as aggravated disorderly conduct, a class A misdemeanor under New York law punishable by up to one year in jail. Disrupting a church service and blocking access to health care both deny basic rights: the freedom to worship as one chooses and the right to medical treatment. Both acts are morally repugnant and can inflict deep psychological scars. Disrupting a church service raises the specter of religious persecution; denying access to health care violates doctor/patient confidentiality.

Senator Perry, I thank you for your staunch support of abortion rights through the years. Increasing the penalty for denying access to medical care through trespassing will help assure those rights. I hope you and your staff draft such a law and that you sponsor it in the Senate.

Sincerely,

Timothy. C. Dewart

Timothy C. Dewart

Discussion

1. What is the proposal? What are the elements of the plan?
2. How does the author aim this proposal at his specific audience? How would he have to change things if it were written for a general audience?
3. What are the author's supporting arguments? What values does he stress?
4. Does he fairly represent opposition viewpoints? Analyze the refutation section (paragraphs 7, 8, and 9). Is it effective? What other objections can you raise?
5. React to the last two sentences in paragraph 5.
6. Is the analogy in paragraph 10 a false analogy or valid?
7. Write a draft letter to one of your local representatives about a law you would like enacted.
8. This letter is long. If you had to cut 25 percent, argue which sections contribute the least.

Note: This essay is a letter the student wrote to her boss, the owner/director of a dance studio where the author worked as a dance instructor

Dear Shirl Bonaldi:

There are a few things I would like to discuss with you. I feel your business needs extreme improvements.

First, your attendance record lacks by a lot. You are the director of a dance studio, and you have put in only two full weeks this whole year. At least one day a week you have cancelled class or gotten another teacher to cover for you. As a result of these constant absences, students have lost confidence in you. For example, one of your most advanced students, Kelly Fisher, refused to do competition because she felt she wouldn't get enough practice. A student can only practice so much on her own. She needs a teacher's advice and corrections to really improve and be successful in competition. Your students are beginning to doubt your ability because they don't see it very much.

Secondly, you have lost your enthusiasm. You used to come to class with your tights, leotards, and proper shoes. Now you wear jeans and sneakers. It is a bad influence on the little kids. Now they come unprepared. When asked where their stuff is, they say, "Miss Shirl doesn't have her things, so why do I need them?" You never dance anymore. You just sit in your chair and dictate what you want done. You make it easy on yourself. You take all the advanced classes and leave the other teachers with the beginner and baby classes. Where is your desire to teach and dance? You have already lost two students, and you will continue to lose more if you don't think about what I'm saying.

There is one last point: the treatment of your employees. I have been working for you for three years, and I've gotten the same pay all that time. I'm teaching as many classes as you are. I also pay $104 a month to take lessons from you. When I finally had the nerve to ask for a raise, you laughed at me. I understand you may not have been able to afford it, but you were inconsiderate.

The students miss how you once were: energetic, enthusiastic, and caring for all of us. You could use these again. Please think about it. Thank you for your time.

Sincerely,

Tina Maenza

Tina Maenza

Discussion

1. Comment on the tone of this letter. How do you think the author's audience would react or feel? Suggest where and how you might revise it for tone.

2. Outline the letter. What are the key arguments? Discuss their validity. Are they supported with sufficient detail?

3. If you have complaints about your boss or place of employment, write a brain-teaser list. In peer groups or in class, discuss how to achieve the proper tone in presenting them.

4. How does this letter's format fall short?

---

10 Hometown Boulevard
Rochester, NY 14611

January 23, 2003

Mr. John Goodman
Chief Engineer
Time-Warner Communications
Rochester, NY 14620

Dear Mr. Goodman:

I'm writing this letter to remind you why I should be promoted to the Master Control Supervisor position.

First, my professionalism and communication skills not only have helped employees perform effectively but also helped the company succeed. Edwin Cowls, the Production Manager, said this at our 2000 award ceremony when he awarded me the plaque for best communication skills. You patted me on that back then too, remember? Your last two quarterly reviews credited my professionalism; both said I was your number one man.

In March, 1997, I was hired for the Master Control Operator position which I still hold. Since then I have obtained the knowledge and hands-on experience needed to supervise the other operators in the department. I am experienced in all the systems in the master control area, including News-play. This system was brought on line during 1995. As you may recall, this was the first digital system in the city to run local and worldwide newsclips 24 hours a day. Most of the system's bugs are now resolved due to my discrepancy reports to the engineers—such as the system freezing so that on air a newscaster looked like someone has pressed "pause" on a VCR.

continues

Louth, the digital system that runs Channel 26 (WB), is also fairly new. But because of my daily troubleshooting and repairs, it's now 98% effective. I was the one sent to learn Seachange, another new system, and you had me train the other operators with it. These are the responsibilities of a supervisor.

You may be reluctant to promote me to Supervisor because I have not been employed as long as two other operators. But I have spoken to them, and they do not want the promotion themselves because they would need to make a shift change. They said I'm already their supervisor and that you should make it legitimate. Both feel I'm the best qualified because I do all the instruction and implementation already. They assured me if I were promoted that there would be no problem.

You may prefer to promote someone from outside who has supervisory experience. But who would train and instruct this new hire on the department's systems? Me. Why go through that and incur needless expense when you have someone In your department to fill the position? You may have forgotten that I do have training in supervision—during my six-year military career, I attended classes in supervision and held a supervisory position my last three years. I am currently attending college, which adds depth to my career file.

I believe I have completely refreshed your memory on my accomplishments and work performance. I now rely on your keen judgment to see that I am the applicant most qualified and suitable for the position of Supervising Master Control Operator.

Sincerely,

Willie F. Nelson, Jr.

Willie F. Nelson, Jr.

Discussion

1. If you were Willie's boss, would you be convinced by this letter? Why or why not?
2. Rewrite any phrases you'd consider changing. Explain why you'd do it.
3. What possible refutations does the author raise and answer? Are there any other possible objections Willie does not raise?
4. Write a letter to your boss, outlining why you deserve a promotion or raise.

Personal Persuasive Letter

October 30, 2003

Dear Greg,

Hi, how are you? Probably scared, shocked and confused. I am too. But I need to talk to you about our future and our baby's too. As I'm sure you realize, our future is now going to be unimaginably more difficult than we thought. I know I can do it, though, and you can too. I have a lot of faith in the two of us. But although we could do it apart, if that's what you truly wish, we both know that it will be a thousand times easier together.

As far as our relationship goes, I don't see any reason why we should break up. Things were really going well between us before. Now you avoid me at all costs and refuse to speak to me over the phone. I am willing to forgive all that. I want us to move forward *together* into this new part of our lives. We should do this for ourselves, but—more importantly—we need to do it for our baby. We need to preserve our relationship for the sake of the emotional support you as a father can provide the baby and me. I need to be strong for the baby, and I need your help. Please try to see this from my perspective. I *can't* run away; I *can't* hide, I really need you now, Greg—more than ever.

The biggest point I want to make is this: *our baby will need a dad*. If it's boy, who's going to teach him to play football, fix cars or handle girls? If it's a girl, who's going to be there to threaten her boyfriends, tell her she's not old enough to wear make-up and that her skirts are too short? Don't deny her the chance to be "daddy's little girl." Now, I know you are probably thinking, "Teach my kid how to handle girls or not to wear short skirts? How can I possibly do that considering the mess I'm in now? How can I teach my kid about the world when I haven't figured it out yet?" But the truth is that no dad ever has. Parents just teach their kids what they *do* know. They try to help them in all the ways they can. You can do that, Greg—I know you can. Remember that fatherhood is as much a learning experience as childhood.

If you don't decide to be part of our baby's life now, think about that someday down the road when you will inevitably run into him. Then you will have to look into your child's hurt, innocent eyes and tell him you didn't love him enough to be his dad—the pain and loneliness you knew you would cause in his life wasn't enough to make you want to stay. And I know you, Greg; I know you haven't the heart to do that. Even if you don't want to be a dad, our baby will want to have you as one. You owe it to him. After

continues

all, you're half the reason he's here. For your own sake, though, think of all you'll miss. You won't get to see your baby's first steps, his first Christmas; you won't know his first words or the look on his face when he tells you he loves you. Imagine your life without your father and all the things he did for you that our baby won't have.

I realize you feel stuck between a rock and a hard place right now. But you aren't, and everything can be fine. Nothing will be fine, though, unless you are willing to put in the effort to make it so. I need you desperately right now, and in eight months our baby will too. I hope you will see past your fears and choose willingly to do what you know is right. Greg, please come back and be a father to our baby.

All My Love, Always,

Britni

Britni (Bellwood)

Discussion

1. Discuss the tone of this letter. How does the author reach past the rage one might expect? Are there any sections where you think the tone could be better for her audience?

2. Write a brief reply to this letter as if you were Greg. He might agree to come back, but if he does not, what reasons might he give? Try not to invent things, but pick up cues from Britni's letter.

PERSUASIVE ESSAY

A Voice Against Needle Exchange

Raymond Santiago

The Needle Exchange Program attempts to reduce the AIDS epidemic by providing sterile syringes to intravenous drug users. Vans usually distribute these syringes in local neighborhoods. Addicts are supposed to give their names, turn in their used needles, and get a new pack. There are about 75 needle exchange programs in 55 cities (Leary 1). However, I believe we need to hear the voice of the inner city. It has plenty of needles, but it doesn't have enough outreach into the streets or good drug treatment facilities. The Needle Exchange Program had to be thought up by people who don't understand the inner-city mentality.

Studies show that this program does slow the spread of AIDS, and that it puts many addicts into contact with health care services, including drug rehabilitation programs. It is reported that the spread of AIDS among intravenous drug users has dropped in every city with this program.

The media, however, has not reported the bad side. I've worked as a volunteer outreach worker in the inner city among Hispanic and black communities with high rates of AIDS. I know from my experience in the streets that chronic heroin and crack addicts are irresponsible and extremely difficult to reach. They don't show up for appointments. Many have lost their families because of irresponsibility. When they need a fix, they use the first available needle. How can these people be counted on to turn in dirty needles or to give their real names to keep track of them?

Here are three other problems. Many dealers sell drugs with needles for extra money. Where do they obtain these needles? From the helpful vans, of course! Second, while we make needles easy for addicts to get, diabetics whose lives are also at stake must pay for their insulin needles. Third, what would happen if someone were to die of a drug overdose while using a needle from a Needle Exchange van, and the family sued the program?

continues

This program means well, but treatment is still the best avenue. Addicts hooked on heroin and crack today have to wait so long for treatment that by the time they do get help, most are already infected with the AIDS virus. And let's remember this: it costs taxpayers about $2,000 a year to treat an addict, but $40,000 to put them in prison, and $100,000 to care for them as they die of AIDS (Garcia 14).

Fresh needles can make other problems worse. A television documentary recently reported on the exchange program in Philadelphia. They stationed the van near schools and children saw them operate. Residents also found themselves collecting pails of discarded used needles from their sidewalks. Cars from New Jersey and Delaware cruised in for needles. This van was stationed in an area plagued with crime, abandoned houses, and economic problems. The residents didn't want the program and these additional problems there. But it was the perfect place for those who run the program: it had no voice, no way of fighting the program.

Corrine Jennings, a woman who lives on the Lower East Side of Manhattan, said addicts "urinate, defecate, and vomit on my steps." She washes blood from her steps after addicts shoot up "with syringes they got from the van down the street" (Monte 6). Residents also complain that drug users come from New Jersey for the clean needles. Yet discarded needles are still picked up in her area—and used again. And the discards endanger everyone. A toddler was found playing inches from a syringe discarded near a church (Monte 6). It's hard to pick them all up, because the program on the Lower East Side dispenses over 20,000 needles each week ("Legalizing Syringes Won't Curb Abuse" 22).

The program came to my city also—against the inner city's wishes. Drug counselors, volunteers, addicts, and ministers spoke against the program at meetings before it arrived. I met the program's promoters. Many seem as if they have never dealt one-on-one with an addict. They showed high education on addiction, but little true knowledge about how an addict thinks, feels, or functions.

Addicts spoke at the meeting, including some already with the AIDS virus. One woman, who had been an addict for years, spoke about the time she shot up with a girl who was eight months pregnant. She told the girl that she had the HIV virus, but the girl responded, "that she didn't care, that she needed a fix right away." So they shared needles. She came to the meeting to speak against the Needle Exchange Program because addicts are desperate, indifferent, and irresponsible. One by one other speakers shared similar experiences and opinions, all falling on deaf ears.

A friend of mine, a drug counselor and ex-addict, said giving an addict needles is like writing him off. I'll translate Julio Cuevas's statement from Spanish: "You don't need a needle exchange program to save their lives. You need to give them hope, and if you give them needles, you're closing down their last hope—that their lives will change" (Cuevas 13). Giving an addict clean needles is like helping him pull the trigger of a gun to his head.

I know many addicts who kicked drugs. I was there once myself   seven years ago—drowning my pain with drugs, trying to hold on to some hope I could overcome this demon. If someone had handed me a needle every time I needed one, I would never have made it out of drug addiction.

continues

Works Cited

Cuevas, Julio. "A Quien Pueda Interesar." *La Prensa Hispana*

　　1 Nov. 1993: 13.

Garcia, Andres. "The Latino Community." *La Prensa Hispana*

　　1 Nov. 1993: 14.

Leary, Warren E. "Report Endorses Needle Exchange as AIDS Strategy."

　　New York Times 20 Sept. 1995: A1.

"Legalizing Syringes Won't Curb Drug Abuse." *New York Times*

　　12 Sept. 1995: A22.

Monte, William. "Neighborhood Report: A Rough New Neighbor in a

　　Rough Old Neighborhood." *New York Times* 19 Mar. 1995: B6.

Discussion

1. The author supports his position with personal experience as well as research. What are you still left wondering about that he could answer either with more research or personal observations?

2. He fairly presents the facts around the Needle Exchange Program in the opening paragraph. But what refutations might the promoters or you raise against his argument?

3. Go through the essay and list the various arguments he uses against needle exchange. What values does he stress? What values would you stress to argue *for* needle exchange?

4. Write a position statement on some issue for which you have firsthand experience. You might use the author's approach: arguing against outsiders who think they know best.

RESEARCHED PERSUASIVE ESSAY USING MLA-STYLE DOCUMENTATION

Genetically Modified Food

Caroline Ward

Somewhere in Southeast Asia, a little girl in a poor village has a problem. She cannot see well anymore, especially at night, and will eventually go blind. She is sick because her immune system cannot fight infections. In fact, there is a fifty percent chance she will die—all because her diet consists mainly of rice, and rice does not have enough beta-carotene for her body to convert into vitamin A ("Vitamin Deficiency" 34). But there is hope for her and the other 800 million people in the world suffering from malnutrition (James 21). Scientists are developing genetically modified foods with nutritional enhancements, such as rice with higher levels of beta-carotene, increased resistance to disease and drought, higher yield, and the ability to grow in salty or nutritionally deficit soil.

"Genetically modified" (GM) essentially means that scientists have taken DNA from one plant or organism that has a desirable trait, like disease resistance, and spliced it into DNA from a plant that does not have that trait. GM foods particularly benefit developing countries, which are the least equipped to feed their people. Much of the soil available for farming in countries like Brazil, Colombia, Venezuela, and Indonesia cannot sustain crops because it is either too acidic or lacks nutrients, and it has been that way since "before humankind appeared on the planet" (Borlaug

continues

135). GM crops that can grow in bad soil and higher-yielding GM crops can provide possible solutions to this problem.

Unlike farmers in the United States and other developed countries, plant disease and drought can completely devastate some farmers in Asia, South America, and Africa. These farmers depend on harvests to feed their families for an entire year. If they lose their crops to disease or drought, they go hungry. If genetic engineering provides crops that are more resistant to disease or drought, those farmers and their families have a much better chance of surviving.

GM foods can also be beneficial to developed countries like the USA. One benefit of herbicide tolerant crops (ones engineered to survive weed-killing treatments) is that farmers should be able to use gentler chemical sprays on the crops. The same goes for insect resistant crops like *Bt* corn, which is modified to produce a natural bacterium that is toxic to some common insect pests. Robert Horsch of the Monsanto Company, a leading manufacturer of GM seeds, also claims that *Bt* corn has a five to fifteen percent higher yield than non-GM corn, because the farmers use gentler chemical sprays (63). Increased nutritional value can also be beneficial. Won't kids (and adults) across the country rejoice if they have to eat fewer vegetables to get the same amount of vitamins and minerals?

Despite these promises, many people are skeptical of genetically modified foods because of the risks. First, they are concerned about possible adverse effects of GM foods on our health. Some claim that a genetically engineered substance designed to make dairy cows produce more milk, called recombinant bovine somatotropin (rbST) or recombinant bovine growth hormone (rBGH), can be dangerous to humans.

Ronnie Cummins, director of the Organic Consumers Association, argues that milk from those cows contains high levels of IGF 1, a protein hormone similar to insulin that has been shown to promote cancer in humans (39). However, protein hormones have no effect when ingested orally, which is why diabetics need to *inject* insulin. Additionally, IGF-I is normally present in milk, and the difference in levels is very small. Therefore, the Food and Drug Administration (FDA) has determined that IGF-I in milk from rbST–supplemented cows poses no significant health risk (United States, FDA, CVM n. pag.).

Some people have also voiced concerns about antibiotic residues in milk from rbST-supplemented cows, because they do have a slightly greater chance of developing udder infections that need to be treated with antibiotics (United States, FDA, CVM, n. pag.). The overuse of antibiotics can lead to germs and bacteria evolving and developing resistances to antibiotics. If that happens, doctors could not fight viruses, making it possible for a common stomach flu to become an epidemic. However, milk from cows treated with antibiotics is discarded for several days, and new milk is tested for antibiotics before it goes to a milk processing plant. If the milk tests positive for residues, it is rejected for human consumption immediately (United States, FDA, CFSAN n. pag.).

Cummins and other opponents of GM foods also worry about the risk of allergic reactions. In 1996, Pioneer Hi-Bred spliced DNA from Brazil nuts into soybeans because the nuts contain an amino acid that natural soybeans have little of, and they were searching for a more nutritious animal feed. But researchers at the University of Nebraska found that the modi-

continues

fied soybeans could cause allergic reactions in people sensitive to Brazil nuts. The company ceased plans for production, and the soybeans never made it onto the market (36). Milk, nuts, fish, and wheat cause most people's allergies (DeGregori 127). However, if the use of DNA from these foods is limited and properly labeled, then the risk of potentially dangerous allergic reactions should be greatly reduced.

Safety testing is essential, as the soybean case proves, but the tests themselves must be conducted carefully. In 1995, the Rowett Research Institute in Scotland hired British biochemist Arpad Pusztai to conduct a government-funded independent study on genetically engineered potatoes. All was well until 1998, when Pusztai announced preliminary findings that the GM potatoes were damaging the lab rats' immune systems and digestive tracts. Support for GM crops and food was already shaky in Europe, and Pusztai's announcement added fuel to the fire. The director of the Institute himself looked into Pusztai's work and discovered the experiments were flawed. The researchers had "included too few animals per diet group, and lacked controls such as a standard rodent diet" (Kuiper et al. n. pag). Pusztai and his team were suspended and the experiments were never completed.

Another issue is the effect of GM crops on the environment and wildlife. In 1998, a study claimed that pollen from *Bt* corn was toxic to Monarch butterflies, who feed on milkweed that grows in and around cornfields. However, this study was done in the laboratory by feeding the butterflies milkweed dusted with *Bt* corn pollen in much higher concentrations than would ever be found in a normal field. After a field study, a group of independent researchers concluded that the actual risk to Monarch butterflies was negligible (Sears et al. 6).

However, there is the possibility, especially with *Bt* crops, of insects and weeds becoming resistant to herbicides and pesticides. Organic farmers have been spraying *Bt* on their crops for years, but they have been careful to use it sparingly, because they knew the insects would eventually evolve and develop immunity to *Bt.* The *Bt* crops, however, churn out their pesticide all the time, regardless of whether or not they have an insect problem. The insects are then much more likely to become resistant, like the antibiotic-resistant viruses previously mentioned (Halweil 142).

Though evolution can't be stopped and eventually the insects and weeds will develop resistance, the Environmental Protection Agency has instituted safeguards to slow the process. Farmers who use *Bt* crops are required to set aside part of their fields for regular crops, therefore allowing "insects that have acquired some *Bt* resistance to breed with those that have not, diluting the resistance trait" (Brown 57). Furthermore, a new genetic engineering technique being developed could help avoid these risks almost entirely, because most insects and weeds are exposed to genetic modification through plant pollen. With this new technique, all of the modified genes would be carried through the plants' female reproductive systems; therefore, the pollen (which is male) would not contain any modified genes (Jung 31).

Some people are also concerned about intellectual property rights (IPRs). Under current IPR laws, private corporations can patent their genetically engineered seeds, making it illegal for farmers to save seeds from their harvest for next year's crop, unlike with traditionally bred plants.

continues

Some companies have employed "terminator" technology that renders the seeds sterile (Cummins 80). Even if the farmers tried to save seeds for next year's crop, they simply wouldn't grow. This means they need to buy seed every year, and while some commercial growers can handle this expense, most small-scale farmers cannot.

Without patents, though, private corporations would have no way to commercialize their product and make a profit on it, and therefore no reason to invest in this research. Without investments from corporations, biotechnology research would depend on the government for funding. Since it cannot usually give science top priority, it is unlikely research would progress much.

Unfortunately, there is no easy solution to the intellectual property rights problem. GM seeds are more expensive than regular seeds and will be for a while. But farmers may be able to eventually reduce their production costs by using fewer chemical pesticides and raise profits by getting a higher yield per crop.

For developing countries, some private companies are working on agreements with foreign governments and researchers to help them reap some benefits of GM crops and foods. For instance, Robert Horsch says that Monsanto is sharing its "intellectual property and technical knowledge" on disease resistant sweet potatoes with Kenyan scientists (63). The U.S. government is also working on bills to aid developing countries in conducting their own GM research. Congress recently held a hearing about funding the National Science Foundation's (NSF) research into agricultural biotechnology, including genetic modification. One of the bills proposed authorized the NSF to establish research partnerships with scientists in developing countries (United States, Committee on Science 2). At the hearing, Dr. Mary Clutter, an assistant director of the NSF, said, "Perhaps the single most effective way to help the developing world . . . is to provide the solid scientific knowledge base and efficient research tools, including trained scientists, that can be applied to local problems" (Clutter n. pag.).

In light of my research, I believe genetically modified foods have great promise, especially to developing countries that desperately need to feed their people. The possible benefits seem to outweigh the risks, especially when I consider the 800 million people in the world like that little girl in Southeast Asia.

With regard to the GM foods already on the market, I believe they are safe for consumers. The companies producing these crops and foods have done extensive analyses that have been reviewed and approved by the FDA. As I have shown, many of the arguments frequently raised against GM foods can be easily refuted. However, I hope more independent studies will be conducted to show skeptics that GM foods are safe and can be beneficial to people through increased nutritional value; higher yield; and resistance to insects, herbicides, drought, bad soil conditions, and disease.

Works Cited

Borlaug, Norman. *Genetically Engineered Food Could End World Hunger.*
   Genetic Engineering: Opposing Viewpoints. Opposing Viewpoints
   Series. James Torr, ed. Greenhaven Press, Inc., CA: 2001. 129–136

Brown, Kathryn. "Seeds of Concern." Scientific American April 2001:
   50–57.

continues

Clutter, Mary. <u>Agricultural Biotechnology Research</u>. Testimony at

   the Hearing on Strengthening NSF Sponsored Agricultural

   Biotechnology Research. U.S. House of Representatives, Committee

   on Science, Subcommittee on Research. Washington: 25 Sept.

   2001. EBSCOhost. EBSCO Publishing. Central Maine Technical

   College Lib. 28 Sept. 2001. <http://www.ebscohost.com>

Cummins, Ronnie, and Ben Lilliston. <u>Genetically Engineered Food:</u>

   <u>A Self-Defense Guide for Consumers</u>. Marlowe and Company:

   New York, 2000.

DeGregori, Thomas R. *Genetically Engineered Food is Not Dangerous.*

   <u>Genetic Engineering: Opposing Viewpoints</u>. Opposing Viewpoints

   Series. James Torr, ed. Greenhaven Press, Inc., CA: 2001. 119–128.

Halweil, Brian. *Genetically Engineered Food Will Not Help End World*

   Hunger. <u>Genetic Engineering: Opposing Viewpoints</u>. Opposing

   Viewpoints Series. James Torr, ed. Greenhaven Press, Inc., CA:

   2001.137–146.

Horsch, Robert B. Interview with Sasha Nemecek. "Does the World Need

   GM Foods?" <u>Scientific American</u> April 2001: 62–65.

Kuiper, Harry A., Hub P.J.M. Noteborn, and Ad A.C.M. Peijnenburg.

   "Adequacy of Methods for Testing the Safety of Genetically Modified

   Foods." <u>Lancet</u> 16 Oct, 1999. Vol. 354, Issue 9187, p. 1315+.

   <u>EBSCOhost</u>. EBSCO Publishing. Central Maine Technical College

   Lib. 8 Oct. 2001. <http://www.ebscohost.com>

James, Clive. *Transgenic Crops Worldwide: Current Situation and Future Outlook*. Agricultural Biotechnology in Developing Countries: Towards Optimizing Benefits for the Poor. Matin Qaim, Anatole F. Krattiger and Joachim von Braun, eds Kluwer Academic Publishers, Netherlands: 2000. 11–23.

Jung, Christian. *Molecular Tools for Plant Breeding*. Agricultural Biotechnology in Developing Countries: Towards Optimizing Benefits for the Poor. Matin Qaim, Anatole F. Krattiger and Joachim von Braun, eds. Kluwer Academic Publishers. Netherlands: 2000. 25–37.

Sears, Mark K, et al. Impact of *Bt* Corn Pollen on Monarch Butterfly Populations: A Risk Assessment. Proceedings of the National Academy of Sciences of USA. 14 Sept. 2000. 3 Oct. 2001. <http://www.pnas.org/cgi/doi/pnas.21132999>

United States. U.S. House of Representatives, Committee on Science, Subcommittee on Research. Hearing Charter: Strengthening NSF Sponsored Agricultural Biotechnology Research. Washington: 25 Sept. 2001. 3 Oct. 2001. <http://www.house.gov/science/research/sep25/res_charter_09250 l.htm>

———Food and Drug Administration, Center for Food Safety and Applied Nutrition. 2000. National Milk Drug Residue Data Base: Fiscal Year 2000 Annual Report. 11 Dec. 2001 <http.//www.cfsan.fda.gov/-ear/milkrp00.html>

continues

————Food and Drug Administration, Center for Veterinary Medicine.

1998. Report on the Food and Drug Administration's Review of the

Safety of Bovine Somatotropin. 2 Dec. 2001.

<http://www.fda.gov/cvm/index/bst/RBRPTFNL.htm>

"Vitamin Deficiency, Dependency, and Toxicity." The Merck Manual of

Diagnosis and Therapy. 17th ed. Merck Research Laboratories, NJ:

1999. 33–51.

Discussion

1. Would more examples like the one in the introduction have improved or detracted from the essay? Explain.
2. What does the author do to show she is an ethical arguer?
3. Outline the essay's main headings. How much is devoted to proposing an idea and how much to refutation? Do you agree with the proportion? Explain.
4. Think of one other worry or concern about GM food that was not raised. Are you more or less willing to accept GM food after reading this research paper?

REVIEW

Dance Rhythmics

Tina C. Maenza

"Dance Rhythmics" was performed at the old St. Agnes Church by the

dancers of Dance Attitudes who ranged from three to fifteen years old.

They performed tap, jazz, and ballet to an almost full house. Despite some interesting dances, songs, and costumes, the recital as a whole was a disappointment. It simply needed more preparation and organization.

Even considering that this was only the second recital for this school and most of the students were beginners, the girls were unorganized and unprepared for an audience. As dances were in progress, a dancer's head would turn to a fellow dancer to imitate moves. They were not in synch and lacked confidence and grace. It distracts the audience when a ballet dancer jumps in the air and lands with a big thud.

The class mothers were unprepared and unorganized themselves. Their job is to prepare dancers before going onstage and show them their way once off. Yet there were long stale breaks between dances. Instead of twenty seconds, breaks lasted two minutes. One could hear chaotic movement behind the curtain. There were no props, so what was the problem? And once the red velvet curtain raised, the dancers were still fidgeting into position.

The mistakes and lack of synch in the young girls were cute, acceptable, and expected in their amusing "Hippity Hoppity Frog" and "Jump Shout Boogie." But the dance teachers' numbers, "Swing the Mood" and "T.B.A. Flipper," were unimpressive, not good examples for the young dancers. The moves were simple and boring and almost easy enough for some students.

The older girls were weak too. In "Fantasia Overture" performed by seven, eleven, and twelve-year-olds, the girls leaped like cattle roaming open land. The hollow stage echoed after each jump. Six of the seven girls were overweight, yet dressed in short red tutus that barely covered their rears. This color was probably chosen to coincide with the music, but only drew viewers' attention to the size of their bodies. Another performance

continues

where appearance made a difference was "Kiss the Girl." The costumes were unnecessarily revealing, for with almost every little bounce their breasts seemed about to burst from their costumes.

Overall, this performance was a disappointment. The commotion in the audience and exiting of people after almost every dance showed they were not interested. With organization and practice, the girls are likely to perform better next June.

Discussion

1. What are the author's standards of judgment in this review?
2. What support does she give for her views?
3. Although the review is negative overall, how does the author strive for balance and fairness? Does she succeed?
4. Write a review of a recent performance you witnessed in sports, the arts, film, or television.

LITERARY RESEARCH PAPER USING COMPARISON AND MLA DOCUMENTATION

Responsibility And The Odyssey

John Barzelay

In the first pages of Homer's *Odyssey,* the Greek God Zeus introduces the theme of responsibility: "Ah, how shameless—the way these mortals blame the gods. From us alone, they say, come all their miseries. Yes, but they themselves, with their own reckless ways, compound their pains beyond their proper share" (Homer 78). The tale will demonstrate how irresponsible men are held accountable for their excesses. It will take twenty years to transform Odysseus from a fearless, irreverent, reckless boy into a responsible, self-controlled man.

Now consider the controversy surrounding attention deficit disorder—and how the *Odyssey* addresses this problem. ADD is used to describe an inattentive, overactive, noncompliant child with poor impulse control (Breggin n. pag.) Four million ADD-diagnosed children each year are pre-scribed Ritalin, a stimulant medication (Diller, "Nearly" n. pag.).

In a letter to the <u>New York Times</u> one physician asks whether vague and subjective symptoms including "often fights with hands or feet or squirms in seat . . . leaves seat in classroom" and "has difficulty awaiting turn" could be explained by something other than a neurological problem. He suggests that many factors may lead children to behave this way: "a spirited, creative nature that defies conformity . . . inconsistent discipline or lack of unconditional love . . . boring and oversized classrooms . . ." In short, the ADD label is "attached to children who are in reality deprived of appropriate adult attention" (Breggin n. pag.). The National Institute of Health admits that there is no valid diagnostic test for ADD (Huffington n. pag.). Neurologist Fred Baughman cites estimates of the frequency of ADD that vary from 1 in 3 to 1 in 1,000 and asks, "Is ADD, after all, in the eye of the beholder?" (Breggin and Breggin n. pag.).

Early in the book, Homer describes the misery that Odysseus's wife and son endure at the hands of brazen suitors who hope to wed the supposed widow, Penelope. Odysseus's son, Telemachus, blames the god Zeus for his misfortune: "Zeus is to blame. He deals to each and every laborer on this earth whatever doom he pleases" (Homer 89). These are the words of

continues

a boy who sees himself as a helpless victim. This self-image perpetuates his victimization.

But growing up means becoming responsible for oneself. And Telemachus's transformation from child to adult begins when the goddess Athena arouses his dormant manhood by instructing him: "Think how to drive these suitors from your hall at daybreak. Summon the island's lords to full assembly, give your orders to all and call the gods to witness. Tell the suitors to scatter sail in quest for news of your father. Then . . . think hard for a way to kill these suitors. You must not cling to your boyhood any longer. It is time you were a man" (86–89). She shows Telemachus he is not helpless, that passivity makes him guilty of complicity.

This same phenomenon occurs with children diagnosed with ADD. Studies show that labeled children tend to hold themselves less accountable for their behavior. The ADD label encourages victimlike passivity or a sense of persecution. One author says, "Self-image for children is highly dependent on peer opinion. . . . Once labeled, it may take them well into adulthood to learn that they have a choice" (Diller, "Culture" n. pag.).

The suitors indignantly deny any responsibility for devouring Odysseus's family's worldly goods by blaming Penelope for being so attractive (Homer 96–99). By fixing blame on her, they rationalize their outrageous behavior.

Just so, we find that diagnosing children as ADD merely relieves us of responsibility. Diller says, "Parents of children who receive the diagnosis often describe the event as tremendously liberating and empowering. The idea that their problems are not of their own making but controlled by skewed brain chemistry and genetics represents salvation from a sense of failure" ("Culture" n. pag). Shockingly, while prescriptions of Ritalin to children diagnosed with ADD jumped 20% since 1989, the percentage of those receiving psychotherapy dropped from 40 to 25% (Huffington n. pag.). Such statistics show that health-care providers prefer relatively cheap drugs to costly therapy. It also demonstrates our lazy culture's inclination to medicate social problems rather than act on them. Diane McGuinness describes the crossroad in the debate concerning ADD: "Research . . . indicates that ADD and hyperactivity as 'syndromes' simply do not exist. We have invented a disease, given it medical sanction, and now must disown it. The major question is how we go about destroying the monster we have created . . . and still save face" (Breggin n. pag.).

The brazen suitors show that to enjoy one's folly, a man will embrace with dogmatic fervor any explanation that relieves him of responsibility, even if the consequences of doing nothing are horrible. Odysseus revenges himself on the suitors, cracking open their skulls and washing the floor in their blood (Homer 448–51).

The failure to correct the ADD fallacy will also have serious consequences. One developmental psychologist at UC Berkeley reports that children on Ritalin are three times more likely to develop a taste for cocaine. The Drug Enforcement Agency reports increasing Ritalin abuse among adolescents. Huffington concludes, "When the government spends $16 billion a year on the drug war, and when more than half those in jail are nonviolent drug offenders, isn't it time we connect the dots between prescription drugs and street drugs? How many more prisons do we have to build to jail offenders who, earlier in life, we have drugged with abandon?" (n. pag.). Not only are we turning out Ritalin zombies; we have made

continues

the concepts of self-discipline and freedom of choice obsolete. This indicts our society, but the real tragedy is the child whose life is needlessly and irreparably harmed.

In Odysseus's encounter with Polyphemus the Cyclops, both Polyphemus and Odysseus first reject responsibility. Polyphemus, the son of Poseidon, harbors no fear of Zeus. For when Odysseus entreats him for hospitality in the name of Zeus who guards all guests, the Cyclops contemptuously eats two of Odysseus's men. Likewise, Odysseus, whose lineage springs from Zeus, blinds the one-eyed son of Poseidon to escape.

As the crew escapes, Odysseus taunts the Cyclops and proudly announces who has humiliated Poseidon's son. Polyphemus groans back: "Oh no, no—that prophesy [was made] years ago. It all comes back to me with a vengeance now! Telemachus warned me all this would come to pass someday, that I'd be blinded here at the hands of one Odysseus. Come here, Odysseus, let me give you a guest gift and urge Poseidon . . . to speed you home. I am his son . . . and he will heal me if he pleases" (Homer 227). Polyphemus realizes his own reckless sacrilege caused his pain. Offering a guest gift shows his respect for Zeus.

Odysseus, however, brimming with indignation and pride, shows contempt for Poseidon in responding, "Heal you . . . Would to god I could strip you of life and breath and ship you down to the House of Death as surely as no one will heal your eye, not even your earthquake god himself!" (Homer 227–28). Odysseus's blind arrogance incurs Poseidon's wrath, and it takes 20 years of pounding, rocking, sea-sickening misery to clear his vision. Home at last, he must face another disaster his blindness allowed to happen—the suitors for his wife's hand.

Like Odysseus, we are no longer blind. Twenty-five years of drifting on a fallacy and sowing the seeds of disaster have passed. As the evidence mounts, we can no longer plead ignorance. ADD simply does not exist as the widespread condition psychiatry once claimed. Society must now decide whether it will acknowledge its culpability and minimize the damage, like Polyphemus, or turn a blind eye to the disastrous long-term effects, like Odysseus. Society should leave behind its fantastic explanations and prescription drugs, stop avoiding responsibility, and liberate itself from victimhood.

Works Cited

Breggin, Peter R. "Whose Attention Deficit Disorder Does Ritalin Test?"
Center for the Study of Psychiatry and Psychology Online.
<http://www.breggin.com/newyork times.html> 2 Mar. 1999.

Breggin, Peter, and Ginger Ross Breggin. "The Hazards of Testing 'Attention-Deficit/Hyperactivity Disorder' with Methylphenidate (Ritalin)."
Center for the Study of Psychiatry and Psychology. Online.
<http://www.breggin. com/newyorktimes.html> 2 Mar. 1999.

Diller, Lawrence H. "The Culture of ADD." Online. n. pag.
<http://www.docdiller.com/html/six-1.htm> 2 Mar. 1999.

Diller, Lawrence H. "Nearly 5 Million Americans Take Ritalin Daily." n. pag. Online. <http://www.docdiller. com> 2 Mar. 1999.

Homer. *Odyssey.* New York: Penguin, 1997.

Huffington, Arianna. "U.S. Attention Deficit on Legal Drug Risk." Center for the Study of Psychiatry and Psychology. Online.
<http://breggin.com/ritalinAH2.html> 2 Mar. 1999.

Discussion

1. Evaluate the sources used in this essay.
2. Is the author's focus primarily on the *Odyssey* as literature or on ADD?
3. Are there any flaws in the comparison between the two?

CHAPTER 16

Handbook of English

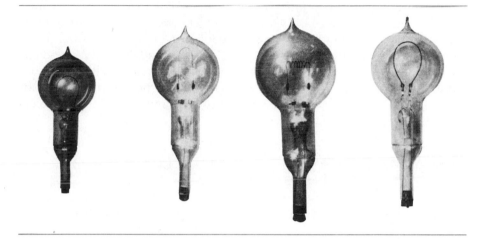

Sanity is perhaps the ability to punctuate.

—W. H. AUDEN

You just can't trust the English language.

—NEDRA LAMAR

There's only one "z" in "is."

—GEORGE S. KAUFMAN

This handbook covers the most common, serious errors in punctuation, sentence structure, and usage. Refer to it *after* you've written your paper. Don't let commas distract you from stringing good ideas together or from searching for vivid, exact words to express your ideas. But *do* use the handbook before your final draft is printed. A great idea described with sentence fragments is like the Mona Lisa smoking a cigar—who could appreciate its beauty? In the résumé that lists your academic achievements, should you stumble over those three stooges—"their," "there," and "they're"—a potential employer may decide you might not be able to tell the difference between a debit and a credit either. When I started as a professional writer for magazines, an editor returned one of my submissions with four or five errors circled. He wrote, "I don't trust a person who can't spell."

CORRECT WRITING AND THE ENGLISH LANGUAGE

Modern English grammar is confusing, but imagine for a moment what it was like before we had a grammar system. William Caxton, the man who compiled the first English dictionary back in 1490, did so because he was fed up with all the varieties of English being used. There were no formal rules for language then, and people became so inventive, Caxton said he couldn't understand a book written in the English of 200 years earlier. The language had changed tremendously even since his own birth. Once, not far from his London home, Caxton grew hungry and knocked on a farmhouse door. He asked the woman who lived there if he could buy some eggs ("eggys") from her. The farm wife answered she didn't speak French. Caxton snapped back that he wasn't speaking French but "goode englishe." They needed a mediator to translate his "eggys" to her "eyren." After many such confusing incidents, Caxton decided the country needed a dictionary to make the meaning and spelling of words the same throughout the land. Over the next 200 years, people decided you should no longer capitalize or punctuate according to individual whims, but only for definite reasons. Grammar "rules" were born.

Rules not only help us understand each other today, but also slow down the historical evolution of English so we can understand our past and so future people can understand us. Study the following versions of the same biblical passage from different years. They are all correct English for their day:

> **About 1000 A.D.:** Ure Faedir, þu þe eart on heofonum, si þin nama gehalgod. Tocume þin rice. Geweor þe þin willa on eorþan swa-swa on heofonum.

> **About 1390:** Oure fadir that art in heuenes, halewid be thi name. This kyngdom come to. Be thi wille don in earthe as in heune.

> **1611:** Our father which art in heauen, Halowed be thy name. Thy kingdom come. Thy will be done, in earth as it is in heaven.

> **1952:** Our father who art in heaven, Hallowed be thy name. Thy kingdom come, Thy will be done. On earth as it is in heaven.

Notice how much more our language changed in the early years? This was largely the result of not having fixed rules. When the Normans invaded England in 1066, thousands of French words, spellings, and sentence structures simply mixed haphazardly with what the native English already spoke and wrote. Different regions went their own way, making governmental, cultural, educational, and even religious communication a nightmare. Caxton's dictionary and, in 1611, King James's Bible, standardized English vocabulary, grammar, and usage.

Notice also that while change has slowed, it hasn't stopped. People are too creative for that. Grammar rules don't squash creativity, but they do make new ways of writing or talking prove themselves over time and across many regions of the country. Otherwise, thousands of new words and expressions like "bad" (meaning "good"), "gag me with a spoon," or "interface" would quickly have become entrenched and made our communication problems worse. If new ideas weren't tested over time, a common ungrammatical expression such as "alot" (a lot) might be accepted as standard English. Fine, except then future generations would need a new rule like this added: "You use an article ("a") before nouns except in the case of 'lot,' where it is incorporated into the noun itself." If millions of people do decide to break the current rule for several decades, "alot" will probably become standard English, and future students will ask, "What was wrong with those people?"

Many accepted contradictions exist as it is. It's spelled "realize" in Chicago, but "realise" in London. "The government *have* decided . . ." is correct in England because the British see collective nouns as plural. Americans see collectives like "government" and "committee" as singular, so they say, "The government *has* decided. . . ." English can be plain weird: quicksand is slow, a boxing ring is square, and we park on a driveway and drive on a parkway. More than half our language's vocabulary came from other languages—words like "bureau" (French), "spaghetti" (Italian), and "mesa" (Spanish). More than any other language, English is the language of democratic inclusion, and the price we pay for such acceptance of other languages is contradiction.

■ **PRACTICE 16-1:** Think of five contradictions in local, regional, or international English spelling, word meanings, or usage.

Rules of language are a *convenience*. There's no reason why "cat" can't be spelled "rat," "hat," or "lypd." The letters and sound of the word have no logical connection to the object they represent. **Language is simply an agreement people make that they will share these arbitrary definitions.** Communication and complex thoughts would be impossible without such an agreement. That agreement is called "standard English" and it is *the language used for government, education, business, and publishing—in other words, the language that provides a person with money, prestige, power, and status.* Other, nonstandard forms of English, including "street" language, black English, teen slang, and others, compete with standard English for the "vote" of agreement about what means what. Nonstandard English is often creative and dramatic, but incorporating it into standard English complicates an already difficult system.

PUNCTUATION

Punctuation is a quiet signal to an experienced reader. You don't stop to think "What does that comma mean?" You absorb the punctuation without thinking, as you do with small words like "if" or "and."

When you mispunctuate, a reader can usually figure out what you intended to say. But you make her read twice what should only have to be read once, and you may give her an entirely wrong idea. For instance, reread the first sentence in this paragraph without the comma. Doesn't it sound for a second that you're punctuating a reader? Sometimes punctuation errors can be more serious. Look at these two sentences:

- All foreign fruit plants are free from duty.
- All foreign fruit, plants are free from duty.

The first means that young trees and bushes that will bear fruit may enter the country without paying an import fee. The second means all fruit as well as plants are duty free. The comma in the second sentence means two items are duty free. Number 1 was what Congress intended in a law it passed. But a congressional clerk punctuated incorrectly as it is in 2 and the error cost the United States $2 million in lost import taxes before the law could be reapproved without the comma.

❥ Comma

❥ **1. USE A COMMA TO SEPARATE AN INTRODUCTORY CLAUSE OR PHRASE FROM THE MAIN SUBJECT AND VERB OF THE SENTENCE.** The comma signals the end of introductory words and the beginning of the sentence's main subject **(S)** and verb **(V)**. For example:

Subject   Verb
S   V

Since starting her new job, Cindy has been promoted twice.

The typical English sentence starts with its subject (a noun), tells you what the subject does (the verb), and usually ends with a modifier **(M)** that further explains what these two are up to.

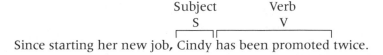

Subject Verb   Modifier
S   V   M

Amy reads science fiction novels.

```
      S    V        M
     ┌────┐┌─┐┌──────────────────┐
     Jeremy hit a home run yesterday.
```

```
          S    V                        M
         ┌────┐┌──┐┌──────────────────────────────┐
     My friend Diana wore a silver wig at the café after work on Tuesday.
```

Even when sentences are longer, the "normal" pattern still holds.

However, when the modifier comes first as it does in the sentence you're reading now and you're desperately looking for the main subject and verb, the writer must help by marking the end of the introductory words with a comma (after the word "verb" here. "Writer" is the subject, and "must help" is the verb). **Hint:** If the following words begin a sentence, you will usually need a comma at the end of the introductory words:

If	**Since**	**When**	**Because**
As	**Although**	**Before**	**After**
In	**On**	**At**	**With**

Verbs ending in "ing"

```
            Intro              S      V
     ┌──────────────────────┐┌─┐┌──────────────────┐
     If I get an "A" in Chemistry, I will explode with joy.
```

Because he was running late for his mid-term exam, John dashed out of the locker room wearing only his sneakers and a smile.

Wearing only his sneakers and a smile, John dashed out of the locker room.

If it's a very short introductory phrase, there's no need for the comma because a good reader can see the entire sentence as a unit.

```
        Intro       S    V    M
     ┌──────────────┐┌──┐┌──────┐┌────┐
     In a moment we will join you.
```

Before the film Jackie told us the whole plot.

At noon we'll go home.

Even if it's short, however, introductory words that would confuse a reader if unpunctuated need to be separated:

Next to Janis, Bob is ugly. (Bob looks ugly when compared to Janis. If the comma followed "next," it would mean that Janis thought Bob was ugly.)

■ **PRACTICE 16-2:** Write five sentences about any subject. Start them with these five words: if, when, since, although, as.

❜ **2. A COMMA SEPARATES ITEMS LISTED IN A SERIES.**

> Mario walked into the faculty locker room by accident and found a pile of moldy papers, a textbook, and a retired Latin professor on the floor. He dropped his sneakers, socks, and towel.

The comma before the conjunction is preferred, but not necessary.
This rule also applies to a series of adjectives modifying the same noun—but *only* if you can substitute an "and" for the comma.

> The Latin professor gave a musical, sputtering snore. His nose was a pinkish red and matched his pink, red, and tan socks. (The commas after "musical" and "pink" could each be replaced by "and." An "and" cannot be put between "pinkish" and "red," so that gets no comma.)

Wrong: The professor gave a most, musical snore. (An "and" cannot be substituted for the comma.)

■ **PRACTICE 16-3:** How would you punctuate these sentences:

A television "survivor" needs a lack of fear a lack of inhibition and a lack of brains.

The dean recited an amazing itemized list of Jill's violations of college policy.

❜ **3. A COMMA SEPARATES TWO GROUPS OF WORDS THAT COULD BE PUNCTUATED AS SEPARATE SENTENCES WHEN THESE SENTENCES ARE JOINED BY A CONJUNCTION.** These are the conjunctions:

and	**nor**
but	**for**
or	**so**

This comma tells readers a complete thought has just ended, and they must regroup to look for a new subject and verb.

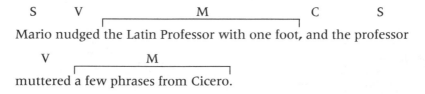

He could scream for help, or he could leave quietly and say nothing.

If the reader sees an "and" or other conjunction and *no comma,* the signal is different. It tells the reader that whatever is on the other side of the conjunction still refers back to the subject or verb on the first side:

```
  S     V              M              C              M
```
Mario asked if the professor was hurt or if he could get him a Latin text.
("Mario asked" applies to both "if" clauses.)

The professor grunted and asked if he was in Rome. ("Professor" before
the "and" applies to both verbs "grunted" and "asked.")

Hint: When you come to any conjunction, separately read what is written
before the conjunction and what is written after the conjunction. If *both* are
complete sentences, you need a comma. If either part is less than a complete sentence, don't use a comma.

■ **PRACTICE 16-4:** Punctuate the following:

Cruella kicked the dalmatian in the side and then laughed wickedly.

Paul Bunyan had a giant blue ox named Babe and they traveled together deci-
mating forests and calling it progress.

**4. COMMAS SEPARATE NONESSENTIALS FROM THE MAIN SEN-
TENCE.** This is one of the uses of commas that frequently occurs when you
hear pauses in a sentence, but you will do two stars better if you understand
the logic behind it. When you have a *parenthetical comment*, a comment like
this one that sounds as though it belongs between parentheses, you need to
separate it from the main sentence. It signals to the reader that we are making a side trip into a less important area. To test whether you need commas,
see if the sentence makes sense if you leave out the words in question.

```
  S           M              V              M
```
Mario, his pulse starting to race, began backing toward the locker room door.
(First modifier can be left out without damaging the main idea of
sentence—commas needed.)

The Latin professor, who wore only gray tweed undershorts, shouted,
"*Illiterati non carborundum.*"

Mario, however, was racing for the health office.

**Remember, if the words in question are essential to understand-
ing the sentence, *don't* use commas; commas set off nonessential information.** The following are both correct as they are:

George Smith, who plagiarized a term paper, was expelled from college.

All students who plagiarize term papers should be expelled from college. (In the
second, "who plagiarize term papers" cannot be dropped from the sentence—it is
essential to the meaning, so there are no commas.)

The following sentences are both correct as they stand. Explain how the meaning changes when we add the comma:

The president of the college says the professor is misinformed.

The president of the college, says the professor, is misinformed.

How would this sentence from *The Wall Street Journal* change if we removed the comma?

In the past decade small stocks returned 13 percent, above their 12 percent annual gain since 1926.

A group of words at the end of a sentence can also be considered extra information. If the words are necessary to the main idea in the sentence, *do not use a comma.*

Write all test answers in the blue book, remembering to skip lines. ("Remembering . . ." is extra information.)

The war is over because we starved the enemy into submission. (The *reason* the war is over is the key idea, so "because . . ." is necessary.)

Don't leave the party if you've been drinking. ("If . . . " is necessary.)

Placemarker words or phrases are considered nonessential and always set off with commas. Place markers are expressions like "thirdly," "in conclusion," "therefore," "farther to the left," "next," "however," and "on the other hand."

■ **PRACTICE 16-5:** Punctuate the following:

Senator Windbag on the other hand voted for the law.

Meeting Tony Blair the Prime Minister of England was the big moment of the trip.

Directly witnessing child abuse however can change a person's mind about its seriousness.

❜ 5. USE A COMMA TO SEPARATE QUOTATIONS FROM TAG LINES. (See the section on quotations on page 438.)

Gloria told the class, "Julius Caesar was a Roman geezer."

❜ 6. USE A COMMA AFTER THE GREETING IN A PERSONAL LETTER. BUSINESS LETTERS USE A COLON.

Dear Wendy,

Dear Senator Cumulous:

❜ 7. USE A COMMA TO SEPARATE DIRECT ADDRESS OF SOMEONE.

Sarah, would you come here?

I wish you'd look at this, Doctor.

❜ 8. USE A COMMA TO SEPARATE THE DAY FROM THE YEAR IN A DATE:

September 19, 2003.

❜ 9. USE A COMMA TO SEPARATE WHAT WOULD BE SEPARATE LINES IN AN ADDRESS:

I visited my former lawyer at Cell Block 33, 12 Dawson Street, Sing Sing Prison, San Francisco, California 92758.

■ **PRACTICE 16-6:** Illustrate the first five comma rules by creating a sentence for each that uses commas correctly.

■ **PRACTICE 16-7:** Comma Exercise. Correct any comma errors in the following:

TO: ALL STUDENTS   OCTOBER 3 2003

FROM: DR. R. J. FACTOTUM

          Dean of Academic Studies

RE: Graduation Competency Exam

The college is instituting a competency examination which must be passed   5
to graduate so all students should study the following questions carefully.

BIOLOGY PRACTICUM, Part 1. Create life with your Bunsen burner a test tube and two spoonfuls of the cafeteria's Jell-o.

Part 2. After your professor approves your life-form you should make it evolve to the level of an earthworm or a TV talk show host whichever   10
comes first.

BIOLOGY WRITTEN TEST. The platypus lays eggs like a bird, swims like a fish, and has hair like a mammal but it has no wings, gills, or eyelashes. If a female platypus were to mate with a polar bear what would be the genetic makeup of the offspring?   15

PHILOSOPHY. Using Socratic and Aristotelian methods of inquiry you must explain life. What will humans assuming they still exist then believe life means in the year 2050? Be concise, and specific.

ENGLISH. From memory, rewrite *Moby Dick*, also called *The Whale* or *Hamlet*.

MATH, Part 1. Applying the principles of probability studied in Math 151   20
you must defeat your math professor at blackjack poker or gin rummy. A deck of unmarked unopened cards must be supplied by the student.

Part 2. Students must divide any number by zero, and record the result if they live.

Answer Key to Comma Practice 16-7

Line

1. Separate day from year in date. ". . . 3, 2003 . . ."

6. Separate two complete sentences joined by a conjunction. ". . . graduate, so . . ."

7. Separate items in a series. ". . . burner, a test tube . . ." Comma after "tube" is optional, but be consistent.

9. Separate introductory words. ". . . form, you . . ."

10. Separate nonessential information. ". . . host, whichever . . ."

12. Separate two complete sentences joined by conjunction. ". . . mammal, but . . ."

13. Separate introductory words. ". . . bear, what . . ."

16. Separate introductory words. ". . . inquiry, you . . ."

17. Separate parenthetical, nonessential information. ". . . humans, assuming they still exist then, believe . . ."

18. No comma before conjunction unless there are two sentences. ". . . concise and . . ."

19. Separate end of parenthetical material. ". . . *Whale*, or . . ."

20. Separate introductory material. ". . . 151, you . . ."

21. Separate items in a series. ". . . blackjack, poker . . ." Comma after "poker" is optional.

22. Separate items in a series. ". . . unmarked, unopened . . ."

23. No comma before conjunction unless there are two sentences. ". . . zero and . . ."

■ **PRACTICE 16-8:** Exchange drafts of a paper with another student and work together to correct each other's comma use.

; Semicolon

; **SEMICOLONS CONNECT TWO COMPLETE SENTENCES THAT ARE CLOSELY RELATED.** To test whether a semicolon is correct, read the words on each side of the semicolon; each side must stand independently as a complete sentence.

Hawaii has the Liberty Bowl; Florida has the Gator Bowl.

We can satisfy almost all our energy needs with solar power; the main energy needed is the effort to pass the laws.

Wrong: Our soccer team lost by a 7–4 score; even though they had twice as many shots on goal as our opponents. (What follows the semicolon is not a complete sentence.)

Wrong: There are two billion hungry people on earth, that's more than all the people who lived in the entire nineteenth century! (The comma should be a semicolon because there are two complete sentences.)

Do *not* use a semicolon when two sentences are joined by a conjunction; a comma is used there.

Wrong: The boss wants sales; and he wants them now.

***Do* use a semicolon if two sentences are separated by what's called a conjunctive adverb.** You don't need to memorize that term, but recognize the most common ones, which are "however," "therefore," "yet," and "nevertheless."

Colorado River University may have carp in its river, but Colorado Creek College has trout in its pond. (comma comes before the conjunction.)

Colorado River University may have carp in its river; however, Colorado Creek College has trout in its pond. (semicolon before a "however" joining two complete sentences.)

Colon

A COLON'S MAIN USE IS TO EMPHASIZE A SHARP BREAK BETWEEN A STATEMENT AND SOMETHING THAT FOLLOWS: A LIST, A COMMENT, A QUOTATION, A QUESTION, OR AN EXPLANATION. Hint: think of a colon as meaning "that is" or "namely." If one of these sounds right, a colon is your best choice.

Three things would make the Student Union perfect: a popcorn vendor, sawdust spread on the floor, and a ringmaster.

Everyone should remember Henry David Thoreau's last words: "Moose, Indian."

Because the colon is used only when you want to make a dramatic break, do not use it when your list or explanation follows *smoothly* from what comes before:

Wrong: This handbook consists of: rules, rules, and more rules.

■ **PRACTICE 16-9:** Create a sentence using a semicolon correctly and another correctly using a colon.

Other Punctuation

EXCLAMATION POINT: They're overused! They shout too much!! Save them for big moments!!! Don't use more than one!!!

—— **DASH:** You are never required to use a dash—commas, colon, or parentheses can always substitute for the dash, for it **separates a nonessential part of the sentence from the main idea** (see comma rule 4). A dash has more flair than commas, so poets—Emily Dickinson, for instance—like to use them.

> Professor Snerdman—a burly bull of a man with a flaming shock of red hair—charges into his lectures just looking for a student foolish enough to wave his hand.

- **HYPHEN:** A hyphen indicates **a word split** at the end of a typed line. *Only* divide words at syllable breaks—which are indicated in dictionaries. Hyphens also **connect groups of words that function as a single unit:** a happy-go-lucky boss is not a happy boss, go boss, or lucky boss. If you can substitute an "and" at the problem location, use a comma.

> sister-in-law
>
> my thirty-first birthday
>
> two-thirds vote
>
> the hairy, old horse

( ) **PARENTHESES: Parentheses separate nonessential information** (definitions, citations for sources, or by-the-way comments like this) from the main text. No punctuation marks should precede a parenthesis, and all punctuation that normally would come at that point should follow the end parenthesis mark. (The exception is a parenthetical statement that is a complete sentence, like this one.)

> When General Motors fired the Flint auto workers (7,000 in August and another 6,000 in October), the city's tax base collapsed.
>
> General Motors fired 13,000 Flint auto workers in August and October. (The city's tax base collapsed.)

" " Quotation Marks

" " **1. Put quotation marks around the titles of short works** (poems, articles, chapters of books), but use italics or underlining to indicate works long enough to be published on their own (books, long plays, magazines, newspapers).

> In his research paper, Michael documented the following sources: *The Missoula Times-Union,* O. Henry's "The Gift of the Magi," *Jaws,* a Newsweek article called "Bloodshot in Boise," and the entry "Worms" in *Encarta.*

Sacred works (Bible, Koran) and **public documents** (The United States Constitution) are *not* italicized or underlined.

" " **2. Use quotation marks to indicate speech reported word for word.** If you're doing research, you must record exactly what the writer wrote. If you want to leave out some of what was said, use **ellipsis marks** (3 or 4 dots). Three dots mean you've left out part of a sentence; four dots mean you've left out a sentence or more, or you've left off the end of the sentence you're quoting.

> The press secretary reported, "President Nixon left 3,500 hours of tapes, 10,650 pages of diary . . . and 45 recorded dinner conversations with his wife."

> Joseph Campbell's best advice was, "Follow your bliss."

If you're writing **dialogue in a narrative,** you also must use quotation marks around what the speakers say. If you don't feel you can report accurately, summarize and *do not* use quotation marks.

> "What a blast!" Billy yelled as he lit the fuse.

> **OR** As he lit the fuse, Billy said he was having a blast.

If people speak aloud in anything you write, these guidelines clarify what's happening:

- Never quote two or more people in dialogue in the same paragraph. If a second person speaks, start a new paragraph, even if only for one word.
- Use *tag lines* to identify speakers. A simple "he said" is usually better than "he threateningly implied." In dialogue between only two people, you may leave the tag lines out once in a while if it's clear who is speaking.
- Punctuate tag lines with commas.
- People's thoughts are *not* put in quotation marks.

Sample Dialogue, Taglines, and Thoughts

> Greg approached the registration counter waving a letter. "This says I can't graduate," he said.

> "That's right," the secretary said. "See, you haven't completed your program's new course in witchcraft."

> "Witchcraft! I'm going into telecommunications."

> "Well," she said, "maybe the college curriculum committee thinks you need a broader perspective." Great, Greg thought.

■ **PRACTICE 16-10:** Write three lines of dialogue in which two speakers exchange ideas. Have fun with it, but punctuate correctly.

66 99 **3. Use quotation marks around a word or phrase being referred to as a word.**

> The word "computer" comes from "compute."

> I want to examine the term "software."

❛ ❜   **4. Use single quotation marks for quotations within a quotation.**

> Doctor Seaver says, "We must understand poverty, not simply 'pity the suffering of the poor,' as my colleague stated."

Single quotation marks are made with the apostrophe key.

❝ ❞   **5. Punctuating quotations.** At the end of quotations, periods and commas go before the quotation mark; semicolons and colons follow it. Question marks and exclamation marks go before the end quotation if they are part of the quotation, after it if they apply to the sentence as a whole.

> Merle said, "trick or treat"; then he snapped open his suitcase.
>
> How can we elect a man who says, "Kiss my grits"?
>
> Darren's last question was, "What's for supper?"

Do *not* combine a comma with other punctuation marks in quotations.

> **Wrong:** Ingrid asked, "Where's my scented soap**?",** and Brian confessed he thought it was Halloween candy. (The comma after the question mark must be deleted, even though it is required by comma rule number 3.)

❜ Apostrophe

❜   **1. Use an apostrophe to form a contraction;** the apostrophe is located where the missing letters normally would be.

> don't (do not)
>
> who's (who is)
>
> it's (it is)

❜   **2. Use an apostrophe to form possessives.** To form the possessive of *all singular nouns* (including those already ending in "s") and *plural* nouns *not* ending in "s," simply add " 's."

> Pete's ball
>
> James's hat
>
> men's cars
>
> people's park

For plural nouns already ending in "s," only add an apostrophe.

> schools' rules
>
> enemies' weapons
>
> cats' tails

What does the following sentence mean? "I saw cats' eyes staring at me from the woods." It means more than one cat was staring. If it had been "cat's," only one cat was staring.

When grammarians codified the English language, **the apostrophe's two uses ran into conflict where they overlapped: at the possessive pronouns.** The grammarians awarded the apostrophe to the contractions—who's (who is) and it's (it is)—and allowed the possessive pronouns to be possessive even though they don't have apostrophes: whose, its, his, ours, hers, and so on.

It's raining outside. (it is)

The sky let loose its heavy rains. (possessive it)

Who's coming to the party? (who is)

Whose party is it? (possessive who)

■ **PRACTICE 16-11:** Write a series of sentences that correctly use a dash, a hyphen in a compound word, titles of a chapter and a book, a quotation, a contraction, and a possessive plural. Circle each use.

CAPITALIZATION

1. Capitalize the first word in every sentence or intentional sentence fragment.

2. Capitalize the first letter of all words in a proper noun.

A proper noun is the name of a specific person, place, thing, organization, or event.

Frederick Douglass	October
South Carolina	the Northwest
Orange County	Kodak Corporation
Cobb's Hill	*Webster's New World Dictionary*
Lake Ontario	Tuesday
the planet Earth	Grandma (but "my grandmother")

Do *not* capitalize the seasons (winter) or general directions (Go northeast a mile).

3. Capitalize the first word and all important words in a title.

The Moon and Sixpence

A Dance of Thieves

"Rommel the Desert Fox"

■ **PRACTICE 16-12:** Punctuation Exercise. Correct any errors in punctuation and capitalization in the following:

May 2, 2003

12 Pit Road
Citrus, FL 32881

Marla G. Snooker
President   5
Snooker sales corp.
17 Lemon Lane
Citrus, FL 32881

Dear President Snooker,

I regret that my wife Loretta and I will not be able to attend the companys   10
annual dinner dance at the Elegant Memories diner. Since Loretta returned
to college full time I'm living with a human volcano and its tough keeping
up with her. She tears through four classes, and three hours in the library.
When Loretta and I arrive home she's still full of energy, however, I'm
ready for a nap.   15

All of a sudden she knows about Psychology and even talks to me in spanish. She wants to discuss "Hamlet" and Ode to Joy with me. It's wonderful
she's learning so much but I'm worn out listening. At 2 A.M. she'll be reading that yellow marker attached to her hand.

"Do you feel like discussing picassos paintings?" she'll say. "It's 2 A.M.!" I'll   20
groan. "Put some zip in your life," she'll say.

A four-hour party will kill me and Loretta has to finish her research paper
about illegal whale hunting. There's one thing I need most rest. I hope that
you our president will understand.

Sincerely,   25
Boris Backwater
Boris Backwater

Key to Practice 16-12

Line

6. Capitalize proper nouns. ". . . Sales Corp."

9. Colon used in greeting of formal letter. ". . . Snooker:"

10. Separate interrupter with commas. Dashes acceptable instead of commas.
    ". . . wife, Loretta, and . . ."

10. Possessive requires apostrophe. "company's"

11. Capitalize proper noun. "Diner"

12. Comma separates introductory material. ". . . time, I'm . . ."

12. Comma separates two complete sentences joined by conjunction.
    ". . . volcano, and . . ."

12. Contraction, not possessive. "it's"

13. Comma before conjunction *only* if it joins two complete sentences. There's just one here. ". . . classes and . . ."

14. Comma separates introductory words. ". . . home, she's . . ."

14. Semicolon joins two complete sentences when "however" or "therefore" is used. A comma would be used if "but" had been used. ". . . energy; however . . ."

16. It's generic, not a proper noun. "psychology"

16. Capitalize words derived from proper nouns (Spain). "Spanish"

17. <u>Hamlet</u> should be underlined or italicized as a book-length work.

17. "Ode to Joy" must have quotation marks around it—title of a short work.

18. Comma separates two complete sentences joined by conjunction. ". . . much, but . . ."

19. Comma separates nonessential information (unless she's really reading the marker). ". . . reading, that . . ."

20. Capitalize people's names and use apostrophe for the possessive. "Picasso's"

20. New paragraph before "It's." A new paragraph starts when there's a second speaker quoted.

21. New paragraph before "Put."

22. Comma separates two complete sentences joined with a conjunction. ". . . me, and . . ."

23. Colon (or dash) should mark the sharp break. ". . . most: rest."

24. Commas separate nonessential interrupters. Dashes OK too. ". . . you, our president, will . . ."

SENTENCE STRUCTURE

Sentence Fragment

The "normal" English sentence has a subject, verb, and possibly a modifier. Anything less is a sentence fragment or incomplete sentence. Why do English teachers make a big deal about it? Because it shows whether or not you recognize the basic unit of the language.

Most sentence fragments are not like the following: "John the house early" or "Left the house early." Most fragments occur when a writer who is nervous about writing a long sentence makes a break even though there's no grammatical reason or when a writer confuses a verb *form* with a main verb. Look at these examples:

Fragment: Margaret put away her teddy bear, kissed her goldfish goodbye, and tore up the photos of her high school boyfriend when she headed off to college. Which turned out to have more fish than good-looking guys.

Fragment: The first college guy she dated reminded her of her guppy. Because he puckered every time she looked at him.

Both examples are typical fragments that should be attached to the previous sentence. The first example lacks a subject in the second part—it needs to refer back to "college" to make sense. The second fragment does have a subject and verb, but it also begins with a "because," which turns what follows into a *dependent clause*. It *depends* on the first part to have complete meaning. There's no theoretical limit to the length of an English sentence (James Joyce may hold the record with a 50-page sentence in *Ulysses*).

Beware of these key words:

- because
- since
- if
- although
- as
- who
- which
- verbs ending in "ing"

If any of these words begin a sentence, it should be in an introductory phrase or clause with a comma separating it from the main subject and verb. If there is no such place, you've probably written a sentence fragment.

How to fix a sentence fragment:

- Attach the fragment to the previous sentence if it completes the thought.
- Add a subject and/or verb if needed.

Legitimate uses of sentence fragments: to answer your own rhetorical question or to create a fragmented impression in dramatic scenes.

Legitimate Fragment: Why do politicians lie to the public? Because the public wants to be lied to.

Legitimate Fragments: Whack! The stick caught the side of his head. Whack. Dizzy. Spinning images of the windows. Whack! Sal went down.

Run-On Sentence (Comma Splice)

A run-on sentence is two sentences joined together without proper punctuation. What difference does it make? Here is an actual invitation some professors at my college received for an end-of-the-semester party: "Come to the party and forget your exams, spouses and other attached persons are welcome." We all thought it was going to be a wild party until realizing, at the end of the sentence, that we were only to forget exams. In this case the writer should have either substituted a semicolon for the comma or put a period there and capitalized the "s" in spouses.

> **Run-On:** From the parking lot, Emily listened to the roar of the jets landing at the airport she wished she were going somewhere. (Second sentence begins after "airport.")

> **Run-On:** Tom's biology experiment had an unexpected result, his frog grabbed a scalpel and hopped for freedom. (Second sentence begins after "result.")

> **Run-On:** The security guards pursued the frog toward the student cafeteria, however, the amphibian made good its escape. (Second sentence begins before "however." If a "but" had been there, a comma would be proper.)

How to fix run-on sentences:

- Use a period between the two sentences. This can be used in all three run-on examples.

- Use a semicolon between the two sentences. This can be used in all three run-on examples.

- Add a comma and conjunction (and, or, but, so, for, nor) between the two sentences if it sounds logical. An "and" could be used in the first run-on example and a "but" in the third, instead of "however." None of the conjunctions seem to fit the second example.

- Make the second sentence a dependent clause attached to the first sentence by adding one of these words between the two sentences: because, since, if, when, although, as. You should NOT use a comma if you use this option. "When" or "because" could be used in the second example.

It may help you to understand sentence structure better if we examine the **three types of sentences: simple, compound, and complex.** The following abbreviations are used:

S—subject of sentence

V—verb of sentence

M—modifier

C—conjunction

DCl—dependent clause

        S   V   M

Simple sentence (SVM): Tran Loc wished to study English.

        S   V   M

Compound sentence (SVM, C SVM): Tran Loc wished to study English,

C S V   M

but it was painfully slow work.

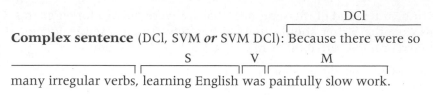

Complex sentence (DCl, SVM *or* SVM DCl): Because there were so

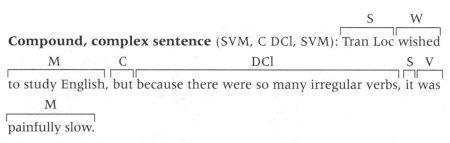

many irregular verbs, learning English was painfully slow work.

Compound, complex sentence (SVM, C DCl, SVM): Tran Loc wished

to study English, but because there were so many irregular verbs, it was

painfully slow.

■ **PRACTICE 16-13:** Write one sample sentence of your own to illustrate each of the four types of sentences. Label the parts as illustrated here.

Misplaced Modifiers

A modifier is a word or group of words that describes or adds details to another word or group of words. The italicized sections in the examples are modifiers:

> Chantel played the *Baldwin grand* piano.

> *With tenderness,* Randolph rocked the *beautiful, bald* baby.

The modifier must be placed next to the thing it modifies, or it may accidentally describe something else with comic results:

> **Misplaced:** For Sale: One maple table by elderly lady *with chipped legs.* (an actual newspaper ad)

> **Misplaced:** I was on my way to the doctor's *with rear end trouble* when my car's rear axle gave way, causing the accident. (from an actual insurance claim form)

> **Misplaced:** The accident was caused by a little guy in a small car *with a big mouth.*

The placement of one modifying word can change the meaning of a sentence. How do the following sentences differ?

> In the poker game John almost won $500.

> In the poker game John won almost $500.

Consider this gruesome, unintended meaning I once found in a paper:

> **Misplaced:** The police arrested a man in the Mt. Hope Cemetery who said he was digging up corpses trying to make some extra money.

Corrected: The police arrested a man digging up corpses in the Mt. Hope Cemetery; he said he was doing it to make some extra money.

■ **PRACTICE 16-14:** Correct any sentence fragments, run-ons, or misplaced modifiers your professor marked on your last paper.

■ **PRACTICE 16-15: Sentence Structure Exercise.** Correct any run-on sentences, sentence fragments, or misplaced modifiers in the following:

What Your Professor's Office Tells You

A Campus News Special Report
Angela Johnson, Social Editor

So you're thinking about visiting your professor in his office? Cornering the lion in his den. As a veteran faculty-watcher, let me tip off incoming freshmen about what to expect.

Relax if you see family pictures on the professor's desk, a child's hand-made pencil holder or a finger painting means you're in real luck. You might even be offered a cup of coffee, this professor is a pussycat, no lion. With chubby, sticky cheeks, your professor loves children; how can you go wrong?

But covered with debris and centuries of dust, the professor in the messy office will be a trial. You won't be able to sit though, he'll have the chair stacked with old magazines and memos. Which he can't find time to read because he worries about the meaning of life and where his grade book is.

Professor Neat, is a steel trap. Beware! A polished desk, an empty wastebasket, and a coat hung on a hanger instead of flung over a chair are warning signs, you should enter with care. Because Professor Neat plans to vacuum clean your mind with ruthless efficiency.

AGREEMENT

"Agreement" means the parts of a sentence are in harmony so readers are not confused. Here are three kinds of agreement to strive for.

Tense

All verbs must agree in tense unless you clearly prepare a reader for a time shift. Generally speaking, if your essay starts in the past tense, it should use the past tense throughout. Stay in the present if you start there.

José *came* to my house and *asked* to use my encyclopedia.

José *comes* to my house and *asks* to use my encyclopedia.

José *came* to my house often, but now that he *has* his own encyclopedia, he *stays* away. ("Now" prepares us for time shift.)

Wrong: José *came* to my house and *asks* to use my encyclopedia.

Subject–Verb Agreement

Subjects and their verbs must agree, meaning singular subjects require singular verbs and plural subjects require plural verbs.

For college students, the most common source of mistakes is a **collective noun**—which is a subject that includes more than one individual but is thought of as a unit, so it requires a singular verb.

> The wolf pack devours deer. (collective singular)
>
> Wolves devour deer. (plural)
>
> The community is going bankrupt. (collective singular)
>
> Many area businesses are going bankrupt. (plural)
>
> The government decides who is drafted. (collective singular)
>
> Bureaucrats decide who is drafted. (plural)
>
> Everyone is writing a paper this week. (collective singular)
>
> All students are writing papers this week. (plural)

Dual subjects require a plural verb:

> Sheri and Rolfe study two hours each night. (But Sheri studies two hours each night.)

Noun–Pronoun Agreement

Pronouns represent nouns and must therefore be of the same gender and number (singular or plural) as the nouns they represent.

> Paul wants *his* paper typed.
>
> The dog doesn't care if *its* paper is typed.
>
> Everyone wants *her* hair short these days.
>
> **Wrong:** Everyone wants their papers typed. (his/her/one's)
>
> **Wrong:** A paper should show their writer's style. (its)

SPELLING

I am a bad speller. I *need* a dictionary so I don't look stupid. For the past 35 years I have had to say to myself "i" before "e" except after "c" every time I've spelled "believe" or "receive." (And it took me another ten years to learn that this does not apply to "foreign" or "neighbor.") Spelling just doesn't "come" to some people, and I'll always rely on a dictionary more than most people do.

For the same reason people judge others based on looks or clothes, readers judge ideas and writing skills partly by the surface appearance of the paper.

Fair or not, it's done. So the final task before typing any paper is to check the spelling of all words you're not 100 percent certain about. It'll be worth the two minutes it takes. If you simply can't find a word, look up a synonym in a dictionary or thesaurus and your word may appear in the definition.

By the way, don't rely on your word processor's spell-checker to catch more than 75 percent of your misspellings. "My hat was a white pail" looks just fine to most computers, even though you meant, "My cat has a white tail."

Numbers

Spell out numbers under ten and spell out all numbers (even those *over* ten) that start sentences. Numbers over ten can be written as numerals. *But* if you compare numbers, both numbers must be in the same format. If you spell out the number, you must also spell out "percent," "degrees" and "cents" instead of using the symbols %, °, ¢.

- At the conference, five women arrived late.
- Twenty-five customers complained yesterday.
- Another 15 people left after lunch.
- By Christmas, only 20% of our merchandise remained.

WEIRD WORDS

Weird Singulars and Plurals

Singular Form	Plural Form	Singular Form	Plural Form
analysis	analyses	medium	media
crisis	crises	mouse	mice
datum	data	sheep	sheep
deer	deer	species	species
fish	fish	thesis	theses

Irregular Verbs

Normally you add "ed" or "d" to verbs to form the past and past participle (action that began in the past and continues):

Base Form	Past Tense	Past Participle
I walk	I walked	I have walked
We implore	We implored	We have implored

But some English verbs are rebellious. Here are the most common irregular verbs:

Base Form	Past Tense	Past Participle
awake	awoke, awakened	awakened, awoken
become	became	became
begin	began	begun
bite	bit	bitten
blow	blew	blown
break	broke	broken
bring	brought	brought
build	built	built
buy	bought	bought
catch	caught	caught
choose	chose	chosen
come	came	come
creep	crept	crept
deal	dealt	dealt
dig	dug	dug
do	did	done
draw	drew	drawn
dream	dreamed, dreamt	dreamed, dreamt
drink	drank	drunk
drive	drove	driven
eat	ate	eaten
fall	fell	fallen
feel	felt	felt
fight	fought	fought
find	found	found
fly	flew	flown
forget	forgot	forgotten, forgot
forgive	forgave	forgiven
freeze	froze	frozen
get	got	gotten, got
give	gave	given
go	went	gone
grow	grew	grown
have	had	had

Base Form	Past Tense	Past Participle
hear	heard	heard
hide	hid	hidden
hurt	hurt	hurt
keep	kept	kept
know	knew	known
lay (place)	laid	laid
lead	led	led
leave	left	left
lie (recline)	lay	lain
lose	lost	lost
make	made	made
mean	meant	meant
pay	paid	paid
read	read	read
ride	rode	ridden
ring	rang	rung
say	said	said
see	saw	seen
set	set	set
shake	shook	shaken
show	showed	showed, shown
sing	sang	sung
sink	sank	sunk
sit	sat	sat
speak	spoke	spoken
steal	stole	stolen
strike	struck	struck
swear	swore	sworn
swim	swam	swum
take	took	taken
teach	taught	taught
tear	tore	torn
think	thought	thought
throw	threw	thrown
wear	wore	worn
write	wrote	written

ODD PAIRS

Adapt means to modify to fit: Professor Cruz adapted his lecture for a class of elementary pupils.

Adopt means to accept as one's own: Professor Cruz adopted a less-formal attitude toward the children.

Bring is used only for movement closer: Bring the cat here.

Take is used for all other movement: Take the cat with you when you leave.

Can is used when the *ability* to perform a task is the issue: Can Merwin swim across the bay to the island?

May is used when *permission* to do something is the issue: His mother says he may not try the swim.

Conscience refers to one's sense of morals: My conscience won't allow me to eat lamb.

Conscious refers to being aware or awake: I'm just too conscious of how farmers mistreat lambs.

Lose means to be defeated or misplace something. It is a verb: Gina will lose her tennis match.

Loose is an adjective meaning detached: Gina stepped on a loose ball and twisted her ankle.

Sensuous refers to situations that have rich appeal to our five senses: It was a sensuous night with balmy breezes, fireflies, and the aroma of fresh cut hay.

Sensual also refers to arousing the senses, but in a distinctly sexual way: The sensual night in the garden stirred Romeo's and Juliet's passions.

Set is used when you place an object down: Franz set the plate on the counter.

   Wrong: Grandma said Franz should set awhile with her.

Sit is used only if the subject seats itself: Franz would sit by his sick guppy for hours.

Who is used when referring to subjects in sentences that *perform* actions. "Who" stands for "he" or "she": Who entered my room last night? (He entered.)

Whom is used when referring to objects that *receive* actions and stands for "him" or "her": You left with whom? (You left with her.)

   To whom are you speaking? (Receives action)

   The man who drove the car was drunk (Performs the action)

MECHANICS

Foreign words: Use italics for words from foreign languages: *bon voyage, cerveza, prosit, et al.* **Note:** if a word has been officially absorbed into English (lasagna, aloha, gung ho, kangaroo), do **not** italicize. A good dictionary will indicate if a word is still considered foreign or has been adopted.

Common abbreviations and symbols:

Apt. (apartment)

rpm (revolutions per minute)

¢ (cents)

° (degrees)

P.M. *or* p.m. (noon-to-midnight): Three p.m.)

A.D. (*anno domini.* Precedes year: A.D. 975)

Two-letter postal code (for states)

Rev. (reverend. Place before name: Rev. Smith)

M.D. (place after full name: Mary Smith, M.D.)

e.g. (for example. Followed by a comma and example)

c. *or* ca. (about. When referring to dates)

mph (miles per hour)

$ (dollars)

% (percent)

A.M. *or* a.m. (midnight-to-noon time reference: Six a.m.)

B.C. (Before Christ. Follows year: 58 B.C.)

No. *or* no. (number)

mg, km (milligrams, kilometers)

Dr. (doctor. Place before name: Dr. Smith)

Ph.D. (doctor of philosophy. Place after full name: Mary Smith, Ph.D.)

i.e. (that is. Followed by a comma and an explanation)

vs. *or* v. (versus)

Format for College Papers

Paper: white, 8½ by 11, one side only

Font: 12 point Courier or New Times.

Ink: Black

Margins: Left justify with one inch on all sides

Heading: Your name, course title, and date in upper-left corner

Title: ¼ down the page, centered, all in capitals. Separate title page common only in papers of ten pages or more.

Double space

Paragraphs: Indent five spaces

Number pages in upper right

Staple: upper-left corner

DICTIONARY OF USAGE

The 25 Most Commonly Misused Words in English

advice, advise
Advice is a noun, meaning "guidance."

His father's advice was to study liberal arts.

Advise is a verb, meaning "counsel" or "give advice to."

His father advised him to study liberal arts.

affect, effect
Affect is a verb that means "influence."

The president's budget cuts affected public television.

Effect may be either a noun or verb, although it is used as a noun about 99 percent of the time. As a verb, it means "accomplish."

The president's public television cuts effected a $2 million savings nationwide.

As a noun, *effect* means "impact" or "result."

The cuts have had two effects locally: longer auctions and longer membership drives.

all right
"Alright" is not standard English. Would you write "alwrong?"

a lot
This is the only way it appears; don't use "alot" in such sentences as this: "Don't make a lot of spelling mistakes."
The word "allot" is a verb, meaning to "distribute shares."

among, between
Between is used with two items or persons.

After graduating, he had to choose between a career in business and working for his father.

Among is used with three or more items.

After graduating, he had to choose among a career in business, working for his father, or continuing for a master's degree.

amount, number
Amount is used with uncountable things.

An amazing amount of work goes into completing a college course.

Number is used with countable things.

> What number of hours do you study for an average college course?

Amount applies to sand, weight, and volumes. But if you count the grains of sand in your navel someday, it will be a number, not an amount.

Number applies to people, years, and dollars.

Being that, being as

Use "since" or "because" instead.

> Since it rained so hard, we stayed home from college.

> **Wrong:** Being as it rained so hard, we stayed home from college.

etc.

Try to avoid *etc.* It sounds lazy. If you do use it, italicize it because it is Latin and don't write "and etc." *Etc.* means "and others."

farther, further

Farther means "a greater distance" and should be used only to refer to space and time.

> If I have to travel any farther between classes, I'm going to wear roller skates to school.

Further means "more" or "besides." It's used with ideas or abstractions.

> Our professor is always saying, "Let's go into that further." And after we exhaust the topic, he always seems to say, "Further, we should consider . . ."

few, little

Few is used with countable items.

> Few students know this college was once a prison farm.

Little is used with uncountable items.

> Some would say how little the place has changed.

good, well

Good is an adjective and should always modify a noun, never a verb.

> Her essay made several good proposals.

> **Wrong:** She runs good. She feels good. She talks good.

Well is an adverb and should modify a verb.

> She runs well, feels well, and talks well.

its, it's

Its is the possessive of "it"; *it's* means "it is."

> It's a shame a deer can't shoot back at its hunters.

lie, lay

To lie means "to recline" and should be used if the reclining object or person can be thought of as doing it under its own power.

> He lies down. The dog lies in the shade.

To lay means "to put in place" and should be used if another person or force puts the object in that position.

> Dad lays the baby in the crib. I lay the book on the table.

Lie and *lay* are complicated because they're irregular verbs and the past tense of *lie* is the same as the present tense of *lay*.

Lie	Lay
I lie down. (today)	I lay it down. (today)
I lay down. (yesterday)	I laid it down. (yesterday)
I have lain down.	I have laid it down.
I am lying down.	I am laying it down.
I was lying down.	I was laying it down.

mad, angry

Mad means "insane." A person can be mad, but not "mad at" you. Use "angry."

might of, could of, would of, should of, must of

These verbs do not exist. "Of" should be the helping verb "have."

> Inez should have used "have" when she wrote the note to her teacher that said: "I must of got a hundred on the test—I studied all afternoon."

We may confuse this because the contraction "might've" (might have) sounds like the incorrect form.

myself

A pretentious word to avoid.

> **Wrong:** Janet came with myself to the airport. (Use "me" instead)

> **Wrong:** I myself did not believe him. ("I" alone says it.)

prejudice

This requires a "d" ending when used with a helper verb—"is," "was," "are," or "were."

> Dorothy is prejudiced.

raise, rise

You *raise* an object or person, but you *rise* yourself.

> Bill raised his fist when he won the 100-yard dash.

> Peter had to rise from where he'd fallen on the track to see his opponent celebrate.

than, then
Than is comparative.

Alaska has fewer people than Rhode Island.

Then refers to time.

Then we drove home.

that, which, and who
Who should be used to refer to people. *That* and *which* are used to refer to things or ideas.

Amy, *who* led the team to the state finals, broke her ankle in the final minutes of the regular-season game, an accident *that* cost the team its playoff game.

Wrong: The man that lives next door is bald.

there, they're, their
There refers to a place, *they're* is a contraction for "they are," and *their* is the possessive of "they."

They're going to take their tennis game over there on court three.

to, too
If you mean "very" or "also," use "too." **Hint:** The extra "o" suggests excess.

It's too hot to go anywhere; it's humid, too.

try to
People often say "try and" when they mean *try to*.

We'll try to start the engine.

Wrong: Let's try and go to the party. (You're not doing two things, only one.)

unique
Unique means one of a kind, not just unusual.

Moe is unique if he has antennae and speaks Martian.

your, you're
Misusing these is a professional embarrassment. *Your* is possessive; *you're* is the contraction for "you are."

You're going to get in trouble if you misuse your words, but you're going to be a star if your writing is correct as well as lively.

■ **PRACTICE 16-16: Word Usage Exercise.** Correct any errors of usage and spelling:

ATTENTION!! JOB OPENING!!

COMMUNICATION MANAGER FOR SMALL COMPANY

Young company desperatly requires writing advise. We do alright with manu-facturing, but our lack of a communications manager has begun to effect sales alot.

Forward you're résumé to us by June 15. Depending on the total amount re-cieved, we will notify applicants of interviews by July 1. Applicants that are suc-cessful should of written reports, letters, etc.

We'll look farther into the qualifications of the best three applicants at the in-terview. Their going to lie down ten rules for good writing and than demonstrate what affect each rule will have on business communications. The person we hire should speak good and be ambitious. The best between the three finalists can start immediately. We need all the help we can get.

CONTACT: Personel Department

Wordsmith.com

■ **PRACTICE 16-17: Summary Exercise.** For each of the following, write a sentence that:

1. Starts with "because," "since," or "if."
2. Has a "however" in the middle.
3. Contains two sentences joined with an "and."
4. Contains an "and" but does not contain two complete sentences.
5. Uses a colon.
6. Includes a quotation.
7. Uses a singular possessive.
8. Uses a plural possessive.
9. Contains an interrupter phrase.
10. Has a dash.
11. Is followed by a legitimate sentence fragment.
12. Includes two words in the usage section that you have had trouble with.
13. Includes a semicolon.
14. Includes two words you frequently misspell.
15. Uses "in conclusion" or "lastly."

■ **PRACTICE 16-18: Summary Exercise.** Correct any errors in punctuation, sentence structure, spelling, or usage in the following:

December 3, 2003

Wade Biggs
Personnel Director
Fudge Motors, Inc.
Detroit, Michigan 11391

Dear Mr. Biggs,

Attached to this letter you will find my résumé. Which lists my employment and academic background. I hope your still considering me for the job in the swedish division of the company.

I used to make alot of errors in English but I received some good advise from one of my prof's at college, and now I write good. My prof told me the kind of affect bad grammar has on a potential employer who has hundreds of people to choose between. I know I'll go farther if I know how to use a semicolon; as in this sentence. Its important, to, knowing the difference among words like "amount" and "number." When you study wrighting since Third Grade as I have you soon learn to punctuate and use correct sentence structure. Although its hard sometimes if you hav'nt lain the rules down in front of yourself.

Commas for instance should mark two sentences connected with a conjunction. They also set off interrupters, these words block the flow of a sentence. Sitting like a frog flattened in the road, my prof told us to watch out for the sentence fragment. "Beware the galloping run-on he lectured us and shun the frivolous, comma." After I memorized these rules I knew I'd be an employee any company would of been proud to hire.

Sincerely,

Gustov Osterly.
Gustov Osterly

■ **PRACTICE 16-19:** Write a letter to the students who will take your writing course next term. Give them advice that will help them do well, and close by explaining two grammar or usage rules they must know. Give an illustration for each.

■ **PRACTICE 16-20:** Correct the punctuation and usage in the first draft of "How to Get Back the Family You Lost" on page 380.

■ **PRACTICE 16-21:** Exchange papers with a fellow student for peer review. Read each others' work once only for punctuation, a second time only for word use, and a third time only for sentence fragments and run-on sentences.

Note: Additional practices in mechanics are in *The Instructor's Manual.*

MYTHS ABOUT ENGLISH

Myth #1: You cannot begin sentences with "and," "but" or "or" because these conjunctions must join two things. **Reality:** Prestigious writers and publishers often start sentences with these words because they're great transitions. Computer grammar checks pounce on this because it is something they *can* do. Ignore them.

Myth #2: Put commas where you hear a pause. **Reality:** Do this and you'll be wrong about half the time because pauses come where semicolons, colons, dashes, periods, and no punctuation are right. Commas indicate where key elements of sentences must be separated for clarity. Learn the rules in the handbook.

Myth #3: Don't use "I" because it makes your writing sound too personal. **Reality:** Which is better: "I think" or "One might think"? The impersonal "one" is a tone-killer in all but the most formal writing, and an "I" hides behind it anyway. Don't shout "Me! Me! Me!" at readers, but don't worry about squashing every "I."

Myth #4: Computers will fix your errors. **Reality:** Use spell-checks and grammar-checks, of course! But learn enough yourself to catch what computers miss—especially commas and usage errors—and to know when your computer gets spooked by our illogical language and finds errors where there are none.

Myth #5: Your job as a writer is to avoid mistakes, and your professor's job as a teacher is to correct mistakes. **Reality:** Your job is to say something worth saying with the most vivid details and most accurate words and to keep mistakes to a minimum so they don't interfere. Your professor's job is to help you do all three. Grammar mistakes irritate readers and teachers, but what they care about most are great ideas, details, and language.

Myth #6: Passing this course proves you have mastered English. **Reality:** Passing is one step forward in your lifetime of writing. Enjoy the journey.

InfoTrac® College Edition:
Readings on Punctuation, Usage, and Grammar

For tips on using *InfoTrac®* College Edition, see page 464.

Russell Baker. "How to Punctuate." *Scholastic Update.* 16 Nov. 1984.

Comma, colon, semicolon, dash, parenthesis, quotation marks, and apostrophe with examples.

Paula LaRoque. "Comma Coma." *The Quill.* Mar. 1996.

Comma rules explained in a different way.

"Errors of Our Way." *Community Care.* 21 Mar. 2002.

A dozen common usage mistakes not covered in Ideas and Details.

Lorraine Ray. "Does Gramm-tik You Off?" *Business Communication Quarterly.* Mar. 1997.

Where computer grammar correction software programs fail and why.

CHAPTER 17

Twelve Million Sources: *InfoTrac®* College Edition Access

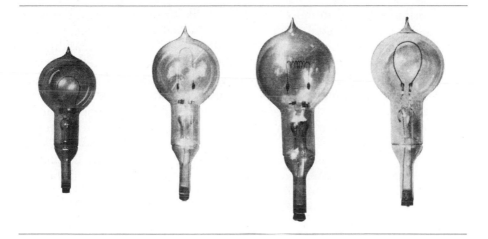

Books are humanity in print.

—BARBARA TUCHMAN

When you purchased *Ideas and Details*, you received a four-month subscription to *InfoTrac®* College Edition, a college-oriented database of more than 12 million articles on subjects from Shakespeare to terrorist attacks, music reviews to sports, AIDS research to financing college educations. You will discover that *InfoTrac®* College Edition has several big advantages over using Internet search engines. Unlike the Internet, *InfoTrac®* College Edition is selective—choosing to include only material that has already appeared in leading publications. Some articles are scholarly and some popular, but all have been screened by editors, so you are likely to read more reliable information than appears on most web sites. Unlike Internet sites, there is no advertising, it is updated daily, articles rarely disappear or change, and the index has been set up specifically for college students doing reading and research. Imagine *InfoTrac®* College Edition as a window from *Ideas and Details* to a wider world of resources for writers and readers, far more than I could ever hope to cram into this book—or even 10,000 books!

By accessing *InfoTrac®* College Edition articles listed here, you can learn how to write résumés or to write for publication; learn more about topics like honesty or creativity covered in *Ideas and Details;* read professional samples of the kind of writing you're asked to do in *Ideas and Details* (such as narratives or persuasion); and do research or class projects with all the bibliographic information your professors require.

HOW TO USE *INFOTRAC®* COLLEGE EDITION

Access it at this web site: www.infotrac-college.com

Log on with your access code.

Type in either a subject or keyword, and you're off!

Hints:

- Try the **Easy Trac Subject Search** first—this often lists subdivisions of your topic, so you can see how it is organized and learn new ways of asking for information.

- If you use **Easy Trac's Keyword Search,** and you get 400 hits, use the **Limit Search** (limiting "By Word" is usually most helpful).

- **Power Trac** lets you use an **Advanced Search** to limit sources by author, date, title of article, and other features. Use this *after* you get a feel for your topic's structure on Easy Trac or if you have specific articles you want to read—such as those recommended in *Ideas and Details*.

- If you don't get enough hits, describe your topic in a new way.

- You can print articles, save them to disk, or e-mail them.

- You can read issues of one magazine, starting with the latest issue, by asking for it by journal name (jn) on Advanced Search.

- Lists of articles appear in chronological order, the newest ones appearing first on your screen.

■ **PRACTICE 17-1:** To familiarize yourself with *InfoTrac*® College Edition, log on and find an article on any subject that interests you. Write a one-sentence summary of the main point and list two new things you learned from reading.

InfoTrac® College Edition: Readings on How to Write a Résumé and 21 Other Forms of Writing

You will find the following sources on *InfoTrac*® College Edition. These explain how to create types of writing not covered in depth in *Ideas and Details*. Most articles appeared in trade magazines for professional writers. **Hint:** Search for the article by using "Advanced Search" and limiting by "Title." Do not enclose title in quotation marks.

Writing a Résumé:

Robert Greenly. "How to Write a Résumé." *Technical Communication.* Feb. 1993.

Lee H. Bender. "Résumé Writing and Introductory Skills for Getting the Job You Want." *Orthopaedic Nursing.* May/June 1997.

Writing a Letter of Recommendation:

Kenneth C. Petress. "Letters of Recommendation: Their Motive and Content." *College Student Journal.* Dec. 1999.

Writing a Letter of Complaint:

"Kvetching on: How to Complain Constructively When a Product or Service Disappoints." *Chatelaine.* Feb. 1990.

Job Application, Cover Letter, Thank-You Note, Acceptance Letter, E-mail Protocol:

Sandra Hagevik. "Job Search Correspondence." *Journal of Environmental Health.* Jan/Feb. 1998.

Writing Proposals: There are many types of proposals. Enter "Proposal Writing" and click on "subject guide" for more specific categories of proposal writing. Here are two samples that are well done:

Thomas Couch; Ruth Knack. "Get that Grant: How to Write a Winning Proposal." *Planning.* 1996.

Rebecca Dudley. "Grant Writing Superstars." *Wenatchee Business Journal.* April 2001.

Writing a Business Memo:

Thomas Clark. "Encouraging Critical thinking in Business Memos." *Business Communication Quarterly.* 1998.

continues

Report Writing:
Philip Vassallo. "Using the 4 S Plan." *ETC: A Review of General Semantics.* Winter 1998.

Writing a Letter to the Newspaper:
Kathiann M.Kowalski. "Dear Editor . . . " *Cobblestone.* Feb. 2001.

Writing an Editorial:
Tom Dennis. "Awash in Hogwash." *The Masthead.* Winter 1996.

Newspaper Reporting:
Richard B. Stolley. "Our Staff as Vacuum Cleaner, and Other Ways We Find Stories." *Life.* Aug. 1983.

Writing a Personal Ad:
Kim Pittaway. "Up Close With Personals." *Chatelaine.* Aug. 1998.

Writing an Ad to Sell Something:
Linda Westphal. "Before & After: Ads Made Better." *Direct Marketing.* Sept. 1998.

Magazine Writing:
Michael J. Bugeja. "Learning From Magazine Writing." *Editor & Publisher.* Oct. 1998.

Deborah Newton. "Writing Personal Experience Articles." *The Writer.* Aug. 2000.

Writing a Letter Asking a Magazine to Read Your Work:
B. J. Bassett. "The Three-Step Query Letter." *The Writer.* Sept. 2000.

Speech Writing:
Matt Hughes. "Tricks of the Speechwriter's Trade." *Management Review.* Nov. 1990.

Playwriting/Scriptwriting:
Jeffrey Sweet. "Playwrights' Corner." *Back Stage.* Jan. 1997.

"A Wedding of Worlds." *American Theatre.* March 1997.
  Explains differences between playwriting and scriptwriting.

Writing Poetry:
Mary Baron. "Let Your Poem Breathe." *The Writer.* March 2001.

Linda Batt. "Here Are 10 Ways to Jump-Start a Poem." *The Writer.* Aug. 2002.

Writing Fiction:
Thomas Fleming. "Visions and Realities." *The Writer.* July 2000.

Writing Song Lyrics:
> Jas Obrecht. "Jimi Hendrix: Messages to Love." *Guitar Player.*
> Oct. 1993.

Nature Writing:
> Richard Yatzeck. "Walk on the Wild Side." *The Writer.* May 2001.

Writing Children's Literature:
> Sam McCarver. "Common Ground: Writers of Children's Books Can
> Take Their Cues From Adult Fiction." *The Writer.* June 2002.

Journal Writing:
> Debra Allen. "All About Journalizing: Sites That Instruct and Inspire
> Writers of Various Types of Diaries." *Link-Up.* May 2002.

■ **PRACTICE 17-2:** Read one of the articles above and list its main points.

■ **PRACTICE 17-3:** Read one of the articles above and write a sample according to its guidelines.

INFOTRAC® COLLEGE EDITION RESEARCH PROJECTS AND ASSIGNMENTS

Personal Research Projects

Do you wonder what your salary will be once you graduate from college and start your career? Or how exactly you'll be spending your workday? Have you thought you'd like to visit Tahiti or dive the reef off Grand Cayman Island, but want to know more before you buy your ticket? Do you get frustrated when television reports that fiber is good for you and salt bad, and then read a newspaper story the next day that questions both reports? How painful and effective will it be to remove that dragon tattoo from your arm? How can you rebuild the old Ford Mustang in the garage? You can use *Info-Trac®* College Edition to find answers to these personal research questions.

As with academic research topics, you'll be happier with your results if you do some thinking first. **Make a preliminary list of research questions you want answered.** Besides focusing your attention, this makes you aware of new keywords you can enter in the *InfoTrac®* College Edition search engine. **Enter a broad topic first, so you can see how *InfoTrac®* College Edition subdivides the subject and learn more key search words.**

■ **PRACTICE 17-4:** Look up one of these topics and find three pieces of information that you think most of your classmates will not know but will find interesting.

- A place you love (or hate)
- A place you have dreamed about visiting
- Your favorite athlete, musician, or actor
- A topic of health care interest to you: steroids, fiber, acne, yoga, heath clubs, running, hormone replacement, cancer risks, second-hand smoke, caffeine, salt, fat, the drug Ecstasy, or warts, for examples
- Body decoration: makeup, hair dyes, tattoos, piercings, fingernail art.
- A future career issue (if you're considering the medical field, try researching malpractice suits or insurance; a future law enforcement officer may research false charges of police brutality or working with the canine unit)
- Your hobby or sport
- The dating scene: newest club gimmicks, dating services, online singles chat rooms
- Any other topic of personal interest

Possible Papers:

- An informative research report
- An analytical or critical thinking paper in which you explain the significance of what you learned
- A personalized research paper in which you relate what you learned to your own experience
- A persuasive paper that argues a point about the topic (e.g., fiber is overrated; I will never visit Nassau)

Bibliography Project

InfoTrac® College Edition can help you create a bibliography (a list of sources about a topic). Follow guidelines for proper Works Cited format in Chapter 14. Unlike the Internet, *InfoTrac*® College Edition provides all the documentation information required. An **annotated bibliography** explains in a sentence or two what each article covers and what its thesis is. Here is a sample:

Robertson, Stephen. "The Age of Consent Law and the Making of Modern Childhood." <u>Journal of Social History</u> 35.4 (2002): 781–800. *InfoTrac.* Online. 30 Oct. 2002. <http://www.infotrac-college.com>

Robertson argues that when New York City enacted the first age of consent laws in the early twentieth century to protect children from predatory sexual abuse and prostitution, it created a new idea—a safety zone around childhood.

■ **PRACTICE 17-5:** For your source from Practice 17-4. Write an annotated bibliography entry with a one-to-two sentence summary of the main points.

Possible Papers:

- A bibliography of sources to demonstrate mastery of format
- An annotated bibliography to demonstrate mastery of format and of reading
- A preliminary step toward writing a research paper

Debate Project

Two research teams of students will debate a controversial issue before the class. Each team should research supporting reasons, facts and statistics for its position as well as opposition refutations (see Chapter 12), so it can anticipate them and prepare responses. The team ought to meet before the debate to assemble arguments and supporting detail and to strategize about how to present ideas and handle refutations.

Debate format usually consists of an opening statement by a moderator explaining the topic, then presentations by each team, followed by responses by the other side. There is often a brief final refutation and conclusion by each team. In addition to long-argued topics such as abortion, legalizing marijuana, gun control, and medically assisted suicide for the terminally ill, here are some newer controversial topics you can research on *InfoTrac*® College Edition:

- Censorship on the Internet
- The rights of accused terrorists
- Legalizing homosexual marriages
- Banning cloning of human beings
- Restricting paramilitary groups

Possible Papers:

- Group paper in which each person writes the section he/she researched.
- Summary report written by the "audience" members of the class. This would outline the main points on each side and may conclude with an opinion about which side presented the strongest case.
- Individual papers written after the debate. These can be persuasive papers that argue the same position taken in the debate. Or they may be reaction papers that evaluate how the debate went by reflecting on the strengths and weaknesses of both sides and stating how you would do it differently next time.

Informative/Persuasive Projects

The following topics can all be successfully researched on *InfoTrac*® College Edition. I suggest starting with the narrow subtopics (or inventing your own) rather than the broad topics.

- **Women and Men**

  Sex and power

  Wages of male and female athletes

  Female and male evangelists

  Male and female body decorations

  Parenting styles of men and women

- **Saving Children**

  Effects of divorce on children

  Youngest child/oldest child

  Teenage drug use

  AIDS and children

  Causes of autism in children

  How safe is day care?

- **Culture Conflicts**

  Choose two cultures (African, Western, Middle East, Oriental, Native American) and research how they compare on one issue:

  - Religious beliefs

  - View of nature

  - Attitude toward war

  - Sexual practices

  - Family life

  - Political structures

- **Food**

  Starvation

  Pesticides and pollution

  Eating disorders

  Irradiation

  Effects of microwaves on attitudes toward food

- **Historical Topics**

  Witches/witchcraft trials

  Funeral traditions in a different time and/or culture

  War crimes trials then and now

  Myths about George Washington, Winston Churchill, Queen Elizabeth I, or other "great" people

- **Technology Today and Tomorrow**

  What great inventions are being created now for the future?

  Are electric-powered automobiles any good?

  What happened to wind and solar energy?

  What's next in computers?

  If we did clone a human being. . . .

- **Nature**

  An endangered species (humpback whale, tiger, orangutan)

  A dangerous beast (shark, tarantula, West Nile virus, rattlesnake)

  Rock climbing

  Fishing

  Sea kayaking

  Nature photography

- **The Arts**

  Your favorite artist, musician, or writer (life story or technique)

  An artistic, literary or musical movement (e.g., Expressionism, Minimalism, Hip Hop)

■ **PRACTICE 17-6:** Pick a broad category that interests you, then either select one of the subcategories listed or create one of your own and list five or six research questions you would like to answer about the topic.

■ **PRACTICE 17-7:** Locate four good sources on *InfoTrac*® College Edition and write one or two sentences describing what you learned from each.

■ **PRACTICE 17-8:** Make a tentative thesis statement for your paper and a rough scratch outline. Then return to *InfoTrac*® College Edition and gather more in-depth information from your original and new sources—trying to decide as you read which heading on your scratch outline each good piece of information best fits. If something does not fit one of your existing headings but it seems important, add a new heading to your outline.

The Real Rules for Writing Classes (and Maybe Life)

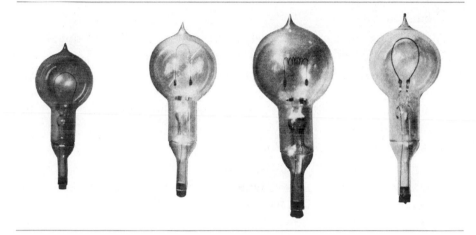

- Show up.
- Play hard—it's the only way to have fun and improve.
- Figure out what you're good at and exploit it; figure out what you're weak at and work on it.
- An honest effort does not guarantee an "A," but it almost always prevents failure.
- Thou shalt not steal.
- Each day is a chance to start fresh. If you tell yourself, "I'm no good in English," you chain the weight of the past to your ankles.
- Bad things happen to everyone; those who succeed find a way to keep going.
- Writers live more in 24 hours than most people because they look intensely at things.
- Smart people ask for help before it's too late.
- Do more than the minimum required.
- Defensive living and defensive writing ensure only mediocrity. To accomplish anything outstanding requires some risk.
- Love far more things than you hate.
- Parties last one night; your grades last a lifetime.
- Inspiration is rarely luck; it knocks on the doors of people who try hard and care about what they're doing.
- A hard assignment is an invitation to be better than you are now.
- Write a rule of your own here:

  _____

- Write one of your professor's rules here:

  _____

- Ask a person you admire for a rule and write it here:

  _____

- Life is often unfair and will break these rules when it chooses; you can persevere anyway.

A TROUBLESHOOTING GUIDE TO WRITING

Note: Many of these "problems" are normal procedure for most writers.

Problem	Possible Causes	Possible Cures	Chapter Reference
I don't know what to write about.	Unclear about assignment or purpose in writing.	Reread text. Reread assignment. Ask professor.	
	Unclear about audience.	Visualize an audience and write to it.	1, 12 13, 14
I can't get started.	No ideas or vague ideas. Insufficient detail or visualization.	Brain teasers.	2–3
	Introduction jitters.	Start with main idea. Use intro brain teaser.	6
	Insecure about thinking. Fear of risk.	Overcome blocks and strive for honesty.	1, 3
I start but then stall.	Ideas fuzzy or incomplete.	More brain teasers.	3
	Poor writing environment. Fear of messiness/risk.	Overcome these blocks.	6
I can't put my ideas or notes together.	You need a main point or headings.	Work on thesis/outline.	5
I keep writing around the same idea— going nowhere.	Insufficient ideas/details.	More brain teasers.	2–3
	Redundancy.	Cut to essential idea.	7–8
I know what I want to say but not how to say it.	Word paralysis.	Freewrite, loop, or try oral composition. Talk to peers.	5–6